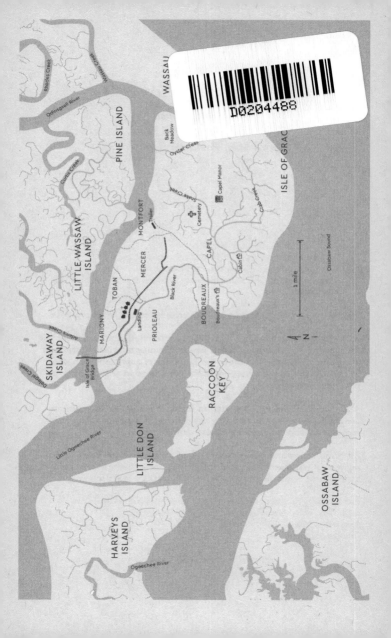

PROLOGUE

"THE MAN BOWED." SARAH MUNRO HIKED HER STRAW BAG higher on her shoulder and followed the officer down the Savannah Police Department's hallway. He held a cell phone to his ear, and she yanked his arm. "And a woman *died* tonight."

He nodded, but his deep frown, as well as his dismissive wave, told her he wasn't too concerned about the murder. Or the fact that Sarah had found the body in the Savannah Preservation Office's courtyard fountain.

Was a death in the historic district so commonplace that it didn't warrant its own investigator? Frustrated, she followed him around the corner toward the second-floor landing when her cell phone buzzed. A text from her father. Where are you?

She halted near the stairs, her fingers hovering over the phone's keyboard. She debated how much to tell him. Then again, he probably already knew.

She texted, *I'll be home soon.*

Someone bumped her as they passed, and she moved closer to the vending machine that carried only rows of Coke cans. Her officer stood nearby, talking on the phone, while federal, state, and local LEOs congregated in groups around the open area. Her father had told her that the city had numerous task forces, all trying to combat the rising crime rate. She and her dad had returned to Savannah nine months ago, and in that short time, they'd both noticed the uptick in drug use and violence.

It's dark. I'll come get you, her father texted back.

No. Not only did she not want her father worrying about her, he wasn't supposed to drive. *I'm leaving soon. Drink your tea.*

I hate that tea. It tastes like sh*t.

Despite the ache in her chest, she smiled. Yes, he hated the tea. Yet it was the only thing that helped with his recurring seizures. And if he thought that being even more cranky than usual meant she'd ease up on the herbal leaves, he was wrong. *I don't care. Drink it.*

She glanced at her officer—who was still on his phone—and debated leaving. If the cops wanted her statement, they knew where she worked. The same place where a woman had been *murdered*. "I'm leaving, Officer. But I know what I saw."

He ignored her, and she turned toward the stairs.

"Sarah?" A male voice cut through the station's din, ringing phones, and metal chairs scraping along seventy-year-old linoleum.

She blinked one man into focus. Tall, broad shoulders, long blond hair tied at the base of his neck, angular face, and deep, ocean-green eyes. The kind a girl could lose herself in. "Nate?"

Was that her breathy voice? She swallowed, and a warm flush rose from her neck to her cheeks. She wasn't sure why, but since meeting Nate Walker yesterday, she'd felt shaky and incoherent and…restless.

Does he know what I did to his map?

"I heard what happened." He touched her arm before shoving both hands in the front pockets of his jeans. His biker jacket stretched across his shoulders, the black leather rustling with the movement. "Are you okay?"

"I wasn't hurt." She stared at the red-and-white vending machine and blinked. Adopted daughters of cops didn't cry. They *endured*. "This is my fault, Nate. I'd asked my assistant to do some research for me. I had no idea she was staying late."

"This isn't your fault." He leaned in closer, the scar on his cheek appearing deeper and more ragged. His pine-scented aftershave tickled her nose. "I'm sorry."

She wiped her palms on her chiffon skirt, relieved he didn't seem to realize she'd secretly photographed the seventeenth-century map he'd brought to the preservation office for her to look at. The map included the only layout she'd ever seen of the remote, colonial-era Cemetery of Lost Children on the Isle of Grace. Even though the property's owner—and Nate himself—had both told her to stay away, she was determined to visit as soon as possible.

She was a terrible person. "My dad was a police chief in Boston, so unfortunately I'm used to things like this. I'd just hoped Savannah was safer."

"Nate?" A man built like a wrestler with long, black, braided hair yelled from the lobby on the first floor. "We gotta go, man."

Nate ignored him and kept his attention on her mouth. "I couldn't help but overhear. What did you see?"

She licked her lips. "You'd never believe me." She wasn't sure she believed it herself. Loud voices downstairs distracted her. Two military policemen in full uniform and carrying weapons had entered the station. "That's odd. What do you think they want?"

Nate took her hand and led her into a nearby alcove. "What did you see?"

She pressed her hands against his chest. His heart pounded, and he radiated heat like an engine revving. "What are you doing?"

"Nate?" The man with the braid ran up the stairs. "Time to go. Now."

"Please, Sarah. *Tell me.*"

The MPs were right behind Nate's buddy.

"In the shadows, I saw a man bow."

She heard Nate's sharp inhale right before he kissed her, his gentle hands on her shoulders at odds with his demanding lips. His warmth wrapped her in an erotic haze and he tasted like mint and summer breezes.

Had she moaned? *Good golly Moses.*

"Excuse me, ma'am."

Nate broke off the kiss because the man with the braid had taken his arm and dragged him down the hallway to the emergency exit, the MPs on their heels. Chills scurried along her arms, and she wrapped her sweater around herself. She touched her swollen lips, still stunned. Still tasting his peppermint mouthwash. Still inhaling his scent that reminded her of freshly cut grass and pine trees.

Nate glanced at her before he hit the metal exit and disappeared. The door slammed shut with a loud reverb. Apparently, he'd locked it as well. When the MPs couldn't force it open, they turned and ran past her, one of them brushing her skirt as they headed toward the stairs.

What do MPs want with Nate Walker?

"Miss Munro?" The officer who'd been ignoring her touched her elbow. "I'm ready for your statement."

She pulled away, her attention on the MPs racing out the front doors. She was a woman who sought the truth in both her professional and personal life. But tonight's revelation was more than a cheap magazine tell-all. It was an earth-shattering event that stripped away the delusions she'd been carrying her entire adult life. One delusion in particular: when Nate's lips had touched hers, she discovered she'd never truly understood what it meant to be kissed.

"Ma'am?"

She nodded. She'd give her statement. Then go home to her father. But as she followed the officer into an interrogation room, she couldn't help but wonder if she'd ever see Nate again. No. If she was being honest with herself, which she always tried to be, she wondered if she'd ever kiss Nate again.

CHAPTER 1

TWO WEEKS LATER, SARAH WAS LOST. THE PIRATED ISLE OF Grace cemetery map on her phone was useless. And the rustling and grunting sounds she'd heard from the woods told her she wasn't alone.

She clutched her camera and studied the seventeenth-century headstones and crosses leaning every which way in the sandy soil. Ancient oaks layered with Spanish moss hid whatever—or whoever—had made those noises.

The hand-painted sign TRESPASSERS WILL BE SHOT. THEN PROSECUTED. NO KIDDING. nailed to a tree reminded her to keep moving. She couldn't leave before photographing Saint Michael's statue.

The headless archangel stood at the central tomb in the Cemetery of Lost Children, on a four-foot plinth with one hand raising a sword to Heaven and the other clutching his shield. She snapped a picture. He was naked, quite unusual for a colonial-era tomb, but she was more interested in the initials *TT* carved below his feet.

Sarah adjusted her hood and knelt on wet wildflowers to take more photos, her jeans soaking up the dampness. The rustling and grunting started again. A tingly feeling spread through her body. "Who's there?"

A nearby group of blackbirds took flight.

She stood. "Hello?" Her voice echoed in the empty spaces around her.

A deer appeared from behind a limestone crypt, stared at her, then slipped into a copse of pecan trees.

Her shoulders dropped in relief. *What is wrong with me?* She wasn't usually so jumpy. Maybe it was the cemetery's creep factor. Maybe it was stress over her father's health and their meeting with the social worker later today. Or maybe it was the fact that she couldn't sleep without remembering the pressure of Nate's lips against hers.

It'd been two weeks, and she couldn't stop thinking about him. Or the MPs following him. Or that perfect, once-in-a-lifetime kiss. She touched her lips and studied Saint Michael again. He protected acres of defenseless, centuries-old headstones with a confidence she envied. If she had half his courage, she might not have ended up trespassing in an abandoned cemetery, at seven a.m., in the rain. Then again, he'd lost his head while she, at least, still had a job.

For now. She needed these photos for her grant proposal, and if she didn't take them today, there wouldn't be another chance.

"Lady Sarah." The British-accented voice coming from behind her was heavier than a whisper but lighter than a question. "Have no fear."

Her mouth went dry, and she turned, ready to use her camera as a weapon. Five yards away, a man emerged from behind a crumbling vault, too far for her to hit him with her camera but too close for her to run and not get caught. A green jacket covered black jeans, and his black boots crushed white daisies. He came forward.

"Who are…" She paused because his walk belied his height and width. It had to take tremendous strength to maintain control over every muscle so he could move with that eerie-yet-elegant fluidity. Before she could speak again, he swept his arm forward and bowed at the waist.

OhGodOhGodOhGod

"You're…a…" She couldn't even stutter the words *Fianna warrior*. Many believed that the Fianna had disappeared in 1149, after the Second Crusade, but she knew the truth. She wiped a sweaty palm on her hip and pretended that speaking to a man who'd committed his life to an army of merciless assassins dating to the Roman invasion of Britain was normal. Because, seriously, if he was here to kill her, she'd be dead already. "Aren't you?"

He nodded and said in a modulated voice, "My Prince calls me Cassio. I carry a message."

How long has he been watching me? "What message?"

Cassio shoved his hands into the pockets of his coat. The shoulders of his coat were darker than the rest, soaked through. "You must stop your unholy toil."

"My toil?" She removed her camera from around her neck and knelt to pack it away in her camera bag with her rolls of film. Her hands shook, betraying her calm and casual demeanor. "You mean my job at the Savannah Preservation Office? It's only temporary until I return to the Smithsonian."

"No, my lady." Cassio pointed to Saint Michael.

Oh. *That.* "I'm just submitting a grant proposal. To restore a seventeenth-century diary." She stood and inhaled the damp air, but the sting of mildew and decay burned the inside of her nose. She took another step away. "Not a big deal."

He raised an eyebrow, deepening the scar across his forehead. "The Prince has requested you leave this diary, and the love story it hides, alone. 'Tis a sad fable, best forgotten." Cassio held out his hands palms up. "No good comes from retelling old tales."

So the Prince, leader of the secret army of assassins called the Fianna, was taking an interest in her research. What did such a powerful, dangerous man want with the diary of a seventeenth-century teenage girl? She exhaled and straightened her shoulders. A million thoughts raced through her mind, but one was uppermost: he hadn't bowed all the way to the ground—the sign of imminent execution—yet.

She offered a pedantic smile, as if she was talking to a student in a graduate seminar. "The seventeenth-century love story between the brutal pirate Thomas Toban and his Puritan lover Rebecca Prideaux is *not* a fairy tale."

"You are correct, my lady. Fairy tales don't end with the hero killing the heroine because she betrayed him."

His smile reeked of condescension, and she fisted her hand to stop herself from slapping him. Because hitting a ruthless assassin? Really bad idea. "You're wrong about Thomas and Rebecca's love story."

"Yet your ideas about the lovers have been rejected." He crossed his arms and gave her the same kind of narrow-eyed glare her boss had perfected. "By your peers, no less."

The Prince had read her article in *The British Journal of Eighteenth Century History*? And knew about her Great Betrayal? Wonderful. "I don't understand. As you say, my reputation is in tatters and I'm barely hanging on to my job. Why does the Prince care about my research involving Rebecca's diary? I'd think, as leader of the Fianna, he'd have better things to do."

"This is his better thing." Now Cassio's voice resonated with a darkness that sent shivers along her spine, burning and chilling at the same time. "The Prince won't ask again, my lady."

"I—"

"Sarah, don't say another word." The deep male voice came out of the shadows off to her left. "Cassio, back the fuck up. Slowly."

Nate?

Sarah couldn't move. Her limbs were frozen in place, partly from Cassio's death threat and partly from Nate's sudden appearance. *What is he doing here?*

Nate emerged from the shadows in a black field jacket, jeans, and combat boots, pointing a gun at Cassio. His long blond hair was tied behind his neck, and he didn't stop moving until he stood between Sarah and the warrior.

"How now, brother?" Cassio tilted his head. "Let there be no fray between us this day."

Nate moved his aim from Cassio's chest to his head. "I told you I was taking care of this."

"Yet you weren't."

Nate's rough laugh could shred paper. "It's been fifteen fucking minutes."

"What's going on?" Sarah stood to the side behind Nate while the two men appeared locked in some kind of fierce, silent battle.

Her breaths were so shallow, she felt light-headed, just now realizing the danger. Trespassing, defying her boss's orders, and putting her job in jeopardy had been exhilarating until Cassio had showed up with threats and Nate appeared with a weapon.

None of this had been in the plan this morning when she set out for the Isle of Grace. And the last thing she wanted was for anyone to get hurt.

"Please, Nate," she said softly. "Cassio was just—"

"I know what he was doing," Nate said sharply, more to Cassio than to her since he hadn't even glanced in her direction. "Now it's time for him to leave."

Cassio kept his attention on Nate, who was making his point in a physically dominant way. Sarah had spent enough time with men to read Nate's stance. From his steady arm and the fact that he stood inches taller and wider than Cassio, Nate's nonverbal cues implied that if he lowered his gun, it was because he was going in for a fistfight.

Cassio lifted a shoulder as if he'd examined the threat and found it wanting. "You understand the consequences?"

"I told you I did." Nate nodded toward the damaged vault that someone had covered in plastic sheeting. "Now go."

Branches cracked behind Sarah, and she spun around. *Was that grunting?* "Do either of you hear that?"

"Cassio?" Nate said. "I still see you. Why aren't you leaving?"

Yes, she was sure she'd heard grunting. Almost like a snorting. "Nate?"

Cassio hit his fist against his chest and bowed his head. "As you wish, brother."

"Nate!" Sarah pointed to the woods. "I hear—"
Something loud whizzed by her head, and the reverb shut
down the chatter of bugs. *Gunshots.*

"Sarah!"

She headed toward Nate and tripped over a grave
marker. Her ankle turned, and pain shot up her leg. Nate
ran over, and Cassio vanished. That's when she heard footsteps behind the trees and another gunshot.

Someone was shooting at her.

Nate yanked her arm and dragged her along with him.
"*Run.*"

CHAPTER 2

NATE GRIPPED SARAH'S WRIST AND RACED TOWARD THE crumbling crypt covered with torn plastic. Adrenaline gave him the speed and strength he needed, though his head throbbed with one mother of an incoming headache.

He led Sarah behind the vault, avoiding rusted rebar sticking out like knives, and pressed them both to the ground, his chest against her back. She shifted, touching his arms. He bit his lower lip until he tasted blood. His arms, covered in a burn salve and wrapped in gauze, hurt like they'd been brushed with razors. It had been two weeks since Nate and his buddies had ended up in a shoot-out with Remiel Marigny's men at Capel Manor on the Isle of Grace. A battle that, despite Nate and his unit winning, had ended with a crashing helicopter and subsequent fire. That night had left Remiel defeated, but not out of the game. While Nate had mostly recovered from his cuts and scrapes, his charred arms were talking longer to heal. And he knew, deep in his combat-hardened heart, that while he'd been recuperating, Remiel had spent the same time rearming.

"Nate—"

He covered her mouth with one hand and could feel her shallow breaths. Despite her squirming, she didn't seem to be hurt. Except now her scent encompassed him. *She still smells like gardenias?* His body hardened, and he stirred in embarrassment. *Sing the ABC's. In your head. Backward.*

A minute later, he released his hand and whispered, "Remember to breathe."

She nodded, and he adjusted his body to aim his weapon, the shift bringing his hips higher on top of hers. He traced the trigger and counted down another minute. Then two more, until he heard nothing and saw no one. Of course

Cassio—that fucker—had left them alone. Because the Fianna's SOP was to issue insane orders then leave when things got hot.

The shots could've come from one of the Marigny boys who lived on the isle and poached on Capel land. Or had Cassio been right? Was Sarah in danger? Nate prayed not.

"Whoever was out there is gone." He stood, shoved his weapon in his waistband, and helped her stand. She stumbled until he caught her. "Are you hurt?"

"No." She scanned the cemetery. "You're sure they're gone?"

"Yes." He waited until she put weight on both feet. When she grimaced, he asked, "Did you turn your ankle?"

She hobbled over to a tomb, and he held her elbow as she sat. "I'll be okay. Did you hear those grunting and snorting sounds right before the shooting started?"

"No." His focus had been on Cassio. "Probably animals. Maybe wild boars. The shots could've come from hunters."

"Probably." She chewed her bottom lip, and he exhaled.

Here he was, in front of the woman who'd haunted his daydreams for the past two weeks, and he could barely speak. It's a good thing his buddies weren't here to see his pathetic self. That pack of former Green Berets, especially Pete, weren't likely to have much sympathy for his instant attraction to a die-hard historian he'd just met two weeks ago, regardless of how smart and beautiful she was. He'd never fallen so hard for a woman. Then again, he'd never ventured into a preservation office. If he'd known…hell, he would've run there in record time.

The jackhammer in his head made him nauseous, and an aura clouded his vision. He closed his eyes and squeezed the bridge of his nose with two fingers. No seizure. Not now.

"Nate?" She tapped his arm. "Are you alright?" Her soft voice floated over him.

"Fine." He even opened his eyes to prove how *fine* he was. "What are you doing here?"

She gripped the edges of the tomb until her knuckles turned white. Her brown hair had been braided, but strands now framed her face.

"Sarah?" He knelt in front of her. This wasn't how he'd envisioned their first meeting after their first kiss. "Is that your truck I found half a mile from the cemetery gate? I know you know this is private property. So you couldn't be trespassing."

She watched him from beneath long eyelashes. A breeze wafted through the graveyard, causing the mist to drift around the headstones.

"Alright." She threw up both hands. "Yes, I'm trespassing. Yes, the owner, Juliet Capel, told me not to, and I did it anyway. And yes, if my boss finds out, he's going to fire me."

Nate admired her reluctant honesty. "Why would your boss fire you?"

"Because he told me I wasn't to trespass on anyone else's property. No more investigating seventeenth-century graveyards or remote coastlines. No more losing Smithsonian-issued SLR cameras down eighteenth-century wells. My boss has this *thing* about breaking the rules."

She looked so irritated, like a teenager trying to explain a speeding ticket; he tried not to laugh. Yet he could also relate. "I have a boss like that too."

She tilted her head. "You have a boss?"

Now he'd said too much. "Everyone has a boss." He scanned the area again. His first concern was getting her out of this damn cemetery. His second would be figuring out how to protect her, as he'd promised Cassio he would.

And while Nate had been receiving secret orders from Cassio, Nate's men were at Iron Rack's Gym with their boss, Kells. None of them had a clue where Nate was, but by now he would definitely be missed.

Their gazes met again, and she looked away. Was she thinking about their kiss? He sure as hell was, because apparently he was still in high school. A mass of emotions settled in his gut. He hated the queasy adrenaline after-shocks that left his hands and feet with the shakes.

How am I going to get her to agree to my protection?

He could threaten, maybe throw around some physical intimidation. But he wouldn't do that to a woman. And never, ever, *ever* to Sarah.

Despite her dirty jeans, raincoat, mud-covered leather boots, and smudges on her pale cheeks, a shudder rocked his body. A man could lose himself in the depths of her brown eyes, and he stopped himself from reaching for her. Although maybe she'd accept a comforting hug and thank him for being a gentleman. After which she'd throw herself into his arms. Naked.

Yeah. That would be nice.

"Nate. I'm leaving now."

Sarah's voice drew him out of his stupor, and he shook his head to clear the erotic images. He had work to do. Cassio had been clear on Nate's nonnegotiable assignment. Protect Sarah. Stop her research. Don't tell Kells.

Earlier that morning, Nate had gotten a text from Cassio to meet him in the cemetery. Nate had almost pulled a no-show because his relationship with the Prince was not only complicated, it was a secret from Kells. But if Nate hadn't shown, Cassio would've hurt someone Nate cared about.

Unfortunately, his meeting with Cassio had left Nate in an untenable position. Although he was duty-bound to his CO and honor-bound to their men, Nate was now also an agent of the Prince—a.k.a. the leader of a covert army of highly trained assassins. It was a difficult sitch, and he hadn't had time to work it out yet. What with the gunshots and lying to Kells and saving Sarah.

"Wait a second." Leaving her sitting on the bench-like tomb, Nate headed toward the naked angel and found her camera bag on the ground. He'd been watching her while she'd taken photos. Not in a stalking way. In a figuring-out-how-to-let-her-know-that-she-was-in-danger kind of way. He'd been doing those mental gymnastics when Cassio appeared.

Nate hurried back to her. "I'll walk you out. I can't let you leave alone."

"Why? I thought you said it was safe."

He slung the bag on his shoulder, not surprised by her question. Her beauty was surpassed only by her stubbornness. And as frustrating as that trait was, it was also one of the things about her he found so damn attractive—except during a mission. During a mission, orders had to be followed or people died. "I'm here to protect you."

Sarah stood, but her ankle didn't like that, so she sat again. *Why do these things always happen?* "That hunter is gone. I'm sure he's halfway across the isle by now."

The truth was she didn't need Nate's protection. She had to figure out how to get to her truck. If either her father or her boss found out what had happened, she'd be in for some serious lectures. And a firing.

It didn't help that she could still feel Nate's hard body on top of hers and had been picturing him less…clothed. She let out a long breath. What was wrong with her? She could barely breathe. Forget thinking or talking or walking. When Nate was around, she became a blubbering mess.

"That hunter could be anywhere, and his carelessness could get us both shot." He carried her camera bag; his other hand still held his weapon. "What were you photographing?"

She took a ragged breath. "Tombs for my research."

Nate knelt, placing the camera bag and his gun on the ground next to him. Then he took her boot with the sore ankle and placed it on his thigh. Tenderly, he untied the laces and slipped it off.

His hands wrapped around her foot, and she felt his warmth through her pink sock. His fingers rubbed along

the sides, and she wondered about the scars on his hands.
She'd never ask, but they did make him appear even more
masculine. "What"—she dragged in more air to form her
words—"are you doing?"

"Checking your ankle."

Despite his gentle hands, his physical size overwhelmed
her. If she sat next to him, her head would only come to his
shoulder. And his thighs were bigger than her waist.

He rotated her foot. "It's a slight sprain. Nothing's torn,
and it's not broken."

It didn't hurt as much now that it was free, but it was still
tender. "Nate? What are *you* doing here?"

"Looking for trespassers."

His refusal to meet her gaze told her he was lying. "That
night we saw each other at the police station. You ran away
from those MPs. Why?"

"The MPs were searching for...someone else." He
finally looked at her with green eyes that drank her in like
she was frozen lemonade on a summer afternoon. Then he
laughed. The deep tone reverberated in her stomach.

She straightened. "What's so funny?"

"You are. Not funny." Now he smiled with perfect
teeth and a cheek dimple. "Just...surprising."

She wasn't sure how she felt about any of this. "You
talked to Cassio before I saw him. I believe your exact
words were *I told you I was taking take care of this*."

Nate's ears turned red.

"*This* meant *me*. Am I right?"

His eyes betrayed a heat that told her he remembered
their kiss. She licked her lips, but when his nostrils flared,
she dropped her gaze. She had to get home. Her father
needed his anti-seizure meds.

"How does it feel?" His hands on her ankle sent heat
through her body.

She swallowed before saying, "It hurts, but I can walk
on it." He massaged the tendons above the sprain. His

movements relieved the throbbing. "You haven't answered my question."

"I need to wrap the ankle to keep the swelling down." He pulled a white handkerchief out of his back pocket and unfolded it. Strawberries had been embroidered in the corners. "This was my mom's. I carry it for good luck."

"I hate to take it—"

"It's not a gift." He refolded it lengthwise and wrapped it around the bottom of her foot and her ankle. "It's a loan."

That meant she'd have to see him again. She wasn't sure how she felt about that either.

The handkerchief was large enough to encase, tie off, and keep her ankle stable. "This will help with the swelling until you get home. Ice it as soon as you can."

Once he finished, he put her boot on and laced it. She stood. The throb was now a low ache.

"Cassio knew I was taking photos for a research grant I'm applying for. He told me I needed to stop."

"That's a good idea." Nate studied the tall cross to their left. "You know what Cassio is?"

She swallowed. "He's a Fianna warrior."

"Then you also know his orders come from the Prince and what the Prince's warriors are capable of?" Nate took her hand, raised it to his lips, and dropped it.

Did he almost kiss my hand?

"I do." She shoved her hands in her raincoat pockets, trying not to be too disappointed. "Except I don't know why the Prince or his warriors care about my research."

"The why doesn't matter." Nate's voice sounded resigned, as if he'd dealt with assassins before and was tired of the whole thing. "Do you want me to drive you home?"

"No, thank you." If Nate drove and she left her truck, her father would find out she'd been trespassing. "What did Cassio want from you?"

Nate led the way. She followed slowly, and he reduced

his pace to let her keep up. "Cassio wants me to stop you from completing your research, which is probably that grant you're applying for."

"Why?"

"No idea." He adjusted the camera bag. "Why were you using a film camera?"

"My digital SLR is broken." She'd heard it crash when it hit the bottom of the eighteenth-century well she'd been investigating. On private land. After dusk. "I'm using my dad's camera. He's an eBay junkie with tons of film."

Nate held a branch so she could pass under it. "My uncle bought and sold on eBay too."

"Was he a photographer?"

"No." Nate frowned as if a bad memory had surfaced. "He collected knives."

"How interesting." She honestly wasn't sure what else to say and fell into silent step next to him. When the path out of the cemetery tightened, she let him lead the way. Except as she watched him walk, studying his shoulders flexing beneath the jacket, she couldn't stop thinking about their kiss two weeks ago. Was he thinking about it as well?

Thirty minutes later, she was too sweaty and breathless to care about the kiss. Nate had kept up a slow-but-steady pace, holding so many branches for her that she'd lost count.

Once at the truck, she tried to unlock the door but her shaking hands couldn't get the key in the lock. Then she dropped it. They both went down together. She found it first and stood quickly, only to bump her head on the rear-view mirror.

What is wrong with me?

Nate wrapped one strong arm around her waist and took the key with his free hand. He kept her close, her back to his chest, all six-plus feet of solid masculine warmth behind her as he unlocked the truck. His breath tickled her neck. His pine scent, reminding her of summer days, made breathing difficult.

What would happen if she turned around, slipped an arm around his neck, and lifted her lips? Instead, she slid into the driver's seat, praying he wouldn't notice her trembling.

Before she could close the door, he grabbed the door-frame. "Why don't you let me take you home?"

"I'll be okay." She tried twice before she got the key in the ignition.

He took her camera bag off his shoulder and handed it to her.

She'd almost forgotten. "Thanks." She tossed it onto the passenger seat.

"Sarah." Her name came out with a Southern drawl, and he put his muddy combat boot on the edge of the cab floor. "I have something of yours. If you want it back, you'll answer the phone when I call. And you'll meet me where and when I say." His granite jaw told her he wasn't joking.

"What are you talking about?"

He held out her rolls of film. He'd taken them from her camera bag.

"Give me my film." She used her firmest voice—the one she saved for her undergrads. "I need them developed today."

He shoved the film into his coat pocket. "Then you better get home so I can call you."

She caught another whiff of his scent and shivered. "Please get your foot out of my door, or I'm taking it with me." *Did I really say please?*

"I need your number."

She threw out each digit and started the truck. Unfortunately, it took a few tries to engage the clutch. Once she had the truck in gear, she glared at him, striving for calm, cool, and collected. Had she really considered kissing him again? What was wrong with her? "I have to get those photos sent off tonight. I'm on a deadline."

"So you're still applying for your grant?"

"Yes." The future of her career depended on winning that grant. If she won RM Foundation's money, she could restore Rebecca's diary enough to read it. If she could read it, then she could redeem Thomas and Rebecca's love story and, eventually, her own professional reputation. She released the parking brake and put the truck in reverse. "If anything happens to that film, the Smithsonian will hear about it." The lamest threat ever, but the best she had.

"I promise you, Sarah. I will call." He pointed to the dirt road behind her. "Now go."

She shifted to see behind her and stepped on the gas. Because of the narrowness of the road she'd taken—which had ended abruptly in a thicket of palmetto trees—she'd have to drive the entire way off Capel property backward. And the last thing she wanted was to hit anything and embarrass herself in front of Nate Walker.

CHAPTER 3

ZACK TREMAINE LEFT THE LOCKER ROOM OF IRON RACK'S Gym, freshly showered and changed after having spent two hours clearing the tunnels beneath the building. He passed the front desk painted with a Jolly Roger flag and headed into the front office. Thank goodness it was empty and the coffee hot.

The past two weeks had been hell, and caffeine was the only thing keeping his temper down. The fact that Luke, the youngest member of their unit as well as their office manager and tech guru/god, kept the grounds percolating 24/7 was more of a public service than a nice gesture.

Zack wasn't proud of his temper, but there was a lot he wasn't proud of at the moment. Including his shiny, new dishonorable discharge, which matched his new uniform of worn jeans and whatever T-shirt he scrounged up for the day.

It'd been a long five years since two of their unit's A-teams had been accused of the Wakhan Corridor Massacre and ambushed by a tribal warlord in the Pamir River Valley. A battle that left half of their men, including Nate, in a POW camp for two years. Once rescued by Zack and the remaining members of their unit who'd been in the command post at the time, Nate and the other rescued men had returned home only to be convicted of all sorts of crimes and sent to prison. Or, in Nate's case, a military psych hospital.

And a few weeks ago? Zack and his men who'd led the rescue had been, for some made-up, bullshit reason, dishonorably discharged. Hence their new digs in a run-down pirate-themed gym in Savannah. Because where else would a bunch of ex-Green Berets with no money, no connections, and no family hide out?

"Hey." Pete White Horse appeared in the doorway in a black T-shirt with a white skull and crossbones. The bones were barbells, and printed below them were the words: *Lift or Go Home.* The tee matched his long black braid and the tribal tats covering his biceps. "Kells wants this staff meeting started. Pronto."

Zack poured coffee into an Iron Rack's black-and-white logo mug. "Can I say no?"

"Nope." Pete checked his watch. "I gotta teach a Krav Maga class in forty minutes in the same space."

Zack poured sugar into his coffee. He normally drank it black, but what the hell. A new day, new job, new life. Isn't that what Kells had been spouting since they'd landed in Savannah after leaving Fort Bragg? "I'm coming."

"Hmmm." Now Pete was texting.

"What's wrong?"

Pete shoved his phone in his back pocket, and Zack followed him toward one of the two training rooms on the other side of the open gym that consisted of a few treadmills and a ton of lifting stations. A boxing ring had been dropped in the center, and the space was decorated with kitschy pirate flags nailed to the walls.

Pete's frown was frownier than usual. "Nate's not here."

"Maybe he went on a donut run." As the recently returned XO of their unit, Nate provided the carbs for their meetings, always hoping to distract them from Kells's bad moods. It never worked. It just spiked their insulin and set them up for late-afternoon sugar crashes. But no one asked Nate to stop. No one wanted to hurt his feelings when he had so much shit to deal with. Nobody came back from Afghanistan unscathed, but after years in that POW camp, Nate was both mentally and physically scarred worse than most.

"Nate took a vehicle."

"Nate can't drive. What about his seizures?"

Pete snagged a clipboard as he passed the desk. "He's still having them. He's still not sleeping because of those nightmares. And he's still spending half his awake time in that damn ring, fighting whoever'll take him on."

Yeah. Zack had noticed the time Nate spent in the gym, mostly getting beat up. "What'll you tell Kells?"

Pete stopped near the door with a window. "No idea."

Zack studied the four men sitting in fold-up chairs, waiting for the meeting to start. Thanks to the U.S. Army's secret counsel, their unit was down to the eight who weren't in prison and had no families to return to. "Nate will show."

"I know." Pete checked his phone again. "I just don't know when. Kells will see through any cover story. He's got that damn internal bullshit meter."

"Leave it to me." Zack had an idea where Nate might be. "I'll return in five. Ten max."

⟡

Fifteen minutes later, Zack entered the training room, hoping to slip in quietly. Except the door squeaked like a rusted outboard motor scraping concrete, and every head turned.

"You're late." Kells stood at the front of the room, arms crossed. He wore his daily uniform of tan combat pants with a white T-shirt. While he'd polished his combat boots, he hadn't shaved in a week, and his reddish beard emphasized his ginger status. His dark-gray eyes and his buzzed red hair—not to mention his height, which made him the tallest man in the unit—added to his intimidating Celtic/Viking/Angry Scot appearance. "Did you find Nate?"

Zack sat in one of the chairs set up in a semicircle, between Luke and an empty seat. Cain, Ty, and Vane sat opposite. "Nate will be here soon."

Pete, who stood behind Kells, rolled his eyes.

Yeah, it was a crappy excuse, and it even bordered on a lie. Nate hadn't been at the grungy nightclub he worked at, the same place he'd once bought his illegal anti-seizure drugs. Since spending time in an Afghan warlord's shithole prison wasn't enough hell for one man, Nate had come home suffering from convulsions, seizures, and nightmares. Unfortunately for the few weeks that Nate and Pete had been on their own in Savannah, before the rest of the unit showed up, Nate has started self-medicating. The irony was that it took a battle with Remiel Marigny, their psychotic, arms-dealing asshole enemy, to get Nate clean. So whatever Nate was doing? It was for the good of the unit. That's the kind of brother Nate was: loyal, trustworthy, and determined to redeem all of their lives.

"Does anyone know where Nate went?" Kells asked the group.

"No." Cain's legs were stretched out, his booted feet crossed, hands clasped on his stomach, and he stared at the ceiling. He'd shaved his head. Again. "His bike's still here. He couldn't have gone far."

"Nate will return," Ty said in a voice that couldn't sound more bored. Or depressed. Or maybe just not giving a fuck. With Ty, the poster boy for the blond-hair/blue-eyed/perfect-looking-people society, it was hard to tell the difference. "Where else is Nate going to go?"

Vane, in an Iron Rack's T-shirt and his long brown hair tied at the base of his neck, glared. "How about jail?"

Zack leaned forward until his elbows cut into his thighs. Vane had served with Kells the longest and, because Kells trusted Vane completely, had developed an entitled attitude. As much as Zack wanted to like the brother who was always willing to do the hard things, Vane's know-it-all vibe got tiresome.

Ty looked at Kells directly. "What's Vane talking about?"

Kells's gaze fired a metaphorical round at Vane. "Nothing."

From the finality in Kells's word, Zack knew the *nothing* was bullshit. He prayed that Nate wouldn't have to go back to the U.S. military's prison hospital, a.k.a. the army's secret psych ward, in Maine. Considering Nate's emotional shape, Zack wasn't sure his friend would survive.

"Zack." At Kells's command, Zack met his boss's stare. "I was saying that the renovation of Prideaux House is taking longer than expected, so we're stuck living above the gym for a while."

Vane moaned the loudest. "One bathroom for the eight of us?"

"Dude." Ty's impatience brought out his Tennessee accent. "We have an entire locker room to ourselves after hours."

"And who has to do all *that* laundry and cleaning?" Vane asked.

"We do," Luke said, taking notes on a clipboard. "There're seven of us, so each of us takes a housekeeping day."

Zack scanned the room. There were eight of them, but no one was going to make Kells take over the suds and dryer sheets. Not because he was their CO and two weeks ago had been a full colonel in charge of a Special Forces Brigade. He just sucked at laundry. He didn't separate lights and darks.

"How're we on classes?" Kells asked Pete.

"Good." Pete clamped his clipboard to his chest. "Vane and I are teaching two classes a day, six days a week to civilians. One is for women. And it's only half full. Since this place has historically been all male, we need to get the word out. I also want to update our own self-defense skills. I'm instituting mandatory classes three days a week just for us. Vane and I will alternate instruction."

"When are we supposed to do that?" Ty said. "Between running this place and doing laundry and clearing those damn tunnels, there's no time."

"And the club reopens tonight," Pete said. "We'll be taking turns working security."

"You mean bouncers at that goth strip joint down by the river?" Ty smiled at Cain. "Can't wait to see you in leathers."

Cain gave Ty a middle finger.

"No dressing up," Pete said. "I couldn't handle seeing you all in leathers that tie up the crotch and ass." He handed out spreadsheets. "Nate made schedules. They include everything except for when to piss. Learn them. Love them. The first one who bitches goes to the tunnels."

Zack groaned. Every moment was accounted for. All the jobs in the gym, from wiping down equipment to disinfecting the locker rooms, were laid out by day, time, and name. The morning hours were marked for clearing the tunnels. Because, unbeknownst to most normal people walking around the historic district, Savannah had been built upon an eighteenth-century underground system of tunnels and cisterns. Of course, they were in ruins and filled with rubbish and rats, because that's how their luck was going lately. But Kells's thinking was if they got the tunnels cleared, they'd have a battlefield advantage in case Remiel attacked their unit in the city. A situation Zack didn't even like to consider. Still, he didn't mind the work. Since it was summertime in Savannah, it was cooler below the city than above.

The club required two bouncers at night, and Kells's name wasn't on that roster either. That meant they each had to work two nights a week. Zack had to give Nate credit. The schedule, while exhausting, was fair. And the workout schedule would help manage their pent-up frustration. Besides a weight-lifting regimen, Pete had them taking classes on different self-defense disciplines including Krav Maga, jujitsu, and… "What's Dirty Defense?"

"Street fighting," Pete said. "Standard defense moves with knives, chains, broken bottles. I'm teaching that one."

Zack grimaced.

"Trust me," Pete said. "We're going to need it."

"Since Pete and I are the only ones qualified to teach," Vane said in that annoying, *knowing* way that drove Zack insane, "we need more instructors so we can offer more classes to make more money. The gym memberships barely keep the AC on. I'll be talking to each of you about teaching specific courses."

Zack and Luke shared a glance. *Oh, yeah*. He felt the same way about teaching civilians: he'd rather stick hot pokers up his nose.

Pete handed out another paper. "Money's an issue. Calum Prioleau owns this place, the nightclub where we'll start working as bouncers, and Prideaux House, where we'll eventually live. He's paying for the renovations and isn't charging us rent, but the money we make here and at the club pays for our expenses. Since none of us are drawing a salary from Uncle Sam and our accounts are still frozen *and* we want time for our mission, we need to make this plan work."

"Why are we working at the club again?" Cain asked. "Because the money's not that great."

"Since Nate and I came into town a few weeks ago," Pete said, "before the rest of you arrived, that club was our only source of intel. It also provides off-the-books cash income."

"To put it bluntly," Kells added, "we need information and cash. We're running on empty. Empty gas tanks. Empty wallets. Empty gun chambers."

Zack knew the dismal state of their nonexistent finances and had no answers. Their dishonorable discharges, along with their unit's reputation-destroying scandals, had left them unemployable, with bank accounts seized by the U.S. Army. They weren't even eligible for contract gunslinging work. They'd once been proud Green Berets and now were blackballed.

Cain crumpled his schedule. "What about our mission? How are we supposed to find out why our A-teams were set up and our men sent to prison if we're working the gym, the club, and clearing tunnels?"

"When Nate gets here, we'll talk about it." Kells sounded

more frustrated than defeated. Or maybe that's what they needed to believe right now. "When is Charlotte arriving?"

Zack prayed that Charlotte—the only wife left in the unit—would get here soon. Cain, although one of the best combat-tested soldiers in the room, was moody as shit. And the only cure was Charlotte, his beautiful psychiatrist wife who was in North Carolina until she could leave her job and come to Savannah.

"Next weekend," Cain said. "She has an interview at a local hospital. If she gets the job, we'll rent an apartment nearby." Cain grinned at Vane. "You'll only have to share the john with six men."

Vane snarled. "Living with your wife doesn't get you out of cleaning duties."

Cain bared his teeth. "Never said it did."

"Is there anything else?" Kells asked the group.

"No," they said simultaneously. Without Nate to run interference, no one wanted the meeting to last longer than necessary.

"Good," Kells said. "Dismissed."

CHAPTER 4

NATE WAS NO GENTLEMAN. IN FACT, HE WAS AN ASSHOLE. Hadn't Vane, just yesterday, called Nate on his assholeness after handing out housekeeping assignments?

As Nate watched Sarah's truck disappear beneath a canopy of trees, he wished he could bring her back and… do what? Kiss her again? Stare into her brown eyes? Act like a lovesick fool?

In his defense, he'd told her to stay off Capel land. That cemetery had seen its share of violence, and it hadn't been confined to the eighteenth century.

A breeze dried the sweat on his neck. *Is that grunting?* He hadn't been joking about the wild boars. They roamed the more remote areas of Capel land and could be seeking prey farther inland.

When nothing charged him, he started the hike to the SUV parked near Pops Montfort's trailer on the edge of Capel land. While the Montforts didn't own as much property as the Capels, Pops and his buddy Grady Mercer— another patriarch of the isle—were the current caretakers of the Capel land roads that comprised more than half of the Isle of Grace.

The drone of buzzing insects and chirping birds brought life to this desolate land best known for centuries of tragedy and death. The scent of honeysuckle thickened the air, and the heat-fueled humidity felt…*unholy*. Nate kicked a rotted log out of the way, slapped a mosquito on his neck, and fought his way through a hedgerow of thistles. Somehow, he'd lost the trail in the boggy ground. He'd love to strip off his coat, but there was no way he'd expose his burned arms to the blood-sucking bugs.

Although it wasn't even eight a.m., he was hot, sweaty,

and tired. He didn't want to return to town and face Kells with his *you're not supposed to drive* concerns. Yeah, his buddies were worried about him. Hell, he was too. But for the moment, he craved the isolation of the woods, the peace of not having to deal with all the bullshit in his life.

He climbed over a split live oak tree eaten by termites and jumped a stream, grateful for his boots. Then he wiped his face with the edge of his T-shirt. Why hadn't he thought to bring water? Or a machete? Maybe he'd be killed by a boar, and then he wouldn't have to worry about his deal with Cassio, about Sarah's safety, about his men's situation, about lying to Kells, about returning to that prison hospital.

Shit. He hated self-pity, but it was better than thinking about Sarah. Figures he—a man who followed every command ever issued—would fall for a woman who did as she pleased. A woman who smelled like gardenias and stared at him with those beautiful brown eyes.

He was fucked.

Despite his annoyance at her apparent inability to follow orders, his body heated up as he envisioned her wearing nothing but a warm, inviting smile. Sweat dripped down his neck and arms, making the healing skin itch.

He felt for the handkerchief in his back pocket—which he'd given to Sarah—and reached for the medal around his neck that wasn't there anymore. Sighing, he avoided a prickly branch with thorns that looked like razors. He'd either make it to Pops's by noon or land in the Black River. But one thing was certain: he'd missed Kells's staff meeting. And his boss would be pissed.

∽

Forty minutes later, Nate arrived at Pops's red barn, situated behind a double-wide trailer. The yard held a variety of classic American cars, mostly from the fifties and sixties. It was hard to tell exact models since the grass reached his knees.

Ratatatat. Ratatatat. Ratatatat.

The sound of rapid gunfire sounded from the other side of the property, where Pops and Grady had a rifle and pistol range. As much as Nate wanted to join the ex-Marines in pounding rounds, his brain felt like it was being crushed by his skull, a sure sign of an oncoming migraine, the kind that led to a seizure. He needed to return to the gym while he could still drive.

Once at his SUV, he found his cell phone in the glove box and reinserted the SIM card. He'd gotten into the habit of taking the SIM card out because he was sick of being tracked by everyone and everything. It didn't take long for Pete's texts to appear.

> Where the fuck are you!?! Kells is pissed. Call
> me. ASAP!!!!!!

Then there was Zack's text. *Give me a story and I'll cover for you.*

Nate leaned against the SUV's door. Why was he so fucking restless? Was it because he was lying to Kells and his men? Was it general anxiety about his future and these damn headaches? Or was he worked up because of Sarah? He took a roll of film from his pocket. He couldn't lie about what he needed. Not the way his body threw off heat. He wanted to see Sarah again, in a seriously sexy and horizontal way. But he was one breath above being homeless and jobless.

He tossed the film through the open window onto the passenger seat and pressed his forehead to the vehicle's hot metal. He had no money. No prospects. Had serious problems with migraines, seizures, and his long-term memory. *Aaaaaaaaand* even though he still had weeks to worry about it, there was the whole prison hospital thing. Yep. He was real prince material.

A raindrop hit his forehead, and he raised his face to

the sky. The musty scent of rain hitting the soil burned the inside of his nose. A storm would be a welcome relief to all of this heat and stress.

When his phone rang, he answered on speaker. He couldn't put off Pete any longer. Nate might be a screwup as a soldier, but he wasn't a dick. "Hey, brother. I'm on my way—" The words dried in his throat, and he pulled out his gun.

A man stood in front of the SUV in the shadow of a massive oak tree. In dark jeans and with a black hooded sweatshirt hiding his face, he held a nine-mil, barrel pointed down. Yet he didn't bow.

When had that become a good thing?

"Nate?" Pete asked.

The hooded man's finger twitched on the Glock's trigger. From the man's stance, he was a quick draw.

"What do you want?" Nate asked.

"What?" Pete asked. "Where are you?"

"At Pops—" Nate's vision splintered.

"Nate!" Pete's voice crackled over the phone's speaker. "What's going on?"

Nate couldn't speak. The agony in his head had moved in with knives. He fell to his knees. And threw up.

"Shit!" Pete's voice blasted. "Zack and I are on our way. Don't fucking move."

Not a problem considering the IEDs exploding in Nate's head meant an incoming seizure. Colors burst in front of his eyes, and he shut them to keep all extra light out. He regulated his shallow breaths and, as he faded into black, kept one vision anchored in his mind. A sexy woman with brown eyes framed by long hair. *Sarah Munro.*

⁓

An hour later, Sarah parked in front of her house in Savannah's historic district. The rain hadn't hit the city yet, but clouds hovered on the outskirts. She closed her eyes and stretched her foot. Her ankle ached, and her shoulders felt as if she was holding Atlas's burden.

Thunder hit, and she opened her eyes to find her father standing on the brick stoop. *What is it with men and the hands-on-the-hips thing?*

Her father waited, with a scowl marring his face. In jeans, boots, and a red flannel shirt, he looked more like a Cape Cod fisherman than a Georgia retiree. Next to him, in the same stance and wearing jeans, a black T-shirt, and a College of Charleston baseball cap pulled down low over his eyes, was a man she hadn't seen since her dad retired. Detective Hugh Waring. Her father's former partner in Boston until an IA investigation ruined both their lives. Six foot with short brown hair and penetrating hazel eyes, he was one of the few men her father still respected, trusted, and remembered.

The moment she shut the car door, her father's voice boomed, "Where have you been, and what have you been doing?"

She gave him her fakest smile and tried to come up with a story. Although, having been caught in many a lie, her story fizzled. At least the look in his brown eyes was of annoyance, not pain. She reached for his hand.

"Sorry I'm late, Dad. I had a run-in with the pharmacist." She paused as Hugh took her bag off her shoulder. For some reason she didn't want to identify, she noted that Hugh wasn't as tall as Nate. "What are you doing here, Hugh? I thought you were still in New York."

Hugh kissed her cheek. "Hey, Sarah—"

"Hugh left the NYPD," said her dad. "Now he's a detective in Charleston. Homicide. And he's here to talk to me."

"Will you stay for the auction tomorrow, Hugh?" she asked, hoping to deflect her dad's questions. "It's at the Mansion Hotel on Forsyth in downtown Savannah. It's for those pirate weapons I authenticated. Seventeenth and eighteenth century."

"No," her dad answered instead. "Hugh has to be in Charleston by noon."

She and Hugh exchanged eye rolls as she limped into the tiled foyer. "Coffee?"

Hugh winked. "Yes, please."

"Dad, did you have your tea yet?" Almost a year ago she'd found a recipe for an herbal tea in her grandmother's recipe box that was supposed to help with migraines. Now she made sure her father drank at least two cups a day. Although four would be better.

"No." Her father shut the front door and frowned at Hugh. "It's horse piss."

Ugh. "Dad," she said, heading into the kitchen. "It's been helping your headaches and your seizures." And his memory, but she didn't want him to worry about that. She wasn't sure how aware he was of his memory lapses.

"What happened, Sarah?" her father asked. "You're muddy."

Hugh followed behind them as if he knew to stay out of the line of fire. He dropped her camera bag on the counter near a package. Her name was on the front with no return address.

"I'm fine." She took the new pill bottle out of her purse and gave it to her father, hoping he wouldn't notice her scratched hands. Then she put on water for his tea. "Hugh, have you had a chance to check out that name I gave you a few weeks ago?"

"Nate Walker?" Hugh poured himself a cup of coffee. "I ran a prelim search. You were right about him being ex-military but I don't have any military contacts anymore."

"I'll text you the name of mine." Her father used a knife to pry open the lid. After swallowing one pill, he said, "Sarah, why are you limping?"

Hugh added, "What happened to your hands?"

Why did her dad and his best friend have to be detectives? Why not dentists?

She gave her father a glass of water and filled a tea ball with her special herbal concoction. "I fell and hurt my ankle." She then poured herself a cup of coffee. Now all she needed was a shower so she could erase Nate's sexy scent.

"Hugh." She added boiling water to the tea ball in her father's mug. The scent of bacopa leaves and feverfew filled the room. "What are you doing here?"

Hugh drank his coffee before saying, "Have you heard about the heroin?"

"Of course she's heard," her dad said. "But she hasn't answered my question."

His eyes had that certain hooded gaze that meant he'd reverted to *Joe Munro. Chief of police for the fine city of Boston. Retired.*

"Might as well tell him, Sarah," Hugh said.

Heaven save her from bossy men.

She added honey to her father's cup and checked the steeping. If it was too strong, it could cause vomiting.

"*Sarah.*"

"Okay." Sticking to the edges of the truth might get her through this unscathed. "I met a man."

Hugh took a vibrating cell out of his pocket. "Excuse me, Sarah."

"You can take it out on the patio," her dad said. The moment Hugh left the room, her dad continued his interrogation. "This man—how did you meet him?"

She handed him the tea, and he scrunched his nose. He didn't like it, but he slept so much better when he drank it.

She stirred more sugar into her coffee. "I tripped over a tombstone, and he helped me."

"Oh." Her father finished his tea in three large gulps, grimaced, and placed the mug in the sink. "I was worried."

She hugged him, and he kissed her head before pulling away. Since he was a proud, stubborn ex-cop, these moments were rare. She'd remember every one for both their sakes. It didn't matter that he'd adopted her after marrying her mother. He was her father, and she'd do everything in her power to protect and care for him.

She picked up her coffee and left the kitchen. "If you're feeling okay later, we could develop my pictures in your darkroom. I have to send them to the granting agency tonight." Once she got the film back, of course.

He sent a text on his cell phone and followed her through the family room. "These pictures wouldn't be a ploy to keep my mind off today's appointment with the social worker?"

She shook her head. There was no more room in her heart for sadness and worry.

Her dad took her elbow. "Someone left that package for you. It must've been delivered last night. Felt like a book."

"Probably someone wanting me to authenticate something." Not knowing if he was feeling weak or just wanted to touch her, she led him through the French doors. Since returning to Savannah, she'd taken over the walled garden and his study. He hadn't said a word about either, which only spoke to his lack of energy.

She stepped onto the flagstone patio lined with pink geraniums and gardenias and sat at the iron table.

"No," Hugh said. "Tell Mrs. Pinckney I'll come by this afternoon."

When Hugh ended the call, her dad asked, "Everything okay?"

"A missing person case." Hugh glanced at his buzzing phone. "Thanks for the contact info, Joe."

"Of course," her father said.

Hugh removed his baseball cap, balancing it on the raised brick edge of the pond. His movements, so efficient and careful, reminded her of that moment in the courtroom when the Boston DA had dropped all charges against Hugh and he'd turned around to mouth a thank-you. Her father had taken the blame to save the younger man's career.

She gripped the coffee cup, using the heated ceramic to

re-center her emotions. So much had happened to them in the past three years between the drug-bust-turned-bloodbath, her dad's resulting blackouts and seizures, and her own job debacles. That life in Boston didn't seem real anymore.

After her father sat, Hugh joined them, his foot tapping beneath the table in time to the water fountain. With the worn leather chest holster holding his weapon, he resembled Nate. Except where Nate had been all strength and determination and control, Hugh seemed like a viper waiting to strike.

"Sarah," her dad said with a smug smile. "Hugh wants my help."

Hugh nodded, and she appreciated the gesture. Retiring early, under suspicion, from the Boston police force was the hardest thing her dad had ever done, and helping Hugh might get her dad through today's evaluation. His memory lapses had become so frequent, the neurologist and the social worker had mentioned in-patient therapy.

"Don't wear him out, Hugh," she said. "My dad's cranky even when he's not tired."

Hugh laughed, and in his eyes, she saw the truth. He was also here to say goodbye in case the next seizure wiped out her dad's memory completely. Her vision fogged, and she checked her fish in the pond. The birds treated her koi as snacks.

"Very funny," her father said. But his rare smile told her he was flattered by both their attention and their worry. "Now. Hugh. What do you need?"

"This heroin is killing us, Joe. It's been laced with some unidentified compound that causes blackouts and comas." Hugh reached for the black leather briefcase he'd carried outside. "Luckily, I caught a break in my investigation."

Her dad leaned forward, his hands clasped, his eyes crystal clear. Sarah didn't know if it was excitement over being needed or if his pain meds had taken effect. But she loved seeing his eyes flash with intelligence and clarity, and she grabbed his hand.

Her dad squeezed back. "Have you caught any dealers?"

"None. I spoke to Detective Garza here in Savannah, and the SPD hasn't caught any either." Hugh found a photo in the briefcase and laid it facedown on the table. "The only clue I have is a dead dealer found yesterday on a Charleston wharf. He'd been shot, and someone cut his palm."

Her father's eyes darkened. "That wasn't on the news."

"No," Hugh said. "I made sure it wasn't."

Sarah sipped her coffee. "How do you know this dead dealer is connected to this new drug?"

"An informant," Hugh said. "But it's still hearsay because I have no evidence."

The doorbell rang, and she hurried to answer it. But when she opened the door, no one was there. An intense tingling in her arms told her something was wrong. Tourists sauntered by with cameras, a large man walked his tiny dog, and two boys were trying to skateboard on cobblestones.

Then she saw a man near the street corner beneath a magnolia tree. Average height, black T-shirt. She raised a hand to shade her eyes. She raised a hand to shade her eyes and blinked. Cassio wrapped one arm around his waist and bowed.

She ran inside and locked the door. Her heart beat so fast she could only take shallow breaths. Before she could peek out the window to see if he was still there, her phone buzzed on the kitchen counter. When she read the message, she realized the new text came from a blocked ID.

> Lady Sarah, thou must cease thy unholy bother to save thy noble father.

CHAPTER 5

SARAH PRESSED THE PHONE TO HER FOREHEAD. IT WAS HER second warning from the Fianna. Despite the blocked ID, the text had to have come from Cassio. Only Fianna warriors spoke and texted in Shakespearean verse. From what little she knew about them, their fierce reputation came not just from their violent deeds but from the severe penances and acts of self-discipline they forced themselves to endure. Including, but not limited to, memorizing all of the bard's plays. But why did Cassio—and the Fianna—care about her research? What could a tragic seventeenth-century love story have to do with a secret army of assassins?

The whole thing was ridiculous. Except for the fact that she'd received two warnings—no, three. Nate had warned her as well.

She started another pot of coffee. While she measured the grounds, voices carried through the open French doors. Both men sounded loud and animated, and Sarah smiled until she heard the detective say, "Joe? It's Hugh. Remember? I'm your friend."

She placed the coffee scoop in the sink. Dry heaves rumbled in her stomach.

"Are you sure?" her father said.

"Yes, Joe," Hugh said. "We're talking about that heroin bust behind O'Malley's Pub in South Boston? Three years ago? The one that cost us our jobs? That's why I'm here. I think that case is related to the heroin we're dealing with now."

"I don't remember."

The scent of brewing beans filled the kitchen, and her stomach cramped.

"It's okay, Joe," Hugh said. "Tell me about your garden."

She ran to the bathroom and slammed the door. The cold water on her face helped, but her mascara, not as waterproof as the label promised, made her look like a deranged raccoon.

A few minutes later, her father knocked. "Sarah? It's okay."

Unable to hide any longer, she came out. Her father took her in his arms and squeezed. She hugged him back, knowing it would never be okay again. "Is Hugh still here?"

"Yes." Her father's face was translucent, the skin drawn tightly over his cheekbones. "I'm looking for something in my study."

She breathed deeply and tried on a smile. "What does it look like?"

"A green folder, in one of the boxes I took when I left the department."

After promising to find it, she headed for the study. Her history books and maps—everything she'd once kept in her office at the Smithsonian—covered all horizontal surfaces. She went to the closet where she'd shoved her dad's boxes. Once she found the folder, she returned to the patio and handed it to her father, who was studying Hugh's photo.

"This case ruined our lives, Hugh. And neither one of us remembers how we both ended up passed out behind O'Malley's Pub next to four dead police officers and two dead drug dealers."

"Each of those murdered dealers had a cut in his hand like the man I found yesterday."

Her father slid the folder across the table, and Sarah clasped his shaking shoulder. If his agitation grew into a panic attack, he could take days to come out of it. And they both had to keep it together for the social worker's visit. "Hugh? Do we have to do this now?"

"Yes." Hugh opened the file, and his face paled. "It's the same person, Joe. Whoever's pushing this stuff now, it's the same as before."

"Let me see." Her father's voice sounded tired, but he took both photos and laid them on the table next to each other.

"Sarah," Hugh said, "I'm not supposed to show my photo to anyone. It's from an active crime scene, and I'll lose my job. Again."

"I promise I won't say anything." She stood over her father, one hand on his shoulder, and studied the photos. "Besides, no one believes me anymore. *The British Journal of Eighteenth Century History* made sure of that." In both photos, the victims had been shot in the chest and blood covered their left hands. "How come I didn't see this photo at the trial?"

"Our defense attorneys didn't think it would help our case," Hugh said.

Her father placed his fingers on the two photos. "Both vics were hit in the same exact spot, and both left hands were carved up."

"They were carved with the letter *B*," Hugh said.

Sarah studied the older photo taken behind O'Malley's Pub. She'd seen plenty of crime scene photos in her life but had never gotten used to them. She met Hugh's gaze as the realization hit. "If you find this killer, you and my father could be exonerated?"

"We weren't found guilty," Hugh said, "but our reputations could be restored."

A miracle she'd been praying for for three years. She studied her father's photo again, this time noticing a thirteen-digit alphanumeric sequence printed on the sides of the drug packages. "What are these numbers?"

"No idea," her father said. "We were never able to ID them."

She wiped her palms on her jeans. Her body felt cold despite the rising humidity. "These letters and numbers are part of the seventeenth-century Prideaux pirate cipher that may have also been used during the Revolutionary War."

"How could you possibly know that?" Hugh asked.

"I studied the Prideaux pirate cipher for years. Until I almost lost my job." She tossed the photo onto the table. "No one's ever solved it."

Hugh frowned. "What's the cipher for?"

"It designated the locations of underground rooms built along the southeastern coastline and used to hide contraband. Or, during the Revolution, military matériel." She pointed to the photos. "Those hide sites have never been found because the cipher has never been solved. It's legendary because it's unsolvable."

"You mentioned this cipher almost cost you your job." Hugh tilted his head. "Was your article in *The British Journal* about this cipher and these hide sites?"

"Yes. Along with the love story behind how the cipher went missing."

"If someone has solved the cipher," her father added, "it's possible that same someone is using these hide sites to move this heroin."

The doorbell rang, and Sarah rose. If Cassio was still playing games, she'd do some serious yelling. "Excuse me."

"Seventeenth-century ciphers?" Hugh started stacking photos. "Crazy."

She left the patio in full agreement. But crazy didn't make it not true. She opened the door to find Miss Tidwell, her dad's social worker, on the stoop. A white van was parked behind her car in the tight, semicircular brick driveway, with two men in white uniforms standing beside it.

Sarah blew out a breath. "You're early, Miss Tidwell. I thought our home visit was later this afternoon?"

Miss Tidwell pushed her way into the foyer, and the two men followed. "There's been a complication." The social worker wore her standard outfit of blue pencil skirt, white blouse, and sensible black flats. Today, her short white-blond hair was slicked with gel, her lips stop-sign red.

Sarah shut the door, not caring that the force caused the hall's chandelier to shake. "What kind of complication?"

Miss Tidwell walked into the kitchen, waving a piece of paper. "We're here for your father. We believe he's in danger in this home."

Sarah followed, took the paper, and scanned the document with the State of Georgia seal. Her heart rate revved, and her shaky hands tore the edges. "What is this?"

Hugh came in from the patio and took the paper. "This is an involuntary commitment order for Joe Munro. Why?"

"We believe"—Miss Tidwell rested her skinny butt against the counter—"that Mr. Munro's seizures are caused by trauma and the decline in his memory is due to poor nutrition."

"*What?*" Sarah spat out the word, and Hugh gripped her shoulder.

"The commitment paperwork is legal," Miss Tidwell said. "I have the right to remove Mr. Munro and commit him."

Her father appeared. "What's that racket?"

Miss Tidwell gave Sarah's father a simpering smile, as if she cared for his well-being. As if she didn't have a heart the size of a Lyme-infected tick. "Mr. Munro—"

Joe retreated until he hit the wall next to the refrigerator. "Stay away from me, you evil cow."

Sarah moved in front of her dad. "You're not taking him anywhere."

Miss Tidwell shrugged. "We can, and we are."

"Sarah!" Hugh shook her arm. "They have the paperwork. They've followed the procedures and made their case. Their commitment forms are legit—"

"Their premise for committing him is wrong. The seizures are causing his…lapses. Not poor nutrition." She nodded toward the two men in white who'd taken her father's arms.

Hugh released her and lowered his voice. "You need a lawyer. Do you know anyone in town?"

She wiped her face with her palms. Her cheeks felt tender, and her eyes burned. "I know someone I can ask for a recommendation."

"Let go of me!" her father bellowed.

"Miss Tidwell," Hugh said with an edge in his voice that could slice diamonds. "According to your paperwork, you can take Mr. Munro to a specified psychiatric facility for one week."

"Yes."

"Yet there's nothing in your document that says Miss Munro can't appeal the order."

Miss Tidwell blinked. "There's a procedure for that."

"You're also required to tell us where you're taking him."

"St. Joseph's Hospital. He'll be in the short-term psychiatric unit."

"You're not taking me anywhere." Her father kicked one of the orderlies, and Sarah saw the other slip something out of his pocket. A syringe.

She ran to her dad and cupped his face in her hands. "Please, Dad. Go with them. I know who can help us."

"Screw that." Her father spat in Miss Tidwell's direction.

The orderly stabbed the syringe into her father's neck.

"No!" She grabbed the orderly's arm, but it was too late. Her father's eyes rolled before his head slumped forward. The orderlies almost fell to the floor under the deadweight of her father's body.

Sarah faced the social worker. "You'll be hearing from my lawyer today. I'll get my father released. And expect to be sued."

The orderlies laid her father on a stretcher they'd brought in without her noticing. They carried him out, and Miss Tidwell followed with no word of comfort.

Hugh stood next to her. "Don't worry. Joe will be okay. I'll grab my things and follow them. I want to make sure they're taking him to where they say they are."

She was so grateful for Hugh's help. "We have to save him." She sniffled, found her phone on the counter, and started dialing. "We have to."

"We will, Sarah. I promise." He squeezed her hand. "I owe your father for my second chance."

She nodded and swallowed. Why did anger and frustration taste like vinegar? On the second ring, Calum Prioleau answered.

"Sarah, so nice to hear from you. Are you looking forward to the auction tomorrow? Carina told me you've done a wonderful job with the Prioleau/Habersham collection."

She rubbed her forehead with her free hand. She'd forgotten about the auction, her photos, and Nate. Her ankle started aching again. "Actually—" Hugh handed her the involuntary commitment paper and went to the patio for his bag. "I have a legal problem I'm hoping you can help me with."

"Tell me."

Hugh placed the green file on the counter, waved to her, and left.

A few minutes later, after laying out the situation, she said, "Do you know of a lawyer in town who can help me?"

Calum chuckled. "I don't mean to be rude, Miss Munro—"

"Please, call me Sarah."

"As you wish, Sarah." His Southern accent had a lulling, protective sound to it, and for the first time since the doorbell rang—no, since seeing Nate Walker earlier—she felt like she could breathe again. "I'll take on your father's case. If you fax me the commitment letter, I'll have my office begin right away."

"Thank you so much, Mr.—"

"Please, call me Calum. After all, you're in charge of my financial future."

Despite the stress, she laughed. The auction might bring

in a few hundred thousand, but that was nothing compared to the Prioleau fortune.

"Thank you, Calum." She closed her eyes. "How long will this take?"

"Hopefully not long. In the meantime, go to Dessie's Couture and find a dress for tomorrow. Charge it to the Prioleau Foundation."

Dresses were the last thing she cared about right now, especially those she couldn't afford at Dessie's, the most exclusive dress shop in town. "Thank you, but I don't need a new dress."

"Considering the company at the auction, you'll feel better armed in a Dior."

Unfortunately, he was right. Usually, as the authenticating historian, she was in the background at these events. But since this was a local show and her boss wasn't here, she'd have to take a more active role. They might even want her to speak a few words. Something she should've thought about before today. "Thank you for the offer."

"You're welcome. I'll call you as soon as I have any information. Try not to worry."

"Okay." Could she sound any more despondent? "Calum, there's something else. I read on the commitment paperwork that since I'm adopted, I don't have any legal rights to care for him at all. Which is absurd. I couldn't love him more if he were my birth father."

"I'll check." Calum paused. "Sarah, have you seen the Prioleau sigil painted around town?"

"Yes." She'd been noticing it for weeks. A white cutlass held by a white skeletal fist with red blood dripping down the blade's edge. "It's from the original pirate flag flown by the Prioleau pirates in the early eighteenth century, not long after they changed their name from Prideaux to Prioleau. I believe it predates the Jolly Roger."

"Yes, it does." Calum's voice carried a subtext of laughter. "Did you notice the words?"

The drips of red blood formed words beneath the image. *Sans pitié.*

Sarah smiled for the first time in hours. "No mercy?"

"That's why you don't need to worry."

After hanging up and faxing the form to Calum, she pressed the heels of her hands to her eyes and prayed the day wouldn't get any worse.

She took a few deep breaths and opened the green file folder. It contained her father's original photo as well as a copy of Hugh's photo. A handwritten note in messy writing read:

> *I want to talk more about this cipher and those hide sites.*
> *Call when you get a chance.*

Her phone buzzed with two different texts from two different unknown numbers.

The first read: If you want your film, meet me at Screamin' Perks coffee shop. Two hours. N.

But it was the second text that made her hands go cold. *If you continue in this endeavor the ensuing chaos will last forever.*

CHAPTER 6

"THANKS, DOC." NATE HANDED THE BURNER CELL PHONE to Dr. Bennett, who stood near the bed. Nate had no idea what'd happened to his phone or his shirt, but he recognized the room in Pops's trailer. Considering the superhero stickers on the dresser near the window, the room had once belonged to Pops's two grown sons. "You're a peach for coming all the way out here."

Doc Bennett chuckled and put the phone in his old-fashioned black doctor's bag. "When Calum Prioleau pays you to be at his beck and call, you beck when called."

"So true." Calum kept the doctor around because of his discretion and willingness to work beneath the bureaucracy that was insurance-based health care. Nate and his men didn't have insurance or money, and didn't want medical records that could be traced.

Nate sat higher against the headboard and smelled peppermint. Doc Bennett had taken off Nate's shirt to rub salve on his arms, and now he smelled like a damn breath mint.

Doc Bennett shoved his hands in the pockets of his white lab coat. "I took more blood. I still can't identify the substance that may or may not have been in those Z-pam pills you were taking. And who knows what the docs were giving you in that prison hospital in Maine for the past few years."

"Meaning"—Nate closed his eyes—"you have no idea why I'm still having seizures and memory loss?"

"Correct." Nate opened his eyes at the doc's hushed tone. "You need an MRI."

"Unless we can do that without a paper trail, the answer is no."

Doc Bennett sat on the edge of the bed. "Nate, there are regulations regarding MRIs that require paperwork. We need to figure out what's going on in your brain. Despite the new meds I gave you, the seizures are getting worse."

Nate shook his head and for the first time heard voices in the other end of the trailer. Pete and Zack were talking to Pops and Grady. Having his buddies here, and knowing they'd all had to carry him inside, made everything worse. "They're less frequent."

"Yet getting more severe." Doc Bennett picked up Nate's wrist to feel his pulse. "How's your memory?"

"My short-term is okay, but I still don't remember much from the night my unit was attacked in Afghanistan. I have vague memories of the POW camp. The prison hospital memories are a blur of white walls, gray jumpsuits, and seagulls. When I don't have headaches and I'm not puking from the migraines that precede a seizure, I'm okay."

"Pete says you're not sleeping. That you're having nightmares."

Thanks, Pete. "I'm a soldier. I don't need much sleep."

"You need those REMs to heal. Next time you wake from a nightmare, write down what happened. It could help."

Nothing about Nate's nightmares could help.

Doc Bennett added, "Your pulse is fast, and you're pale. You're also dehydrated. Are you eating?"

"Yes." At Doc Bennett's frown, Nate added, "Sometimes I get nauseated."

"I'll give you an anti-nausea prescription." Now the doc held Nate's trembling hand. "Any withdrawal symptoms?"

He yanked his hand away. "I get shakes and sweats at night." Along with the horrible dreams. "Fighting in the ring helps with the restlessness."

"Do you crave those Z-pam pills?"

The illegal ones he'd bought on the streets until two weeks ago? "Sure. They worked." He paused before reminding the doc, "They're legal in Canada."

"They're also addictive." Doc Bennett raised an eyebrow. "What about the anti-migraine pills I gave you?"

"They're shit."

Doc Bennett shook his head. "I'm worried. You were out for thirty minutes today. Your next seizure may put you into a coma or worse." Doc Bennett stood and smoothed down his white coat. "Any chance you'll stay here and rest?"

Nate yanked off the blanket. Thank God he still had on pants. "No." He swung his legs over the side of the bed and stood. Then he groaned. His headache had eased, but every joint ached.

"Tomorrow, Nate."

"Excuse me?" He hadn't realized the doc had still been talking.

"Come to Calum's mansion tomorrow. I want to check your blood pressure." Doc Bennett's cell phone rang, and he excused himself, saying, "I'll leave your new prescriptions with Mr. Montfort."

"Thanks." Once the doc grabbed his bag and left, Nate found clean clothes laid out for him.

Thank you, Zack. Pete would never have thought of that.

Nate showered in the trailer's small bathroom, not an easy task while trying to keep his arms dry. After toweling off, he dressed in jeans and a long-sleeved navy T-shirt and used the hair dryer. Then he tied his hair with a rubber band. Many years ago, Kells had ordered Nate to grow his hair for a mission. Although he hated having long hair, he couldn't cut it until Kells said so.

When ready, he headed for the kitchen because that had to be where the smell of fried fish was coming from. He still wondered why Calum was helping him and his unit, but since Nate couldn't afford to question it, he didn't. He also had no recollection about how he had gotten to the trailer. Nate wasn't only at the mercy of others, he was indebted to them too. Which sent things from worse to shit.

He found Grady, Pete, and Zack in the family room next to the kitchen, all eating off paper plates with plastic forks. "Hey." Nate cleared his throat. "Thanks."

"Doc just left," Pete said with a mouth stuffed with fried fish.

Zack placed his plate on the coffee table near a brown paper bag, and grabbed a mug. "How're you feeling?"

"Better." It was the truth. Although Nate felt like he'd been beaten with many hammers, he didn't welcome death anymore. He had to embrace the nondestructive feelings when they came.

Pops stuck his head out the kitchen doorway. "You hungry, Nate?"

"Yes, sir." He shoved his hands in his back pockets and realized that he was, actually, starving. He couldn't remember the last time he'd eaten.

He took his hands out again and flexed his fingers. Then he went over to the linoleum-topped table near the window. Someone had laid his jacket on top, along with his cell phone and gun. He picked up his weapon. First, he popped the bullet out of the chamber, then he released the clip.

"You okay, son?" Grady wiped his lips with a paper napkin. "You seem agitated."

Nate reloaded the single bullet and slammed the mag in. "I'm fine."

Grady harrumphed. "I'm calling bull on that shit."

Nate placed his gun on the table to face the older man. Grady and Pops had been Marines, Third Force Recon, during Operation Desert Shield. They'd fought in Task Force Ripper, a.k.a. the Hundred Hour Bloodbath. So when Grady and Pops, who was coming out of the kitchen with a plate of fried fish, called bullshit, it meant something.

"I haven't been sleeping." Nate took his plate and plastic fork from Pops, ignoring the four missing fingers on Pops's hand. "Doc Bennett gave me some new pills." He took a bite of the fish and closed his eyes. Between the seasoning and the light frying, it was the best thing he'd eaten in forever. It sure as hell beat the Hamburger Helper he and his men had been living on for the past two weeks.

Pops moved toward the window, one hand in a pocket of his overalls. "Why are Sheriff Boudreaux and Calum Prioleau here?"

"I called them," Pete said.

Nate popped another bite in his mouth. Then another, only to realize he'd finished the meal in four swallows. "*Why?*"

"Because," Pete said in his you're-such-a-dumbass voice, "I thought you were in trouble."

Pops opened the door so Calum and Sheriff Jimmy Boudreaux could enter.

Jimmy took off his uniform hat and pointed at Nate. "You took a car?"

Yeppers. Nate put his plate on the table. "I thought I'd be fine. I hadn't had a seizure in almost a week." Okay. Three days.

Calum went into the kitchen and came out with a mug of coffee. In his tan seersucker suit, blue tie matching his eyes, and gold signet ring, he was the personification of perfection. Not a tough feat considering he could buy the entire southern U.S. "Nate," Calum said around a sip, "do you even have a license?"

"Yes. From North Carolina."

Jimmy hit his hat against his thigh. "Is it valid?"

"Does it matter?"

"It does to the next cop who pulls you over for reckless driving because you're having a migraine and can't control the car. Then it will really matter when he discovers you're an ex–Green Beret suffering from combat-induced seizures who shouldn't even be behind a wheel."

"When I'm in Savannah, I'm on my bike." Yes, *loser* was spelled B-I-C-Y-C-L-E. "I swear."

"Leave the man alone." Grady collected everyone's empty plates and went into the kitchen. When he returned, he handed Nate a cup of coffee.

He savored the hot, bitter drink that scorched his throat

and made his eyes water. He couldn't have fucked up this day more if he'd tried, and it wasn't even noon.

"It's a matter of safety," Jimmy said to Grady. "Nate's and the public's."

Grady waved a dismissive hand and returned to the kitchen.

"Nate." Calum cleared his throat and leaned a shoulder against the wall closest to the new flat screen that sat on an old turntable. "What happened? And please tell us you didn't see anyone bow."

"No bowing. Just a seizure. No biggie."

Pete stood. "You asked someone what they wanted. Then everything went silent. When Zack and I got to Pops and Grady at the range, it took us twenty minutes to find you passed out near the SUV, clutching your loaded weapon."

And he was busted. "I saw…a man. With a gun."

"Did you know this man?" Jimmy asked.

"No."

"You saw an armed man on my property?" Pops's frown deepened the creases on his weather-weary face.

Grady reappeared with his own cup of coffee. "One of the Marigny boys?"

"I don't know," Nate said. "He wore a hooded sweat-shirt, and I couldn't identify him. Then the migraine came, the seizure hit, and I blacked out."

"A delusion?" Zack appeared with the coffeepot and started around-the-room refills. "Sometimes you have them before your seizures."

Nate held out his mug for a top-off. "I haven't had a delusion since I left the prison hospital." Once he'd stopped taking the prison hospital meds that kept him semi-comatose most of the day.

"Did any of you," Calum said directly to Pete, Zack, Pops, and Grady, "see an armed man while you were searching for Nate?"

All four men said, "No."

"*Sheeeeeeeeit.*" Jimmy hit his thigh with his hat again. "Pops? Grady? You up for tracking? We need to go before it rains."

Pops grabbed his rifle where it had been propped near the door. Grady went into the kitchen and returned with a .22 rifle.

Jimmy nodded. "Right." Then he said to Pete, "We may be gone a while. But keep me in the fucking loop. You got it?"

Pete took his cell phone out of his pocket. "Yep."

After Jimmy, Pops, and Grady left, Pete tossed his phone to Nate. "When the fuck were you going to tell us about this?"

Nate read the text sent to Pete.

> To mourn a mischief that is past and gone is
> the sure way to draw new mischief on.

Zack read over Nate's shoulder. "What does that mean?"

Pete stared at Nate. "I want to know who it's from."

"I'm not sure what it means," Nate said as he reread the text, "but it's from Cassio."

"Who the hell is Cassio?" Zack asked.

"*Fuuuuuuuck* this," Pete said. "Is that why you left this morning?"

"Yes. Cassio summoned me to the cemetery on the Isle of Grace and told me to protect Sarah Munro."

"You didn't kiss her again." Pete sent him a sideways glare. "Did you?"

Nate scowled. "Of course not." Although he had thought about it.

Calum took out his own phone and started texting. "I thought we were done with *them*?"

Zack crossed his arms. "Is someone going to tell me what the fuck is going on? Or do I start hitting?"

Pete paced the room while Calum commanded his

world from his phone. Nate didn't say anything. He, along with Pete and Calum, had promised never to speak about their past involvement with the Fianna.

Zack tapped the cell with the text message. "How about I go to Kells and tell him you've been in contact with the Prince and his fucking Fianna army, those soul-sucking assassins who kill not only without remorse but with a brutality that would shame the fucking warlord who kept you prisoner and tortured you—along with half of our men—for years."

Nate closed his eyes. He'd made so many mistakes. The last thing he wanted was for more of his buddies to be dragged into this. He also knew Zack couldn't abide secrets. Secrets had ruined his life, and Nate would never want to cause his friend more pain.

Allowing Zack into the group with Pete, Calum, Garza, and himself meant Zack would be forced to keep a secret from Kells and the rest of their men. But maybe keeping a secret was easier on the soul than being a victim of one.

Nate opened his eyes. "Two weeks ago, before you and the other men arrived in Savannah, Pete and I had some trouble with Remiel." Nate raised one arm. "I got burned, but what you don't know is that the Fianna helped us out. In return, we promised the Prince we'd not mention their involvement to Kells. And we haven't."

Now it was Zack's turn to pace. "This is fucked up."

Pete threw his large, muscular body onto Pops's couch, and it groaned beneath the assault. "From what does Cassio want you to protect Sarah?"

"I'm not sure. Cassio also ordered me to stop her research. When I found Sarah in the cemetery, someone shot at us."

"Who?" Calum looked up even while his fingers tapped the keyboard.

"Don't know." Nate stared out the window at a white cross near the tree line. "Maybe the hooded man. Maybe the Marigny boys. I'm meeting Sarah soon. I still need to figure out how to get her to agree to my protection without telling her anything."

"Good luck with that," Pete said grimly. "Sarah is PhD smart. She'll smell bullshit before it leaves your mouth."

No kidding. "I'll talk to Kells about Sarah, but I can't tell him the entire truth."

"I don't like it," Zack said. "Secrets always bite us in the ass."

So true, brother. So very fucking true.

"You should know," Calum said, slipping his phone into his jacket pocket, "Sarah has had quite the morning herself. Her father, Joe Munro, has been involuntarily institutionalized."

Pete stared at Calum. "Why?"

"Joe suffers from dementia and headaches along with seizures. He was Boston's chief of police until a scandal forced his retirement. His doctors believe Joe's worsening seizures have more to do with poor nutrition than any medical condition."

Nate hadn't realized Sarah's father lived in Savannah. "Are you helping her?"

"Yes. From the paperwork Sarah faxed me, it's a straightforward involuntary commitment order. Joe is in a locked psychiatric facility for his own safety." Calum's smooth Southern drawl finished with a strained hitch.

"What else is wrong?"

"I just discovered that my twin sister, Carina, tried to get Sarah fired from the Smithsonian almost a year ago."

"How'd she do that?" Zack asked.

"Carina is a U.S. senator for the state of Georgia," Pete said before standing to face Calum. "Why?"

"I don't know," Calum said. "I also discovered that Carina has pressured Sarah's boss to cancel one of Sarah's current research projects. What's even stranger is that Carina was on the Prioleau/Habersham collection committee that chose Sarah to be the authenticating historian for the auction tomorrow."

"What auction?" Pete asked.

"The auction of rare seventeenth- and eighteenth-century pirate artifacts that will open the Savannah Summer Arts Festival."

"So now what?" Zack asked.

"Now," Nate said with quiet determination as he put down his coffee, "we return to Iron Rack's, and I talk to Kells before I see Sarah."

Pete took the paper bag off the coffee table and tossed it to Nate. "Your new meds. And Doc Bennett wants to see you tomorrow at Calum's mansion. Three p.m."

"Got it." Nate paused, the self-disgust burning in his gut. "I need a ride."

CHAPTER 7

Nate went into the office of Iron Rack's Gym and waited. Kells sat at his desk covered with papers from the previous regime, and Luke stood nearby, handing him documents to sign.

Kells squinted at an invoice. "What's this for?"

"Wholesale cleaning supplies." Luke's eyes widened when he saw Nate. "The other one is for a grocery delivery service. We don't have time to go food shopping, but we don't want to live on takeout. It was Nate's idea."

While Kells and Luke talked, Nate went to the window and focused on the closed-up T-shirt shop across the street.

"Where are we going to cook?" Kells asked.

"In that galley kitchen on the top floor of the gym," Luke said.

Nate hid a grimace. He wouldn't consider that closet with a hot plate and a sink a kitchen.

"Alright." Kells signed the docs and handed them to Luke. "Remember, I hate broccoli."

"We know that, sir." Luke put his papers into a file folder and headed out. "Good luck," he whispered as he passed Nate.

Nate nodded and moved to the front of Kells's desk. He stood, while not quite at attention, with his shoulders straight, his hands behind his back.

Kells glanced at Nate, then bent his head over a notebook on his desk. "You missed a staff meeting. A meeting you wrote the agenda for."

"Yes, sir. It won't happen again."

Kells threw down his pen. "Want to tell me why?"

"I took a car this morning."

To his credit, Kells didn't slam a hand on the desk. He

just watched Nate with his intense gold-speckled brown eyes. "Pete said he and Zack found you unconscious, and you saw Dr. Bennett."

"Yes. The doc gave me another prescription. But that's not all. Something else happened." Nate told Kells about meeting Cassio in the Cemetery of Lost Children as well as Cassio's demand that he protect Sarah Munro. He left out the part about Cassio working for the Prince. In Nate's story, Cassio could be one of Nate's contacts from the club. He ended with "I set up a meeting with Miss Munro."

Kells went to the window overlooking the street. Instead of using blinds, the previous owner used Jolly Roger flags to cover the lower part of the windows. He fixed his gaze at some unknown thing outside. "You met Miss Munro two weeks ago, before the rest of us arrived?"

"Yes, sir. She helped me with some research that proved crucial to the mission."

"You trust Cassio?"

Good question. "On this issue, yes."

Kells faced Nate, his jaw hard and unrelenting. "Does Cassio work for the Prince?"

Nate held his breath in his throat. If he answered yes, the Prince would kill Nate and the entire unit. It wasn't some idle threat by a no-name gunrunner. This was the Prince. The leader of the deadly Fianna army. Highly trained, soulless men who followed extreme rules in their mission to…well, Nate wasn't sure what their mission was, but the Fianna didn't bluff. They stated their intentions with no ambiguity or passive-aggressive bullshit. A situation Nate both admired and feared.

"Nate?"

He met the eyes of his CO, one of the toughest commanders in the Special Forces community. Could Nate lie to Kells? Break the trust of the brotherhood? Could Nate *not* lie to Kells and put them all in danger?

Pete and Zack appeared in the doorway.

"Sir," Pete said. "Luke said you wanted to see us?"

"Yes." Kells sat down again. "Nate told me about Cassio's demand that Nate protect the historian Sarah Munro."

Pete and Zack entered yet stayed silent.

"While I would normally consider Nate's request to protect an innocent woman, and I'd also normally demand more information about this Cassio—" Kells paused. "We have other things to worry about."

Nate stepped forward. "Sir—"

Kells held up a hand. "I understand your need to help a woman who helped you, but you're not going to be able to do that because you're not going to be here."

"Why?" Pete asked. "Where's Nate going to be?"

"Nate is returning to the prison hospital in Maine."

Nate gripped the metal chair in front of him and made sure to inhale and exhale. He'd known his reprieve had been temporary, but he'd hoped for more time. He'd honestly thought he'd get at least another six weeks. If not more.

Zack stood next to Nate, their shoulders touching. But neither Pete nor Zack spoke.

"What about Sarah?" Nate was proud of his voice's even tone when everything in him wanted to scream at the thought of being forcibly drugged with meds that made his muscles melt and his mind splinter.

"Until we have more intel about Miss Munro and any danger she's in, we can't spare a man to watch her."

Nate sat in the chair, his head beginning that oh-so-familiar pounding.

"How long before Nate leaves?" Zack asked.

"I've made arrangements for Nate to be transported on Sunday afternoon."

"Today is Friday," Pete said.

"I know," Kells said.

"How long is he going back for?" Zack asked.

"Seventeen years. Twenty minus the three years he's already served."

Nate had spent two years in a POW camp. Three years in the psych ward of the U.S. military's secret prison hospital. And had been granted two precious months of liberty. He dropped his head and pressed the heels of his hands to his eyes. Colors danced behind his eyelids. Now he only had two days of freedom left?

"Nate." Kells's firm voice made Nate's head snap up. "Meet Sarah and end this."

Nate stood on wobbly legs. "Even if it leaves her in danger?"

"Yes," Kells said. "I want her out of our lives. Today."

Etienne Marigny climbed the ladder from the johnboat onto the *Brigid* and adjusted his stance to the rolling deck. His cousin's yacht was anchored outside the beautiful-yet-remote Dead Man's Hammock in Wassaw Sound.

"I need to see him," Etienne told a crew member who ran over with a towel to clean the muddy footprints he'd left on the deck.

"Mr. Marigny knows you're here." The crew member laid out another towel so Etienne could wipe off his boots.

He finished as the Warden came from the stateroom. "How is Remiel?"

"The same." The Warden marched over in a black hoodie and jeans. "Did you fire shots at the historian and Walker this morning?"

"A few. For fun." He'd wanted to take out Walker but hadn't yet been ordered to kill him. Although it went against Etienne's instincts, he'd only shot a *no harm, no foul* warning.

The Warden gripped the railing and stared across the marsh. White egrets skimmed the surface of the water beyond the seagrass. A peaceful sight at odds with the monster below. "I also saw Nate Walker this morning. No wonder the Prince wants to recruit Walker. He reminds me of Rafe Montfort."

"Both of whom are still alive while Eddie is still dead." Etienne took an apple out of his jacket pocket and bit into it, using his fist to wipe his chin. The fact that Montfort and Walker were allowed to walk this earth while Etienne's eighteen-year-old nephew lay in a grave on the Isle of Grace told Etienne everything he needed to know about justice in this world. Simply, there wasn't any for people like him. People with no power or money or connections.

But since his cousin had arrived in town, the *old way* of doing things had started to change. By the time his cousin fulfilled his plans, those with power and money and connections would be begging Etienne for mercy. Except there wouldn't be any. For the first time in his life, he'd go all *sans pitié* on *their* asses. He'd teach them not to screw with the Marigny family.

"Eddie died from his own stupidity and pride." The Warden paused to watch a pelican dive for its breakfast. "Don't make the same mistake."

"My nephew died because Walker and Montfort refused to back down from a fight. It wasn't the kid's fault."

The Warden shrugged. "You'll have your chance to avenge your nephew's death."

He pitched the apple core into the water. It bobbed until floating into the marsh grass. "You don't know that."

"Remiel promised." The statement exuded indignation. "Isn't that enough?"

"For now." Etienne's phone buzzed with a text from Remiel, and he headed down to the stateroom. "I just hope my next assignment is to kill Walker."

Etienne entered the stateroom. Light streamed in from windows, exposing highly polished wood furniture and a carpet woven in intricate floral designs.

His cousin Remiel sat in his leather chair and took a strawberry from a silver bowl on his desk. He bit the berry off its stem and wiped his fingers on a linen napkin.

When Remiel reached for another, Etienne stood at

attention. Although his cousin wasn't especially tall, he was—even by male heterosexual standards—exceptionally handsome. He'd inherited intense blue eyes, black hair, and a strong jaw from his mother's side of the family. Unlike Etienne who'd inherited the Marigny dark eyes and sharp, beak-like nose that resembled a black crow plague mask. Or so he'd been told.

Remiel ate two more berries before addressing the man tied in the chair on the other side of the desk. "Mr. Pinckney, we have a situation."

Stuart Pinckney, president of the Bank of Charleston, groaned.

Etienne didn't understand why Stuart was upset. He was still alive while his cohort was dead. And Etienne should know, since he'd just killed the cohort.

Remiel wiped his hands again and lifted a silver chain with a Saint Michael the Archangel medal. It shone in the sunlight. "Maybe we misunderstood each other, Stuart. Maybe you're working on the Julian timetable and not the Gregorian calendar?"

Stuart Pinckney shook his head.

Remiel tossed the necklace onto a book. "You know what I want?"

Stuart nodded.

"Good." Remiel slapped his hands on the desk and stood. "This afternoon one of my men will return you to your bank in Charleston, and you will give him what is mine. Do you agree?"

Stuart struggled with the ropes, and Remiel raised a take-care-of-this eyebrow at Etienne.

He slapped Stuart's head. *Idiot.* Was a simple nod too much to ask for? It's not like he'd been tortured today. And the nub, where Stuart's left ring finger had been before Remiel cut it off, had stopped bleeding.

Etienne knelt before the banker, who was tied to the chair, his mouth covered with duct tape. His blue-striped seersucker suit and white shirt, which two days ago had been pressed and pleated, were now a wrinkled mess. The most surprising thing was Stuart's eyes. His bright blues had become shadows of their prior beauty within hours, not days, of beginning the torture. Now Stuart's nine remaining fingernails dug into the chair arms, leaving behind small half-moon marks in the wood. Remiel would want the chair destroyed.

Etienne had a lot of shit to do today, and dealing with Stuart was the least of his chores. "Just nod, Stuart. It will ensure your wife's safety."

Stuart started to cry. Didn't Stuart realize that as long as he served Remiel, his life had meaning? "Do we have a deal?"

Stuart nodded as the cabin door flung open and banged the wall.

"Sir," a merc in combat pants with a nine-mil on his hip said. "The banker's body has been found."

"Already?" Remiel asked. "By whom?"

"Two old men on the isle."

"Pops Montfort and Grady Mercer." Etienne rose. Those old geezers were always up in his family's business. "We knew this would happen."

"Not this soon." Remiel's voice dropped an octave.

"Sheriff Boudreaux is handling the situation," the merc added.

"Now the Prince will get the message," Etienne said. That was the plan, after all.

"Indeed." Remiel stared at a photo on his desk of a beautiful woman with long red hair before lowering the silver frame until it lay face down on the wood. Maybe so he wouldn't have to face the condemnation in her green eyes? Etienne and his brothers had always wanted to know about the mysterious woman, but none of them had ever had the courage to ask.

"Cousin." Remiel spoke as he regarded Stuart's

trembling body. "It's time to inform Miss Munro about her part in my plan."

"What about Walker?" Etienne planted his fists on the desk. "The Green Beret needs to suffer for Eddie's death."

"Not to worry. Walker is falling in love with the pretty historian." Remiel glared at Etienne's fists until he removed them. "And love always causes a man to suffer."

CHAPTER 8

SARAH WALKED DOWN INDIAN STREET, PHONE TO HER EAR, convinced her boss complained more than her father. Quite a feat considering her father had turned griping into an Olympic sport.

"I understand." She passed Iron Rack's Gym and adjusted her straw bag on her shoulder. She avoided a homeless man sleeping on the sidewalk. The scent of wet asphalt and gas and urine irritated her nose. "Senator Carina Prioleau came to see you, and now you don't want me to submit my grant request to restore Rebecca's diary. Got it."

"Does that mean you're going to stop this quest of yours?"

Now her boss sounded like Cassio. "I guess." At least her boss didn't know about her adventure this morning. He just suspected because...well...she *was* known for trespassing. "Why does Senator Prioleau care about my grant proposal?"

"The *why* doesn't matter as long as she has the power to cut our funding."

Because everything always comes down to money. "Can we talk later? My father—"

"Will be fine. You have a lawyer?"

She blinked. "I do." She pushed open the door to Screamin' Perks coffee shop and inhaled the aroma of beans and cinnamon. She dropped her bag onto an empty table. The warmth and scents reminded her of her mother's kitchen in Boston. "I'll call when I learn more."

"Good. In the meantime, don't submit your grant request, and stay off private land. If you're caught—" He paused, but Sarah heard the silent *again*. "I can't save you."

The thing was, she'd never asked him to.

She ended her call and ordered an iced latte. Her table

gave her the best view of the coffee shop. The café was in a more industrial area with fewer tourists, bookended by auto repair shops and laundromats, with Iron Rack's Gym in the center. Unlike the other streets in the historic area of Savannah, no flowers hung from cast-iron lampposts. No horse-drawn carriages rolled by. The sidewalks were cracked with weeds, many storefronts were closed, and a few of the cars parked along the curb were missing tires.

According to the mayor, this area near the river and train tracks was up-and-coming. If this café didn't have the best coffee in town and if it hadn't been daytime, she never would've come.

Once her iced latte arrived, she sat and checked her phone. Although what she really wanted to do was throw it against the wall and scream *damn them*. *Them* being Cassio, her boss, and Senator Prioleau.

What she didn't get was why her boss, a U.S. senator, and a Fianna warrior cared about Rebecca Prideaux's diary. Rebecca had been a sixteen-year-old girl, born in the seventeenth century, who'd been burned as a witch. *What kind of trouble could that cause?*

Sighing, she scrolled through her messages. She'd heard from Hugh Waring. Her father had been admitted to St. Joseph's psych ward and was comfortable. Meaning they'd drugged him so he wouldn't retaliate. Hugh also mentioned she couldn't visit until tomorrow morning. A fact she'd fight once Calum's office called her and she knew more about her dad's legal status. She also reread the weird texts she'd gotten from Cassio. She had no idea what they meant, and the frustration made her cranky.

She put her phone away and took the package she'd found in her kitchen from her straw bag. She yanked the envelope tab and pulled out an *old* book. She turned it over. It had to be eighteenth century, if not earlier.

She sipped the sweet, cold coffee and, after wiping down the table, placed the book on a napkin. There was no note in the envelope. No clue who'd sent it. Although she really should've taken it to the Savannah Preservation Office to study it under controlled conditions, she was too impatient. Carefully, she opened it to discover a ledger.

The front page had *Capel Cemetery* written on the top. The ledger was in surprisingly good condition. None of the pages were stuck together, although the script was hard to read and some words were faded.

Using her pencil's eraser end, she turned the pages and saw columns with headings for *date of purchase, deceased, birth date, death date, payor.* The ledger listed all of the tombs, headstones, and mausoleums purchased for Capel Cemetery, a.k.a. the Cemetery of Lost Children.

She immediately scanned through the dates of purchase. She didn't see anything for Rebecca Prideaux in 1699, but as she flipped forward to 1712, she saw a number of entries paid for by *T. Toban.*

Her stomach did that clenchy thing she hated, and her hands began to sweat. She shoved her pencil in her hair and kept reading. She didn't recognize any of the deceased names, but one thing stuck out. T. Toban had paid for the tomb of an unknown person, with *My Soul's Joy* written in the margin.

My Soul's Joy? Sarah squinted. That's what her mother used to call Sarah as a child.

"Sarah?"

She looked up. Nate stood in front of her in jeans and a long-sleeved navy T-shirt. His hands were shoved in his front pockets. When he rolled on the heels of his black boots, wide shoulders filled the shirt and chest muscles flexed beneath the cotton.

Her breath caught in her throat. It wasn't only his physical size that made her toes curl. It was the way he looked at her with those green eyes. A combination of hungry and desperate with a side of longing. And from his sigh when he dragged out the chair, a touch of despair?

She wiped her hands on her skirt. "Hey." *Wow. Inarticulate Sarah strikes again.* "You…" *Changed? Look good? Want to make out again?* She swallowed and finished with "seem different."

Which was the truth. This morning he'd been in control, with orders and demands. Now, after asking the waitress for a coffee and two blueberry muffins, his demeanor was quieter.

"I showered." He scanned the room. He wasn't obvious about his perimeter check. He just studied the area with the same attention her father used to. Finally, he said, "Thanks for meeting me."

"You have my film?"

He slid something across the table.

She read the white receipt. "You had my film developed for me?"

"You said you needed it by tonight. And there's a photo place in a drugstore not far from the Savannah Preservation Office. It's already paid for."

"That was nice." She took another sip of coffee, not sure what else to say. She was surprised he'd remembered, and she appreciated it. "Thank you."

"The least I could do."

She put the receipt in her bag. "I want to return this to you." She took out the folded handkerchief and laid it on the table. "I washed and ironed it." She looked away. "Thank you."

Was that the only thing she could say?

"Does your ankle feel better?"

"Yes." Although it still throbbed a bit. "Wrapping it helped." She took another sip of coffee while he slipped the handkerchief in his back pocket.

"I'm glad." He reached for something around his neck but then dropped his hand. When did things get so awkward between them? Was it because of that kiss that neither of them seemed capable of mentioning?

"Thanks," she said for the third time. *Good golly Moses.*

Were they going to talk about the weather next? Or maybe he was done talking? She'd gotten her film and given him his handkerchief, and maybe he was ready to leave. Or maybe he was waiting for her to give him a hug or kiss him on the cheek. Would he expect that? Would he want that?

"Sarah?" He reached over to take the pencil out of her hair.

Heat rose up her neck. "Yes?"

He dropped the pencil into her bag. "Why was going out to that cemetery so important to you today?"

She waited until the waitress delivered Nate's coffee and muffins and left. "I wanted to find Rebecca Prideaux and Thomas Toban."

"Prideaux?" He used a plastic knife to cut one muffin in half. "Any relation to the Prideaux pirates you mentioned a few weeks ago? When I showed you that map?"

"Yes. Rebecca is also related to Calum and Carina Prioleau. The Prideaux name changed to Prioleau in the early eighteenth century." She played with the straw in her iced latte. "I believe Rebecca and her fiancé Thomas are buried in that cemetery on Capel land."

Nate offered the second muffin to her. "Eat this."

"No…" Her stomach growled. "Okay. Thanks." She took a bite, appreciating the sweetness. "Have you heard the story about Rebecca and Thomas?"

He ate half his muffin and wiped his fingers on a napkin. "No. Is it related to the story of Anne Capel you told me about at the preservation office? That Puritan woman who was accused of murdering forty-four children?"

"Kind of. Anne Capel was older than Rebecca." Sarah savored another bite of her pastry. "Years after those children died and Anne was acquitted, Anne encouraged Rebecca to run away with Thomas."

He reached over to wipe a crumb from her cheek. "I'm guessing Rebecca's family wasn't happy with her boyfriend?"

"They weren't." Sarah's face felt hot, and she found her

napkin. "The men of Rebecca's family were vicious pirates who forbade Rebecca from seeing Thomas. By 1699 the Prideaux pirates, as they were known, had become the wealthiest family in the area. They felt Thomas, who came from a family of carpenters, was beneath Rebecca. The young lovers were forced apart by their families and met a tragic end."

"Sounds Shakespearean."

"It was." She finished half of her muffin and brushed the crumbs off her skirt. "It began when Rebecca, with Anne's help, became a Puritan against her family's wishes."

Nate popped another piece into his mouth. When he was done, he said, "I bet that annoyed Rebecca's parents."

"It did. Things got worse when Rebecca fell in love with Thomas Toban. Anne, who hated the Prideaux family, encouraged the love affair and helped them elope. Two weeks before her seventeenth birthday, Rebecca and Thomas ran away to catch a ship to Virginia where they'd start a new life. The night the couple left, they were caught and people accused Rebecca of witchcraft."

"By *people* you mean her family?"

"Yes, along with other families of the isle."

He paused mid-bite. "Why?"

"When Rebecca left to meet Thomas, she stole something belonging to her family. She knew her family would hunt for her, so she needed leverage."

"I know all about leverage. Mostly not having it." Nate finished his muffin, then his coffee. "What did she steal?"

"Evidence about her family's illegal pirate empire. Unfortunately, this evidence also proved that other families in the area—including the Tobans—were active accomplices in the illegal trade that helped move the merchandise stolen from ships."

"These other families agreed to murder a sixteen-year-old girl to cover up their own guilt?"

"Yes." Sarah played with the edges of her napkin.

"After her family caught the lovers and found the evidence Rebecca had stolen, these families wanted her dead. They accused her of witchcraft, burned her at the stake, and made Thomas watch."

"That's brutal."

"The worst part is that, according to historians, Thomas is the reason they were caught. He set up their capture to save his family."

"Why?"

"Thomas realized the leverage Rebecca had on her family would indict his as well. If the evidence was released, his father and uncles would be arrested and hanged. Apparently, once he learned she was willing to betray his family along with hers, he turned on her."

"How did Thomas find out about this evidence?"

"No one knows." Sarah stared into the melting ice in her cup. "Some say Anne told him."

"Sounds like you don't believe the story."

She tilted her head. "Why do you say that?"

"You always state things clearly and definitely. You take responsibility for your facts and knowledge. Yet you just said 'according to historians,' 'apparently,' and 'some say.' That tells me you don't believe Thomas betrayed Rebecca."

Sarah had to give Nate credit. He paid attention. "I don't believe Thomas betrayed Rebecca. I believe someone else, maybe Anne, betrayed the lovers."

Nate clasped his mug and stared into it. "What happened to Thomas after Rebecca died?"

"After her death, he disappeared for two years only to return as a vicious pirate who went sword to head with the Prideaux pirates and any other pirates who'd take him on. As time passed, the Prideaux pirates became even wealthier and changed their name to Prioleau. Thomas grew angrier and more bitter. He was determined to destroy the Prideaux family."

Nate covered her hand with his, and she let him. His

fingers were still warm from clutching his coffee. "This happened centuries ago. And I'd wager most people have never heard it. Why is this story so important to you?"

"My mother was from Savannah and told me all about the legends of pirates and witches and ghosts. I can't explain why, but because of my mom, I feel connected to Rebecca. She's lost in history and can't find her way home. I have this sense I'm meant to prove their love was real, that they didn't betray each other."

"Sarah." Nate squeezed her hand, and heat spread along her arm. "You know finding the truth won't help your father. Right?"

She yanked her hand away. "What do you know about my father?"

CHAPTER 9

NATE LEANED BACK IN HIS CHAIR AND KEPT HIS FOCUS ON Sarah's face. If he didn't, he'd stare at the rest of her. She'd changed into a white tank top and sweater over a long, flowy pink skirt. When she crossed her legs, the slit in her skirt briefly exposed her bare legs. Instead of hiking boots, she wore brown sandals that showed off her pink-painted toenails.

He shouldn't have said anything about her father. Yet, while she'd talked about Rebecca and Thomas, there'd been a sadness in her voice that Nate wanted to ease. Except now he'd just killed Calum's trust after swearing not to say anything. Nate was becoming quite good at betraying people he cared about.

"Nate?" Sarah's voice sounded higher and pitchier. "How do you know about my father?"

"A few weeks ago, after we met, the young woman at the SPO's front desk said you'd left early for a family emergency."

The same woman who'd been murdered the night he kissed Sarah. "I remember that." She stood and shoved books into a straw bag. "I need to go—"

"I'm sorry." Nate rose. "I didn't mean—"

"It's fine." Except from her short, clippy tone it wasn't. "You reminded me that I need to check on my dad. He's been hospitalized." She bit her bottom lip. "But you already know that."

"Is there anything I can do?"

"No." She put her bag onto her shoulder and passed by him, her skirt brushing his jeans. "I'm sure I'll see you soon. You have this way of appearing in my life."

"Actually—" The word sounded hoarse, like it'd come out sideways. "I'm leaving town."

She stopped to look at him, her eyes less wary and more…concerned. Sorry, maybe? A man could only hope.

"Will you be gone long?"

He paused and stared out the window. Across the street, a man in a black hooded sweatshirt stood with his hands in his pockets. Nate couldn't see the man's face but could feel his intense stare.

"Nate?" Sarah prompted.

He shook his head and said, "Yes. I'll be gone for…I'm not sure if I'm coming back."

"Oh." She adjusted the bag, and her gaze darted around the café. "I didn't know."

"I have two favors to ask."

"Of course." She smiled, and every part of his body heated up. *Is this woman ever not beautiful?*

He glanced out the window. The man in the hoodie had disappeared. "First, I need you to promise not to go out to that cemetery alone." He took a twenty out of his wallet and threw it on the table. It was too much, but in a few days he wouldn't need money, so it didn't matter. "Second, you have to stop your research into Rebecca Prideaux and Thomas Toban."

Her face scrunched in an adorable way that made him want to kiss her again. "Why?"

"Well, for starters, Cassio—a Fianna warrior—asked you to. Second, I believe you're in danger from other quarters as well. I'm not sure of the details, but I am sure I won't be here to protect you."

"Nate—"

He placed a hand on her arm. "*Please*, Sarah. Promise me."

She covered his hand with hers. Where he was hot, her fingers were cold. "I won't go to the cemetery alone." She regarded their hands, one of top of the other, and made no move to pull away. "But I've spent most of my career studying Rebecca and Thomas."

He bent in close enough to smell her gardenia perfume,

his hand tightening on her arm. "The Fianna want you to stop what you're doing. And they won't hesitate to go after the ones you love. It's no coincidence that after our meeting today your father was involuntarily admitted to the psych ward. The same day Senator Prioleau warned your boss about your research."

Her eyes widened, and he could hear her breath stutter. "My boss just told me about the senator's warning. How do you know about my father and those things?"

"I just do. And I'm not the only one." He focused on her lips and lowered his voice. "Please, Sarah. Take your father and leave town. Forget about Rebecca and Thomas. Save yourself while you still can. If I could go back in time and save myself and my men, I would."

Despite the sadness in her eyes, she said, "Alright. I won't send in my grant request." The strain in her voice matched her deep exhale, as if she'd just lost a fight with herself.

The relief left his muscles trembling. When she dropped the hand covering his, he wrapped an arm around her waist, drew her close, and kissed her. Her bag hit the ground with a thud.

It took a moment before she melted into him, another before her arms wrapped around his neck. Her lips softened beneath his, and he used one hand to keep her head still while his other arm brought her even closer. Her breasts, barely covered by her tank top and sweater, were pressed against his chest, and their hips made contact. He didn't care if she could feel his reaction to her. He didn't care about anything other than having her in his arms one last time.

His eyes burned behind his eyelids as his lips moved over hers. He chose a rhythm that dominated yet allowed her to respond. The kiss was wet and hard and wonderful—until someone wolf-whistled.

He raised his head to see her closed eyes and slightly swollen lips. It wasn't until he kissed her forehead that she left his arms, her hands on her stomach. When her gaze met his, his heart felt like an IED had exploded in his chest. Strands of hair framed her face; her sweater had shifted, exposing a bare shoulder; her rapid breath pushed her breasts higher above her shirt's neckline. Unable to control his breathing, his thinking, or his deepest needs, he left. He couldn't bear to see the questions in her brown eyes. He couldn't bear to say goodbye.

Sarah couldn't move. She couldn't adjust her sweater or find her straw bag. Even her breath couldn't find a normal rhythm. Nate had done it again. He'd kissed her and then walked away, leaving her a trembling mess.

Aftershocks made her shiver, and she fixed her sweater. She'd heard the whistle, but now everyone had returned to their phones and conversations. She found her bag and touched her lips. She'd never, in her entire life, been kissed the way Nate kissed her. She'd never been held so tightly against such a hard body. She'd never been made to feel so…desired. She closed her eyes and took three deep breaths. *How could he kiss her and walk away? Again?*

After clearing the table, she left the café. Although his kiss had gifted her the moon, his sad eyes had told her he didn't want to go wherever he was going. His demeanor was more than despairing. It was defeated.

Including today, she'd met Nate six times. And in the first five, he'd been a man of determination and force, asking questions, making plans, issuing orders. And always incredibly polite. But the man who'd just asked her to abandon her life's work, kissed her, and walked away? That wasn't Nate. That was a man who'd lost.

What changed since she'd seen him earlier?

She headed toward her truck. Had she just agreed not to restore Rebecca's diary? Had she just agreed not to reclaim her professional reputation? Apparently so. The decision hurt more than she'd expected. Or maybe the pain was from Nate's habit of kissing and leaving. Either way, she wanted to go home, curl up on the couch, and critique the next episode of *Drunk History*.

As she neared Iron Rack's Gym, she saw Nate on the sidewalk talking to the friend with the long black braid. The same man she'd seen at the police station two weeks ago.

Nate's friend laid his helmet on top of his motorcycle and put his hand on Nate's arm, but Nate threw it off. Clearly, they were arguing, though she couldn't hear what they were saying. A third man came out of the gym and joined them. This one had dark brown hair tied at the base of his neck. While the man with the braid had tribal tattoos on each bicep, barely visible beneath his T-shirt, the new man had tattooed arms. When he clasped his hands behind his head, the underside of the tats showed. They were full-circumference inked sleeves.

What was she doing? Spying on Nate and his friends? For what reason? Because Nate was hot. Because she craved his arms around her one more time. Because he'd been kind to her, saved her, and then paid for her photos.

And made me walk away from my life's work.

Now she was standing in a dingy street, lusting after a man she barely knew who probably belonged to a biker gang and who'd asked her to give up on her career. She moved into the closest alley and closed her eyes. *What is wrong with me?*

A bottle smashed, and she opened her eyes. Two guys jostled each other at the other end of the alley. She got into her truck, and saw a man in a black hoodie in an old service station near Iron Rack's. He hovered beneath the faded Texaco sign, staring at Nate and his buddies.

She didn't like the way the hooded man looked at Nate.

Nate's buddies went inside, but Nate stayed outside, eyes closed, face to the sky as if wanting to feel the sun's rays for the last time. Finally, he followed his friends. A moment later, the hooded man crossed the street and slipped something through Iron Rack's door mail slot.

Once the man left, she headed home. New construction projects around the city and detours for tomorrow's opening of the Summer Arts Festival snarled traffic the entire way.

She had no business interfering in Nate's life. Yet, as she drove around a garden square, she made a U-turn. It took another twenty minutes before she parked in the same spot she'd vacated. The moment she got out, her phone hummed with a text.

> Lady Sarah, the past is but a battle lost. Leave
> it be or risk the cost.

"Dammit, Cassio." Seriously. What had Rebecca and Thomas ever done to him?

She grabbed her bag and locked the truck. After looking both ways, she crossed the street and entered Iron Rack's Gym.

CHAPTER 10

IN THE GYM'S LAUNDRY ROOM, ZACK TOOK A PILE OF laundry out of the dryer and dumped it in the basket. After he loaded the dryer with another wet pile, he filled the washer again and hit Start. Then he carried the basket into the adjacent locker room and dropped it onto a table against the wall.

"Hey," Ty said, coming into the locker room. "You texted?"

"Yes. Where are the others?"

"Dunno." Ty threw himself onto one of the benches in between a row of lockers. He rested his head on his clasped hands, bent his leg to place a boot on the wooden seat, and stared at the ceiling. "Who else did you ask to this clandestine meeting?"

"It's not clandestine."

"If the CO and the XO aren't invited, it's clandestine."

Vane appeared, with Luke and Cain following behind. "Got your text. But I have a class in a few minutes."

Of course he did. Zack hid his irritation. There was no reason to be annoyed by Vane, other than the fact that he was always annoying.

"Where's Nate?" Luke carried a clipboard and sat next to Ty's head.

"He just got into the ring with some unlucky civilian." Cain's shoulder held up the nearest locker. "Nate's in a mood and was looking to pound flesh."

"Or get pounded in return." Pete came in last with a frown the size of Idaho and straddled a metal folding chair someone had left near the table. "Make it fast. Once Nate takes down his sparring buddy, he'll be checking to see if we're following his chore chart."

"I like Nate's chart," Luke said. "It's organized and fair."

Ty sighed. Zack knew every day that passed without more intel about how they'd landed in this nightmare made it more difficult for Ty to offer any emotional responses other than sarcasm.

In fact, Zack couldn't remember the last time any of them had laughed or had fun or watched a horror flick together with popcorn and beer.

Zack took a deep breath and started. "We have a situation—"

"Nate is returning to that psych ward," Vane said, "isn't he?"

Zack put his hands on his hips. A safer place than around Vane's neck, squashing his smug, self-satisfied voice. "Yes."

Ty sat up, straddling the bench. "Excuse me?"

"Kells just told us." Zack kept his attention on Cain, whose red face and fisted hands didn't need commentary.

Pete added, "Nate leaves in two days."

"Why?" Cain's question came out loaded with confusion, frustration, and anger.

Pete rose and stood next to Zack. Apparently they were going to address the men together. "Because Nate's release had never been anything but temporary."

"This is bullshit." Cain paced the room, running his hands over his shaved head. "Do we know who helped Kells get Nate out? Maybe we can talk to whoever that is."

"No," Luke said. "Kells's source is a secret."

"That military prison hospital," Pete said, "is on an uninhabited island off the coast of Maine. All of the men stashed there have powerful enemies."

"As do we," Ty reminded them.

"So now what?" Vane asked. "Do we let Nate go? Ghost him? Fight for him?"

"We can't ghost him," Luke said. "Whoever helped Kells get Nate free also made it so we were dishonorably discharged without jail time."

"Meaning," Cain said, "if we help Nate escape, then we go to jail?"

"Yes," Luke said. "The person helping Kells has all the leverage."

"I have an idea," Zack said. "It's why I wanted to meet alone."

"I don't see any way out of this." Vane looked at each of them for optimal theatrical effect. "Maybe it's for the best. Nate is still having seizures and delusions."

A moment later, Pete's fist slammed into Vane's stomach. Vane doubled over, gasping for air. Cain yanked Pete away, tossed him into the chair, and stood guard.

Zack gripped Vane's shoulder, helping him up. "You okay?"

"No." Vane spat on the floor. "What the fuck was that for, Pete?"

"For questioning Nate's sanity." Pete shifted until Cain crossed his arms.

"I'm telling Kells," Vane said.

"Do it," Pete said sullenly. "Asshole."

Vane made to leave but Zack grabbed his forearm. "Not yet." Then Zack looked at every man in the room. "Nate needs our help. And I have an idea. But it'll only work if we work together and agree to keep this quiet."

"From Kells?" Vane snorted. "After what's been happening the past few months, the last thing we need is secrets between us."

While Zack would normally be the first to agree, this wasn't a secret from the world. Just from Kells. "For now, Vane. We only have a few days, and if it doesn't work, then it won't matter. If it does, Kells won't care. This is what we're going to do." Zack straightened his shoulders, spread his legs, and put his hands on his hips. "Luke, you're the linchpin to this plan."

Luke held up his clipboard. "Always am."

"First, I want to see those files you were compiling with all the info for our defense in case we went to trial."

Luke nodded. "I just transferred everything to a remote secure server."

"Second, I want you all to write down everything you can remember for the past five years."

Vane scoffed. "You can't be serious."

"I am." Male voices sounded outside the locker room, so Zack lowered his own. "I need each of us to record everything we can remember from the night Nate's and Jack's teams were ambushed in the Pamir River Valley. Anything you can recall from the recorded messages we received, planning their rescue, their return to the States, and their trials and convictions, up to two weeks ago when we were finally discharged."

"Everything?" Cain rubbed his fist on his chin. "That's a lot of writing."

"I know." Especially for a man like Cain who'd rather do than write. "Ask Charlotte to help. Her perspective could be important. She might remember something we missed."

Cain nodded.

"I'll call Abigail Casey," Luke said. "I'm sure she'd do anything to help us."

"Great." Abigail was married to Liam Casey, one of the ten men in their unit imprisoned in Leedsville. Unfortunately, at the time of the ambush five years ago, only three wives were left in the unit.

"What about Kate?" Ty asked. "She was still married to Kells when this nightmare started."

The room went quiet. The truth was no one wanted to touch that mess. Kells was still dealing with the emotional aftermath of his wife leaving him.

"I'll do it," Vane said. "Kate may help us. She always liked me and Nate."

Everyone liked Nate. "Great." As much as it killed Zack to say it, he managed a short "Thanks, Vane. Nate leaves in two days. Time is critical."

After agreeing to write out their memories as quickly

as possible, the men left, except for Pete. Zack found the basket he'd filled earlier and started folding, stacking the clean clothes and towels on the table. Halfway through the pile, he asked Pete, "What's wrong?"

"I know someone who might be able to ID Kells's contact who got Nate a temporary reprieve from that prison hospital." Pete threw the T-shirts on the table, defeating the entire concept of folding. "Maybe we could convince this contact not to send Nate back."

"That's a lot of *mights* and *maybes*." Zack paused while rolling washcloths. "Who's your contact?"

Pete dropped a towel on the floor, picked it up, and chucked it into the basket. "The same man who uncovered classified intel on me and Nate when we first came to town. Detective Garza."

Nate struck a right hook into his partner's jaw and savored the pain shooting through his knuckles and forearm. The guy's head swung back, but he regrouped with a left jab. A move that left the guy open to a liver punch.

Nate obliged, and the adrenaline surge left him strong and clearheaded. The constant movement and physical violence kept him focused and alert, almost like when he'd been on those Z-pam pills. Fear didn't drive his fights. Just a need to control something. And he could control his hits.

His partner returned with a series of punches to Nate's face, which he protected with his gloves. The muscles in his shoulders contracted, and he bit down on his mouth guard. One of the things he missed about the previous owner? They'd been allowed to fight barefisted without safety gear. A sitch Kells had nixed on the first day Nate's unit had taken over the gym.

Nate found an opening and threw an upper cross jab. His opponent stumbled. Nate almost swung a roundhouse kick, but Kells had forbidden MMA-style workouts as well.

His opponent grunted and followed up with a left hook. Nate took the hit but returned with a punch to the jaw. His partner swayed, and Nate went in again. And again. The more he hit, the more aggression he felt. The more aggression, the more alive. The more alive, the more hope that maybe his life wouldn't be spent in a zombie state in a prison hospital at the ass-end of the world.

He heard a whistle but hit one more time, with more force than he'd realized. Pain rocketed up his arm. His opponent landed on his ass, staring at silver stars painted on the black ceiling.

The ref, a member who'd volunteered for today's fight, dragged Nate away, still blowing the damn whistle. Nate bent over, leaning his forearms on his thighs. His breath sounded like the coal train that rumbled along the river every morning at four a.m. His heart felt like it was breaking out of his chest.

"What the hell is wrong with you?" The ref grabbed Nate's shoulder, forcing him to look up. "When I blow the whistle, you stop." The ref left Nate to check on his opponent. "Asshole."

Nate took off his gloves and then his helmet and teeth protection, only to see Vane and the ref helping the guy stand. Nate's opponent wobbled, but when the guy got his gear off, he said, "You beat me again, Walker."

"You don't make it easy." He'd not meant to hurt the guy. In fact, he was grateful to have anyone to spar with. He didn't have as many partners as he'd once had.

"You okay?" Vane asked Nate's opponent.

"Just got my bell rung." The guy nodded at Nate. "Prefer it when men don't hold back."

"It wasn't a fair fight." The ref threw down his whistle and left the ring.

Vane grabbed the whistle. "We need to talk."

"No." Nate sure as hell wasn't going to listen to one of Vane's endless lectures. "Don't you have a class to teach?"

"I gave it to Pete." Vane's phone rang, and he turned to answer.

Nate held a hand out to his opponent. Once they shook, Nate helped him out of the ring.

The guy packed his duffel. "I hear there's an amateur fight tournament coming to town." He carried the bag on his shoulder, limping yet determined not to show it. "Will Iron Rack's be involved?"

"Not sure. I'll have to ask our business manager."

"Great. See you tomorrow." The guy headed for the locker room.

Nate found his water bottle and drank. As the water hit his parched throat, he forced himself to remember all of this. The smell of male sweat. The endless chore list. Calum's garbage and rat-infested tunnels. The ability to drink a damn glass of water whenever he wanted, at the temperature he liked. The memories of spending time with those he loved. Even this gym with the crazy pirate flags and ceiling painted black with night-sky constellations.

The time to pursue the woman he wanted. The freedom to kiss Sarah. He savored all of it because soon he'd be in a far-off land with only memories to keep him sane.

"Hey." Vane appeared again, snapping his fingers in front of Nate's face. "What the *fuck* was that about? We're not supposed to kill our members."

"He was up for it."

"You can't go all *Fight Club* in here. We have new rules." Vane stalked away.

Zack appeared next to him, holding a plastic bin of dirty towels, until their shoulders almost touched. They watched Vane confront Luke, who, instead of hitting Vane over the head with the clipboard, turned and went for Kells's office.

"Ignore Vane." Zack offered the advice as if it'd matter in a few days.

"Always do." Nate peeled off his T-shirt and tossed it into Zack's basket. "Is Kells here?"

"No."

Just as well. "I need to adjust the chore and job charts," he said as they both headed for the locker room. If he had to leave his men, he'd make sure their new situation was as organized and orderly as possible. "Let's go with a laundry service. And I'll contact that payroll company with those new socials Calum got us. And we need help at the desk during the busiest hours—" Nate paused when he noticed someone standing in the shadows near the front desk. A beautiful woman in a pink skirt, her long hair in a ponytail, and holding a straw bag. She stared at him with deep brown eyes rounder than moons. *Sarah.*

CHAPTER 11

SARAH TRIED HARD NOT TO OGLE NATE. BUT HIS ALMOST-nakedness made her mouth dry up and her hands clench. He'd taken off his shirt and wore only gym pants that rode low on his hips. His long hair was bound behind his neck, and his upper body shone from sweat.

God had put him together in layers of muscles and tendons, all stacked and shaped into a perfect male form. Even the random scars and tight, red skin on his arms that looked like burns seemed like they belonged, like he'd earned them. His green gaze widened, and his chest undulated with the force of all of that heavy breathing.

Probably from beating a man until he was almost unconscious. Nate had just kept hitting as if not aware of what he'd been doing or what was happening. She'd been around men her entire life, so straight-up virility didn't frighten her. But she'd never seen this kind of raw, masculine action. Although the force of Nate's attack concerned her, Nate's opponent had acted like it wasn't a big deal. So maybe it wasn't.

"Sarah." Her name came out on his exhale, heavy with surprise.

"Hi." *Good golly Moses.* "I, uh, wanted…" She swallowed and clutched the letter she'd found on the floor near the front door. "Could we talk alone?" She nodded to his friend whom she'd seen outside earlier, the one with the long brown hair and tatted arms.

Now that she was closer, she realized the ink formed a dragon that started on one wrist and went up his arm and down the other arm.

"Of course." Nate ran a hand over his head and led the way until stopping suddenly. "Would you wait in the office while I change? I'll only be a minute. Zack will take you."

"Sure," she said.

Zack's smile brightened his dark, intense demeanor, and she breathed for the first time since seeing Nate in the ring.

When Nate disappeared into the locker room, Zack put down his laundry basket. "This way."

"Thanks." The office was in the front corner, overlooking the street. Inside, she saw another man sitting behind the desk, typing on a laptop.

"Luke? This is *Sarah*." She glanced at Zack. Had there been an emphasis on her name? "*Sarah's* waiting for Nate."

Yes. Definite emphasis.

Luke shut his laptop. "Oh." He blinked before smiling. "Okay. I'll be at the front desk."

With his short brown military-style haircut—so different from Zack's—and Atlanta Braves T-shirt over shorts, he seemed out of place with Nate's buddies. Nate and Zack seemed like mercenaries, while Luke was…less threatening.

As Luke passed with his laptop under his arm, he said, "Nice to meet you, Sarah."

She nodded, and Zack waved to a metal chair in front of the desk. "Nate will be in soon. No one will bother you, and you're welcome to whatever's in the coffeepot."

Once alone, she dropped her bag on the chair and studied the room. Concrete walls and floor had been painted gray. Plastic bags from a hardware store lay in the corner, still filled with cords and plugs and cables. Cardboard banker's boxes lined the perimeter.

A bookcase behind the desk held notebooks with years printed on the spines. Most of them were from the eighties and nineties. It was as if someone had just moved out and the someone who'd moved in had dumped the new on top of the old.

One wall was a picture window half-covered by Jolly Roger flags. Two other walls had corkboards filled with posters of boxing matches, MMA fights, and brochures advertising protein drinks. The last wall—the one not visible from the doorway—was decorated with the largest map of Afghanistan and Pakistan she'd ever seen.

She found her glasses and realized it was a topographical map, with the mountains and valleys outlined in green concentric circles. Pins with colored-glass tops were clustered in different areas, but all of the red pins were in one area: the Pamir River Valley. The yellow pins were grouped around the Wakhan mountain range.

Blue, green, purple, and black pins were stuck over the rest of the map but didn't appear to be in any order. One gray pin was off on its own, in the northern part of the country, near the Hindu Kush. To the east, ten orange pins were stuck in Islamabad.

She ran her fingers over the orange pins. What a strange thing to find in a run-down gym on the edge of the not-nice part of town. Male voices sounded near the gym's front desk, but no one came into the office. She placed her palms on files stacked on a plywood credenza to get a closer look.

She remembered, maybe five years ago, that an entire Wakhan village had been brutally massacred. But she hadn't heard anything about it since it'd happened.

Male laughter made her turn, and she knocked files off the credenza. She picked up the folders and had to fish under the desk for a stray paper. It was a list of names written in teacher-perfect handwriting. Beneath the title *LMCF*, ten names were grouped into five pairs and marked with an alphanumeric code in sequential order.

The first two names were Jack Keeley and Tank Wofford. 3C-115. The second two names were Liam Casey and Quinn Jones. 3C-116. Sarah scanned the other three pairs until seeing two single names on the bottom. *Alex Mitchell*, 1A-102. Below that was *N. Walker* next to a phone number with an area code from the state of Maine.

None of this makes any sense.

She opened the top file and was about to toss in the list when she noticed something. A photograph from O'Malley's

Pub, similar to the one she'd found for her father earlier. Carefully, she lifted the photo only to realize there were more beneath. All of them were different pictures from her father's crime scene that she'd never seen before.

She sifted through them only to get the second shock. Beneath the pictures of the crime scene that had destroyed her father's and Hugh's careers was the same photo Hugh had shown her. Below that was the third and biggest shock of all: photographs of her working at the Savannah Preservation Office. Of her talking in the garden with Nate when he'd brought her the map to authenticate. And one of them talking in the police station moments before he kissed her.

The last page, written in perfect penmanship, was about her: where she'd gone to school, her degrees and scholarships, her dissertation, her work experience, and the reason for her demotion to contract work, a.k.a. *forced leave* due to that article in *The British Journal of Eighteenth Century History*.

When the lights in the room began to spin, she forced herself to breathe. She needed to find the safe spot between shallow breaths and hyperventilating. She needed to get the hell out of there.

Using her phone, she took photos of the map, the list of names, and the O'Malley's Pub pics and sent them to Hugh with a text.

Any idea what this all means?

She slapped the file shut, shoved it and her phone in her bag, and spun around only to find a man standing in the doorway, arms crossed, biceps almost as large as Nate's.

His black sweats and Iron Rack's T-shirt matched the fierceness in his brown eyes. He wasn't as tall as Nate or as handsome, but his deep frown and long hair tied at the base of his neck told her he wasn't the type a woman could flirt with or cajole to get out of trouble.

"What did you put in your purse?" He pounded out the words in a direct statement.

She hiked her bag on her shoulder and rose on her toes to maintain maximum height. "None of your business." Then, because she was annoyed, added, "I'm leaving now."

"I can't let you do that."

Really? "Then what are you going to do about it?"

Nate entered the locker room to find Ty mopping the floor.

"Hey, Nate. Win your fight?"

"Yes." Nate hated seeing his friend scrubbing the gym when he should be leading an A-team halfway across the world. But this was their life now, and to feel bad about it would leave him stuck in the sea of self-pity with the Sirens luring him to their shores with the *Song of the Fuck-up.* The song that'd already stolen years of his life. "You okay with the chore chart?"

"It's cool." Ty swished the broom around benches between lockers. "Better than prison."

Amen, brother. "I'm just going to shower and get out of your way."

"Whatever."

Nate found his jeans and a black T-shirt folded on top of the dryer in the adjacent laundry room. Then he sucked in his stomach, dropped his gym pants, and turned on the water. After untying his hair, he got in. When the heat hit the tight muscles in his back, he closed his eyes. He'd stripped the gauze off his arms before his fight and now let the water rinse off the salve. He was sick of the smell. Turning, he lifted his face to the waterfall.

Since leaving the prison hospital, he'd been exercising like death was chasing him. Despite the ongoing seizures, his body had responded to the new activity by forming muscles he'd never seen before. The irony was that he was returning to the psych ward while he was in the best physical shape of his life. If there'd been a time to meet his enemy and save his men, it would be now. But since his wishes always went to shit, he just soaped up as the water turned cold. The chill helped with the tension in the lower half of his body.

He opened his eyes and noticed Ty straddling a nearby bench. "I need to tell you something. Something I should have said two weeks ago."

After he turned off the water, Ty threw him a towel. Although Nate wanted to get back to Sarah ASAP, he recognized compassion and maybe a bit of sadness in his friend's face. Ty ran both hands over his crew cut and clasped them behind his head. A restless gesture Nate knew often preceded a lecture.

Nate finished drying before asking, "What is it?"

"Whatever happens, it'll be okay."

Shit. "You know. About my returning to the prison hospital."

"Yeah." Ty sighed. "Zack and Pete told us."

"Perfect." Nate tossed the towel toward the gray hamper. It hit the edge and fell onto the floor.

"Because of you and Pete, we know the name of our enemy. That's more intel than we've had for the past five years."

"Is it okay for me to leave even though we don't have a plan to work the mission? Is it okay for our men in prison? Is it okay that our exit papers were stamped *dishonorable discharge*?" He ripped open his jeans and shoved his legs through.

"None of us can see the future," Ty said. "But maybe the army will let you go for good behavior or some shit like that. Trust me, man. It'll work out. It has to."

Nate zipped up, found his socks and boots, and put them on. Then he reached for a brush and attacked his hair. He wasn't used to Ty being the optimistic one. Positive thinking was Pete's domain. Besides, since Nate's release from that psych ward, he and Ty only talked about work. While they'd once been closer than brothers, now they were nothing more than teammates. And Nate wasn't sure what to do with Ty's sudden concern.

Nate brushed out his hair and tied it back. His heart hurt at the loss of the friendship. At the loss of his brothers. His parents were long dead and his sister was unavailable, so his buddies had been his only family. He slipped the black T-shirt over his head. "Thanks." Although he'd no idea where all this emotion was coming from.

"No prob." Ty stood, his blue eyes crinkling. "We've started a new life in Savannah. We have a second chance to make out with our demons."

Nate had missed Ty's bad jokes. "Make amends, bro. Not make out."

Ty's smile transformed his face from a hard-core operator into someone approachable. "Not when your demons wear a black leather mini, a lace bustier, and swing a whip."

Maybe not so approachable. Nate laughed and found his towel to toss it into the basket. "Can we trade demons?"

"Not a chance, brother." Ty started mopping again. "That bitch is mine."

Their laughter lessened the ache in his chest until Luke ran in. "Hurry, Nate. Vane and Sarah are arguing in Kells's office." Luke smiled. "She's kicking his ass."

CHAPTER 12

NATE RAN OUT. AS EXECUTIVE OFFICER, ONE OF HIS JOBS was to keep order and peace. Which included, but wasn't limited to, breaking up fights. He'd just never had to stop a fight between a soldier and a historian before.

He passed the fighting ring and halted in the office doorway. Vane, all in black, and Sarah, in her pink skirt, faced off in the room. She wore her glasses, clutched her straw bag on her shoulder, and tapped a sandaled foot. Zack stood near the window, arms crossed.

Nate shut the door as Vane said to Sarah, "What did you put in your purse?"

"Nothing that concerns you."

Vane took a step forward. "I want to see it."

Sarah refused to retreat. "No."

Vane lowered his arms, and Nate threw Vane against a cabinet. "What's going on?"

"Your girlfriend stole something from Kells's desk."

Nate pushed Vane again. "She wouldn't do that."

"Actually, I did." Sarah spoke in the most unapologetic voice Nate had ever heard. "And I'm not sorry."

Nate let Vane go and faced the beautiful woman. She'd buttoned her sweater, but it only emphasized her figure. She'd also reapplied the pink lipstick he'd kissed off earlier. When she shifted, the slit in her skirt opened. He swallowed, hating that his throat felt so dry. "Excuse me?"

"You've been tracking me for weeks. Following me and my father. Searching for information about our life. I trusted you, Nate Walker. And while I'd love to know why my life is so important to you, I'm leaving now, and I never want to see you again."

Nate looked at Vane. Then at Zack. "What is she talking about?"

Zack shrugged.

"Who the hell cares?" Vane pointed at Sarah. "She's a thief and a liar."

Sarah scoffed. "Says the man who intimidates women."

Nate faced her. "Sarah—"

"No, Nate. I don't want to hear anything from you. I just want to leave." She picked up a picture frame from Kells's desk, muttering, "Serves me right for wanting to help you."

Nate exhaled and balanced his weight on both legs. How many times had he forced order out of chaos? Too many to count. But this situation with a beautiful woman was a first. "No one leaves until I know what the hell is going on."

"Fuck this, Nate." Vane's hands landed on his hips.

"Watch your language," Nate ordered.

"I don't need your protection, Nate." Sarah waved an arm toward the map. "You lied to me, and I'm not interested in what you have to say."

"Nate doesn't lie." Every head turned toward Zack. "I don't know what you think you know, Miss Munro, but Nate didn't lie about it."

Sarah turned the frame so they could see the photo. "Nate told me he worked in a gym."

Nate groaned. Damn Kells and his stupid camera. It was a photo of them in combat gear outside a Quonset hut at Fort Bragg. Nate was front and center, surrounded by Ty, Zack, Cain, Pete, and six other men who were currently in prison. "We were in the army. Now we work here."

"I'm not stupid, Nate. See that sign on the Quonset hut? I can read Latin. Not only do I know what *De oppresso liber* means, I know what it stands for." She pointed to him, then Vane and Zack. "You're Green Berets."

He swallowed hard. In their anger and frustration, they'd let their physical and operational security go. Even Kells was guilty of poor OPSEC. Since she deserved an answer, Nate offered, "We *were* Green Berets."

"And now you run a gym?" She shook her head. "You think anyone believes that? It doesn't seem like any of you *work* here. The locals run the place while you clean and look busy. You have a map of Afghanistan in your office, and you've been collecting photos of me and my father. I'm not believing the past tense, Nate. Something's going on, and somehow my father and I are involved."

No one responded.

She scoffed. "You all manage this gym now?"

"Yes," Nate said.

She put the frame on the desk. "Then who is Iron Rack's named for?"

He glanced at Zack and Vane. With their matching blank stares, they looked as clueless as he felt.

"Seriously?" She stared at the ceiling. "It's named after Captain Calico Jack Rackham who designed the Jolly Roger flag and was hanged in Jamaica." Now she stared at them as if they were throwing spitballs in a high school history class. "Jack's lover, Anne Bonny, almost hanged as well until she claimed to be pregnant. There's no record of her execution. I checked the Port Royal library as well as the eighteenth-century Jamaican records in the British Library in London."

"Nate?" Zack asked quietly. "Why is she talking about pirates and libraries?"

"I think," Vane whispered loudly, "because she's a librarian."

Her sigh might as well have been an eye roll. "I have a PhD in early colonial history, a degree in archival studies from Harvard, and a Master in Letters from St. Andrews University in Scotland. But, of course, that's old news to you."

Vane coughed. "Kells said you went to Boston College."

She lifted her chin. "Undergraduate degrees in classics and history."

Nate turned to Vane. "How do you—or Kells—know that?"

A flush flooded Vane's face.

Zack moved until his fist hit Vane's chest. "Sarah is right? You and Kells have been following her? Digging into her life? Her past?"

Vane lifted both hands. "I've no idea how Kells knows anything."

"Yet," Nate said, "you and Kells were talking about Sarah."

Vane gave a short nod.

"They've been following both of us." Sarah dropped her bag on Kells's desk and retrieved a file folder. From that, she handed Nate two photos. One of them sitting together outside the SPO. The other of the two of them in the police station moments before he kissed her.

He faced Vane. "What the *fuck* is this?" The words exploded before Nate could stop them.

"No idea, brother." Vane shoved his hands in the pockets of his sweatpants and put on the *poor me* act that Nate despised. "Kells was talking about Sarah the other night, totally out of context. He was stressed and needed to vent."

It always irritated Nate when Vane threw out the Kells-and-I-are-so-fucking-close-we-sit-around-and-confide-in-each-other card.

Zack took the photos. "This is bullshit."

Agreed. But right now Nate's main concern was Sarah, who, while she had every right to be pissed, might be in even more danger than he realized. Why else would Kells have her—correction, *them*—followed?

Sarah glared at all of them. "I'm leaving."

"No, you're not." He checked his watch. "I'm changing the chore chart. Zack, take Vane to the tunnels. We're behind on getting them cleared. Especially the one leading to the club."

Vane sputtered. "I'm working the front desk."

Nate ignored Vane. "Luke has the desk until Pete is done with his class. And tell Cain he's on housekeeping duty until I return. Ty has grocery and dinner duty tonight."

"Got it." Zack handed the photos to Sarah, grabbed Vane's arm, and dragged him from the room.

Once alone, Nate released a deep breath and focused on Sarah. Without the men in the room, she seemed smaller. Maybe because she wasn't trying so hard to look fierce.

She put the photos in the file and returned it to her straw bag. "I'm not sorry I took that file—am taking the file. And I'm mad that you lied to me."

"I know." He shoved his hand in his pockets. "You mentioned there were other photos?"

"Yes." She spoke softly now. Less commanding, less certain. A few minutes before, her eyes had fired lasers; now she wouldn't meet his gaze. "I need to leave. I've got things to do."

"I have an idea. We go to neutral ground. You show me the file, and I promise to answer your questions the best I can."

After a long pause, she said, "My father's house."

Was everything with her going to be a negotiation? Until now, he'd never truly appreciated that his men did what he told them to do. There might be fussing but never rebellion. He took her hand, and when she didn't run, he squeezed. "Alright."

She removed her glasses and watched him from beneath those dark lashes. "Did you know about the photos?"

"No. My not knowing about the photos means I've been betrayed also." Her brown eyes shimmered. She'd been hiding the fact that she was about to cry, and that sent his heart into a tailspin. "I don't like being betrayed."

"Then let's go." She yanked her hand out of his and led the way.

"Sarah." When she turned, he said, "Wait at the front desk. I'll be right back."

"Hurry." She adjusted her bag on her shoulder. "I have a million things to do."

While she waited, he ran upstairs to the room he shared with Pete to grab his coat and his gun. Nate always felt better when he carried his own weapon. When he met her downstairs, Sarah walked out. He followed, texting Luke. *Tell Ty to get new burner phones today. And don't tell Kells where I've gone.*

I know nothing, Luke texted.

None of us do, brother. None of us do.

಄

Thirty minutes later, Zack entered the Savannah Police Department. He'd left Vane in the tunnels with the excuse that they needed water and more garbage bags. Not a lie, but not the entire truth. Considering what Zack had learned about Kells having photos of Sarah and Nate, partial truths seemed to be part of this new mission. A situation Zack didn't like. The further away he and his men moved from their time as active-duty Green Berets, the less their unit appeared to value virtues like honesty and patience.

Zack still wasn't sure about trusting Detective Garza. Why would a city cop cover for a group of ex-soldiers living covertly in his city? But since Nate and Pete trusted him—and those two trusted few people—Zack was willing to go with it.

Once inside, he double-timed it up the stairs, rounded the corner, and entered chaos. Groups of people stood around whiteboards while others sat with heads down at tables. He found Detective Garza seated at his desk, typing on a laptop.

"Detective Garza?"

Garza raised his head. "Yes?"

Zack held out his hand. "I'm Zack Tremaine. Nate's friend."

Garza blew out a breath. "Right." He shut his laptop

and led the way through furniture that must've been new in the nineteen fifties. He stopped at a vending machine and punched the button for two Cokes. "You okay with sugar and caffeine?"

"Lunch of warriors."

Garza handed him a cold can and opened a door with a *#2* painted on the outside.

"Is this necessary?" Zack asked as he took a seat at the table across from a one-way mirror.

"Yes." Garza hit a button on the wall. "There's no one watching or listening."

"Is that a problem here?"

"It hasn't been, but I'm not taking any chances."

"One might think you're afraid."

"One might think I've seen a man bow." Garza opened his can and drank the initial fizz. "Calum told me you know that Nate and Pete met a Fianna warrior."

Zack raised his can. "Just found out."

"Is that a secret you can keep?"

"Do I have a choice?"

"We all have a choice." Garza sat in a metal chair and kicked back until his ankles were crossed on top of the table. "Question is what will yours be?"

"I'm choosing to support Nate."

"Even if it means not telling your CO?"

"For now."

"Huh." Garza took another drink before asking, "What do you need?"

"How much do you know about what happened to Nate before he arrived in Savannah?"

"I know about your unit's ambush in the Pamir River Valley and being accused of the Wakhan Corridor Massacre. I'm also aware that the two ambushed A-teams were sent to a POW camp for two years. Once rescued, they came home to be convicted of murder and other things and sent to prison."

Zack exhaled and took a long drink of the sweet soda.

"Then," Garza continued, "two weeks ago, the A-team that'd been in the command center during this entire mess—*your* team—was dishonorably discharged but not sent to prison."

Zack stared at the green linoleum floor. Garza knew more than Zack realized, but that made this easier. "What do you know about Nate specifically?"

"After being rescued, instead of being sent to one of the army's correctional facilities, he went to a military prison hospital in Maine where they treated him for headaches, delusions, and seizures."

"Did you know that Nate's release was temporary?"

"No." Garza put his can on the table. "I didn't know that."

"Apparently, whoever helped Kells get Nate out of prison could only do so on a short-term basis. Nate returns to the prison hospital on Sunday."

Garza dropped his legs and sat forward, elbows on his thighs. "What do you know about Kells's contact?"

"Nothing. Kells is close-mouthed about everything. I was hoping if we could ID this contact, I could talk to him, see if there's a way to keep Nate out of prison. Cut a deal."

"And you don't think Kells has already thought of that?"

"Like I said, Kells doesn't share. So I don't know what to think." Zack finished his soda and put the can on the table. Seeing those photos of Sarah and Nate in Kells's office had brought up a whole new set of questions, not the least of which was who was telling the truth and who was lying. "Pete told me you have contacts who were able to find out classified black ops information, a few weeks ago, when you first met Pete and Nate. You did background checks."

"I did due diligence. It's a good thing, too. Otherwise I wouldn't have realized the importance of staying away from men who bow."

"Can you help?"

"I can make a call."

Good. "There's something else. I just found out that Sarah Munro—"

Garza raised his head, eyes wide. "The historian from the Savannah Preservation Office?"

"Yes. Someone was following her and Nate two weeks ago, taking photographs."

"Shit." Garza ran a hand over his head. "Shit. Shit. Shit."

"I've no idea who'd do that. Or why. The only thing I do know is that my CO had the photographs in a file in his office."

"Could Kells have hired the tail?"

"I don't know." Zack's voice barely came out above a whisper. Maybe because he didn't want to hear the suspicions rolling around in his mind.

"Hell." Garza ran a hand over his hair until short strands stuck up all over. "I'll see what they can find out about Kells's contact. In the meantime, I'll call Calum Prioleau. Nothing happens in this city without his knowledge."

"And he'll keep quiet?"

"For Nate's sake?" Garza nodded. "Absolutely. Calum owes Nate…everything."

Zack exhaled deeply for the first time in hours. "I need to get back to the tunnels."

A knock sounded, and Garza opened the door. A cop dressed similarly to Garza stood outside. "Sheriff Boudreaux just called."

"I'll be right there." Once the man left, Garza said, "That's Detective Elliot. He's not a fan of Nate's." Garza collected both cans. "Stay away from him."

Zack followed Garza to his desk, grateful for the cooler air. "Thanks for the warning."

"I'll call you as soon as I hear something." Garza tossed the cans into the recycling bin. "You have my number?"

Zack scrolled through his phone. Nate had programmed in numbers, many with unusual monikers. "Are you Copper?"

"It's pronounced *Coppa*. With a New York accent."

Zack laughed. "Aren't you from New Jersey?"

Garza clapped Zack's shoulder. "If your men don't fuck up my city, I'm going to like you."

CHAPTER 13

NATE'S HEADACHE RETURNED BECAUSE FATE LIKED TO watch him vomit and pass out. Hopefully, as long as he didn't have a seizure, he'd be okay.

He waited on the sidewalk for Sarah to park her truck in her driveway. He'd told her he was following behind when the truth was he'd ridden his bicycle and hidden it in a nearby alley. He didn't want her to know he wasn't allowed to drive. Male pride and all that.

While he waited, he scanned the surroundings, especially the house. White columns supported the antebellum brick home graced by an elaborate stone-and-cast-iron staircase. Creeping fig covered the stone walls protecting the enclosed garden. The scent of jasmine wafted by on the warm breeze while pots of pink flowers stood as sentinels on each step. He rubbed his damp hands on his jeans and wished he'd polished his boots. Then he noticed Sarah's skirt and sleek ponytail. He always felt underdressed around her. "This is a beautiful home."

Sarah rummaged through her straw bag. "It was my mother's. She inherited it from her parents." She found a key, led him up the steps, and opened the door. "My great-great-grandparents lived in the original building, but that burned down in the nineteenth century."

The door opened silently, and she led the way. A free-standing circular staircase dominated the cool, dark foyer. He appreciated the silence and was hesitant to unsettle the stillness the house demanded. On his right, he passed a sitting room with two club chairs, a fireplace, and built-in shelves. To his left, the dining room had a polished table, sideboard, and six dining room chairs on an embroidered carpet. Even the crystal chandelier looked original.

He inhaled deeply. The house smelled like orange oil and gardenias. It smelled like home. "You need an alarm."

"You sound like my dad." She led him past the staircase, down the hallway, into the kitchen and family room. The open area with white cabinets and black granite counter, clearly an addition, had windows overlooking the garden with a raised fountain. The eating area held a round table, and a desk sat in an alcove near a couch and coffee table.

"We came home less than a year ago, and I haven't had a chance to install an alarm." She dropped her bag on the desk and took off her sweater. "Would you like water or a soda?"

He threw his jacket on the table and closed his eyes. "Water, please."

"Nate?" When he opened his eyes, she was in front of him. She touched his hot face with her cooler hands, but her gaze was focused on his neck. "Are you alright?"

"Sure." He didn't move because he didn't want her to stop touching him. She was so close, he could smell the gardenia scent in her hair, see a tiny scar on her forehead that he had a sudden desire to kiss. Her cool hands alleviated the heat building in his body.

"Do you have a headache?"

Among other ailments. "Is it that obvious?"

"Yes." She left him to fill her teapot with water. "My father suffers from seizures and headaches. I have an herbal tea that helps."

That sounded iffy. "Do you have ibuprofen?"

She found a metal card catalog from behind the toaster and opened it. The box looked like it'd belonged to the original Betty Crocker. "That stuff will destroy your stomach." She flipped through cards and took one out. "I also have a homemade salve that will help with the burns on your arms." She read the card. "You're not allergic to buckthorn oil or beeswax, are you?"

He almost laughed, but she looked so serious he just said, "I don't think so."

She stared at his chest until he cleared his throat.

Turning away, she tucked her hair behind her ear. He could've sworn her cheeks looked redder than before. "Sarah, I swear to you I had no idea about those photos in Kells's office. I know what it's like to be betrayed, and I'd never do that to you."

She nodded, switched on the gas range, and set the teapot to boil. He ached to go to her, to take her in his arms, but she had to decide on her own if she trusted him. The next move had to be hers. The only sound came from the gas flame and the hiss from the water. "Are we okay?"

Whatever answer she gave him, he'd hold in his heart and carry to the prison hospital.

"Yes," she said softly as she took a mug out of a cabinet. "We're okay."

He released a loud breath. She hadn't looked at him, but it was a start. "That's...good."

She grabbed a *Chocolate de Paris* tin on the counter and popped off the top. An unsettling smell drifted out. "I know this is an unusual request," she said as she filled a tea ball with herbs from the tin. "If you take off your shirt, I'll put salve on your arms while we wait for your tea."

Whoa. He'd not expected that, especially since she still hadn't met his gaze.

He hesitated and then yanked off his tee. Why the hell not. In forty-eight hours he'd be on his way to the psych ward. He had to make the most of his time left. "Now what?"

She popped the tea ball into the mug and took a glass jar out of a cabinet. "My burn salve is made with aloe vera, rosewater, sea buckthorn oil, coconut oil, honey, and beeswax. I'll massage it into your arms to ease the tightness." The teapot whistled, and she poured water into the mug. Then she added a big dollop of honey.

"What's that smell?"

She smiled. "Bacopa and feverfew and a few other herbs." She came over with the lotion. "The honey makes it taste better."

He doubted it. "I don't think that'll help."

Now she chuckled. "You sound like my father." She held out the salve container so he could sniff. "This one smells nice."

It reminded him of summer picnics, which led to visions of Sarah in a bikini, which led to clenched hands and a raging hard-on. "It does." He still wasn't sure about her salve, but he said yes. If it meant she was volunteering to touch him, he was all in.

He sat on the stool while she dipped her hands into the container and rubbed her fingers together. "I need to warm it."

"I don't mind if it's cold. I'm always hot."

She kept her attention on his arms. "Tell me if there's any irritation."

He didn't say anything because her hands were on his shoulder and slowly working the salve around his biceps and forearm and down to his wrist. The cream felt cold on his tight skin, and he closed his eyes.

"Are you alright?"

He nodded because he had no words to describe the sensation of her hands running up and down his arms.

"My grandmother and mother left me these recipes." Sarah spoke in such a low voice, he opened his eyes as if that would help him hear her better. "They believed in homeopathy. Many of their recipes date to the seventeenth century, to Anne Capel."

"Besides being an accused murderer and a romantic who helped teenagers elope, Anne was a seventeenth-century healer?"

"Yes." Sarah finally met his gaze, and he was relieved to see her brown eyes had lightened, that the tight lines around her lips had disappeared. "Some recipes don't work, but others do."

He swallowed instead of answering. The sensation of her hands on his arm felt hypnotic and wonderful and erotic at the same time. He prayed she wouldn't look down and notice his arousal. It's not like he could hide it or help it. And while he didn't want to make her uncomfortable, he wasn't ashamed either. "Did your mom teach you to make herbal remedies?"

"Yes. One of my most vivid memories is an argument my mother and grandmother had about whether ginger or roasted dandelion root was better for an upset stomach." She paused in her massaging to wipe a hand on a towel, take out the tea ball, and hand him the cup.

He tried hard not to notice her breasts through her white cami. The AC in the house had kicked on, and she seemed oblivious to her own reaction. He looked away because he was a gentleman. But *daaaaaaamn.*

He took a sip and tried not to gag. "It tastes like sh—sludge."

"If you finish it, I'll do your other arm."

He pinched his nose with one hand and drank it in three gulps.

"Nate! It's hot!"

Oh, yeah it was. The skin in his throat had burned away, but it was worth it if she'd touch him again. He put the mug on the counter and held out his other arm.

She shook her head and smoothed the salve on his skin. "These are serious burns."

"From an accident." He didn't want to lie to her, so he didn't say anything else.

She sent him a questioning glance yet didn't ask for details. His shoulders dropped in relief, and he sank into the sensation of her hands on his skin while she worked the miracle cream from his shoulder to his wrist.

"How does this feel?"

Unbelievably erotic. "Wonderful. And my headache isn't as bad." Which, amazingly enough, was true. "Thank you."

"You're welcome. You should wait a few minutes before dressing. The salve needs to dry." When she was done, she put the lid on the jar and washed her hands. Then she went to the fridge and got out two water bottles. "You need to drink water after your tea."

"Why?"

"The tea can sometimes upset your stomach."

He opened the lid and took three long swallows. That's when he noticed they were on opposite sides of the granite counter. Adversaries where they'd once been friends. Or at least colleagues. Who'd kissed. Twice. "Do you want to show me what you took from Kells's office?"

"Do you want to tell me why a group of ex–Green Berets are pretending to run a gym in Savannah?"

He moved away from the counter and pulled out two kitchen chairs. He deliberately put them close enough for their knees to touch if she wanted. Which, since she still stood, she didn't.

"I've no idea why Kells did that, but I can tell you what I know. My friends and I recently got out of the army and needed a new life. Since few of us had families and Calum had just bought Iron Rack's, we're running the place for him." Nate took another drink of water. So far, his stomach felt fine. "Nothing sinister in that."

"Maybe." She wrapped her arms around her waist. "You said you were leaving town."

"I did." He finished his water and put the bottle on the table. "I leave Sunday afternoon."

"And you'll be gone for—"

"A long time."

She reached for the tin of gross tea. Then she opened a drawer, found a stack of white sheer squares, and counted them.

When she didn't speak again, he switched subjects.

"What did you mean when you said there were photos of your father's last case in Boston?"

She blinked a few times before putting aside the white squares and dragging a folder out of her straw bag. She handed it to him, yet when he grabbed it, she refused to release it. "Two weeks ago, Juliet Capel told me you were a good guy. A man a woman can trust."

"I am."

She nodded before letting go. "I'm counting on that, Nate Walker. I've not had luck with trusting coworkers. If you betray me, I'll hunt you down and beat you with a shovel."

He held his laugh but not his smile. The thought that she could hurt him physically was beyond absurd. "Threat noted." He opened the file and laid the photos and papers on the table.

He separated them into two sections. On the left, he put out the handwritten page about Sarah's life—in Kells's distinctive type A printing—and the photos of Sarah alone. In all of them, she was around the preservation office. Two were taken of her walking to work; the others were of her working at a table in the garden. A pain drove through his molars, and he relaxed the teeth grinding. "Sarah, do you have any idea when these were taken?"

"Within the past two weeks." She came over and pointed to her low-heeled sandals. "I bought those the day before we met."

He took the photo of the two of them in the garden and moved it on the table. "This one is first. Which one is second?"

She added the two of her sitting in the garden. Then the one of them in the police station.

"These two of you coming into work, they happened after that night we met in the police station?" After. The. Kiss.

"Yes. They were taken last week."

He exhaled and moved on to her life story. He scanned the page slowly. Handwritten words always made his dyslexia worse. "Wow. You really did go to all of these schools and get these degrees." She wasn't even thirty. He read the final paragraph. She'd been put on administrative leave soon after the publication of an article she'd written. "What's *The British Journal of Eighteenth Century History*?"

"The peer-reviewed publication that tanked my career? A.k.a. the Great Betrayal?" She pursed her lips. "*The British Journal* published a draft of my thesis without permission."

She stared at the photos with no emotion. Either she didn't care about what had happened or was holding her feelings so tightly, she didn't know how to unwind them. The fact that she'd named the event meant she was probably dealing with the latter.

"How'd *The British Journal* get it?"

Her eyes had shifted from the brilliant brown swirls to a flat, mud-like color. "My colleagues sent it to them."

She'd been betrayed? By those she trusted? "How'd your colleagues get your draft?"

She went to the counter and those white squares. "They stole it. Broke into my computer, actually." Slowly, she used a small spoon to fill the white squares—which were pouches—with tea leaves. The brilliant passion he'd seen this morning with Cassio and again when she'd faced his men had disappeared.

And, apparently, they were playing twenty questions. "How did that happen?"

"My fiancé took my password."

His throat tightened, and he felt nauseated. "You have a fiancé?"

"*Had.*" The disgust in her voice made him want to sing. But publicly celebrating would've been rude. "I never should've gotten engaged. My dad hated Augustus."

"Augustus?" Nate almost laughed, but instead he released his breath in short, relief-laden spurts. He'd love to know more about this loser ex-fiancé who was probably short and out of shape. "Why did *Augustus* and your colleagues betray you?"

She blinked twice. "To discredit me."

"Hacking into someone's computer, stealing their work, and then publishing it is more than simple discrediting." Nate pointed to the photos. "This is personal."

She frowned and took a roll of white ribbon and a pair of scissors from a drawer next to the sink. Carefully, she cut lengths of about eight inches. "I guess."

"There's no guessing here, Sarah. Your colleagues, your fiancé, must've had a reason to do this. Did they want your job?"

"No." She paused in her cutting to look at him. "I'm the youngest in my department. I worked in a different time period, mostly on my own research projects."

And they were back to twenty questions. "Did they dislike you?"

"You mean was I a bitch who deserved a slapdown?" She started cutting again. "No. I worked on private projects helping people sell their collections to the Smithsonian." She dropped the ribbon and came over to look at the police station photos.

Was she remembering that night as well? Had she lost as much sleep as he had?

"I established and confirmed provenance, authenticated and catalogued items—documents, weapons, clothing—from the mid-seventeen hundreds through the end of the Revolutionary War. The only way to stay competitive in my time frame is to publish. By publishing my research before it was completed, my colleagues made me a laughingstock and ruined any chances I had at getting research grants to finish my work."

"I thought the Smithsonian paid for your work?"

"Not all of it. I use private and public grant money to help with certain projects." Now she took the photo of them sitting in the garden on the first day they met. "For this project, I hoped a private research grant would give me enough money to prove myself and my theory."

"But the project was destroyed by your colleagues for no apparent reason."

"No reason I can think of." She laid the photo on the table. "At the time Senator Prioleau jumped on the ruining bandwagon. And she hasn't gotten off. I've no idea why, though, since she also hired me to do the authentications for the Prioleau/Habersham collection auction."

He laid out the rest of the photographs. They were crime scene pics with dead guys covered in sheets and bags of white powder lying around. A sign over the Dumpster read PROPERTY OF O'MALLEY'S PUB. NO DUMPING. CITY OF BOSTON. "When were these photos taken?"

"Three years ago. It was my father's last case where he and his former partner Hugh Waring were falsely accused of horrible things." Her shortened breath raised her breasts enough that he considered asking her to put on her sweater again.

He focused on the photos. "Then what happened?"

"They were exonerated, and my dad took early retirement. Ever since that night behind O'Malley's Pub, my dad has suffered seizures, headaches, and memory loss. It was hard with me in DC and him in Boston. After my thesis was published, I was put on administrative leave and we returned to Savannah. Almost ten months ago."

Nate rearranged the Boston photos again, placing them first, then the handwritten notes, then the photos of him and Sarah. "What is this last photo? Is this another crime scene?"

"Yes. It's from a recent crime scene in Charleston."

"You've seen this picture before?"

"This morning. Detective Hugh Waring, my father's ex-partner, is now a detective in Charleston. He drove down to ask my father about the photo." She pointed to the older ones from O'Malley's Pub. "He wasn't supposed to show it to us, but it's similar to the ones taken in Boston."

"Similar how?" Nate stopped himself from asking about this ex-partner. Like how old he was, whether he was married, or if he was in love with her.

"The dealers in both the old and new photos were shot in the chest, and someone carved a letter *B* on their left palms. And see the heroin bags?" She pointed to the alphanumeric string I9A4B8M5C6 printed on every one. "These photos were taken three years apart."

He placed the new photo at the end of the line, next to the last one taken of Sarah.

"What are you doing?"

"Building a timeline." He pointed to the first photo. "Your father's last case behind O'Malley's Pub, which sent him into retirement. Two years later, your published thesis ruins your career. Almost a year after that, we meet and you're being followed. Then, a few days ago, a drug bust in Charleston unearths heroin bags with the same type of alphanumeric sequence." He put his hands on his hips. "I know there's something connecting us, I'm just not sure what it is."

She dug her phone out of her straw bag. "There is one thing that connects both of us to these photos, but—" She tapped her screen. "Don't be mad."

He wasn't sure he could ever get mad at her. "What is it?"

She gave him her phone. "It's a photo I took of that map you brought me two weeks ago. The one of the Isle of Grace. I'm not supposed to take pictures of artifacts without consent. If my boss finds out—"

"He won't." Nate expanded and contracted the photo as he moved it around. "Did you use this map to find the Cemetery of Lost Children earlier?" It would explain how she found her way out there while experienced hunters—a.k.a. poachers—got lost.

"Yes." She leaned over his shoulder. Her gardenia scent riled up every masculine part of him, and he shifted forward to hide his reaction to her. "Remember the compass rose in the corner? The one with north off by thirty degrees?"

"I do." Two weeks ago, when he'd brought her the hard copy of the map, she'd discovered that the compass rose was "broken." But neither one of them had thought it mattered.

She put on her glasses and moved until her breast brushed his arm. "Below the compass rose. What do you see?"

Sweat lined his brow, and it took all of his strength to read. Below the compass rose, someone had scrawled $P1C3S4L2R4$ in faint script. "It's an alphanumeric sequence. Similar to what's on the heroin bags."

She took off her glasses. "Yes."

He wiped his brow with his arm. Had the AC stopped working? "That map was over three hundred years old."

She touched his arm. "Are you okay? You look hot."

"I'm fine." He pressed his fists on the table. "What connects two heroin busts years apart, a seventeenth-century map of an isolated sea island, and a group of ex–Green Berets?"

"A cipher." She pointed to her résumé. "More specifically, the Prideaux pirate cipher."

CHAPTER 14

SARAH EXHALED THE BREATH SHE'D HELD SINCE LEAVING the gym. Now she struggled to ignore the fact that Nate was bare-chested. With his green gaze following her, he exuded a raw intensity she'd never experienced. Her offer to put salve on his arms had been altruistic. She'd seen how his burns had tightened his skin and knew the salve would help with the pain.

She'd not expected to be so turned on from touching him. He didn't just look like he was made of muscle, he *felt* like it too. Avoiding the scars on his front and back had also been a priority. He'd not mentioned the cuts, lashes, or puckered scar tissue, so she hadn't either.

She adjusted her glasses. "I believe the sequence on the map and the heroin bags are part of an unsolved pirate cipher."

"Excuse me?"

"Most seventeenth-century ciphers were substitution ciphers, except for this one that was originally developed by the Prideaux pirates." She pointed to the map on her phone. "That sequence is only part of the cipher."

"Did you know this when we met two weeks ago?"

"Yes." She scrunched her nose. "As soon as I saw the map, I knew it was connected to my cipher. That's why I took a photo of it." She reached out to touch his arm, but when he inhaled sharply, she dropped her hand. "I'm sorry I didn't mention it at the time."

"It's okay." He clasped his hands behind his neck and studied the photos on the table. He seemed unaware that every time he breathed his chest muscles rippled. She couldn't imagine being so comfortable in such a physically strong body. "Why do you call it *your* cipher?"

"My mother told me about this pirate cipher when I was

little." Sarah sat and smoothed her skirt over her knees. "It was part of my thesis that ended up in *The British Journal*."

He dropped his hands to his hips. "You want to solve this pirate cipher."

"No. It's unsolvable. And probably cursed." She pointed to Hugh's recent crime scene photo of the dead dealer. "These things usually are."

Nate sank into the nearby chair, his head in his palms. "Sarah, you're killing me."

She touched his knee, amazed at the warmth that came through his jeans. When he raised his head, his eyes shimmered with...pain? "Do you need more tea?"

"No!" He shook his head. "I'm sorry. I'll be better when you tell me what's going on."

His thigh muscles flexed beneath her hand, and she removed it. Was the rest of his body as hard as his arms? Heat flooded her cheeks, and she returned to her tea bags. It would be easier to tell the story while moving. "It all comes back to Rebecca Prideaux. When she decided to run away with Thomas Toban, she stole the key to her family's pirate cipher."

"The story you told me earlier." Nate tilted his head. "That was the leverage she had over her family?"

"Yes." Sarah found the cinnamon shaker. Cinnamon would help with the tea's smell, which sometimes caused nausea even before someone drank it. "That cipher key gave Rebecca leverage over most of the families on the isle."

He stood on the other side of the counter to hold open the bags while she sprinkled in cinnamon. "What did the cipher do? Was it a way to encrypt messages?"

"No. The cipher was used to move stolen merchandise."

"How?"

"The Prideaux pirates were wildly successful marauders. But they required safe places to hide their goods while they made their deals. Piracy was one thing. Dumping stolen goods onto the open marketplace was a different venture."

Nate chuckled. "I've never thought about how difficult it was for pirates to sell their goods."

"More difficult than people realize." She took a cut ribbon, and with Nate holding the pouch, she tied it closed. "This is where things get…controversial. I believe the Prideaux family built hide sites along the coasts of South Carolina and Georgia to protect and move their merchandise."

"Cellars?"

"Kind of." She handed him another pouch. "More like underground rooms, with tunnel access, beneath mausoleums in private cemeteries on isolated sea islands and along deserted coastlines."

"These coastlines are below sea level. Nobody has basements around here."

"They were built underground, along tidal estuaries." She spoke as Nate held the other bags and she filled them with tea and cinnamon. "Each hide site would be lined with an oyster shell–like waterproof concrete called *opus signinum*. It's what the Romans used to line their aqueducts. Drainpipes were added to the hide sites to help the water fill and drain."

"Huh." Nate tied two bags.

"The hide sites would fill and drain depending on the season, the weather, and the moon phases. Different hide sites were in use at different times, but no one person ever knew which ones hid what merchandise and which ones were flooded. Hence the cipher."

"Now you lost me."

"I believe each sequence is a reference to a specific hide site under a specific tomb. Because the Prideaux pirates didn't want anyone to figure out where their hide sites were, they encrypted the names of tombs that sat on top, protecting the hide sites."

He studied her for a moment before saying, "If you know the substitution key, you can decode the alphanumeric sequences and learn the name of the tombs?"

"Yes." She cut a few more ribbons. "You still have to

find the location of the tombs and figure out when they're dry, but having names is a great start."

Nate held the last two tea bags. "If a historian solves these sequences, she can find the hide sites—"

"Proving the hide sites even exist—"

"Thereby saving her career."

She glanced at him, not surprised that he'd figured her out. "Yes." She finished tying the bags and put them into a brown lunch bag she found in a lower cabinet.

"What are you doing?"

"These are for you." She handed him the brown bag. "Drink two cups a day. Four is better. Add honey sparingly. If you send me your address, I can mail you more." To keep her hands busy, she sponged off the counter of dried tea leaves and white satin ribbon cuttings.

She wasn't sure why she was going through all this trouble for him, but she couldn't bear the thought of him dealing with those headaches alone. Then she thought of something else: Maybe he wasn't going to be alone.

She threw the sponge in the sink, and a bitter taste formed in her mouth.

He put the bag into the pocket of his jacket. "Thank you." Without looking at her, he stacked the photos and returned them to the file.

"Nate." She left the sink and sank into the chair again. "I wish...I don't know." Her voice drifted away.

"I have to leave." He knelt and took her hands in his. "But I want you to know that I'm going alone. There's no one else. There hasn't been for a long, long time."

Now he could read her mind? She closed her eyes, hating the realization that his long-term single status made her happy.

Nate squeezed her hands until she opened her eyes. "I wish I didn't have to go, but I do."

"I barely know you, yet I don't want you to go." She tilted her head. "Why do you have to leave?"

"It's an army thing."

She withdrew her hands from his. "Oh."

"I need to get back to the gym." He stood. "I have things to do before I leave."

"What about that file?" She rose as well. "And your boss spying on us?"

He found his phone. "I'll talk to him." He tapped a text. "When I get an answer, I'll let you know."

Was this goodbye? She smoothed her hands across her waistline. "And our map and photos and connections?"

"Cassio told you to stop researching all of that." Nate put on his coat, found his weapon, and shoved it in his waistband. He did that so easily, without any effort or thought, that the gun seemed to be an extension of his person. "Don't get into a legalistic argument with a Fianna warrior. You won't win."

She didn't care about the stupid Fianna, stupid Cassio, or the stupid army. All she cared about was when she'd see Nate again. When he'd kiss her again. "Nate?"

He stood inches away, his gaze fixed on her mouth. "Yes?"

"I…uh…" Why was she nervous around him? Was it the way he stared at her? Like he wanted to protect her and devour her at the same time? Or was it his politeness? How he listened to everything as if he cared? "Do you need a ride?" Seriously? That was the opposite of brave.

His eyebrows formed a V. "No—"

"I'm sorry." She laughed away her lack of courage. "What I meant was…your headaches… If you don't want to ride your bike, I can drive you."

A flush flooded his cheeks. "Oh. That—" His phone buzzed, and he checked his messages. "I'm not supposed to drive because I get migraines that cause vision problems."

"I didn't mean to make you uncomfortable." Her ringing phone on the table saved her. The caller ID said *Calum Prioleau*. "Hi, Calum."

"I have news." Calum let out a breath. "I can't get your dad out without a judge's order."

"How long will that take?"

"Not sure. Also…your father suffered a massive seizure. He's in the ICU."

"Excuse me?" Her father was in the ICU and no one called her? "May I see him?"

"Unfortunately, no."

"What's wrong?" Nate asked.

She covered the phone to whisper, "My dad's in the ICU. A seizure."

Nate's eyes widened, and he sat on one of the counter stools.

"Your father isn't allowed visitors," Calum continued. "Even if he was, they won't let you see him without a judge's permission."

"Why not?"

"Sarah…" Calum paused, as if searching for the right words. "Did you not read the admittance papers?"

"Honestly, Calum, I was so stressed, I only skimmed the first part about my father's involuntary commitment. I do remember Miss Tidwell saying something about poor nutrition. Why?"

"They've accused you of elder abuse."

She gripped the counter. "That's absurd. What evidence do they have?"

"They say you've been poisoning him with herbal tea."

Nate took the phone out of Sarah's hand and helped her sit. Her face had paled, making her wide eyes appear not just darker and rounded but more haunted.

"Calum? It's Nate. What's wrong?"

"They've accused Sarah of elder abuse, and she's not allowed to see her father. He's also in the ICU."

"Can you keep us updated?"

"Yes. And please tell Sarah this is my firm's number one priority. We'll get her in to see her father as quickly as possible."

"I will. Thanks." Nate tossed the phone into her bag and took both of her hands in his. They were freezing, and he rubbed them to warm her fingers. "Sarah?"

She stared out at the garden. "They took my father, and I can't see him."

"I know. Calum will fix this."

She withdrew her hands to pace the kitchen. "I may lose my father. I've already lost my mother. Without him, I'm alone."

"I understand, Sarah." Nate met her in the middle of the kitchen and took her shoulders. "I lost both of my parents when I was thirteen."

She inhaled sharply. "Oh, Nate. I'm sorry."

He nodded. "I know. Everyone is sorry."

"It doesn't help, does it?"

He couldn't lie to her. Not about this. "No."

She took his face in her hands and moved in until he could see tiny marks on her forehead. She'd probably had chicken pox as a kid. "I *am* sorry. You were a baby. I was sixteen when I learned what it was like to be lost, when I learned that kind of pain was possible, when I learned that life moved on whether you wanted it to or not."

He covered her hands with his and kissed her forehead. Although he'd kissed her twice now, for some reason this kiss felt more intimate. She closed her eyes and rested her head against his chest. He enclosed her in his arms, rested his chin on her head, and shut his eyes. The constant noise in his head lessened, and his breath evened out. He didn't know what it was about this woman, but when he was with her, his world stopped spinning, and his restlessness quieted.

Life after his parents' deaths hadn't just moved on for him. It had grown in volume and frequency until it spun out of control, throwing him into the army's no-man's land of chaos and indifference. Where he'd once sought order and self-discipline, he'd received violence and suffering. Now all he craved was peace.

Sarah drew away from him *again*, wiping her eyes *again*. He decided his only wish for the future was a time when she stayed in his arms, sought his protection, and ached for his touch.

Since she didn't look capable of choosing tea versus coffee, he took charge. Even if he destroyed his own self-esteem in the process. "If you don't mind, I'd like a ride to the gym."

She raised an eyebrow.

"On the way, I'll call Calum. Maybe he can drop off a bag for your father."

"My dad is in the ICU."

"If your father is as tough as Kells's report says he is, he won't be there for long. I'm sure he'd appreciate anything you want to send him."

She wiped her eyes with the heels of her hands. "Okay. I'll pack his duffel."

"What else do you need?"

"My straw bag."

He put it on the table. It was so heavy it tipped over and something fell onto the floor. An envelope with his name on the outside. "What's this?"

"I forgot." She picked it up and handed it to him. "Someone shoved it through the gym's mail slot, and I found it when I came back to see you. It's *why* I came back to see you."

He turned it over. "What do you mean?"

"The person who dropped it off had been standing in that old service station near the gym, watching you. I drove away, but the creepy guy bothered me. Maybe it was his black hoodie."

"This man in a black hoodie…did you see his face?"

"No. It was covered."

He turned the envelope over. There were no identifying marks other than his name.

"Nate, have you seen the hooded man before?"

"This morning. On the isle. After you left, I…uh…saw him, and he disappeared." The unsealed envelope was easy to open. A single sheet came out, and he unfolded it.

"It's your map. The one you brought to me to study two weeks ago." She smiled at him. "It's the reason we met."

Which made it *their* map.

"How did that creepy man get it?" she asked.

Two weeks ago Nate had traded it to a Fianna warrior but didn't want to talk about that now. "Not sure."

She raised it up to the light. "There's the alphanumeric sequence below the compass rose."

He shook the envelope and saw two lines written on the inside flap.

Hic est finis iter est scriptor

Do not trust Kells Torridan

Nate blinked. The crazy colors flashed behind his eyes again, and his leg muscles contracted. He gripped the counter and his heart, which had been racing a moment ago, doubled up on the beats per second.

She touched his shoulder. "Nate?"

He could barely control each breath.

"Are you alright?" Her cool hand touched his hot neck. "Do you want to sit down?"

What he wanted to do was lie down in a soft bed, in the dark, with her next to him. Instead, he grunted. She took his hand and led him to the couch. Once horizontal, he covered his face with his arm.

"Here." She spoke so softly he dared to open his eyes. "Water."

He lifted his head enough to drink a few sips. He tasted

blood and realized he must've bitten his tongue. When she placed a cool, damp towel on his forehead, he asked, "Do you have coffee or Coke? Something with caffeine?"

"Yes."

After drawing the draperies to darken the room, she returned with a Coke. It was cold and sweet, and he moaned when it hit the back of his throat.

"*Hic est finis iter est scriptor*," she said, from the kitchen. "Does the phrase mean anything to you?"

"*Here is my journey's end*."

"That's right." He knew her voice well enough to know that she was trying hard not to sound surprised. "It's Shakespeare."

Nate had nothing to say to that. In his world, the phrase was attributed to Fletcher Ames, the lead torturer in the POW camp where he'd spent two long years. As for the other line about not trusting Kells, that was just psy-ops bullshit.

"While you rest, I'll go upstairs and get my dad's bag."

She left, and he couldn't help himself. Despite the wretched headache driving nails into his eyes, he tracked her graceful movements as she left the room. Once alone, he pushed the heels of his hands into his eyes. The pressure helped with the light show. The sounds of the house offered a soothing white noise: the AC compressor kicking on and the icemaker dropping cubes.

He'd always wanted to live in a house like this, with a wife, even kids. He'd no idea how a man went about doing something like that, and he'd never come close to meeting a woman with whom that would happen. But it was easier to fantasize about something he'd never have than work through the possibility that Kells couldn't be trusted.

Nate inhaled and exhaled until the caffeine kicked in and the humming abated. The need to fight something drifted away. Even the pain in his temple had retreated, as if surrendering to the power of bacopa and feverfew. Whatever those were.

A shuffling sound upstairs drew his attention to the ceiling. A crashing noise made him sit. Thumping on the second floor had him with his gun drawn, down the hallway, and in the foyer, where he saw Sarah on the stairs in the arms of another man.

Etienne Marigny stood on a step with Sarah in front of him, a knife at her throat. Blood dripped down her arm. "I wasn't expecting you, Walker."

Nate fixed his weapon on Etienne's ugly-ass face with the pointed nose and black eyes. Nate had only met Etienne once, on the Isle of Grace. The violence that'd poured out of him then was even more intensified now. "Let her go."

Etienne smelled Sarah's neck. "No."

"Ugh!" She twisted until he ran the blade against her breast.

"Don't fight him, Sarah," Nate said. "What do you want, Etienne?"

"My coz wants the solution to Miss Munro's cipher. In return, her father will be released."

"My cipher is unsolvable," Sarah said.

"That's too bad," Etienne said. "My coz wants it by Sunday. Or else your father stays put."

Nate moved closer, his sight pointed at Etienne's forehead. "After delivering your message, how were you planning on getting away?"

Etienne smiled, and Nate heard a click and felt a gun barrel forcing his head forward.

"Nate!" Sarah's eyes widened.

"Don't worry." He kept his voice casual. "This isn't the first time I've had a gun to my head." And if God gave him more days, it wouldn't be the last.

"At least you're not on your knees trading things for your men's lives. I wasn't there the night you gave away your medal." Etienne's eyes lowered to Sarah's neckline, where her camisole had been pulled down, exposing the upper fullness of her breasts. "I just heard the stories."

"Release her. If Remiel needs the cipher, he won't want her hurt."

"It's not her we're going to hurt." Etienne's lips touched her hair. "Not too much."

"Who's Remiel?" Sarah struggled until Etienne gripped her ponytail and yanked her head back. She yelped and clasped his hand that held the knife to her throat.

"My cousin." Etienne licked her neck, and she kicked him despite the blade near her jugular. "And he's going to love you. He prefers women who fight."

"Sarah," Nate ordered. "Stay still."

"Drop your gun," the man behind Nate said in a gravelly voice.

Nate placed his weapon on the floor. The moment Etienne glanced at Sarah's neckline again, Nate spun and knocked away the armed man's gun. Nate grabbed the man's arm at the same time as a gunshot exploded from across the room. A bullet ripped through the air and hit the man in the chest.

Sarah screamed, and the body landed on the ground with a loud thud. The man's eyes were still open, but his breathing had stopped. The bullet hadn't exited and the only blood seeped from a small wound. Nate's ears rang, but instead of covering them, he found his gun and aimed it at Etienne.

That's when Nate saw another man on the second-floor landing, his weapon with a silencer pointed at Etienne. Not the backup Nate would have wanted, but he'd take it.

Etienne's hand with the knife shook while he asked the shooter, "Who are you?"

The man bowed at the waist. "My Prince calls me Cassio."

CHAPTER 15

A SCREAM SNAGGED IN SARAH'S THROAT. ETIENNE PUSHED the knife's edge harder against her jugular, and he wrapped his other arm over her breasts. His gaze shifted between Nate and Cassio, both of whom now had guns pointed at Etienne's head.

She forced herself to breathe. Oxygen was the only thing that could combat the light-headedness making her woozy and nauseated.

Cassio came down one step, and she found herself airborne. Etienne had thrown her into Nate's arms. They both landed on the floor, with Nate's body taking the force of the fall. They rolled, and Nate's weight crushed her lungs.

By the time they scrambled to their feet, with Nate keeping her behind him, Cassio had taken Etienne. Cassio held Etienne's own knife to his throat and whispered something. Etienne's face drained of color. His lips turned gray, and his nose looked so sharp it seemed two-dimensional.

When Cassio released Etienne, he stumbled down the stairs toward the door.

Nate was about to block Etienne, but Cassio ordered, "Leave the fiend. He carries a message."

Nate shouldered Etienne as he ran past. When the front door slammed, Sarah's knees turned to tapioca. She sank, only to land within feet of the dead man with the open eyes. The hyperventilating started again, and she scooted until hitting the opposite wall. Her racing heart felt like it'd swelled three sizes, leaving no room in her lungs to inhale.

Nate had almost killed that man to save her.

Nate shoved his weapon in his back waistband. "Why did you let Etienne leave?"

Cassio came down the stairs with the eerie Fianna

gracefulness that almost defied gravity. "Our ways are not your ways, but justice is always served."

"I don't—"

Cassio lifted a hand. "The Prince demands the cipher remain unsolved. If the cipher is solved, one of your men will die."

Sarah dragged herself up by grabbing onto the grandfather clock. Her body ached, and she couldn't stop trembling. "This Remiel person wants me to solve the cipher or else my father will stay institutionalized."

"'Tis a quandary indeed, my lady. But there's a greater risk than your father's life. And sacrifices must be made."

"My father is not a sacrifice."

"Sarah." Nate's voice had lowered in pitch and volume, and he pointed at the dead man. "Don't argue with Cassio."

She clamped down her gag reflex. Cassio had killed without any show of remorse.

"Who?" Nate's hard voice shook the chandelier. "If the cipher is solved, which of my men dies?"

"'Tis the Prince's choice of man, time, and place."

"This doesn't make sense." Sarah fought to keep her voice level. "Why does Remiel, whoever he is, want me to solve the cipher, and why does the Prince care?"

Red and blue lights flashed through the windows. A moment later, sirens sounded.

"Someone heard that shot and called the cops," Nate said to Cassio.

"Leave by the patio," Cassio said. "I'll care for the dead. Go on foot. Return to your lord."

The police cars blocked the driveway, and Detective Elliot got out.

"Go. Now." Cassio grabbed Nate's arm. "Remember your oath. And the consequences."

"Why can't we stay?" she asked. "I met Detective Elliot two weeks ago. I'm sure he'll listen."

"No," Cassio ordered. "To save those you love, you must save yourselves."

∽

Nate took her hand and led her into the kitchen. He grabbed the file, her sweater, and her straw bag, which was heavier than it looked, and dragged her into the garden. At the farthest corner of the property, he helped her climb a four-foot-high stone wall.

"Where are we going?"

They jumped down, crossed the street, and entered an alley. "To the gym." He guided her across another street and found his phone. Before he could dial, Sarah gripped his wrist.

"We have to talk to the police." She pointed down the alley where a cruiser whizzed by. "We need to tell Detective Elliot what happened. Explain about Etienne holding me hostage."

"No." Nate dropped her bag and spun her until her back was to the wall. "Your arm. It's bleeding."

"It's a scratch." Etienne had cut her when he'd come up behind her. "We can't leave. There's a dead man in my house."

Nate took his handkerchief out of his pocket and tied the white cloth over the wound and around her upper arm. "We'll talk to Detective Garza."

"But—"

"*No.*" Her eyes widened, and he cursed. Between the adrenaline burn, his heart pumping wildly, and his frustration over Sarah's inability to take orders, he was having a tough time controlling his emotions.

She hit him in the chest with her small fist. "You don't understand."

No, *she* didn't understand. He moved until his body touched hers, and then he kissed her. His lips tilted over hers, demanding a response. He'd no right to kiss her. And this was the worst time to do so. But he couldn't control himself. One arm circled her waist, dragging her closer, until they melted into one another. And the most amazing thing happened. Despite the violence surrounding them, all the unanswered questions, his pulse evened out. The constant aching in his head lessened. And the humming he'd learned to live with since leaving the prison hospital, the same humming that led to seizures and migraines, eased.

In the empty space left behind, he felt a quiet peace.

She threw her arms around his neck, and he increased the pressure, unable to do anything other than take all she was willing to give him. Kissing her was a more powerful drug than anything he'd bought on the street or found in the fighting ring. Kissing her made him feel strong, healthy, and whole.

He moved one of his hands to hold her head. He didn't care if she felt how she affected him. He wasn't ashamed or embarrassed. His body had woken up, and now the erection demanding attention could be seen from the space station. His lips over hers, her lips softening beneath his, became his entire world. A whirlwind of desire, a maelstrom of need, an aching for more. Yet, in the midst of those emotions, he found an island separate from his life of chaos and violence. A single moment of grace. Something he never would've dreamed would be possible for him again.

Sarah broke the kiss and whispered, "Nate?" The word came out soft and low, her breath skimming over his sensitive lips. He moved to kiss her again.

"Nate!" She stared at something over his shoulder.

Reluctantly, he turned to look down the alley toward the street. Two cop cars had stopped.

Sarah was right. This was no time to— He inhaled sharply. A man in a black hoodie stood in the shadows, eerie as shit, watching them.

Nate was torn. If he'd been alone, he would've confronted the man—fought him if necessary—to figure out what was going on. But he couldn't fight this man and protect Sarah at the same time. "Sarah, we're going to run.

And we're not going to stop until I say." He squeezed her hand and adjusted her bag on his shoulder. "Ready?"

At her nod, he took off, dragging her behind him. They raced through a courtyard and down a dark alley, crossed a street, and entered a garden square packed with people. He paused behind a live oak tree and waited. Sarah stood next him, breathing heavily.

He counted to ten and…bingo. The hooded man had followed.

Sarah pointed to the sky. A police helicopter hovered. That meant the cops realized there'd been a shot fired at Sarah's house and were looking for a gunman. That also meant the cops would block off roads.

"Do you have sunglasses?"

She nodded and also found a sunhat and a scarf in her bag. Once she tied the silk scarf around her neck and put on the hat and glasses, he took her hand, weaving between tourists and horse-drawn carriages. He made a quick detour into a souvenir shop where he bought a black baseball cap and a shopping bag decorated with palmetto trees into which he dropped Sarah's straw purse and his jacket.

A few alleys later, they hit their first roadblock at the Reynolds Square garden. Keeping to the shadows between the ivy-covered buildings, they worked their way into the edges of the crowd, with Sarah's smaller body behind his. He had to get to the opposite side of the square.

Another helo swirled overhead, and his cell phone buzzed in his pocket. Trucks of local news crews cut off a horse-drawn carriage, and people gathered on street corners.

He hiked the heavy bag higher on his shoulder. *What did she keep in it? Rocks?*

Sarah pointed to a cart selling bottles of water. "Can we get some water?"

He bought two. As she gulped, a drop of water escaped, and he watched it trail down her chin, along her throat, down to her collarbone. He turned away and took a long drink himself, almost finishing the bottle in one swallow until, fifty yards away, the hooded man appeared.

Nate tossed their bottles in the trash, pushed Sarah into a crowd of people, and headed toward a church. The police had cleared the street of cars and carriages.

She pointed to the stone church that looked like a miniature abbey with side passageways. "I know this cemetery. We can cut through the graveyard to a parking lot."

The hooded man, stuck in the crowd, stood on a bench, scanning the area.

Nate followed Sarah through an ornate iron gate, into the overgrown churchyard, and down the crushed-shell path. It wound through an undergrowth of wildflowers, palmettos, and broken headstones. He heard snapping twigs and loud breathing, not sure if it was his, Sarah's, or the man behind him. He rounded the corner of a large mausoleum and saw the ten-foot-tall iron gate leading to a parking lot. The gate was locked. They were trapped.

His mind ran through every scenario, all of which ended with a violent confrontation.

He looked back. The man's hooded head bobbed as he searched the cemetery.

She tugged his arm. "What are we going to do?"

Fight. He handed her the bag and found his gun. "Hide behind that—" Something caught his attention. Graffiti on the church's door. A white skeleton hand holding a black cutlass. "Follow me."

He ran toward the door and barely stopped before pushing it open, thanking every angel in Heaven that it wasn't locked. Once Sarah was through, he shut the door and turned the dead bolt. It was dark in the hallway, and the wall switch didn't work. It took a few moments for his eyes to adjust. When she turned on her phone's flashlight, he said, "Look for a door."

They moved down the stone hallway, dodging chairs and boxes.

"There!" Sarah pointed down a flight of stairs.

He stepped carefully, his weapon ready. Water and mold coated the walls and made the stone floor slippery. It took a few pulls before the latch released. It was even darker and danker inside the passageway.

"I'm not sure about this." Her voice trembled. "Where are we going?"

"To a tunnel beneath the city." Although he'd no idea where it would lead or if it was even passable. He and his men had been clearing out tunnels between the gym, the club, and Prideaux House. Although the tunnels ran underneath the entire historic district, Kells had chosen these three to clear first and, eventually, set up an underground command post. Since all of the men worked at the gym and the club and would eventually move to Prideaux House, Kells figured that if Remiel attacked them in the city, the tunnels would give them a safe place to regroup and plan their counterattack. Unfortunately, of the tunnels needed minor work; others were filled with metal bed frames and debris from a nearby hospital. Some had trash and rats.

The one thing they had in common was the graffiti found near each hidden entrance: The Prioleau family sigil of a skeletal hand gripping a cutlass with the words *sans pitié* written below. Calum, in his uniquely arrogant-yet-not-obnoxious way, had claimed ownership of this underground network that most of the world, except for the city's water and power workers, had forgotten about.

"How did you know the entrance to the tunnel was here?" She raised her phone's flashlight to expose at least twenty stone steps heading down. "Or about the tunnels at all?"

"Long story." He paused to take her bag. She'd removed her hat and her sunglasses. "Hold the railing. The stairs are wet." Once off the bottom step, he turned right. "This should take us toward the river." He saw her worried face in the shadows. "Do me a favor?"

"What's that?"

"Don't forget to breathe."

CHAPTER 16

ZACK STARED AT THE GUY IN FRONT OF HIM. IT WAS ZACK'S turn for desk duty, and he'd hoped to work on his evidence to help Nate. But Zack had had no idea the desk was so busy with fielding phone calls, complaints, and questions about bathroom facilities. "Excuse me?"

"*Duuuuuude.*" Antoine, with bottle-blond hair and a red running suit sporting neon-green stripes down the side, dropped an elbow on the raised counter. "It's always been this way. My guys use your backyard garden for our business transactions, and we offer protection."

"You and your salesforce deal—"

"Sell." Antoine took out a cigarette but Zack pointed at the NO SMOKING sign.

Jeez, did this guy even know what decade it was?

Antoine put the cigarette away. "These are cash-and-carry transactions. You get a cut and our protection. The previous owner appreciated our help."

"Protection?"

Antoine's smile showed off two gold grills. "It's bad out there, man. Did you see what happened to that hotel two weeks ago? And those fires along the river?"

"No, thanks." Zack used his friendly-yet-go-piss-off voice. "New management. New rules. And one of our partners is a cop."

Antoine's smile did a U-turn. "Cop?"

Zack smiled. "Yep."

Antoine pursed his lips. "My *boiiiiiis* aren't going to like this."

Zack pointed to the door. "They'll like jail even less."

When Antoine left, Ty appeared from the door that led

to their living quarters. He'd just returned with groceries and now clasped a legal pad. "Where's Luke?"

"Kells's office," Zack said. "Why?"

Ty dropped the pad onto the desk. Handwritten notes about the night of the doomed Afghan operation. "We don't fucking need this right now."

Zack tucked Ty's pad into a folder with Luke's spreadsheets. "Need what?"

"I was listening to the police scanner, and I think Nate might've been shot."

Nate held Sarah's hand as they moved into the tunnel. She didn't mind; she just didn't want him to notice that she was shaking all over. Partly from the adrenaline, partly from the kiss.

"Sarah, tell me a story. Talking will help keep the fear away."

"I will if you tell me who Remiel is and why he wants my cipher solved."

"Remiel…hates me and my men. I don't know why, and I have no idea why he wants what he wants. I've never even met him."

Oh. Not exactly what she was expecting, but his sincerity told her it was the truth. She coughed and stepped carefully over uneven stones. Why did dark air always smell stale and moldy? "What kind of story do you want?"

"How did your mother learn about the cipher?" With Sarah's wobbly phone light, they walked down a dim hallway until reaching a stone staircase. He dropped her hand so they could descend in single file.

Her sandals *clip-clopped* on the steps. "When my mom was in high school, she and her friends were obsessed with collecting Anne Capel's seventeenth-century natural remedies. They spent hours researching in the SPO library and duplicating recipes in my grandmother's kitchen. Then one day at the SPO, in a moldy box, they found Rebecca Prideaux's diary.

"The diary was—is—ruined and hard to read. Since the girls knew about the tragic love story of Thomas and Rebecca, they read what they could of the diary. What little they learned made them believe that Rebecca hadn't betrayed Thomas and that he wasn't responsible for her death." A landing appeared, and Nate took the light so she could step down. "Their teenage obsession shifted from Anne's recipes to redeeming Rebecca and Thomas's love story." After three more steps, they turned left.

"And did they?" Nate asked. "Redeem the love story?"

"No. Only a few pages of the diary are readable. But my mother couldn't let the story go."

"Why?"

"A year after finding the diary, my mom discovered a *Georgia Pirates* book at the SPO. This book has the only peer-reviewed discussion of the Prideaux pirate cipher with examples. But the most interesting thing is the book's chapter on Rebecca Prideaux. The author claimed that Rebecca transcribed the cipher in her diary to take with her when she eloped with Thomas. The diary was her leverage. And it's the diary the mob used as evidence in her trial."

"Wasn't she burned as a witch?"

"Yes. Her family couldn't kill her just for stealing the cipher. Since Rebecca's diary was filled with Anne's herbal remedies and Anne, years earlier, had been accused of witchcraft for using these remedies to kill forty-four kids, the mob used the diary to prove Rebecca was a witch. The trial was a farce."

When they neared a steel door, he walked through first, weapon out. *What was that rustling sound near the walls?*

Nate must have heard something as well because he shut the door behind him and took her hand. "What happened after your mom found that book?"

"She and her friends continued to collect evidence, visit

cemeteries—until my mom turned sixteen. And got pregnant." Sarah's voice cracked. "With me."

Nate paused at the tunnel's split. Metal building debris blocked the right tunnel. Rocks partially filled the left. He dropped the bag, took her phone and laid it down, and held her to his chest while one hand traced her spine.

"When I was three"—her words sounded muffled—"my mom and I moved to Boston. She married my dad, and he adopted me. Then when I was sixteen, she died in a car crash."

He tightened his arms, and she buried her face into his warmth. He didn't say anything. He hugged her as if knowing that this was something she rarely spoke about. He'd suffered the same kind of loss and understood how powerless words were in the face of intense grief.

Still, she was a grown woman and didn't like standing in the dark with squeaky sounds getting louder. Pulling away, she wiped her eyes. "Are we there yet?"

He chuckled and found her bag and phone. "Almost."

He helped her scramble onto the blockade while she held her skirt to prevent it from getting torn. Once he was on the other side, with her bag and the light on the ground, he put his hands on her waist and swung her down. He stood there, his hands on her waist, in the shadows. "Is that why you became a historian? Because of your mother?"

Sarah placed a hand on his chest, amazed at how strongly and powerfully his heart beat beneath all those muscles. She felt so...fragile next to him. "My mom kept that *Georgia Pirates* book, and I memorized the stories in it, from the poisonous Capel lily to the deal General Francis Marion made to get the Prideaux pirate cipher and find the hide sites."

"General Marion? From the Revolutionary War?"

She nodded. "It's never been proven, but the *Georgia Pirates* book claimed that General Marion used the Prideaux pirate hide sites to move men and matériel during the war.

After reading those stories, I knew that was the time frame I wanted to study."

"You want to find the hide sites and redeem Rebecca and Thomas's love story."

"Yes. My thesis, the one published prematurely, hypothesized that not only did the hide sites exist—because you'd be surprised by how many don't believe they do—but that Thomas Toban solved the cipher and his nephew, who became a pirate as well, offered the hide sites and the cipher to General Marion. I also claimed that Thomas didn't betray Rebecca. I just couldn't prove it." She waited for him to laugh at her and was surprised when he didn't.

Instead, he kissed her, collected her bag and phone, and led her down the tunnel. "And your grant proposal that Cassio doesn't want you to submit?"

"If I win the grant, I'll have enough money to restore the diary properly. Since my boss doesn't want me to fuss with the hide sites anymore, I thought that I could go about it a different way—by reading Rebecca's diary and finding out the truth."

"You have the diary?"

"It's in a safe at the SPO." She heard squiggly sounds and hoped she wouldn't step on anything that moved. "The plan was to restore the diary and Rebecca would tell me how to find the hide sites and redeem her love story."

"That's a hell of a lot to ask from a diary of a sixteen-year-old Puritan girl."

"Which is why *The British Journal* destroyed my career when it published my draft thesis. Of course it was supposition and hearsay," she scoffed. "I hadn't restored the diary yet."

He held her elbow as they turned a corner. The air smelled like moldy cheese and old bathrooms, making her sick. The tunnel widened, and something ran over her toes. "Ick!" She had to wear sandals today? "Where are we?"

"Almost out." He raised the light higher, and she could

see a door at the end. "There are tunnels under the entire river walk. I've heard they were used by pirates."

"They were built in the nineteenth century by the textile factory owners to store raw cotton and linen. But your story is more romantic."

"I bet Augustus never would've made it through these tunnels."

She laughed, just now realizing how talking about her mother had lifted a darkness that had shrouded her heart. A darkness she hadn't even known was there. Despite the stench, she breathed deeply, more grateful for Nate's presence than she'd ever be able to admit. "Augustus is an academic historian, not a field historian. He'd never have gone out to the isle or traveled underneath a city. With *rats*."

They halted before the oak door. When Nate opened it, she used her hand to shade her eyes from the blinding daylight. They were along the river, and she inhaled the fresh air. Crowds moved in and out of shops and restaurants. Helicopters flew overhead, and thunder rumbled in the distance. No one noticed they'd appeared out of nowhere. And it seemed to have gotten ten degrees hotter.

Nate turned left and walked with his arm wound possessively around her waist. She clutched the bag on her other shoulder and shivered, despite the heat, at the realization she'd not only accepted his protection, she'd told him things about herself she'd never told anyone before.

Not even Augustus.

Nate led Sarah across the street, sure he'd lost the hooded man. Now that he was out of the tunnels, his buzzing phone was giving his ass a massage. No doubt one of his men had seen the police helicopters. No doubt Ty had heard something on the police scanner he'd set up in the bedroom he shared with Luke. No doubt Garza was freaking out. But Nate didn't have time to chitchat.

He kept her close while dodging a tour bus and a police cruiser. They were only a few blocks from the gym. He'd considered taking her through another tunnel, the one between the club and the gym, but it had rats that could take down a medium-size dog.

Instead, he headed for another stairway leading from the river up to the street. He glanced at Sarah, still keeping up with his brisk pace. She had dirt smears on her face, and her hands were scratched. At least the handkerchief around her upper arm hadn't bled through. It had been a small cut, and he tried not to think about how much worse it could've been. When he found Etienne again, the bastard would pay for even looking at Sarah.

Nate stood on the stairs and held out his hand. "Ready?"

She put on her hat again and took his hand.

"One more thing." He didn't have the time to give her details, but his friends' lives were on the line.

She squeezed his hand. "You can trust me, Nate. I know what it's like to be betrayed. I won't do that to you or your friends. I promise." She adjusted the bag on her shoulder until he took it from her. The strap had left an angry red mark.

She tried to take the bag. "You can't carry that and reach for your gun."

A zinging in his head forced his eyes closed, and he dropped the bag. *Not now. Not here.*

He kicked all of his physical and mental strength center and front. He would not collapse in front of Sarah. Sweat dripped down his neck, and his fingernails tore into his palms until he felt a soft touch on his arm. He opened his eyes only to see Sarah's brown gaze in his line of vision.

"Are you alright?"

He pressed a hard kiss against her soft mouth. He'd lost count of how many kisses he'd stolen. And, honestly, he didn't care. She tasted as sweet and warm as fresh-picked strawberries.

When he raised his head, she laughed, but her eyelashes lowered. "I guess."

He adjusted the bag's weight on his shoulder. He thought about apologizing, except he wasn't a bit sorry and intended to do it again. "Let's go."

They hurried up the stairs, headed down the street, and slipped into an alley. That led them behind a service station parking lot. They crossed the asphalt broken by weeds and roots and made it into another alley. Little sunshine ever made it here, and the lack of light left the cobblestones covered in a slick green mold.

She slipped, and he wrapped his arm around her waist. The gym's back door was ahead. Only another sixty feet— then a shadow blocked his way. It was tall and dark and held a nine-mil.

Sarah stopped.

"It's alright," Nate whispered. "It's Ty."

Ty came on them fast, keeping her between their large bodies. "What took so long?"

"A tail."

Nate handed Ty the bag in return for an ammo clip. They entered the garden, which consisted of two palmettos and an azalea. "Zack is on the roof."

Nate slipped the clip in his front pocket. "Take her inside."

"Will do." Ty took her arm as another man came out the back door. "Hey, Pete."

Pete didn't answer. He just grabbed Nate's arm and dragged him to a fire escape ladder leading to the roof.

CHAPTER 17

WHERE WAS NATE GOING? WHEN PETE FOLLOWED NATE UP the ladder, Sarah noticed a knife tucked in Pete's back waistband.

"Miss Munro?" Ty tugged on her arm.

She followed Ty into the gym's storage area but tried to get one last peek before the door closed behind her.

"This way, Miss Munro."

Ty was near an opening on the other side of the room, which led to the main gym. She squared her shoulders and followed. The storage area was stuffed with gym mats, punching bags, folding chairs, and moldy boxes. It was also dimly lit by a few hanging bulbs. *Was that a rat?*

As they made their way through the gym, she ignored the stares of the men who were working out. She found Luke in the main office, sitting at the desk, typing on his laptop. She took off her hat and laid it on top of a ledger.

Luke shut the laptop and stood. "Hello, Miss Munro."

Ty dropped the shopping bag on the chair. "Would you like something to drink, Miss Munro?"

"Water would be nice."

"Where's Nate?" Luke asked Ty.

"Roof." Ty went to the mini-fridge with the coffeepot on top and found two cold bottles.

After opening her water and drinking two long sips, she asked, "What is Nate doing?"

Ty's smile stopped two miles from his eyes. "Making sure you two weren't followed."

"With extra ammunition?"

"Just a precaution." Ty cleared his throat and took a long drink from his bottle. He ran a fist over his lips. "*Sooooooooo*...are you and Nate...you know?"

She tilted her head. "Are we what?"

"Fucking."

Her mouth opened and shut. She didn't know what to say.

"Jeez, Ty. Shut the hell up." A woman came into the room and held out her hand to Sarah. "I'm Samantha. We met a couple weeks ago at Juliet's Lily." Juliet's Lily was the most exclusive landscape architecture firm in the city, and Samantha had consulted with Juliet Capel—the owner—on some old documents.

Sarah tried not to stare at the slender woman with wild blond-red curls that almost reached her waist, black leggings, combat boots, and purple lace tank top. "Nice to see you again."

Samantha pointed to the handkerchief on Sarah's arm. "Ty, get Pete's medical kit and some hot water."

Ty finished his bottle in four gulps. "That's not on my chore list."

"I'd like to apologize for Ty." Luke, with his laptop, moved toward the door. "Ty's been under serious stress, and he's concerned you're not Nate's type."

"That's enough from both of you." Samantha stared at Ty. "Go. Now."

Ty tossed his bottle into the trash and left the room.

Once Ty disappeared, Sarah asked Luke, "When you said 'Nate's type,' did you mean the *breathing type* or the *easy type*?"

Samantha laughed.

Luke clasped his laptop against his chest like a shield. "I didn't mean...I don't think you're *that* type. You're the *other* type."

"Luke!" Samantha's higher-pitched voice carried in the small room. "You should stop talking now."

Luke hurried out.

Once the men were gone, Samantha moved the bag so they could sit in the two chairs across from each other. "Are you okay?"

Not really. "Yes. Thank you." Sarah took another drink of water, unsure of what to say or why Samantha was asking.

Ty appeared with a medical kit, a towel, and a bowl of water and placed them on the table.

"Where are the rest of the men?" Samantha dipped a towel into the water and squeezed out the excess.

"Zack, Pete, and Nate are on the roof. Cain is clearing a tunnel. Luke is at the front desk. Vane is teaching, and I'm"—Ty's gaze rested on Sarah before skittering away—"managing the main gym."

"And Kells?"

"Out."

Samantha put on blue plastic gloves and unwrapped the handkerchief around Sarah's arm. "You should probably return to the floor."

Ty left the room again.

"Don't take anything Ty says personally." Samantha washed the cut on Sarah's arm with the wet towel. The cut stung more than Sarah had expected. "He's always in a bad mood."

"Oh." Sarah held Nate's handkerchief edged with strawberries and now stained with blood. She'd have to wash it again before returning it. "Does my arm need stitches?"

"No."

Thank goodness. "Didn't you tell me two weeks ago that you're dating a man named Pete? Would that be the gym's Pete?"

Samantha's smile transformed her face. "Yes. Pete and I met at the club. I was…am…a cocktail waitress there."

"Club?"

Samantha found a tube of antibiotic ointment in the kit and used a Q-tip to apply a small amount to Sarah's arm. "Rage of Angels."

"Down by the river?" Sarah didn't want to say *strip club*

or *that dump*, but she was pretty sure that place was both. "I thought the club closed."

"It's reopening tonight." Samantha wrapped the Q-tip in a tissue she found on the desk and tossed them in the nearby garbage can. "I'm torn about it though. I hated working there, yet I could use the money. And the time is flexible, so I can keep my other jobs."

"How many do you have?"

"Three." Samantha squinted at the wound. "Juliet's Lily, the club, and I give ghost tours."

"Really?" Sarah tried not to wince as Samantha applied a Band-Aid to her arm. "I've always wanted to go on one of those." She hadn't because she'd always been afraid of correcting the tour guide. No one liked a know-it-all.

"Anytime you want, I'll take you." Samantha yanked off the gloves and smiled again. "Keep an eye out for infection. You never know."

Sarah shoved the handkerchief into her straw bag and slipped on her sweater. "Thank you."

Samantha started putting away the bandages and ointment and rearranging the other things in the metal first aid box. "Sarah? How much do you know about Nate and his men?"

"Not much." Sarah picked up the photo on the desk of Nate in front of a Quonset hut. "I know they were Green Berets and now they work in a gym."

"You know you have to keep their backgrounds secret, right?"

Nate had implied that. "Why?"

"Because"—Samantha pointed to the map of Afghanistan on the wall—"bad things happened to them."

Sarah placed the photo on the desk. "Is that why Nate always seems...worried?"

"Nate suffers." Samantha stared out the window, as if thinking of something else. "They all do, but Nate most of all. And he'd kill me for telling you this."

"He mentioned his migraines."

Samantha stood and closed the first aid box. "He also has seizures."

"Which is why he can't drive?"

"Partly." Samantha smoothed down her lace top a few times. Her fidgeting continued until she whispered, "Their lives depend on our discretion."

"What do you know about a man named Remiel?"

"He's a monster who hates Kells and all of his men. Pete told me Remiel is their greatest enemy."

"Even more than the Fianna?"

Samantha whispered, "We're not supposed to talk about them."

Sarah nodded and sighed. She would've liked to learn more about this Remiel who held her father's life hostage, but based on Samantha's frown, that info would have to come from someplace else.

Sarah stood and met Samantha's concerned gaze. "I have no one to tell and no reason to hurt Nate and his men. Not even Ty."

Samantha grimaced, then smiled. "Yeah, Ty is interesting. They all are. Luke is the sweetest. Vane is the most annoying. And Zack is the most unreadable. He's nice, but I think there's a temper there that can be volatile."

"And Nate? Juliet said he was a man worth loving."

"Nate carries everyone's burdens. And it's killing him."

"What about his boss, Kells? He's been having me and Nate followed." Sarah quickly told Samantha about the photos taken of the two of them, leaving out everything else.

Samantha's exhale sounded like a teenaged eye roll. "Kells is an ass."

Sarah tried not to laugh. "Have you known Kells and his men long?"

"I've known Pete and Nate for six weeks, the others, including Kells, two weeks."

"And you're confident in your assessment of Nate's boss and friends?"

Samantha chuckled and moved the first aid box from the desk to the floor. "I'm a cocktail waitress in the sleaziest club in town. I'm an expert in sorting the goods from the bads."

Sarah nodded, not wanting to admit she was relieved. "Thanks."

A knock sounded, and both women turned to find Detective Garza opening the door. "Do either of you know where Nate is?"

Pete appeared behind Garza and said, "Nate will be here soon. What's up?"

"Gather your men in a training room. Calum is on his way." Garza's voice dropped to what seemed like a dangerous level, and he looked at Sarah and Samantha. "I'd like you both there was well."

"What for?" Pete asked.

"We have a problem."

༄

Etienne stood on the *Brigid*'s deck, flexing his hands and cracking his knuckles. A stalling tactic because he didn't know how to tell his coz what had happened. He also wasn't sure what to do with the info about the historian that he'd just learned from Cassio.

That intel was explosive. Just a thing Remiel would want to know. But also a thing, if kept to oneself, that meant leverage.

A crew member appeared. "He's waiting."

Etienne pushed his breath in and out a few times before heading to his cousin's office.

Remiel had changed into black dress pants, black silk shirt, and tie. His hair was wet, as if he'd just showered. He stood by a window, arms crossed. A gold ring glinted on his left middle finger. Stuart was gone, along with the chair.

And the strawberry bowl was empty. "Our last mercenary is taking Stuart Pinckney to Charleston."

"Will Stuart give you what you need?"

"Yes. For his wife's sake." Remiel used a finger to draw the letter *B* in the window's condensation. The script was oddly elegant until he wiped it off with his fist. "Now. Tell me how another one of our men not only is dead but was killed by a Fianna warrior?"

"Did you have the Warden follow me?"

"Yes." Remiel glanced at Etienne with those blue eyes framed by freakishly long lashes. "Apparently you saw Walker and ran out of the house like your ass was on fire."

"That's not what happened." Etienne flexed and curled his fingers in an ongoing rhythmic motion that kept his temper under control. He'd proven his worth so many times there was no reason for anyone to question his commitment to his coz. "Why did you send the Warden?"

"We have work to do, yet you're focused on revenge."

"Because Walker killed my nephew Eddie." Etienne pointed at Remiel. "Your cousin."

"Reminders aren't necessary. I can assure you I've kept track of every wrong done to our family. Done to you. Done to me. But work comes before revenge." Remiel waved to a chair in front of the desk. "Tell me what happened."

Etienne refused to sit. Instead, he paced the room. "I told Sarah the deal. Solve the cipher or see her father die in the psych ward. Then Walker appeared. As the merc and I were getting down to business with Walker, a Fianna warrior appeared and killed the merc."

"But not you."

"No. Cassio wouldn't let Walker touch me."

"Cassio?" Remiel stared out the window at the river beyond the yacht's moorings. "*Othello.*"

Whatever. "Cassio said that the Prince won't allow Miss Munro to solve the cipher."

Remiel laughed softly. "Of course not."

"To ensure Walker prevents Miss Munro from solving the cipher, the Prince put a price on one of Walker's men." Etienne swallowed and was about to say more when Remiel held out his left hand to study his palm. An ordinary gesture, except Etienne knew it was a tic. A *thing* his coz did before striking.

"The Prince has pitted the lovers against each other," Remiel whispered. "How very clever. How very Shakespearean."

The yacht rocked, and Etienne grabbed a bookcase. "Will Walker care more about his man than his girl?"

"Depends on the man." Remiel sat behind his desk and began writing on a piece of paper with a dip pen he'd lowered into an inkwell. "Right now the Prince's leverage is bigger than our leverage. That means I need to offer Walker a reason to betray his men and side with the girl."

"Then I kill Walker, right?" Etienne moved toward the desk. "Walker needs to die for what he did to Eddie before the Prince recruits him."

"Excuse me?" Remiel lifted his head, his pupils two pinpoints in a blue sea. Deep, dank, and dead.

Etienne retreated two steps. "Didn't the Warden tell you? The Prince wants to recruit Walker. Although I'm not sure how killing one of Walker's men will make him want to join the Fianna."

Remiel dipped the pen into the inkwell, clicked the nib on the glass, and wrote again. "Because you don't understand the Prince at all."

"I know he and his men are psychotic freaks."

"Hmm," Remiel muttered under his breath. "Since you let one merc die and the other is in Charleston, you'll have to deal with Leroy alone."

That crazy-as-fuck Russian? Etienne swallowed, but his throat was so dry his spit got stuck. "Okay."

"After seeing Leroy, return here." Remiel used a metal

shaker to sprinkle sand over the inked paper. Then he blew off the excess. "And for fuck's sake, stay away from men who bow."

"And the incoming shipment? We only have one hide site online. The other is flooding."

Remiel handed the page to Etienne. "Here's a temporary site. It should appease Leroy's worries."

Etienne folded it and shoved it in his pocket. He'd manage the Russian. But his patience had worn thin with waiting to kill Walker. He wanted *eventually* to be *now*.

When Remiel waved a hand in dismissal, Etienne went up on the deck and heard a moan. A man lay near the stern beneath a thin blanket, his hands cuffed to the railing.

Etienne lifted the blanket and gagged at the stench coming from Fletcher Ames. The man who'd once been Remiel's trusted head of security and lead torturer. Fletcher raised his head, and a tear trailed down his cheek. The scars around his eyes had scabbed over but gave him the appearance of someone who'd almost had their eyes dug out with broken beer bottles. A bloody bandage had been wrapped around his head, covering where his ear had been cut off. "Kill me."

Etienne didn't answer. They all knew the consequences of working for Remiel. Great rewards came with great personal risk. And only God knew why Fletcher, one of the top guys in the org, had betrayed Remiel.

Etienne dropped the blanket and went for the ladder. Right now, he wasn't concerned with rewards. Right now he was only concerned with revenge.

Once in his johnboat, he patted the pocket with the paper. Twice. Then slipped his hand in just to make sure and checked all of his other pockets. His heart thumped so loudly he was convinced Remiel could hear it, could know it, and would kill him for it. Etienne's cell phone, and the only way to reach Leroy the Russian, was gone.

CHAPTER 18

IF THE GYM'S PHONE DOESN'T STOP RINGING, I'M GOING TO crush it with a barbell. Nate pushed open the training room door under the threat of another headache. Not a migraine—thank goodness—just a dull thudding. Mostly from having to deal with Pete's lectures and Zack's glares while on the roof doing the watch-and-wait in case he'd been followed.

The day had shifted from *not great* to *all out sucks* with the only redeeming moments being those spent with Sarah. Speaking of which, Nate zeroed in on her and had to stop himself from taking her hand.

Everyone in the room stared at him while he focused on Detective Garza. The only no-show was Cain because he was still clearing out tunnels.

The front desk phone rang again, and Garza breathed with the force of a bull in heat, which meant someone—probably Nate—was in trouble. "Where's Kells?"

Luke answered first. "Kells left town. He'll return tomorrow."

Normally, when the CO went out of town, the XO was the first to know. Nate exhaled loudly. Instead of adding to his pity party, he got the party going. "There's a problem, Detective?"

"You bet your ass there is." Garza's irritated voice reminded Nate of the time, a few weeks ago, when the cop still believed Nate and Pete were criminals. "Were you with Sarah *at her house* when someone supposedly fired a shot this afternoon?"

Nate cleared his throat. "I was. With Sarah. When the shot was fired."

Garza stared at Nate as if he were in preschool. "Care to tell us what happened?"

No. If it'd been just him, Pete, and Zack, Nate would've downloaded the entire sitch. But since he couldn't mention the Fianna in front of the other men, he had to keep to the bare facts. "Sarah and I were at her house when Etienne Marigny appeared with a knife." Nate raised a hand to stop the murmurs. "Etienne, one of Remiel's cousins, is in the family business."

"Jeez," Pete said roughly. "I hate that arms-dealing psycho."

"Wait," Sarah said to Garza. "This Remiel Marigny is an arms dealer?"

"Among other things." Garza took out his notepad and started writing. His eyebrows shifted center. "He's also extremely dangerous."

"Oh." Sarah moved closer to Nate and added, "One minute Etienne had a knife at my throat, the next Nate disarmed the second man—"

"Whoa." Pete stared at Nate. "There were *two* men?"

The front desk phone started ringing again, and Nate put a hand on Sarah's shoulder. "Yes."

Garza closed his eyes and squeezed the bridge of his nose. "What happened to the second man?"

Sarah raised her chin. "Nate fought him until a shot went off. It was violent and scary. I almost fainted."

Garza opened his eyes to study Sarah. Considering his rapid blink rate, his bullshit meter was on overdrive. Nate deliberately didn't look at her. Her attempt to play the frightened girl card would only work if he didn't laugh.

"When Detective Elliot got there, he didn't find any-thing," Garza said. "No body. No blood. Nothing. But multiple people called in saying they heard a gunshot come from your house."

"After the fight," Sarah wrapped her arms around her waist, "Nate and I ran."

Every one of Nate's men stared at him with open mouths.

"You ran away from a fight?" Ty scratched his head. "I don't believe it."

"Bullshit." Pete started to pace. "Bull. Shit."

"Since when do you run away from anything?" Luke asked.

Zack threw in, "Especially a fight."

"You'd pay people to fight you." Vane laced his voice with condescension. "If Kells allowed it."

Instead of answering his men, Nate studied Sarah, who stared at the floor because, apparently, the chipped fake-wood gym floor was the most amazing thing in the world. When the desk phone rang again, he ordered, "Would someone answer the damn phone?"

"I'll do it." Zack stomped out.

"Nate?" Garza's voice sounded strained, as if he were one step away from strangling them all. "Is Etienne the hooded man you saw at Pops's this morning?"

"How do you—"

"Calum told me."

"Etienne isn't the hooded man I saw at Pops's. The hooded man is shorter." Nate heard Sarah's intake of breath and avoided her glares. "After we left Sarah's house, the hooded man followed us."

"What hooded man?" Luke waved one arm like he was trying to catch fireflies. Or a sliver of truth. "You were on the Isle of Grace this morning?"

"Yes. I went to the cemetery to, uh, check on something. Then I returned to Pops's trailer where I'd parked the SUV."

Vane took out his phone to text and offered a Kells-like response. "You *drove* a car and *cut* your own staff meeting?"

Ty looked around the room as if the walls had answers. "How come we didn't know about this?"

"Nate didn't want anyone to know." Pete took Vane's phone away and tossed it onto a stack of gym mats. "Kells is already aware of the situation."

Garza's loud cough stopped the convo. "Nate? Why didn't you tell your men what happened this morning?"

"Zack and Pete know, since they came to get me." Nate ran his hands over his head, hating, for the millionth time, that he had long hair. "I didn't want to say anything to the others because I didn't want them to worry."

Garza frowned. "Does this hooded man work for Remiel?"

"My guess is yes."

Sarah sighed and sat in a nearby metal folding chair.

After a long pause, Garza addressed her. "I talked to Sheriff Boudreaux. He mentioned you were in the cemetery this morning as well?"

Nate answered first. "How the hell does Sheriff Boudreaux know that?" Because Nate was sure he'd only mentioned meeting Sarah in the cemetery to Pete and Zack and...Calum.

Garza glanced at Nate. "I believe Calum told the sheriff."

"Don't say a word, Sarah." Calum, in his starched suit and silk tie, sauntered into the room and stood between her and Detective Garza. Calum, as usual, was impeccably dressed and wandered around his city with perfect timing.

Garza muttered a curse. "You know we're on the same side, Calum. Don't you?"

"Of course I do," Calum said. "It's why I told Sheriff Boudreaux that Miss Munro and Mr. Walker were in the cemetery this morning. It's all on the up-and-up." Calum smiled at Nate, then winked at Sarah. "But you're still not interrogating anyone without a lawyer."

"I'm not concerned about her trespassing. I'm concerned about the fact that Sheriff Boudreaux found a body on Capel land. A man was killed this morning. Shot in the chest and his hand sliced." Garza handed his phone to Nate. "Do you recognize this man?"

The victim wore a blue suit, bow tie, and leather loafers. Someone had propped his body against an old tomb. The carvings along the top of the tomb were so old and covered with moss they were hard to make out, but they appeared to be five-petaled roses and five-pointed stars. The man had been shot in the chest, and his left hand was bloody. "I've never seen him before."

Garza handed the phone to the rest of the men and then Samantha, who all said "no." But when Sarah took the phone, she covered her mouth with one hand.

"Miss Munro?" Garza asked in a voice Nate knew was reserved for women.

"He's a banker from Charleston. He came to the preservation office two days ago. He wanted to know if I had an index of local seventeenth-century tombs with Latin quotations on them. I said no."

Garza started writing in his notebook again. "This tomb where this man was found"—he pointed to his phone in Sarah's hand—"had a Latin inscription carved on the front. *Hic est finis iter est scriptor.*"

The tic above Nate's eye kicked in. "Where was this tomb?"

"Near the river." Garza paused, pencil on paper. "On the far edge of the cemetery. Miss Munro, did you hear gunshots while you were out there?"

She looked at Calum before saying, "Yes. I was photographing tombs when I, uh, saw Nate. Then we heard gunshots, although I'm not sure from which direction they came."

"The victim also had his left hand sliced with the letter *B*. I spoke with Detective Hugh Waring in Charleston." Garza nodded to Sarah. "A friend of your father's?"

"Yes."

"Waring says a dead heroin dealer he found in Charleston yesterday had this same mutilation." Garza cleared his throat. "As did two dealers found in Boston three years ago. The same dealers with whom the city of Boston accused your father of working."

CHAPTER 19

ZACK HUNG UP THE PHONE AND PRESSED HIS PALMS ONTO the desktop. His sweaty hands stuck to the paper membership log, smearing the newest entry. He needed to get himself under some kind of control before he went back into the training room.

"Hey." Antoine appeared, still wearing the terrible tracksuit. "Have you reconsidered our situation? I have a deal going down right now, man. *Right fucking now.* I'm offering a 20 percent cut for our first job together. Whadda ya say?"

If the guy had any clue, he'd realize that Zack's fisted hands and heavy breathing meant he was two seconds away from wrapping his fingers around that scrawny throat and twisting. "See that training room over there?" He pointed to Garza's brown-haired head visible through the training room door's window. "That's Detective Garza. Would you like to ask him about your deal? I'm sure he'll have something to say."

Antoine backed away, hands in the air. "I'm looking out for the newbies. Just don't blame me when Leroy shows."

Zack released the sigh of the damned. "Who is Leroy?"

"Leroy is *the* man, dude. The reason why you need to pay me and my boys for protection."

Awesome. Local thugs and low-level corruption. "Thanks for the warning." Then he waved. "Have a nice day."

Antoine pushed the front door open, pausing to point at Zack. "Don't say I didn't warn you, man. Leroy doesn't like being fucked with. He likes to do the fucking."

Once the door shut, Zack rubbed his neck and stared at the black ceiling marked with silver stars. They glowed in the dark, too. He'd noticed that his first night here when he hadn't been able to sleep and had come down to work off his restlessness. While he didn't fight in the ring like Nate, Zack well understood that desperate need to burn off all the emotions that threatened to drown him.

Kells had told them things here would be different. Different way of life, different jobs, different schedules. But Kells had been wrong about one thing. They were in the exact same situation they'd been in for the past five years: completely and utterly fucked. And their dangerous situation had poisoned everything. Not a man standing, either here or in prison, could say he hadn't lost the things he'd loved the most. Not just their freedom and honor but also everyone they'd loved. Correction: Everyone they still loved.

The clanking of weights hitting metal bars, the grunts coming from the fighting ring, even the hardcore rap music Iron Rack's was known for had become background noise that barely penetrated Zack's dark mood. He needed to go back into that room. He needed to be brave. Except bravery was what had landed them all in this hell in an ironic, first-place kind of way.

Zack pushed open the training room door and saw Nate staring at the ground, arms crossed. The rest of the men stood around looking shell-shocked, like they'd just been told all the beautiful women in the world had been sent to the moon. Sarah seemed paler than before, if that was even possible. And Samantha's gaze bounced between Pete and Nate. "What's going on?"

Pete tossed Zack a cell phone with a photo of a dead man near a tomb. "Can you ID him?"

"Nope. Who is he?"

"A dead banker," Ty said. "With the letter *B* sliced into his hand."

Zack coughed.

"Does that mean anything to you?" Garza said.

Zack dropped the phone into Garza's outstretched hand. "Was it his left palm?"

Garza's head tilt screamed surprise, yet the way he gripped his phone showed defensiveness. "How'd you know?"

"Just a guess. I had a fifty-fifty chance of being right." Although he was tempted to say more, he wanted to get this over with before losing his nerve. "We have another problem."

Pete closed his eyes. Ty exhaled like he'd been asked to bleach the locker room bathrooms again. Luke sat on a pile of gym mats, his clipboard next to his ass. Vane muttered under his breath while Calum texted, which seemed to be a constant thing with him. Garza tapped his pencil on his notebook.

Nate was the only one who met Zack's brown eyes. "What happened?"

"A phone call." Zack's next words were going to change everything, and he wouldn't be able to take them back. "From Leedsville prison. From one of our men. Colonel Jack Keeley."

"Who is Jack Keeley?" asked Garza.

"Jack was the commander of the second A-team the night we were attacked," Nate said. Pete's gaze danced around the room like he was waiting for an ambush. "How the hell did Jack make a phone call?"

"No idea," Zack said. "All I know is Jack is in solitary confinement for his own safety because someone put a price on his head. And he has no idea who or why."

Everyone—except for the women—started cussing until Garza raised his hand and the room went quiet. "What does this mean for your other men in prison?"

"I'm not sure," Zack said. "There wasn't time to talk."

"Now what?" Vane held out his palms in a submissive position that wasn't like him at all. Maybe he was trying to atone for the fact that he was so annoying.

Zack shrugged. "Kells isn't here. And Nate is the XO."

"We work the mission," Nate said. "Luke, where are we on our technology?"

"Nowhere. It's nothing compared to what I had at Fort Bragg. We have a semi-secure server, and I have a laptop.

Our Wi-Fi is spotty, and until I can get more protection, I don't want anyone, including Kells, tying their computers to the system. I've spent most of my time updating the gym's website to take online membership applications. I was hoping that more memberships meant more IT money for us."

"Can you get into any…uh…other systems?"

Luke studied Garza before saying, "If you're asking about my hacking capabilities, it's not a matter of talent as much as equipment. If I do things that aren't completely aboveboard, I'll get caught. I can't afford to protect myself."

"Whatever you need, Luke," Calum said as he texted on his cell phone, "let the IT department at my law firm know. Equipment. Service. Whatever. I'll text you their number."

Luke's eyes widened, and he pulled his buzzing phone out of his pocket.

"And contact the architect who's working on the renovations here and at Prideaux House. Work with him to see what kind of hardwiring you need in both places."

"Wow," Luke said. "Thank you, Mr. Prioleau."

"What about new burner phones?" Nate asked.

"They're in my office," Luke said, "with all of our new numbers preprogrammed. Trade in your old one for a new one. I've already texted the new numbers to Garza and Calum."

"Great," Nate said. "Pete, you and Vane keep up with the classes. We need that income."

Pete put his arm around Samantha and nodded.

Nate went over to where Luke sat on the gym mats and took the clipboard. "Ty, I know you have dinner duty tonight, but for now help Cain in those tunnels." Ty moaned, and Nate added, "If we're going to use them—and trust me, we will—we need them cleared and mapped out."

"What about me?" Zack asked.

"Run the main gym and the front desk." Nate made a few more notes on the clipboard. "You and I are working security at the club tonight."

"How is this us working the mission?" Vane grumbled.

"It's not *you* working the mission. It's me figuring out what the hell is going on so I can tell you how to work the mission."

"That's bullshit," Zack said.

"It's not a request, Zack. It's an order." Nate studied the room. "Each of you is to do your job as if nothing's wrong. We've no idea who's watching us, and the last thing we want to show is panic. When I find solid leads, we'll figure out a plan to take down Remiel."

"Detective," Calum said to Garza, "what about that body on Capel land?"

"Sheriff Boudreaux said he'd handle the on-site investigation, but Detective Elliot was assigned the case. He doesn't know yet about Sarah being in that cemetery, but he does want to interrogate her about what happened at her house."

"Can you stop Elliot's interrogation?"

"Not for long. I can give you twenty-four hours. Max. But no more fuck-ups."

A cell phone started ringing, and Sarah dug through her bag. With a soft "Excuse me," she left the room.

Zack counted silently while Nate tracked her until the door shut. A good ten seconds. Nate's interest in Sarah wasn't good for any of them.

"Are we solid?" Nate refocused on the men. "Can we hold on while I gather more intel?"

"Whatever," Ty said as he left the room.

"See you tonight, Nate," Samantha said as she passed him. "I need to go to Juliet's Lily. Now I'm wishing the club was still closed."

Vane followed, leaving Zack alone with Nate, Calum, Pete, and Garza.

Zack whistled low. "I wasn't completely truthful about Jack's situation. I think you know that, Nate."

Nate looked at each of them before saying, "The Prince

put a price on Jack's head. As long as Sarah doesn't solve some seventeenth-century cipher, Jack will live."

"What cipher?" Calum asked.

Nate quickly told them about Sarah's research into the Prideaux pirate cipher and the hide sites the cipher protects.

"How do you know what the Prince wants?" Garza asked.

"Cassio. I met him in the cemetery this morning. Then he showed at Sarah's house and killed the gunman. I couldn't say anything in front of the other men."

"*Sheeeeeeeeeit.*" Garza shook his head. "There was a murder at Sarah's house today?"

"That's what you're worried about?" Pete scowled. "I'm more concerned about the Fianna warrior following Nate."

"Except," Garza said, "Detective Elliott doesn't know that. Nate, do you think Cassio killed this man in the cemetery?"

"No." Nate took the phone to study the photo again. "This body was staged. The murderer wanted this victim to be found. As far as I know, true Fianna kills are more... discreet."

"And the gunman's body at Sarah's house?" Garza asked.

"Cassio took care of it. Detective Elliott won't find anything."

Pete put his hands on his hips and stared at the ceiling. "This is fucked up."

"There has to be a catch," Garza said. "There's always a catch."

"There is," Nate said. "Etienne told Sarah if she *doesn't* solve the cipher for Remiel, her father will be held in the hospital indefinitely."

"Is that possible?" Garza asked Calum.

Calum finally put away his phone. "Yes. I've read Joe Munro's commitment paperwork. They've built an elder abuse case against Sarah. It doesn't help that she's adopted."

"A criminal case?" Garza asked.

"Possibly," Calum said. "I haven't told her yet because I

didn't want to upset her. Joe had a massive seizure and is in the ICU. I know how worried she is about him."

"I hate keeping secrets, Nate," Zack said, "but I get why you didn't mention Cassio in front of the other men."

"I don't like secrets either." Nate's emerald-colored eyes darkened. "Cassio didn't just shoot one of Remiel's mercs, he also let Etienne go. Cassio wanted Etienne to deliver a message from the Prince."

Calum closed his eyes.

Garza ran a hand through his hair until he looked like a badass porcupine. "I thought we were done with the Fianna?"

"I did too," Nate said. "Except they're not done with us."

"Nate?" Sarah stood in the doorway. "May I speak with you?"

"Yes." Nate clapped Zack's shoulder. "Keep the men busy. I'll return soon with answers."

"I'll leave with you, Nate." Calum nodded at Garza. "Call me if things change with Elliot."

Garza's shoulders rose, then lowered in a silent sigh.

Once Calum and Nate left, the detective took a piece of paper out of his pocket and handed it to Zack. "I got a call from my contact. No word on who helped Kells get Nate out of prison, but he's still looking."

Another dead end? Big fucking surprise. Zack unfolded the document. It was an official form from the Hancock Army Community Health Center. Since Zack could decipher army-speak, he knew what that title meant. It referred to the U.S. Army's super-secret psychiatric prison hospital on the remote and nearly inaccessible Baker Island nine miles off the coast of Maine.

"According to the prison hospital's records"—Garza pointed to the document—"Nate is still a patient. Kells and his mystery helper may have gotten Nate a short-term reprieve, but he wasn't released."

Zack's heart began the super-fast ziggity-zag he reserved

for combat, fighting in the ring, and making love to… "All this time, while Nate's been out—"

"Nate was never truly free."

Zack gave the paper to Garza. "You trust your buddy's intel?"

"I do."

"Shit." Zack hit the mats with his palms, except the sound was more muffled frustration than loud anger. And that's what he felt like right now. Stuck in this stupid situation with this stupid gym. Completely powerless. Except he'd no business dating self-pity and her baser emotions. Because the most powerless of them all? *Nate.*

Zack clasped his hands behind his neck and stretched his biceps until he felt his muscles protest. He had another question but hesitated. Garza's answers offered more problems than solutions.

"What?" Garza refolded the paper and shoved it in his pocket. "I've spent enough time with Nate to know mulling when I see it."

"Sarah mentioned that the man killed on the Isle of Grace was a banker from Charleston."

Garza found his notebook on top of the gym mats and flipped through it. "Yes. The banker, along with a second man, went missing four days ago. The first case is a homicide. The second man is still missing."

A panicky feeling lodged in Zack's gut. "Do you have a name of the missing person?"

"Stuart Pinckney. The bank's president."

Zack clenched his fists. "Can you call Detective Waring? Ask him to look into Stuart's business transactions? Or at least a cell phone check?"

Garza tilted his head. "Why?"

Zack hit the nearby hanging bag. "I need to know if Stuart's wife is in danger."

"Do you think what happened to these men is related to what's going on with Remiel and Nate?"

"Yes." Zack scraped his head with his nails until they dug into his scalp. "I just don't know how."

"I'll call Waring." Garza gripped his shoulder. "Why are you interested in Pinckney?"

Zack didn't want to say this out loud. Hell, he didn't want to think it. Thinking it would strip him of whatever honor he had left. Thinking it would leave him with an even bigger hole in his heart than he already had. "Because Stuart Pinckney is married to Allison Pinckney."

"And?"

"Allison is the woman I love."

CHAPTER 20

SARAH WAITED FOR NATE NEAR THE FRONT DESK, HER STRAW bag lying on the floor, wishing she could curl up on her couch and bury her head in the pillows. She'd just gotten a frantic phone call from her boss. There was a problem with the auction catalog, and he wanted her to fix it. *Now.*

Most of the men had come out and dispersed. Luke checked phone messages behind the desk. Samantha and Pete talked nearby.

Sarah paced the lobby, still dealing with the fact that she was now being manipulated by an arms dealer named Remiel Marigny, who hired hooded minions, as well as the Prince and his Fianna army.

What was it about Rebecca's diary and her family's cipher that made everyone go insane?

Nate stopped at the desk while Calum came over. "I'm going to the hospital to check on your father. I'll let you know what happens."

She touched his arm. "Thank you. I'm grateful."

He covered her hand with his much-warmer fingers. "It'll be okay."

She attempted a smile. "I hope so."

Samantha appeared, Pete behind her. "If Sarah's house is being watched and Nate wants to be near her, they should stay in Rafe and Juliet's apartment above Dessie's dress shop. Since they're on their honeymoon, I know they wouldn't mind."

"It's also across the courtyard from Samantha's apartment," Pete said. "I'll be with Samantha as well."

"Excellent idea." Calum took out his phone and texted.

"That's kind," Sarah said, "but I have things to do."

"I know," Samantha said, "but I also know Nate. He's

not going to leave your side until whatever is going on is over. And you can't stay here. If you think the gym stinks, you should smell the upstairs area where the men live." She pinched her nose for emphasis.

Sarah tried not to laugh. It was hard to imagine a place smelling even more *male* than the gym. "I'm not—"

"It's a perfect plan." Calum smiled at her. "I'll have Ivers bring some things over later."

"*I*," Samantha said firmly, "will pick out Sarah's things. But I'd appreciate it if Ivers could drive me." Samantha took Sarah's hand and squeezed. "I'll leave the key underneath Persephone's statue in the courtyard between Juliet's Lily and the apartment. You can't miss her. She's running away, and she's naked. Because, apparently, when women run away their clothes fall off."

Sarah laughed in spite of her bad mood.

Pete kissed Samantha's head. "I'm all for that."

Samantha smiled wide.

This was moving quickly, and Sarah didn't know these people. While they seemed trustworthy, she'd made mistakes before. And she didn't like being manipulated. "This isn't necessary."

"What's not necessary?" Nate strode over to her, his sheer size and the forcefulness in his green eyes making her feel small and feminine. She was fine with the feminine part, not as comfortable with the small part.

"Samantha," Calum said, "suggested you and Sarah stay at the apartment above Dessie's tonight. Samantha and Ivers will grab a few things for Sarah." Calum frowned and looked out the front window. "You didn't drive here, did you?"

"No," Nate said. "We ran. Both of Sarah's vehicles are still in the driveway. My bike is in an alley down the street."

"I'll get your bike," Pete said, "but won't Elliot notice if one of Sarah's cars is gone?"

"Good point." Calum tapped his lower lip with his index finger.

"They can use the Juliet's Lily truck." Samantha took out her phone and started scrolling. "We don't have any big projects, and no one would question it being driven around town. And Sarah, let's trade cell numbers. That way you can text me with a list of things you need."

"Okay." Sarah had that tight feeling in her chest that told her things were out of control. "But—"

"Excuse us, gentlemen." Samantha took Sarah's arm and dragged her into the office, away from the men. After shutting the door, she faced Sarah with hard eyes and crossed arms. "I know a lot has happened, but don't be the stupid heroine who gets killed because she goes into the basement by herself, at night, in a thunderstorm."

She'd never do that. "Maybe if I knew what was going on—"

Samantha laughed. "You won't know what's going on until it's too late. That's how these things have been working."

"What things?" Sarah didn't have time for this. She had to get to the hotel to check on the auction. Then there was her dad. And it was almost four thirty in the afternoon.

"Scary things."

Sarah went to the door's window and watched Nate talk with Calum and Luke. Nate put *two* cell phones on the desk. Luke found a phone in a drawer and gave it to Nate. She hadn't noticed before, but Nate's jeans were streaked with dirt, and his T-shirt was torn at the shoulder.

"Sarah." Samantha came over. "Nate and his men have a determined enemy, and for some reason you're in his sights. If you want to get out of this unscathed, let them do their jobs. Let Nate protect you."

"It's not that I don't need help." Was that her voice, so dry and scratchy? "I don't know if I can trust him." She waved her hand toward the gym with the pirate flags. "Trust any of this."

"Since you've known Nate, has he hurt you?"

"Of course not! He's been kind." He'd been more than that, but Sarah wasn't sharing.

"And protective?"

Sarah sank into a chair near the desk. "That's his way."

"You saw him in the training room." Samantha took the chair next to Sarah's. "You watched him with his men. He gave orders that made sure they'd be safe, out of harm's way, while he volunteered to figure out what's going on. Alone." She took Sarah's hands and squeezed. "Now tell me what kind of man Nate is."

Sarah looked away. "He's considerate."

Samantha snorted and dropped Sarah's hands. "Nate's only concern is for those he loves. Period. He will go to whatever lengths to make sure they're safe. If you care anything at all about him, don't make his job harder. Let him protect you, and don't get in his way."

Calum opened the door and entered. "Sarah, if Sheriff Boudreaux, Detectives Garza or Elliot, or even that cop in Charleston want to speak with you, call me first. Do *not* speak to them alone."

"Thank you." Sarah stood, not sure how she was going to pay Calum for all of his help. But that was a detail on Future Sarah's to-worry list.

"I have to leave." Samantha stood. "Sarah, may I have your house key? I'll return it with your things."

"I left them on the kitchen counter. The front door is probably still unlocked."

Samantha touched Sarah's shoulder and said in a soft voice, "Everything will work out." A second later, she was gone.

Calum cleared his throat. "Did you know our mothers were once friends?"

Now this was unexpected. "No. My mother rarely spoke about her life in Savannah, except for telling ghost stories."

Calum crossed his arms and tapped his fingers on his biceps. "Our mothers were friends until—"

"Until my mother got pregnant at sixteen and left town when I was three?" Sarah shrugged. "It's okay. I know."

"I'm sorry you didn't grow up in Savannah. We might've been childhood friends."

It was an odd thing to say, but the sadness in his voice made her wonder if he'd not had many friends. "That would've been fun." She added a smile because it was the truth.

He took her hand, kissed it, and left the room. She was glad. She needed the time alone to think. If she didn't solve her cipher, she'd lose her father. If she did—betraying Nate in the process—an innocent man would die. The fact that Nate was leaving town didn't make her decision easier. She didn't want him to leave thinking she'd hurt him.

She picked up the photo of Nate and his men. In full uniforms, carrying weapons, and wearing greasepaint on their faces, they all looked strong, virile, and fearsome. They looked undefeatable. Yet the men in the training room earlier had had drooped shoulders and weary lines around their eyes. They'd looked defeated.

With one finger, she touched Nate's face. Then she studied the man who stood off to the side, away but still part of the group. His ginger hair was longish, and he had a beard. She wondered if it was Kells. Of all the weird things that had happened today, one stood out—the handwritten note from the hooded man: *Don't trust Kells Torridan.*

Sarah returned the frame and paced, thinking through her options. Specifically, her grant proposal. Although sending in the proposal to win the grant to restore the diary wouldn't help her solve the cipher in time, it might give her leverage to negotiate with Remiel. Maybe, once he realized what the grant money would be used for, he'd change the deadline.

And if she didn't win the grant money, neither the Prince nor Cassio nor her boss would ever know.

After double-checking that Nate was busy with his men,

she took her laptop out of her bag and placed it on a filing cabinet next to the printer with a connector cord. Once she plugged in her laptop and opened her document, she hit print. She tapped her foot while a circle spun on the screen.

ComeOnComeOnComeOn.

Her laptop bleeped and…*Ugh.* An error message popped up. She needed a printer driver? Another minute later, she had the driver downloaded. The machine hummed and started printing. Of course it was the oldest, loudest printer ever made, and it rattled on the metal filing cabinet. She ran over to shut the door.

Each page took *forever,* and as they came off she placed them into a worn manila file folder she'd found in the trash. *How long did it take to print ninety pages?*

While waiting, she found the receipt for her photos and called the phone number on the bottom. Thank goodness someone answered on the first ring. "I was wondering if photo order 012383 was ready for pickup?"

"That was picked up an hour ago."

Sarah reread the receipt. "Are you sure? I have my receipt."

"I'm sorry, ma'am." The girl sounded like she was barely sixteen, her voice unconcerned.

There was no point in arguing. The photos were gone because someone was anticipating her every move. "Thank you." She hung up and clutched her phone. She could send the report without the photos. It wouldn't be as strong a submission, but the report would still include her research material, which—thank God—she'd submitted last week. One thing this event did tell her: if Cassio was determined to stop her, the diary was worth studying.

The printer halted, and she used a binder clip she'd found on the desk to keep the document together. Then she unhooked her laptop and stashed it, along with the folder, in her bag. She exhaled and sank into a chair. Now all she had to do was mail it without Nate finding out.

She closed her eyes. It wasn't a great plan, but forward movement nonetheless.

"What did you do?"

Sarah opened her eyes to see Nate standing a few feet away in the open doorway. His narrow eyes matched his tight lips.

"Excuse me?"

"Printing." He waved to Luke, who sat at the reception desk outside the office. "A notice on his laptop screen said a print job was in progress. And no one else has a computer tied to that printer."

She stood and held out her hands. "I printed a report I need."

"This wouldn't be the report you wanted to send to the granting agency tonight? The report explaining why Rebecca Prideaux's diary is worth restoring?"

She straightened her shoulders. "I have a plan that will help both of us."

He came closer until she could see tiny brown flecks around the edges of his green eyes. "I will not endanger one of my men to solve that cipher. Do you understand?"

She did, actually. She got why he was angry and defensive. The problem was she couldn't afford to care. "I have a plan to buy us more time. Would you like to hear it, or would you rather hide in a run-down pirate-themed gym for the rest of your life?"

Does Sarah not comprehend the stakes? Nate grabbed two water bottles from the refrigerator and handed one to her. What he needed was food. But what he *wanted* was for Sarah to follow a damn order.

He knew she was smart enough. It was her stubbornness that was the problem. Clearly, she'd never been part of a team. He took two deep breaths and drank half his bottle in one swallow. Instead of arguing with her, he tamped down his irritation and took the low-conflict path. If he wanted to protect her, he had to get her to work with him instead of against him. "What's your plan?"

She paced the room, her pink skirt flowing around her legs. "If I send in my grant request, then go to Remiel and tell him I'm working on—not solving—the cipher, maybe he'll give us more time to figure out how to protect your men and free my father."

He finished his bottle and tossed it in the recycling bin. "Remiel won't go for it. Neither will the Prince."

She took a sip of water and used her fist to wipe off drips on her chin. "We just give up? Your buddy Jack stays safe in prison while my dad is locked away forever?"

"I didn't say that."

"Why can't you see that Remiel and the Prince are *both* using you." She put her bottle on the desk and used one finger beneath his chin to raise his head. Her sweater, buttoned beneath her breasts, only emphasized her feminine curves.

Sweat beaded on his forehead, and he suddenly hated the Prince and Remiel for screwing with his life and taking him away from what he *really* wanted to be doing.

"Nate," she whispered, "the Prince pitted us against each other. He's hoping we'll betray each other instead of working together."

Nate exhaled until it felt like his lungs were turning inside out. She was right. Remiel hated them. The Prince was manipulating them. And for some unknown reason, Nate and his men had landed ass on the ground in the center of a war between Remiel and the Prince. A war that had started years earlier. A war not of Nate's making. "Sarah—"

"It's not just about the cipher." She stood on her toes until her lips were inches from his. "My research and your map are linked somehow. That murder on the isle this morning is too similar to those heroin dealers killed three years ago behind O'Malley's Pub. Not to mention the Latin phrase on the tomb that matches your envelope."

He scrubbed his face with his hands. He didn't trust himself not to kiss her again. "It's also possible everything is related to an operation my men and I participated in five years ago."

She found her bottle and took another sip. "What could a Charleston banker, heroin dealers, and a Latin phrase have to do with a Special Forces mission on the other side of the world?"

"No idea." And the truth was he had less than two days to find out because there was no way he was leaving behind this mess for his men to mop up.

She played with the cap of her bottle and stared at the map. For a woman who'd had a lot to say, she'd run out of words. Maybe she was in shock. Or just overwhelmed. Hell, he was in a constant state of cortisol-releasing stress. Yet, since their run-in with Etienne and Cassio, Sarah had done nothing but handle things with courage.

A fact that confirmed his first assessment of her. Sarah was a woman who dealt with facts first. The question was how would she deal with the emotional fallout? Because he knew from brutal, firsthand experience—the kind of experience gained in a POW camp—that the emotional fallout was what destroyed the man.

He also could tell, from both spending time with her and reading her résumé, that she wasn't the type to let things go and she didn't trust easily. Small wonder she couldn't follow a damn order.

A ringing cell phone startled both of them, and she pulled it out of her pocket. "It's my boss. I need to take it."

"Of course." He went to the window overlooking the street that would never see a horse and carriage. This area hadn't been gentrified yet, and from the deterioration of the asphalt and sidewalks, it wouldn't happen soon. He didn't mind. The ruin made this place perfect for his men to hide.

He sucked in his stomach. Sarah's words earlier had struck him hard in the chest. He was sick of hiding. And in a few days, he wouldn't just be hiding. He'd be hidden.

"Yes." Nate half-turned to watch her pace. "I'm on my way." She hung up. "That's the second time my boss has called. I need to go to the Mansion on Forsyth Park Hotel. There's a problem with the auction catalog."

"Wait here." He headed for the door. "When I return, I'll take you. And then we'll talk about your report."

"Nate, you don't have to come." She grabbed his arm as he passed her. Her small hands had a remarkably tight grip. "You have things to do too."

"Staying with you is my priority." He kissed her again, making it hard and quick when he'd much rather make it soft and long. As he left the room, he added, "Don't leave without me."

CHAPTER 21

NATE OPENED THE DOOR TO THE LOBBY OF THE MANSION on Forsyth Park Hotel, and Sarah entered. The cold AC made her gasp. The lobby had been constructed from marble, gilt, and mirrors, and she saw her reflection everywhere. Good thing she'd brushed her hair before walking over.

"It's freezing in here," Nate said.

"I have a shawl in my bag if I need it."

"What don't you have in there?" Laughter floated below the words. "That thing is almost as heavy as my rucksack."

"I don't carry history books." She smiled at his teasing glint. They'd come to a truce of sorts. He'd wanted to come along, and she'd let him. But she was still determined to mail her report.

And she had to force herself not to think about his kiss. By now, she should be used to his sudden, impulsive kisses. Each one completely different. The first in the police station, passionate and unexpected. The second on the cheek, sweet and gentle. The third in the café, powerful and overwhelming. The fourth against the wall in the alley, desperate and demanding. And there'd been a few pecks along the way, given as if he thought she wouldn't notice.

But this fifth kiss? Short yet filled with yearning.

She touched her lips and let him walk ahead. He'd changed into black cargo pants and T-shirt, all covered with a biker jacket that, while cleaner than the jeans he'd trudged through the tunnels in, also made him appear more…masculine.

"Nate?" She adjusted the bag on her shoulder. "You gave Luke two cell phones earlier."

He scanned the room like her father used to do. "When I shouldered Etienne as he left your house, I stole his cell phone."

"You did *what*?"

Before he could answer, a slender woman wearing a hot-pink shift and her black hair twisted into a knot came over. The woman defined *stunning*. "Miss Munro?"

In her dirty skirt, dusty sandals, and hair that had been ponytailed for the eighth time that day, Sarah felt like a sad cow. "Yes."

"The auction manager has been waiting for you." The woman spent way too much time staring at Nate, her head moving up, down, and up again. "Come with me."

If Sarah had had nails, she'd have used them to claw out the other woman's brown eyes.

Nate took Sarah's hand before following the woman through the lobby toward the courtyard-pool area. Banging sounded from the second floor, and they stepped over tarps.

"Don't mind the construction," the woman said. "We had an incident a few weeks ago."

An explosion that had killed Miss Beatrice Habersham, a woman Sarah had known well, and injured many before taking down the power grid for twelve hours. From the way Nate's jaw cranked, she wondered if he remembered too.

"Will the construction be finished before tomorrow?" Sarah asked.

The beauty lifted her chin as Sarah imagined the goddess Venus would've done. "Of course."

They moved into the white courtyard with a sparkling blue rectangular pool in the middle. Workmen loaded lounge chairs and small tables onto long carts.

Sarah pointed to the side areas with potted palms, pink roses, and night-blooming jasmine. "Is this where the items for sale will be on display?"

"Yes." The woman's heels clip-clopped on the tile. "There is one item that will only be shown in the hotel manager's office and protected by hired guards." She glanced at Sarah with an eyebrow raise that could be either disdain or helpfulness. The woman's hair was so tightly drawn back, it made her face taut and her meaning unclear. "For security purposes."

"There's nothing in the collection that needs armed security."

"That's why the auction manager would like to see you." The woman led Sarah into an office and then disappeared.

One wall of the room held a window overlooking the side garden. Two black leather club chairs flanked a desk. The room was white-walled with no artwork. A man stood near the window, studying a notebook.

Nearby, an older woman with perfectly coiffed white hair sat on a low settee and checked her phone. Miss Nell Habersham wore a pale-pink knit suit that looked vintage French and matching Louboutin heels. She also wore a diamond rope necklace that had, apparently, been a gift from some long-ago suitor. Her sister Miss Beatrice had offered that bit of gossip one night after one too many champagne cocktails.

"Sarah." Miss Nell stood and held out her arms, and Sarah went into them. "Are you looking forward to your auction tomorrow?"

"I am." Sarah breathed in Miss Nell's floral perfume, surprised Miss Nell would spend any time in the same place where her sister had died. Then, maybe, that was the point.

Sarah held out her hand to Nate. Before she could introduce him, he had Miss Nell in a bear hug, his arms around the small woman, her feet dangling.

"Nate!" Miss Nell clung to his neck. When he put her down, she kissed his cheek. "I didn't know you'd be here today."

Nate smiled, and Sarah couldn't help but stare at the red flush staining his cheeks.

Should I be jealous of Miss Nell? Sarah was kind of silently joking and kind of not.

"I came with Sarah." Nate took her hand again. "I thought you were living with your cousin in Charleston."

"I am." Miss Nell sighed. "I'm just visiting and trying not to regret selling Habersham Mansion. I came a day early, though, because Carina added something to the collection and asked me to check it out. Sarah—" Miss Nell motioned to the short man with fluffy brown hair and wearing a yellow golf shirt, khaki pants, and braided leather belt who finally deemed to look at them. His round glasses finished off the bookish look. "Do you know Dr. Maurice Burns?"

"Yes." *Unfortunately.*

Maurice slammed the notebook shut and put it on the desk. "You're late, Sarah."

She frowned. She didn't answer to Maurice. "What are you doing here?"

Maurice squinted at Nate. "Who's this?"

"A friend."

Nate moved until his shoulder was slightly in front of hers. "Is there a problem?"

"Not unless you get in the way of Maurice's career." Sarah hated the snarky edge in her voice until she remembered what an ass Maurice could be. No, *had been* and probably *still was.* Nate placed a hand on her lower back, and she straightened her shoulders. "Why are you here?"

"I'm clerking the auction." Maurice eyed Nate. "Did your friend need to be fed? Is that why you're late?"

Had Nate growled? She wasn't sure. But there was no denying the darkness clouding his green eyes.

"Maurice," Miss Nell admonished. "That's not polite."

Maurice shrugged.

Sarah touched Nate's arm, and the tight muscles bunched beneath her hand. "Maurice Burns was a thirteenth-century historian with the Smithsonian until he left to work for a private collector. And now, apparently, he moonlights as an auction manager."

"We can't all live on grants. Do you know the situation?"

"There's been an addition to the catalog." Which was

ridiculous since she was the one who'd authenticated the collection, written the historical summaries, and compiled the catalog. "I didn't authorize or authenticate anything else."

"It was added this morning by Senator Carina Prioleau. I believe most of these items come from the Prioleau collection?"

"It's half Prioleau and half Habersham," Miss Nell said. "My sister and I have a collection of seventeenth- and eighteenth-century pirate artifacts worthy of the British Museum."

Nate found an auction brochure on the desk. "The proceeds of the auction are going to the Sea Island Loggerhead Turtle Foundation."

"Yes." Miss Nell smiled. "Are you a turtle fan?"

"Of course." Nate smiled that high-wattage grin of his that made Sarah's knees melt. "May I take this?"

"Yes, dear." Miss Nell took the glossy color brochure from him and opened it to the last page. "We've had gift items, like silk ties and scarves, designed with the foundation's turtle logo. All of the proceeds will go to protecting these special creatures."

"I'll tell my buddy." Nate put the brochure into his jacket. "Cain is a sucker for turtles."

Maurice scoffed. "Does your friend know how to wear a tie?"

Nate's nostrils flared, and Sarah changed the subject "Maurice, if Senator Prioleau added something to the auction, and you were able to authenticate it and print a supplement to the catalog, why do you need me?"

"For your signature." Maurice pointed to a table along the side wall with a book cradled on top. "Don't touch it. There's a pressure alarm underneath."

Sarah went over. A felt book support held the water-spotted leather diary she'd held yesterday. "This doesn't belong to the senator. This belongs to the Savannah Preservation Office. This is Rebecca Prideaux's diary."

Miss Nell came over and tapped Sarah's arm. "My dear, the Rutledge family in Charleston donated the diary to the Savannah Preservation Office years ago."

"Why is it *here*?"

"Because," Maurice said, "Carina Prioleau discovered the diary once belonged to Rebecca Prideaux. Therefore, Carina believes it's within her rights to reclaim the book and sell it."

"Senator Prioleau is *wrong*."

"Sarah?" Nate placed a warm hand on her shoulder. "How did Carina discover the diary if it's been at the Savannah Preservation Office for years?"

Sarah wanted to kick herself. "Last week I sent the grant application with a preliminary description of the diary I wanted to restore. I know Carina somehow saw the application because this morning she gave my boss grief about it." Sarah stared hard at Maurice. "We can't sell this diary because it was *stolen*. From the Savannah Preservation Office."

"Have you filed a police report?"

"No. I only realized a minute ago that it had been taken."

"Can you prove the preservation office owns it?"

"There's a catalog listing, and I'm sure there's donation paperwork around."

"Except Carina does own it, dear," Miss Nell said. "Many, many years ago I helped Louise Rutledge steal it from Carina's grandmother."

"Noooooo," Nate said around a smile. "Miss Nell, you're a *badass*."

Miss Nell nodded at the compliment. "I am. But Carina's grandmother was a mean girl and deserved it."

"I don't understand," Sarah said. "That book belongs to the SPO. The board of directors, including Calum, gave me permission to seek a restoration grant."

"Doesn't matter," Maurice said. "The senator wants to sell it. And the opening bid will be fifty thousand."

"What!" Sarah's screech hurt even her own ears, but she

couldn't help herself. Maurice was betraying her. Again. "You can't sell it until we establish provenance."

Miss Nell patted Sarah's hand. "I've confirmed provenance, dear."

Panic jumbled her words. She couldn't lose her only link to Rebecca and Thomas. Her only link to the hide sites. And the cipher. Her last link with her mother. Her only chance to save her father.

Nate whistled. "Why is it worth so much?"

Maurice dodged Nate's question with one of his own. "Sarah, do you know about the alphanumeric sequences?"

"Of course," she said. "You mentioned them in the foreword when you published my thesis in *The British Journal*."

Nate settled his hands on his hips. "This is the asshole who betrayed you?"

She took a few deep breaths to control her emotions. "One of them."

Maurice shrugged. "Augustus and I believed it was time for you to find a new focus."

She fisted her hands. She could easily find a *new focus*. "Is Augustus in town?"

"No. Augustus now works for a private firm in Boston."

"Sarah." Nate's voice helped her come down from the mountain of bitterness and hurt she'd just climbed. "Breathe."

She exhaled. Nate was right in his simple, silent command-type of way. No wonder his men followed his orders. He had a strong yet quiet presence about him that she was beginning to appreciate. "Why is this diary worth so much?"

Maurice adjusted his glasses on his pointy nose. "This diary is one of the earliest primary accounts of colonial life ever uncovered. Senator Prioleau brought in the diary along with a potential buyer."

"Why didn't she just sell it to him directly?"

"I suspect," Miss Nell said, "Carina would like to see how high the bidding will go."

"I'm not signing anything," Sarah said to Maurice's lying face.

"Would you like to tell Senator Prioleau that?"

Sarah turned to Miss Nell. "Do you have physical proof that the diary once belonged to Carina's grandmother?"

"No dear," Miss Nell said. "Just my word."

And wasn't that a kick in the heart. Miss Nell was one of the most beloved women in the city, and Sarah was trapped.

"I swear," Miss Nell said, "the diary belongs to the Prioleau family."

"Except it's not Carina's to sell." Sarah couldn't sign the letter of provenance. It would mean she'd lose Rebecca's story forever. "My life's work is based on that diary."

"Because that's not pathetic," Maurice said with a slyness that told her how much he enjoyed this.

She moved forward until Nate wrapped an arm around her waist and whispered, "Don't make things worse."

Things couldn't get much worse. "But—"

"I think"—the cord of steel in Miss Nell's voice was a firm yet gracious order—"it's time to change your life's work." She took a piece of paper and a pen off the desk and brought it over to Sarah. "It's time to let Rebecca's story go."

CHAPTER 22

NATE BROUGHT THE TRAY WITH BARBECUE SANDWICHES, dessert, and fries over to where Sarah sat in the Blowin' Smoke café. Her arms were folded on the table, and her head lay on top. Her ponytail hung over her shoulder, shifting as she breathed. He wanted to hold her on his lap, wrap her in his arms, and offer comfort. Instead, he said, "You need to eat."

She lifted her head, and her red eyes proved she'd been trying not to cry. "I'm not hungry."

"I don't care." He went to the counter for their chocolate shakes and put one down in front of her. "Drink this."

"Did you talk to Calum?" She sat up and played with her straw.

"I did. He told me he doesn't get involved with his sister's business and that you should still go to Dessie's to find a dress for tomorrow."

"I don't need a dress because I'm not going to the auction." She sipped her shake. "And my dad?"

"Still in the ICU. No visitors allowed."

She used her palms to wipe her cheeks before taking a bite of her sandwich. She cleaned her lips with a napkin but hid her grimace.

"You don't like it?" He took a big bite as she scrunched her nose.

"It's different. Like mustard and vinegar."

"It's North Carolina style." He rubbed his mouth with a napkin and added, "Mine's better though. I'll make it for you." He paused and took another bite. There'd be no time to make barbecue for her. *Ever.*

She touched his cheek with her hand, then ate her

sandwich. "It's good," she said in between nibbles. "But why is the coleslaw on top?"

He drank his shake and waggled an eyebrow. He needed to improve the mood. "I thought you were from Savannah. Don't you know anything about Southern cooking?"

"Nope." She ate a fry. Then two more. "I grew up in Boston, and we hardly ever came home. I think it was too hard on my mom." She sipped her shake before adding, "In New England, everything is roasted. To *death*."

"Kells is from South Boston, and his idea of dinner is food cooked into submission." Nate's phone buzzed, and he read the message. "It's Luke. I'll take this outside. By the time I return, I want half that sandwich eaten." He left the diner, answering, "Any word from Kells?"

"Nope. I'm still working on Etienne's cell phone. Know anyone named Leroy?"

"No." Nate checked his watch. It was almost eight p.m. "I'm eating now and will head to the club. Tell Zack to meet me there."

"Will do. Any new info on our mission?"

"Not yet." Nate moved off the sidewalk and waited until students in SCAD T-shirts passed by. "I've been thinking— our OPSEC sucks."

"We don't have operational security because we just moved in. I'm not sure that lock on the back door works. The rats are the only thing keeping out thugs."

"That's not an excuse." The Fianna would never have allowed Sarah to wander into the Prince's office and see maps on the wall. "We need cameras on our perimeter, a night watch, and an armory." There were other things on Nate's mental list, but he didn't want to overly stress Luke.

"Dude, the first requires money, which we don't have. The second requires men who aren't working twenty hours a day in jobs they hate, which we also don't have. And the third requires weapons. Again, which we don't have."

Nate frowned. "All of the men have a personal pistol.

Pete has two. Ty probably does too. And there are knives floating around. I'd like a full accounting of guns, ammo, and any other weapons we have. Then we need a place to store them."

"All of those weapons could fit in a drawer of a metal filing cabinet I've been emptying. The one that's been there since Eisenhower was president."

"Use that. And let the men know I want a list of all weapons and ammunition by tomorrow morning. Oh-eight-hundred hours."

"Why the hurry? Oh, right. Sorry."

Because by Sunday Nate was going to be on his way to Maine. "This is important, Luke. It's my job as XO to make sure you all are as secure in this new situation as you can be."

"Got it. I'll let you know when I find anything else on the phone."

Nate ended the call and went inside. Sarah hadn't eaten her sandwich, but she'd not only polished off her dessert, she still had the spoon in her mouth. "Did you like the strawberry pie?"

She nodded and licked the utensil. "It was delicious."

He sat and drank his chocolate shake, appreciating Sarah next to him, the taste of cold chocolate, and fries cooked in oil. He pushed over his piece of pie. "Eat mine." Before she could fuss, he said, "No arguing, not about pie or sending in your report for that grant."

"Why? Because I just gave the diary to the senator who wants to destroy my career?"

He squeezed her arm. He wasn't used to seeing her defeated. "Maybe Miss Nell is right. Maybe it's time to find a new focus." He popped a fry in his mouth. "Like me."

She took a bite of his strawberry dessert. "For an ex–Green Beret who runs a pirate-themed gym, you think mighty highly of yourself."

He took the lid off the shake and took a big gulp. He

wanted to close his eyes and savor it, but he didn't want to lose a moment of looking at her. "Yes, I do."

She laughed. "What am I going to do with you, Nate Walker?"

He blew her a kiss. He was willing to look ridiculous if it meant making her happy.

She shook her head. "Men are all alike."

"Not really. Some have stupid names like Augustus."

She pushed her empty pie plate away, crossed her arms on the table, and laid her head down again. "I want this day to be over."

"I know, sweetheart." He rubbed her neck. The irony was he didn't want this day, or the next, to ever end. "I know."

Zack came downstairs dressed in what he hoped would be clothes worthy of a goth strip club whose previous manager sold prostitutes and tainted heroin on the side. Tonight he wore his leather biker pants and a black tee. He'd strapped a gun to his leg beneath his pants and hidden a knife in his leather coat.

He'd just spent the last hour reading through what the other men had written about the night Jack's and Nate's teams were taken and comparing it to the spreadsheet Luke had compiled for their defense arguments. So far, Zack had found nothing new.

The gym was busy. The ring was occupied, and there was a waiting list. Vane had the beginner Krav Maga class, while Pete had taken an advanced class. Zack had had to hear Vane complain about *that* injustice all afternoon.

Luke sat at the front desk, a cell phone connected to his laptop. Zack went over and dropped a Post-it note on a pile of papers. "Here's my list." The fact that his list fit on a Post-it note told Luke everything about Zack's pathetically small personal arsenal. "One nine-mil. One fully loaded magazine. Two knives."

"Thanks." Luke looked up. "Nate said he'll meet you at the club."

"Great."

"Cain!" Luke waved to Cain, who was leaving the main gym area. "Where's your list?"

"Dudes." Cain wore black sweats and nothing else. From the size of his pumped-up arms, he'd probably finished his daily program of lifting and pull-ups. "One Glock. Three magazines. One empty, one full, one with three bullets."

"And?" Zack asked.

Cain ran his hands over his shaved head. "Three knives. Charlotte has pepper spray."

"Thanks." Luke wrote on the same Post-it below Zack's list.

"No prob." Cain pointed to the desk phone. "Did Charlotte call the gym today?"

"No," Zack said. "Why would your wife do that?"

"Because my phone died and I can't find my charger." Cain walked away, grabbing a towel off a stack on a metal chair. "Let me know if she calls." He moved so quickly the stack toppled over onto the floor. The same stack Zack had washed and folded earlier.

Aaaaaaaand Cain kept moving.

"Sure," Luke threw out after him with all the excitement of a kid waiting for a flu shot.

Cain raised a hand and headed for the stairs.

Zack exchanged a grimace with Luke. Cain shared a room with Vane, who was OCD tidy while Cain dropped shit everywhere. "What are the chances the charger is buried under laundry?"

"Nah." Luke started typing again. "I bet Vane hid it."

"You're probably right." Zack clapped Luke on the shoulder. "What are you doing?"

"Nate took this phone off Etienne today. I'm looking for clues, except some of the numbers are encrypted." The phone buzzed, and Luke squinted at it. "It's a text for a change to a meet-up tonight." Concern carved lines on his face. "Etienne was supposed to meet some guy down the street behind that abandoned service station. Name of Leroy."

∽

Five minutes later, Zack held three beer bottle necks in one hand and walked down the street toward the abandoned gas station He inhaled the night air until he entered the alley, where he gagged on the stench of mildew and urine.

It didn't take long to find the two men who'd been living in this alley since Zack and his men arrived. Despite being high or drunk, they'd not caused problems. The short one had even come into the gym to remind them that trash day was Tuesday instead of Thursday.

"Hey, man." The short man sat on his ass, propped up by the moldy brick wall. "Wat up?"

Zack handed him two of the beers, already opened. "Just being neighborly."

"Cool." The short man whistled, and the tall, thin one appeared. "Brews, bro. On. The. House." He slapped the ground between the latter three words.

Thin Guy stopped near his buddy and took a beer. "*Yo.*"

Zack took a drink. "My friends and I are running the gym now."

"Dude," Short Guy said. "That's awesome. Old goat who ran the place before was a real prick."

And a hoarder. "A man came in today, and I was hoping you two could fill me in on the rules around here."

"You met Antoine." Thin Guy's voice was so weak Zack wondered if he was sick. "Antoine's harmless. A go-between."

"A wannabe," Short Guy said.

Both men clanked their bottles in agreement.

Zack lifted his bottle to his lips, trying to figure out the best way to ask the next question. Except he didn't have to. Thin Guy brought it up on his own.

"Stay away from Leroy. He's involved in serious shit."

"Yeah," Short Guy whispered, "Leroy is a Russian *vor*."

Zack didn't know much about Russian mobsters, but he knew the word *vor*: a dangerous, high-level thief in the Russian mob. "What is a *vor* doing in Savannah?"

Short Guy chugged his beer. "Not sure. Leroy entered the game when that tainted heroin hit the streets and made friends with Antoine. We"—Short Guy nodded to Thin Guy—"thought Leroy was the source of that poison, but then it dried up and Leroy is still around."

Thin Guy nodded as if agreeing with his buddy's assessment.

Zack pretended to look confused. "My buddy was supposed to meet Leroy tonight behind the old service station. Any ideas why?"

"Don't know," Short Guy said.

"Do either of you know a man named Etienne?"

Both men shook their heads.

Great.

"Some neighborly advice?" Short Guy stood. "Whatever's going on, stay out of it. Leroy is bad news."

Zack handed over his unfinished beer. "Thanks, bro. Appreciate it."

Short Guy smiled, showing two missing teeth. "No prob, neighbor. No. Fucking. Prob."

Zack headed to the gym. If Leroy was a Russian *vor* and if he was working with Remiel, Zack and his men would need a lot more Post-it notes.

CHAPTER 23

AFTER DINNER NATE WALKED SARAH TO THE CLUB AND settled her in the security office. He didn't want to leave her unprotected, and the fact that she didn't argue with him meant she was more freaked about what had happened at her house than she'd admitted.

Once at the club, Zack informed Nate of the link between some Russian thief named Leroy and Etienne Marigny. Except Nate, not a great multitasker, focused on the job of the moment. He introduced Zack to the staff members, including bartenders, waitresses, strippers, and Bruce—the manager of the VIP room and main club.

At ten thirty, Nate entered the security office. The screens gave him visuals of every room from every angle, including the front door and back alley. At the entrance, two guards in black leathers counted people coming and going. A heavy-metal screech band played in the main room.

Nate clasped his hands behind his neck and stretched his arms. Bruce, in the VIP room, gave the camera a thumbs-up. Zack had moved into the main bar to handle a potential two-boys–one-girl situation. If Nate could come with Vane and Ty tomorrow night, show them the setup, Nate would feel better about leaving them.

Nate wasn't happy about his men having to work at the club in addition to their other duties. But they needed the steady source of intel and cash income the club provided.

He heard a sound behind him. Sarah was asleep on the small couch, and a book had fallen onto the floor. A pencil was stuck in her ponytail. He took it out of her hair and grabbed the book. It was a ledger written in old-fashioned handwriting.

A knock sounded, and one of the bartenders stuck his

head in. "Was on my smoke break in the alley when a man showed. He wants to see you."

"Who?"

"Not sure. Could be a booze delivery." The man left.

At this time of night? The alley's camera didn't show anything. He slipped on his jacket and put his gun into the pocket. Then he kissed Sarah on the head and left.

Nate let the steel-reinforced door shut behind him. Security lights had been added in the alley, yet there were plenty of shadows. He rolled his shoulders and exhaled. "Show yourself."

A man emerged in a long leather coat over black pants and silk shirt. Tall with sharp features and dark hair, he had to be related to Etienne. The man moved into the light, and Nate's heartbeat intensified. Where Etienne was on the ugly side of average, this man could only be described as classically beautiful. Pale skin, intensely blue eyes, and dark hair swept back from his forehead. All of his stark features in perfect proportion, as if carved by a Renaissance master.

Remiel Marigny?

Nate went for his weapon until he heard a click and felt a gun's barrel against his head. *Shit.* He turned slightly to see the shadow of the large man behind him.

Remiel took Nate's gun and laid it on the ground. Then he kicked it away. "I want to talk."

"Then tell your thug to back down."

"No." Remiel said. "I'm here to offer an incentive for helping Miss Munro solve her cipher."

"I don't—" The man behind Nate pushed the gun even harder against Nate's skull.

Remiel smiled. "I know about the Prince's counteroffer, which has put you in a difficult position. Miss Munro solves the cipher and her father goes free, yet Jack Keeley dies. She doesn't solve it and Jack Keeley lives, while her father's life, as he knows it, is over."

"Fuck you."

"Very eloquent." Remiel's pupils appeared edged with silver. "You're conflicted. You want to kill me, yet if you do you'll never get the answers you desperately need. I'm sure those questions are part of the reason you don't sleep well."

"You don't know shit about me."

"Too bad they shoved so many needles in your arm in the POW camp. If you had your memories"—Remiel shook his head—"we'd have much to talk about."

Nate was too tired for bullshit, and he felt a headache building behind his temples. "What do you want?"

Remiel looked up at the last sliver of moon partially hidden by storm clouds. "If you solve the cipher in time, I will guarantee Jack Keeley's safety in prison. If you don't, then I will have Jack killed."

Nate's harsh laugh startled the rat that'd been scurrying behind the Dumpster. "You mean I should side with you over the Prince. Despite the fact that I've no doubt he has a man inside the prison willing and able to carry out Jack's execution. Yet I'm supposed to believe that you have a way to thwart the Prince's orders?" Nate snorted. "That you have a man inside Leedsville prison as well?"

Remiel smiled, showing off his straight, shiny whites. "You don't believe I can play at the Prince's level? Despite the fact that I managed to take out two A-teams, send those A-teams to a POW camp for years, and set up Kells Torridan's men to take the fall for the Wakhan Corridor Massacre?"

"Nope." Although the word carried confidence, Nate swallowed, hating the doubt that snaked through his mind. He'd recently discovered Remiel's involvement in those horrific events but had still assumed Remiel had had help.

After all, until recently Nate and his men hadn't just known Remiel as a low-level gunrunner. They'd thought Remiel was dead. With all the shit that had happened to Nate's unit during the past five years, none of them had *ever* considered Remiel as the cause.

"Then let's reacquaint you with someone who'll make you believe." Remiel raised a hand, and a flashlight shone behind him. A moment later, the man in the black hoodie came forward with the light in one hand and a rope in the other. He yanked, and someone fell out of the shadows with a noose tied around his neck. The man lay on the ground, in the flashlight's beam, protecting his ribs.

Fletcher Ames. A memory came rushing in, and Nate's gag reflex took over. He fell to his knees and threw up. Once his stomach finished curling in on itself, he wiped his mouth with his sleeve. Fletcher Ames had been the head torturer in the POW camp. Fletcher Ames had beaten so horrifically that one day felt like it lasted years.

"Let me make myself clear." Remiel sank on his haunches nearby. "You and Miss Munro have until noon on Sunday to solve that cipher. If you do, I'll save Jack Keeley from the Prince's assassin, and I will release Joe Munro. If you do not…well, you know the rest."

Nate's palms slipped on slimy brick ground, and he fell onto his side. He could barely breathe. Barely move. Not even when Remiel leaned down and said, "You need to accept that you can't protect everyone. One of the people you love most in the world will get hurt. You get to choose which one, the other you get to betray."

Nate was barely aware of Remiel and the others leaving. Barely aware of time passing. Barely aware of his own breathing. The only things he could do were close his eyes against the seizure's flashing lights, keep his breath as steady as possible, and pray this nightmare would end.

Sometime later, a hand fell on Nate's shoulder and squeezed. "'Tis a sorry state, my lord. I wish it were not so."

Nate rolled onto his back and, with Cassio's help, sat against the alley wall. "What am I going to do?"

Cassio squatted until they were eye level. "Join us. Let us take care of this fiend. Let us save you."

"What about Sarah? And the rest of my men? Jack? I can't leave them unprotected."

"We cannot help them. By joining us, you will become part of something that will put an end to these villains."

Nate shook his head. "Why doesn't the Prince order the Fianna to kill Remiel?"

"That is a question for the Prince."

The last thing Nate wanted was a Q and A with the Prince.

Cassio took a tissue out of his pocket and handed it to Nate. "What will you do?"

"I don't know." Nate wiped his mouth. "But I won't leave Sarah and my men unprotected. I can't."

"You'd offer your life for a woman you barely know and a friend who betrayed you?"

"You've no idea what you're talking about."

"It's you who cannot bear the truth. And your trust will mean your doom." Cassio rose, struck his chest with his fist, and bowed his head. "If you fail, Hell and night will bring this monstrous birth to the world's light."

Meaning? If Nate fucked this up, Remiel's devil-backed plan—whatever it was—would succeed.

Hooah.

What is that ringing noise?

Sarah sat up to find her phone, and her glasses fell on the floor. "Hello?"

"Sarah? It's Hugh. I heard someone fired a gun in your house?"

"It was a misunderstanding." She looked around to realize she was alone in the security office. And the reverb that shook the room was from the band's bass in the main bar. "Is that why you're calling?"

"Yes. Also, I heard from your father's military contact. I'd forwarded him that name you gave me as well as those photos you sent me earlier today."

She'd forgotten about that. "It's okay, Hugh. I don't—"

"The contact called me." Hugh's voiced dropped in tone, and she heard him tapping his fingers on the desk. "Major Nate Walker is involved in serious black ops stuff. He, along with the men whose names were printed on that page in the photo you sent me, were members of the 7th Special Forces Group at Fort Bragg under the command of Colonel Kells Torridan. Torridan, Walker, and the rest of their men are either in prison or dishonorably discharged."

"Excuse me?" Nate hadn't mentioned *that*.

"My contact told me the unit was accused of the Wakhan Corridor Massacre."

She put the ledger, glasses, and pen into her straw bag. Nate hadn't lied to her, he'd just left out all the gray parts.

"The contact discovered two other interesting things. Nate Walker was accused of being the mastermind behind the massacre. His men were ambushed and captured. Because he was sick when he and his men were rescued, Major Walker was sent to a secret military prison hospital for the criminally insane. I'm still waiting for more info but wanted to let you know."

Sarah heard noises outside the room and said, "Thanks for calling, Hugh." After hanging up, she noticed she'd missed a call from Calum. He'd left a message saying that her father was more stable and they were moving him out of ICU into a private room. Calum was hoping he could get in to see her father tomorrow.

She put the phone in her lap and closed her eyes. *Please let my father be okay.*

Her phone buzzed again, this time with a text from Miss Nell. It's done.

Thank you. She breathed deeply so she wouldn't hyper-ventilate. She'd suspected that Nate and his friends had sketchy backgrounds, but nothing like this. Maybe she should go to her house, grab a bag, and drive to Charleston. Hugh would know what to do. Except she couldn't leave her father. And she had to solve that cipher.

With her mind spinning and feeling sick to her stomach, she found the female employees' bathroom, where she washed her hands and splashed water on her face. Then she made her way into the strippers' changing room.

The area was filled with white lockers and low benches covered in feathery boas and glittery heels. One wall had a dressing table with mirrors above and stools below. Brushes and hairspray bottles along with curling irons and hair straighteners filled the counter. She sat on a stool, took the band out of her hair, and stared at her reflection.

What should I do now?

"Hey." Samantha breezed into the room in a black mini circle skirt, patent-leather stiletto boots, and a black satin bustier. She'd somehow restrained her wild reddish-blond curls into a tight bun on the top of her head. Her only makeup was red lipstick. "You're awake."

Sarah clasped her hands in her lap. Did Samantha know about Nate and his men? "I can't believe I fell asleep."

Samantha came over, studied her reflection, and pinched her cheeks. "From what Pete told me, you've had a wretched day."

Wretched. *Yes.* "That's a great word."

Samantha took a brush and held it over Sarah's head. "May I?"

"Not sure it will help."

"I can work miracles." Samantha started brushing.

The rhythmic strokes felt wonderfully hypnotic. If Sarah had known this morning when she'd decided to go out to the isle that this was where she'd end up, learning what she now knew, she might not have gone. But then she wouldn't have seen Nate again.

She wouldn't have *kissed* Nate again.

"Ivers left the Juliet's Lily truck down the street, and I put the keys in your overnight bag." Samantha nodded to a floral Vera Bradley bag on a pink settee. "I got everything you listed in your text. I also found your house keys and locked up."

"Thank you." Sarah took a few deep breaths. "Can I ask you a question?"

"Of course." Samantha put down the brush, found a comb, and started separating Sarah's hair into three big chunks.

"Were Nate and his men dishonorably discharged?"

The comb paused. "Where did you hear that?"

"My father was a cop. His ex-partner did a background check. Did you know they were charged with the Wakhan Corridor Massacre?"

Samantha started braiding. "Pete told me you suffered a serious setback in your career not long ago."

"It's true. I was betrayed by those I trusted the most."

Samantha clipped the end of one braid and started on the second. "It's hard to get over something like that. I speak from experience." Samantha met Sarah's gaze in the mirror. "I also know that that kind of betrayal shuts people down, stops them from making new relationships, keeps them in their heads with the *shouldas, couldas, wouldas*."

Samantha yanked on the braid, and Sarah grimaced. "You're not answering my question."

Samantha started the third braid. "Nate and some of his men were *accused* of the Wakhan Corridor Massacre. That accusation led to a mission that went bad in Afghanistan. That mission led to two A-teams being sent to a POW camp." She used a small band to tie off the last braid. "They suffered there for two years before being rescued."

Sarah winced when Samantha pulled the braids and twisted them together. "POW camp?" Hugh hadn't mentioned that.

Samantha nodded and took some hairpins from a bowl. "From what little Pete has told me, it was beyond brutal.

It's amazing they all survived. Nate suffered the most with seizures and memory loss. He remembers little of his years in the camp. When he returned home, instead of going to a regular military prison with his men, he was sent to a military prison hospital in Maine."

"Why didn't he tell me this?"

"It's classified."

"Yet you know?"

Samantha had worked the three braids into a complicated knot at the base of Sarah's neck and started shoving in hairpins. "Pete is tired of the bullshit and confided in me."

Sarah closed her eyes.

"Nate feels responsible for the disastrous Afghanistan mission."

She opened her eyes. "Why?"

"Because he was in charge that night." Samantha frowned at Sarah's hair and added more pins. "I don't know the details, but Nate's plan didn't work out. Then, a few weeks ago, the men who'd stayed behind were dishonorably discharged. Some of them went home to their families, others went to work at Iron Rack's."

"Why didn't Nate tell me?"

"He's not allowed to. Nate is always kind and considerate to me but also distant and overprotective. Yet, when he watches you, I see something else in his eyes. Something that looks like hope."

"Oh." Sarah studied her clutched hands in her lap. She didn't want to be responsible for anyone else's hope when she'd so little of it herself. It was selfish of her, but Nate's issues seemed much larger than anything she could handle on her own.

Samantha squeezed Sarah's shoulders. "I have a favor to ask of you. Nate has to leave soon, and I was hoping that you two could…" She blushed.

"Are you asking me to sleep with Nate?"

"No!" Samantha's hazel eyes widened. "I'd never do

that. I'm just asking you, for the next two days, to let your guard down around him. Let him in. It's hard after the kind of betrayal you've had, but developing a connection with you may help him where he's going."

"I don't understand. Why does he need help?"

"He's not just leaving town." Samantha's face changed quickly. Her flush now appeared almost gray. "On Sunday, he's going back to that prison hospital."

Sarah's pounding heart competed with the band's bass that shook the room. She couldn't have heard that properly. "He's *what*?"

Zack appeared in the doorway, his hand gripping the frame above. His tattooed arms seemed larger up close, and his eyes were darker. "Have either of you seen Nate?"

"Nope," Samantha said.

Sarah spun around on the stool. Something about Zack's voice made her anxious. "*Why?*"

"Nate is missing."

CHAPTER 24

SARAH FOUND NATE IN THE ALLEY. SHE, SAMANTHA, AND Zack were searching the club when a fight broke out near the band. Zack dealt with that while Samantha checked the front entrance and Sarah decided—despite Zack's order not to—to go out the back door.

Security bulbs highlighted the center of the alley but not the shadows surrounding the club and the brick building next door. Thunder rocked the sky, and a few raindrops hit her face. A storm was coming, and from the flashes of lightning, it promised to be intense.

She searched until a lightning flash exposed the sole of a combat boot. Nate sat against a brick wall, one leg stretched out, the other pulled up with an arm draped over it. His eyes were closed, and his other arm rested on his head. There was a graffiti tag painted nearby: the Prioleau sigil of a skeleton hand clutching a sword with the words *sans pitié* written below.

Nate's position screamed defeat, like he'd fought the battle and was the only survivor.

"Nate?" She held her skirt and scrunched down next to him, resting a hand on his thigh.

"My head hurts," he said harshly. "Oh, God. I'm *remembering*."

"What are you remembering?"

He shook his head, keeping his eyes closed. "I'm not sure. It's all in pieces. I know I saw a Fianna warrior bow that night."

"The night your men were ambushed?"

"On a ridge, at sunset. He wore desert fatigues and tribal clothes with a sword. When he saw me, he bowed." Nate opened his eyes, took her hand off his thigh, and brought it to his lips. Her legs cramped, and she sat next to him, praying the ground wasn't as gross as it looked.

He spoke into her hand, as if needing a buffer between them. "We were patrolling, and the mountain next to us exploded in smoke, roars, and chaos. Two rebel attack helos descended. Their twin machine guns fired at my men. Someone on the ground winged RPGs, and the sound blew out my eardrums."

Sarah didn't move. Nate still held her hand, but his focus had drifted to some distance over her shoulder. He wasn't seeing her at all. He was back there, with his men.

"Another helo hovered on the side of the new crater. We were pinned between their guns and more than a hundred tribesmen who believed we were responsible for that massacre."

He closed his eyes, and she gripped his thigh again. "What happened next?" She wasn't sure why, but she knew whatever he was remembering was important.

"It was impossible to hear anything over the whirring blades. Everything smelled like oil and gunpowder. I raised my head to check out the situation, and when the man on the hill saw me, he bowed."

"Nate? Who did this to you? Who set you up for that massacre and that ambush?"

"Remiel Marigny. The man who wants you to solve the cipher."

Nate pressed his head against the alley's brick wall and kept his eyes closed because he didn't want to face the reality that he'd met Remiel Marigny and seen Fletcher Ames again. Nate also didn't want to let go of Sarah's hand. What he really wanted was to drag her onto his lap, bury his hands in her hair, and breathe in her perfume. Something about her kept him steady. The ever-present humming, which had racked his body since leaving the prison hospital, had lessened today.

"Nate?" she whispered. "Let's go inside. It's going to rain."

He nodded but still couldn't move.

"Wait here." She withdrew her hand, and he heard her soft footsteps. A few minutes later, maybe it was longer, he felt her kneel next to him again. "We're going to the apartment."

He opened his eyes. "No." It was time to stop feeling sorry for himself. "I'm fine."

"You're not fine," another, deeper voice said. Zack stood a few feet away, frowning. "Ty and Cain will take over for you tonight. Samantha will drive you and Sarah to the apartment."

Nate stood and helped Sarah up. "Is Samantha done with her shift?"

"No. I'm sending her home. This place is a fucking crazy-town."

Nate kissed Sarah's hand. He didn't care about Zack's dark glare. "I should get Ty and Cain settled."

Zack scoffed. "We'll figure it out."

Despite Zack's right to be angry, Nate was tired of apologizing for his constant failures. He didn't even care that Sarah was there to witness it all. "What's wrong?"

"Why don't you tell me what the hell happened out here tonight?"

When he couldn't figure out a lie, he went with the truth. "I met Remiel Marigny."

Zack's mouth fell open.

"I'm still not sure what's going on, but I don't want to talk about it. And don't mention it to the others."

"Fuck—"

Nate held out a hand. "I promise to fill you in as soon as I get some real answers. Can I trust you, brother?"

Zack stared at Sarah until she moved close enough for Nate to put his arm around her shoulders.

Finally, Zack said, "If I don't get answers from you by noon tomorrow, I'm telling the other men."

Nate nodded.

"Alright." Zack headed inside. "I'll get Sarah's bags."

CHAPTER 25

THE APARTMENT WAS DOWN AN ALLEY, IN AN OLD BUILDING, on the second floor above Dessie's dress shop. After parking the truck, Samantha had shown them into the apartment before going to her own across the courtyard, above Juliet's Lily. Pete was meeting her there later.

Sarah was grateful that Calum had had the apartment above Dessie's freshened up for them. He'd even had food delivered, fresh towels laid out, and new sheets on the large bed in the master bedroom and the smaller one in the spare bedroom. Each bedroom had its own bathroom.

She'd showered, dried her hair, and put on pink PJ pants with a black cami. She'd also thrown on a blue zippered sweatshirt. The AC kept the apartment in arctic temps.

Lightning flashed outside as she boiled water in the galley kitchen. Nate was taking a shower in the smaller bathroom attached to the spare room. He'd offered her the big bed, and when she'd argued with him, he'd just walked away. She still thought it was ridiculous. He was twice her size. He should take the large bed, and she'd be fine on the twin.

She washed and rinsed his handkerchief, the one that he'd use to wrap her ankle and then her arm, and draped it over a dish drying rack. The handkerchief was important to him, and she wanted to make sure she returned it washed and ironed.

She'd asked him to talk about what had happened in the alley, but he'd refused to explain. While frustrated, she also got it. It'd been a long, physically demanding day. She needed sleep, but her mind wouldn't shut down.

The revelations from Hugh and Samantha had shifted something inside her. At first, she'd been shocked and suspicious because of all of the lies. But after seeing Nate experience a flashback in the alley and then learning about Remiel, she'd made a decision. She was going to help Nate.

She just had no idea how.

She poured hot water over her tea bag and breathed in the scent of lavender essential oil heating in the diffuser. Her burn salve was on the table. Her herbal remedies had given her father some relief, and she hoped they'd do the same for Nate.

Her plan was more emotional and less physical because she wasn't the type to fall into bed with every hot man she met. Not that she met many. And none of them as handsome as Nate. Her problem with men was she had no idea what she wanted or how to go after it.

She added honey to the teacup and stirred. The infusion darkened the water. Maybe her problem was that she'd never met the right kind of man. A generous, patient, strong, incredibly hot, and handsome man…

"Sarah?"

She turned and dropped the spoon on the floor. She'd shut off all the lamps except one, yet it wasn't enough to hide Nate. He stood a few feet away, almost naked. And by *almost* she meant he only wore black sweatpants. The rest of his incredibly hardcore body was unclothed. She'd seen him earlier that day in the gym and when she'd put salve on his arms. But things were different now. The scars, gouges, burns, and bruises carried a darker meaning.

Samantha had mentioned he'd been tortured. Yet, until this moment, Sarah hadn't fully comprehended what that meant. She picked up the spoon and dropped it into the sink. "Your tea will be ready in a moment."

"Take your time. *Really.*"

She smiled and handed him a mug. "I can add extra honey. Augustus would only drink it with four spoonfuls."

"I don't need *any* honey." Nate frowned into the cup. "I bet Augustus was short, too."

She chuckled and put the honey away. "Augustus was almost my height."

"Five-seven?"

"Five-six." Now *that* made him smile.

"No wonder your father hated him." Nate wrinkled his nose. "I also smell lavender."

She pointed to the glass tray over a votive candle. "Essential oil. I asked Samantha to pack it. I'm diffusing it into the air, and it should help with your headaches. Now drink your tea."

He tasted the tea until he started coughing.

"You should drink four cups a day." She turned away so he wouldn't see her smile. "Augustus drank three."

Nate threw his head back and downed it. "Done." He put the cup down with a "*blech.*"

"It's not that bad." While rinsing his cup, she added, "You'll see a difference in a few days."

His face drained of color, and she realized what she'd said. But since he hadn't told her about where he was going, she wasn't sure if she should bring it up. "Nate—"

"It's okay, Sarah. Whatever you were going to say, it's okay."

She spun around and gripped the counter's edge behind her. "I know you're leaving on Sunday. Samantha told me you're returning to that prison hospital."

"She shouldn't have said anything." He shoved his hands in his pockets. But the movement couldn't hide his sudden reaction. His erection tented the fleece. He didn't apologize or turn away. But he wouldn't look at her either.

The blush started in her toes and rose to her forehead. Her entire body was on fire.

"It's almost midnight." He nodded toward the spare bedroom. "We...I...should probably get to bed."

That *sooooooo* didn't help. While she wasn't ready to throw down with him on the sheets, she was too restless to sleep. Samantha's request also haunted Sarah's mind. Maybe she *should* open up to him more, offer him that sense of connection Samantha believed he'd need. "Would you like me to put some more salve on your arms?"

He swallowed. The muscles in his neck contracted, and she couldn't help herself. She allowed herself to visually memorize him. He was so beautiful it caused an ache in her lower stomach. The fact that he had to return to the prison hospital had become a physically painful reality. If she was reacting this way, she couldn't imagine the hell he suffered.

"Come on." She took his hand and led him to a chair near the couch. Once he was seated, she turned off the last lamp. The only light, from the gas lamp in the courtyard outside, draped the room in shadows. She grabbed a dish towel and the salve container from the table and knelt next to him. He closed his eyes and laid his head back in surrender.

She tried not to stare at his chiseled chest. Was there such a thing as eight-pack abs? Or a ten-pack? Exhaling slowly, she took out a fingerful of salve, held the wrist of the closest arm, and gently rubbed the salve into his healing skin. "I hope my hands aren't too cold."

"It feels nice. I'm always hot."

She focused on dabbing salve on his arms and working it in. Most of his arm had new skin that wasn't as red as it'd looked earlier. As she moved up, toward his bicep, the muscles beneath his skin contracted. She used a rhythmic touch to make sure she didn't miss any spots. Once at his shoulder, she used a firmer touch. The skin looked healthier, if a bit more scarred, and the muscles were bunched in knots. She just didn't want to hurt him.

"You're not hurting me."

He could read her mind? She was surprised to see his green eyes open and focused on her. "Your skin…it's healing."

"That salve feels nice."

"I'm glad. Do you want me to do the other arm?"

"Please." He swallowed. "I saw that recipe box. Was that your grandmother's?"

"And my mom's. It's where they kept all of Anne Capel's recipes they could find." Sarah couldn't stop staring at his lips. They were moist and red and partly open as if struggling to breathe. "Nate—" She hesitated, then forged ahead. "What happened to your parents?"

He closed his eyes. "Car ran off the road during an ice storm. My sister and I survived, but my parents didn't. We lived with my uncle…until we ran away. She was eighteen, and I was seventeen. I ended up at UNC Chapel Hill on an ROTC scholarship. I was lucky."

Lucky? That's the last word she'd use to describe his life. And she was sure there were other things that he'd left out. "Was your uncle kind?"

"He was an alcoholic who liked to collect hunting knives and terrorize children." Nate stated the sentence clearly, without emotion, but his lips had tightened and the scar on his cheek looked deeper. She could only imagine what kind of home he'd had until he'd gone to college and joined the army. She also realized that Nate hadn't had a real home since his parents' death.

"You have a sister?" For some reason, she'd believed he was an only child.

"She lives in North Carolina, near Asheville." He opened his eyes, and his gaze found Sarah's mouth. Her breath shortened. "My sister attempted suicide ten years ago. She's been in a mental health facility ever since."

She blinked away the blurriness. Nate had survived a traumatic loss at a young age. No wonder he was always trying to protect everyone.

"Nate." Her words got caught in her throat and it hurt to speak. "I'm sorry."

"I've never seen your hair down. It's beautiful." One hand was on hers, the other played with tendrils that framed her face. "Now it's your turn."

She kept her hands and her focus on Nate's other arm. Otherwise she might cry. "I lost my mother when I was sixteen and she was thirty-two. She used to call me her *soul's joy*. After her death, my father became chief of police, working horrible hours, and I immersed myself in school. Since finishing my graduate degrees, I've worked to make a name for myself in a small, competitive field."

She paused to get another dab of salve and continued on his other bicep. "Then my father's scandal and my betrayal by my colleagues ripped our lives apart." She finished his arm and wiped her hands on a dish towel. Unable to stop touching him, she sat on the chair's arm and held his hand to her cheek. "Why is everything so complicated?"

"You mean why couldn't we have met under simpler circumstances?"

She nodded.

His thumb traced her bottom lip. "Nothing about our lives has been simple."

"You're probably right." She touched the scar on his cheek, feeling the indentation and hard edges. "Even if we'd met before, we wouldn't have noticed each other."

"Oh, sweetheart." His slow-spreading smile brightened his face. "I would've noticed you. I would've taken you away from that short troll Augustus, and it would've led to an incredible one-night stand. After not being able to stop thinking about each other, we would've started a fabulous few weeks of intense dates, each night ending in wilder and wilder sex."

"Wow." She'd no idea what to say to *that*. "You've been thinking about this." Of course, she had too. It'd been pretty much all she'd been thinking about for the past two weeks. Although her daydreams were probably tamer than his.

He dropped the smile. "Then I would've left without being able to tell you where or why or for how long. Our texts would get shorter and shorter until turning into a conversation between emojis and memes. You'd get tired of waiting or insecure about my feelings and pull away."

"I'd never do that."

"When I returned home, there'd be awkward phone conversations. A meeting for coffee where you received a sudden call and had to leave. One night I'd surprise you at your apartment only to find you with another man. A lawyer you worked with. Or the guy from the third floor. Maybe even your ex."

"I'd never do that to you." She held his face in her palms. "Please tell me no one else did."

"I believe you."

She inhaled until her lungs hurt. What kind of woman would betray a man who'd proved he'd do anything to protect those he loved? The thought made Sarah want to take Pete's dirty fighting class and kill the foolish cows.

Just not right now.

Nate lifted her hair off her shoulders and let it fall down her back. She caressed his face with her thumbs, feeling the day's worth of stubble. He unzipped her sweatshirt and used both hands to slip it off her shoulders. It landed on the floor with a *whoosh* that matched her intake of breath. His fingers trailed the camisole straps from her shoulders down to the scoop neckline. Her rapid breathing caused her breasts to rise and fall. His fingers traced the soft curves above the satin edging, and she trembled under the weight of intense anticipation.

As if knowing she couldn't bear his near-touch any longer, he took one of her hands and kissed her palm before laying it on his chest, over his heart. "The memory of every woman I've ever met pales before you."

She swallowed, her mouth suddenly dry. "Nate—"

He pulled her onto his lap. His arms circled her waist, and her legs hung off the armrest. One of her arms went around his neck, her other hand now rubbing his bare chest. "From the moment I saw you in that garden two weeks ago, what few relationships I've had faded away. I can't remember names or events or circumstances."

His heart beat fast beneath her hand, and he'd been right about his being hot. His skin scorched hers, and she half-expected to be left with third-degree burns. She laid her head on his shoulder and breathed in his scent. He usually smelled like the woods, but now he smelled like honey and beeswax. The contracting muscles beneath her hand emphasized his strength; his rapid breath exposed his uncertainty; his erection beneath her hip betrayed his need.

It'd been so long since she'd been this close to a man she'd forgotten how they tasted and what they smelled like. How wonderfully hard they were. How amazing it felt to be held like she weighed nothing. She kissed his neck.

He gasped. "Sarah." The word rolled off his tongue with a deep drawl. She smiled. His North Carolina accent deepened when he was kissing her. "We need sleep."

"Probably." Still, she refused to move. Refused to give up any contact with him. "Except I'm not tired."

"No?" His hands moved until one held her head and the other trailed her spine and rested on her lower back.

She shivered and pressed in closer. "No." She kissed his neck again. His arms tightened, then he groaned. "Nate?"

"Hmm?" His eyes were closed, and his hand moved in circles, similar to the rhythm she'd used on his arms. His erection shifted beneath her, making itself known in case she hadn't noticed.

She kissed his chin. "It's been a long time."

He opened his eyes and held her head so close their lips brushed. "For me too."

She inhaled his scent and let her lips rest on his. "I don't want to wait anymore."

Her hair surrounded them in a world all of their own. In a world where it was the two of them with no drama, conflict, or secrets. No one threatening to tear them apart. Threatening to separate them with opposite goals and cross-purposes. "Are you sure?"

She scrambled off his lap and yanked her camisole over her head, giving him his answer: "Yes, Nate. I'm sure."

CHAPTER 26

NATE STOOD IN FRONT OF THE BEAUTIFUL WOMAN. HE DIDN'T care that his sweatpants did nothing to hide his arousal. He'd rather she understood what she was agreeing to: the moment they started this, there'd be no turning back.

He ran his hands over his head, uncertain and trembling. He'd kept his hair tied, but hers hung in waves over her shoulders, brown curls caressing the curves of her pale breasts and rosy tips. He breathed in the lavender-scented air and attempted to control his rapid breathing. Lightning brightened the room for a second, followed by thunder. Despite the AC humming, moisture tinged the air, blurring the edges, lessening the stark reality of the hellish day.

He fisted his hands against his thighs, conflicted about what he was about to do. He'd be leaving her in less than two days, returning to a world where he only half-existed, where his life wasn't his own and his nightmares were real. Yet he couldn't leave without making love to her. He couldn't leave without making her his.

The problem was it'd been years since he'd been with a woman, and he was terrified of hurting her. He could barely handle his aggression in the fighting ring. How was he to do this without losing control?

"Nate?" She drew back her hair until silky waves hung over her shoulders. "Come to me."

"I want to." The husky words sounded lame, like a boy on his first time. The irony was there'd once been a time when he couldn't—or wouldn't—have gone a week without sex. But that was a different man in a different lifetime.

She hooked her thumbs in her pajama bottoms and slowly drew them down, stopping at the lower curve of her hip bones. Sweat broke out on his face, his neck. Hell, his whole body was about to immolate. Still, he hesitated.

He was a selfish bastard. He *needed* Sarah's complete acceptance. He *needed* her to be his. He *needed* her to understand the violence he was capable of and still want him. It would be a gift more precious than he'd ever hoped for.

She lowered her pants even more, until they were on the floor and she was naked. Her hooded eyes dared him. Her full breasts strained for his touch, her long hair mussed around her shoulders. Perfectly rounded hips and long legs that framed the part of her that made her a woman. A goddess illuminated by flashes of lightning.

OhGodOhGodOhGodOhGodOhGodOhGod.

He moved until her breasts touched his chest. Everything became hazy. Except for her lips. He lowered his head to meet hers. Her sweetness shattered his fragile self-control, and heat exploded through his body. He plunged his hands into the silky tangles of her hair and held her head steady so his mouth could caress and plunder. His tongue demanded entrance, seeking surrender.

Her soft sigh made his arousal jump. Need became an all-consuming thought, a driving force that required one thing. *Sarah.* A hand kept her head captive while the other claimed a soft, swollen breast. He almost cried out at the smooth warmth. He'd forgotten the taste and feel of a woman's skin.

But his body hadn't. It demanded a satisfaction that foreplay wouldn't achieve. With a low growl, his fingers plucked harder at the taut nipple, bringing cries of pleasure. He left her lips to trail his tongue across the upper curves of her breast, and his hand reached lower. Grasping her ass, he held her closer.

She rubbed against him, holding her breast, offering it to him. He took the sweet nub into his mouth, and she shuddered. He forced her to the wall. His body kept her still while his fingers plunged inside her. Her readiness humbled him. She'd been thinking about this as well, wanted him like he wanted her, even after everything she'd learned about him.

That truth made him want to fall on his knees and worship her forever with whatever parts of him she'd take.

His thumb rubbed her most sensitive spot, and she rode his fingers as her own hands worked their way over his tight nipples. Her nails ran through the light hair on his chest, down to the bulge in his pants. He hissed at the unbelievable sensation and slammed both palms on the wall, trapping her. When she slipped the sweatpants off his hips, he stepped out of them.

She clutched his hard length while her tongue darted over his nipples. Her hands began the most sensual massage he'd ever experienced. The slow movement up with a slight twist over the head might have been uncomfortable if the pleasure of it hadn't been so incredible. He didn't want gentleness or soft hands, and he had to stop her or he'd lose control.

With one swift motion, he grabbed her ass and lifted her higher. She gasped and gripped his shoulders. His forehead met hers as he shifted his erection to her moist entrance. "Sarah." The word was ragged, forced.

Her lips were swollen and red. Her breath sounded choppy, as if she couldn't get enough air. Her brown gaze met his, and he began to enter her—until he stopped. The pause almost killed him, but he wanted her to know who was making love to her, who possessed her.

"Say my name." He couldn't remember the last time anyone had spoken his name during sex.

"Nate." She licked her lips, her eyes half closed. "*Please.*"

Her plea was all he needed. He drove into her with far more force than he'd intended, as deep as she'd take him, and stopped again. His balls were so tight they were going to crush themselves into dust. His arms and legs shook, the muscles spasming. Not because he couldn't hold her weight—she weighed nothing—but because he was suspended in a place of profound pleasure he might never find again.

"Nate." Her whisper brushed over his neck where she was gently nibbling. "It's okay."

Those weren't the words he was expecting, but they were the words he needed to hear. He didn't want to screw her into oblivion and then leave her. He didn't want to break her heart. He didn't want her to move on and live a life with another man. He was a selfish bastard who was sure of only one thing: loving her was going to ruin him.

He pulled out for the sole purpose of driving into her again. She moaned, and he began a pistoning motion that increased in speed. She was so tight, so perfect, so beautiful. He found her lips and kissed her fiercely, in a way he'd never kissed any other. He wanted to make sure she'd always remember him, always compare him to any other lovers she might have.

She drew the tie out of his hair and let it fall down around his face. Her fingers tangled in the strands, and she set the pace of the kiss. She gentled it, nipping and licking his lips. "Nate…" She tightened her legs around his hips and squeezed him.

He almost lost his mind. He moved his hands to her hips and spread his legs to widen hers so he could pound into her harder, faster, deeper. She arched her back, and he lightly bit her neck. If she wanted more, he'd give it to her.

He found her breast and sucked on a nipple, then the other, until they were tight nubs. The moment she screamed his name again, he let out a feral growl. He gripped her waist and lifted her up and down over and over again until the pressure in his balls was too much to bear. The tightening started low and built and built and built until he used his next three strokes to release himself inside her. It took another four strokes to realize he'd given her everything he had. And another five before he was able to stop.

With their foreheads touching, he fought to get his

breathing under control. His chest rose and fell, but he still couldn't get enough air. Still couldn't take in enough of her scent, that unforgettable mix of gardenias and satiated woman. *His satiated woman.*

They were both covered in sweat, still bound together because he was still semi-erect and still inside her, unable to leave her.

"*Nate.*" His name fell off her lips with an intensity he'd never heard before. "Don't leave me. I'll be lost forever." The aching in her voice broke something inside of him, leaving him raw and vulnerable and more uncertain than he'd ever been in his adult life.

He gently disengaged himself and let her feet touch the floor. Before she could wrap her arms around him, he swung her into his arms and carried her to the master bedroom. Now it was time to make love to her.

Sarah couldn't stop trembling. Her body shook like her central nervous system had packed up, abandoned post, and left town. Nate carried her to the bedroom and laid her on the king-size bed. The AC in the room chilled the sweat on her skin, forming goosebumps on her stomach and arms. Nate placed a light blanket over her and kissed her again. It was both gentle and firm with promises of more.

She hadn't been lying when she'd told him it'd been a long time since she'd had sex. But, honestly, it wouldn't have mattered when the last time was because no man had ever made love to her like Nate had. No one had ever brought her such physical pleasure.

He nipped her nose. "I'll be right back." He left the room only to return a moment later with tealight candles in glass votives and matches. Still naked, he lit the candles and placed them on the bureau and nightstands until the room was filled with the scent of lemongrass and the lingering diffused lavender oil. As he moved, the shimmering light skimmed over his hard body, highlighting every ripple and curve. Her stomach clenched and her toes curled.

Then he disappeared again.

She sat, drawing the blanket to her breasts. It wasn't that she was being modest, she was just…uncertain. Had he enjoyed it? He'd seemed to. Yet she couldn't help but notice, as he'd lit the candles, the sweat on his upper body outlined corded muscles whipped over bone and that he'd been erect again.

Thunder clapped and lightning flashed. The rain hit sudden and hard, pounding the roof and window. Using a pillow, she propped herself against the headboard and stared outside. A black willow tree stood between the courtyard's gas lamp and the window, casting eerie silhouettes around the walls. *Where was he?*

She heard a door open and then shut. *Had he left?* She started to rise when he returned with his gun and her salve. "Did you go outside?"

"I was checking the locks." He placed the gun on the nightstand on the other side of the bed. "I didn't hurt you, did I?"

She clutched the blanket high, unsure what to do or say. He seemed to be even more aroused than he had been, and a warm heat contracted in her lower stomach. She shifted her legs and used the blanket to hide the swelling of her breasts. "You could never hurt me."

He stared at her, still holding the salve. The candlelight emphasized his perfect, naked form. His blond hair hung long and wild, almost touching his shoulders. Wide, muscled chest, that beautiful V leading to hips and thighs that easily held her aloft. Long, lean legs that had pushed hers apart and now made her blush.

The only things she had trouble looking at were the scars.

"I may have left bruises on your waist and your breasts. May I see?"

She doubted it, but he seemed so concerned she lowered the blanket until it pooled around her hips. "I'm fine."

"Lie down." He opened the salve jar and placed it on her bedside table, and then he smiled. "It won't hurt."

Her head hit the softest pillow ever. The blanket still covered her stomach and legs, but her nipples tightened because the AC compressor had just kicked on again, pushing a gust of cold air into the room. "Really. I think—"

His fingers brushed across one nipple, then the other, and she arched her back. With salve on his fingers, he began a gentle massage of her breasts. Everywhere he'd touched earlier now received attention. "I'm sorry if I leave bruises."

Leave. Not *left.* As in, there might be more? His hands became more confident with their touch and the feel of the cream. And she couldn't remember the last time she'd given up this much control to anyone.

"Stretch out your arms."

She obeyed. Each one of his hands had one of her breasts, kneading and caressing just enough to begin the rising cycle of desire all over again. Then he massaged her arms, shoulders, and rib cage.

"Lower the blanket."

She opened her eyes. He sat on the edge of the bed, staring at her with those intense green eyes. She could even see a small tic above his eye. Her gaze trailed lower, and she saw one hand had salve on the fingertips, while his other… gripped his arousal.

She lowered the blanket. Not all the way, just enough to tease him. "You said you were worried about my stomach and breasts."

"I did." Swallowing hard, he let go of himself and used both hands to massage cream from her ribs to her waist. He swept his fingers around her rib cage and then down to her belly button.

Another fire built inside her; this time the flame was stronger and steadier. He moved slowly as he watched her squirm. Yes, she *was* squirming. The one thing she wouldn't do was scissor her legs to relieve the pressure. He'd started this. It was his to finish.

Finally, his fingers reached the edge of the blanket. "Roll over."

She licked her lips and did as he asked. The blanket shifted, exposing her bottom but still keeping her calves covered. He gently spread her legs before running his hands along her back and rib cage, teasing the sides of her breasts squished on the mattress. He traced her spine up and down, but each time he went down, his fingers went lower.

Just when his fingers teased between her thighs, he shifted until she felt him on top of her, his thighs over hers, one hand planted near her head supporting himself while his free hand ran from her neck down to her most sensitive part. His erection pushed against her bottom while his fingers brushed between her legs in a constant, teasing rhythm. She arched her hips until he placed a palm on her spine. "Not yet, sweetheart."

She nodded, welcoming his weight.

He kissed her neck and lowered himself on top of her. "Am I too heavy?"

"Never," she said in a voice muffled by pillows.

He lifted his hips slightly. "Spread your legs."

She did. And his arousal pushed into her gently, as if waiting to be invited. She really, really wanted to arch her hips, but she waited. He was kissing her back, her neck, brushing away her hair to nuzzle beneath her ear. He raised his body slightly and placed his hands on either side of her breasts.

"Sarah, do you want me?"

She moaned into the pillow, unable to form the words. His erection seemed much larger than before, and it had seemed huge at the time.

"I wanted to go slowly this time." He laughed low, as if to himself. "But that's not going to happen."

Barely a breath later, he lifted her hips and drove into

her so hard her head hit the headboard. He rode her like a man running for his freedom. She heard his gasps, and when she twisted to see his face all she saw were his closed eyes and bared teeth and long hair. He was like a wild man in a trance as he drove into her, pushing himself deeper and deeper until touching her womb.

Every muscle inside her contracted. He filled her until there was no room left, no question remaining as to whom she belonged. Without losing speed or tempo, he lowered himself on top of her, reaching beneath her chest with both hands to hold her breasts. She was caught between his hands and his full weight on top of her, and the intensity was almost too much to bear. She cried out into the pillow and tasted salt, only to realize she was crying, not from sadness but from the absolute pleasure she felt with him on top of her, with him inside her.

He squeezed her breasts and shifted his body lower to spread her legs even more. He drove, she met, and when the pleasure became too intense, she burst into a million flames.

He thrust into her at least half a dozen more times, maybe more, but she welcomed it as another wave of pleasure swept over her. By the time he cried out her name, she was riding a final wave herself. He collapsed on top of her, and she didn't move. She wanted this perfect moment to last forever. She didn't want him to withdraw. She didn't want him to leave. She didn't want him to go to that prison hospital somewhere in Maine.

She didn't want to lose him because she loved him.

And because she loved him, that meant there was only one thing to do. Even if she had to take on gunrunners, Green Berets, a bitchy senator, and the entire Fianna army. Whether any of them wanted her to or not, she was going to solve that cipher and trade it for Nate's life. She was going to defend the man she loved. She was going to save Nate Walker.

CHAPTER 27

THANK GOD THE RAIN HAD STOPPED.

Etienne shoved his hands in the pockets of his hunting jacket and waited behind the old service station not far from Iron Rack's Gym. It was after two a.m., dark as the horse-shit that littered the roads of the historic district, and Leroy hadn't showed.

Etienne couldn't believe he'd been so fucking stupid as to lose his fucking phone. After leaving the *Brigid*, he'd torn apart his room in the skeevy motel down by the river but had found nothing.

He'd made his way here, to the meet-up place, hoping everything would work out. The Russian wasn't much for texting, his directions always spare and vague. Etienne had hoped to arrive first—as directed—and finalize the details of the deal before they ran out of time. The midsummer tides were changing, and there'd been unexpected rain. That meant the new hide site would be flooded by Sunday morning. Weapons and water didn't get along.

He walked the perimeter of the station, avoiding the areas lit by the anemic streetlamp across the road. The traffic light on the corner changed, and a flash of red crossed his path. The old asphalt was broken and pitted with weeds and roots from nearby oak trees trying to reclaim the property. Gravel and glass crunched beneath his boots as he walked the area one more time.

He returned to the shed on the back of the lot. A graffiti tag of a skeletal hand clasping a cutlass had been painted on the side, *sans pitié* written below. Calum Prioleau's sigil was almost hidden by overgrown vines. If one didn't know it was there, one would never find it. This was where he'd been ordered to wait, yet it was forty-five minutes past meet-up time.

He'd been sure about the time and place, which meant that Leroy had changed the plan. Probably sending a text that Etienne couldn't receive and would never get. Bile roughed up his throat, and he scraped his fingernails over his head, grabbing his hair until the pain made him stop. *What am I going to do now?*

He couldn't return to Remiel. Etienne's death by Remiel's hand would be as emotionally and psychologically painful as it would be physical. Leroy wasn't known for his warmth and mercy either. Etienne was truly fucked.

Drunk laughter came from the alley across the street. Beneath the streetlight, the pair of homeless addicts were jostling each other until one smashed a bottle. Etienne had no idea how those two acquired alcohol or drugs or their clothes. They had nothing. They were nothing. The only explanation was that Antoine, the low-level punk who ran the street, provided for them.

Antoine. Etienne chewed the inside of his cheek. *Of course.*

He sucked in the humid night air and headed for Screamin' Perks. Someone at the coffee shop would know how to contact Antoine. Antoine would, in return for cash, help Etienne find Leroy. Wasn't a perfect plan. But it was better than being dead.

A soft buzzing woke Nate out of a deep sleep. He rolled over to grab his phone only to find mountains of pillows and blankets. His body ached as if he'd been stretched on a rack, yet it wasn't the same kind of pain he suffered after a seizure. This current pain felt good, as if he'd been doing the hard, physical work it took to wear out a man's mind and body.

He sat and reoriented himself. The candles had burned out, and the only light came from the courtyard. He reached for the chain with his medal. When he didn't find it, he pulled his long hair behind his neck with two hands. It took him a moment to remember where he was…and what he'd been doing. Correction: what he and Sarah had been doing.

Sarah. He closed his eyes. *Daaaaaaamn*. As the night replayed in his head, he prayed he hadn't hurt her. Or overwhelmed her. Or sent her running away.

He'd no money or job or honor. His courtesy was the only thing he could offer her. So why was it when he took her in his arms, he turned into a sexually demanding brute? That's not how a man treated the woman he loved. *Loved*. When had he fallen in love with her? That day in the garden of the Savannah Preservation Office? The night he'd kissed her for the first time? He'd no idea. It felt like he'd been in love with her forever.

His dick, hard and erect, raised the sheet covering his hips. He chuckled. Just thinking about Sarah had awoken *both* of them, and *both* of them were ready to go again.

What they'd done…he'd been wrong about it ruining him. Falling in love with her was going to *break* him. There was no way he was going to be able to return to that prison hospital in Maine unless medicated into oblivion and surrounded by armed guards.

She was buried beneath blankets and pillows, her hair spread out with curls caressing his chest. The AC worked too well, and water condensed on the windows, chilling the room even more.

The phone buzzed again. He found it on the nightstand between his gun and a rubber band. After tying his hair with the band, he answered, "Luke? What's wrong?"

"It's not Luke."

Nate stared at the eerie shadows of branches and leaves on the walls. "Jack?"

"Yep." Jack Keeley laughed in that self-deprecating way Nate remembered. "It's me."

Nate covered his eyes with his free hand. "Where are you?"

"In isolation with a bounty on my head. And I just spoke to the Prince."

"*How?*"

"Smuggled cell phone. Long story." Jack muttered a curse. "The Prince told me the bounty would be lifted if you don't solve some cipher. That cipher—whatever it is—can't be solved, or some end-of-the-world shit is going to happen."

Nate jacked his body up and kept his voice low. "It's an unsolved pirate cipher possibly used during the Revolutionary War."

Jack's laugh sounded like a bark. "Awesome. Although I'm unsure what this has to do with our men, both in and out of prison."

"That's what I'm trying to figure out." Nate scrubbed his eyes with a thumb and finger like he was digging for diamonds. "Somehow we ended up in a war between Remiel Marigny and the Fianna. Remiel wants that cipher solved, the Prince doesn't."

"What the fuck does Remiel have to do with this? I thought he was dead!"

"He's alive." Nate laid a hand on Sarah's blanket-covered hip. "Pete and I learned that Remiel is the master-mind behind not just our setup and imprisonments but also the Wakhan Corridor Massacre. He's the one responsible for this entire nightmare."

"I don't believe it. The Prince has the money and trained men for a sophisticated operation. Remiel is a low-level gunrunner who couldn't strike a deal with a scout troop."

"It's still true."

"We heard the rest of the unit was dishonorably discharged. Something about a secret congressional committee."

"They were all dishonorably discharged. Most are living in Savannah and are busy setting up the new command post." Hell of an understatement. "Now Kells is gone, and I don't know where he is."

"Interesting." Jack paused, and Nate pictured him sitting,

head against the wall, tapping his fingers on the concrete floor. "Wasn't Alex Mitchell, that Army Ranger buddy of yours, convicted of Remiel's murder?"

"Yes. Although I'm not sure if Remiel's living status is known to the rest of the world."

"Kells knows. Earlier tonight, Kells was here, and when he left, he took Alex."

Nate got out of bed, padded into the main room, and found his sweatpants. He needed to pace to think, and the air was freezing his balls off. "Kells was at Leedsville?" Keeping the phone between his chin and shoulder, he tugged on the fleece. "And he got Alex released?"

"Oh, yeah."

Why wouldn't Kells tell me? Nate walked the room, moving between the window seat on one end and the kitchen on the other. His bare feet left damp imprints on the cold wood floor. "Did you talk to Kells?"

"Nope. And he made no effort to contact me."

Nate noticed his handkerchief on the drying rack near the sink. Sarah must've done that. "Kells is protecting you."

"Probably." Although from Jack's dejected voice, the word sounded more like a *maybe.*

Nate started another lap around the room. Would Kells bring Alex to the gym? The men all knew Alex, and no one liked him. Except for maybe Zack. Alex and Zack, along with Nate, had gone through Ranger School together.

He inhaled sharply. He'd just remembered... "Jack, Kells *is* protecting you. I can't tell you why because I made a promise, but I'm sure of it. Kells needs Alex as leverage in this war with Remiel and the Prince. Kells got Alex out before the Prince could."

"Why would the Prince care about Alex?"

"Trust me on this. The Prince cares. A lot."

Jack sighed. "Alright."

"I'm doing everything I can, bro. I'm going to make this right."

"Don't solve that cipher." Jack snorted. "I'm not even sure how one would do that."

"Jack, do you remember a man in the POW camp named Fletcher Ames?"

"That fucker was the camp's lead torturer. You spent more time with him than anyone else. He'd take you away, and we wouldn't see you for days. Sometimes weeks. He even took your medal. Do you remember that?"

Nate reached for the chain around his neck, then dropped his hand. "No." He stopped at the window seat overlooking the courtyard and closed his eyes. Maybe it was a good thing his memory was shit. "Will you tell the rest of the men in prison about Remiel? Or Alex's release?"

"Eventually."

"They've a right to know. They may know something about Remiel that could help us."

"It's too late for that."

Nate sat and pressed his forehead on the cold glass. "It's never too late."

"I have to go, brother, but if you uncover any memories, make them about what you were and who you are. And, for fuck's sake, remember who trained you." The phone went dead.

Nate stared out the window, but in his mind's eye he saw himself in a dirty cell, naked and bruised, fingers dislocated and swollen. Since they were images unattached to emotions, it was like watching a movie.

After another thirty minutes of reviewing horrible, silent memories, his phone buzzed, and he checked the text. From Cassio.

> If your intentions do not affect the outcome
> in this matter, sacrifices will be made and
> you will suffer the cost. You will be the one
> to be lost.

Nate wanted to throw his phone. Instead he glanced out the window. Near the light that illuminated the fountain, Cassio stood in the shadows. In one elegant move, he wrapped his arm across his waist and bowed.

CHAPTER 28

"ARE YOU ALRIGHT?" SARAH'S SOFT VOICE MADE HIM TURN. She stood there with the blanket wrapped around her breasts. She'd tied it off to the side, and it hung to the floor. Her long hair was tossed around her shoulders, and even in the dim light he could see her lips were still swollen. "I woke up and thought I was lost. That you'd left me."

His pulse ratcheted up into heart attack territory. She was the most beautiful woman he'd ever seen. He strode over and took her face in his hands. "I'd never leave you if I didn't have to."

"Nate." She touched a strand of his hair that had fallen forward. "We have to solve the cipher, and I have an idea that could save us both."

He moved one hand behind her neck and held her still. He kissed her the way he wanted to, the way he'd dream of kissing her once he was in the prison hospital. His lips caressed hers, his tongue demanded entry, and he set a rhythm he wanted her to remember.

"Nate, we—"

He picked her up with one arm around her waist, the other still holding her head for more kisses. It only took him a few steps to press her against the wall near the window seat, his lips on hers. He wanted as much light as he could get without turning on the lamps. Harsh lamplight meant daytime and reality and leavings. Filtered courtyard light meant dreams and promises and stayings.

It was a choice of *possibilities* instead of *inevitabilities*.

Just like earlier, he used his physical size to keep her in place. But unlike earlier, she wasn't undressed completely. He found where the blanket parted and caressed her bare hip. The skin was so smooth it made his own feel rough.

His other hand hit the wall for leverage. A few kisses later, he lifted his head. Her eyes were hooded, and her arms wrapped around his neck.

"Sarah, kiss me the way I kissed you."

She raised herself up on her toes, clutched his shoulders, and took over the kissing. Very quickly, she picked up the rhythm he'd set, with her tongue playing with his. Meanwhile, both of his hands found the insides of her thighs. He trailed his fingers up until they barely met in the center, then down again. She trembled, and her kisses halted. Her breathing was so rapid her breasts threatened to break free from the blanket tucked around her.

His body tightened. Would he ever get enough of her? "Do you want me to continue?"

She nodded.

"Then kiss me."

She blinked before tightening her arms around his neck and meeting his lips again. Now he used the back of his hands to explore the soft skin of her inner thighs. He brushed up and down. When he was sure she was ready, he lifted his head.

"What are you doing?" she asked harshly.

Her hair hung around her face, a veil of brown silk he wanted to feel spread across his body. He was torn. He was committed to fulfilling this fantasy, yet he wanted to take her to bed so she could ride him until they were both drained.

"You'll see." Keeping his gaze on hers, he knelt.

Her eyes widened, and he heard her breath hitch. The blanket was open enough for him to see her soft stomach, her gorgeous legs, and everything in between. He gently spread her legs and lifted one until it draped over his shoulder. He used his palms on the inside of her thighs to keep her still while his thumbs caressed the tender skin.

His lips took over the motion of his hands, and he kissed and nipped his way along both sides. Her soft sounds made him even more confident, and he increased the speed and pressure. When his tongue entered her center, her hands clawed the wall. A guttural cry ripped from her throat. Her hips bucked, and he positioned them at the perfect angle. He licked and suckled and drew her into him. He explored every part of her, using the same rhythm with which he'd kissed her. The same rhythm with which she'd kissed him.

His goal was to bring her to a climax she'd never forget.

No, his real goal was to ensure she'd never forget what they'd shared. He wasn't a tender lover. He was a selfish bastard. He wasn't going to let her forget him. He wasn't going to let her solve that cipher. He was going to leave. And all of it was going to kill him.

But for now, his mouth was fucking her, and she tasted like strawberries. The very fact she was letting him do this made him want to conquer the world and offer it all to her. He felt her body tighten and increased the action and speed until she gripped his head and screamed his name.

When she collapsed, he used his strength to help her sink to the floor. She ended up on his lap, the blanket still tied around her breasts but the rest of her body open to him. She wrapped her arms around his chest and tucked her head beneath his chin. Every breath had a ragged edge, and she shivered.

He shifted until he found the wall and imprisoned her against his heart. His erection jumped beneath her hip, and he ignored the pressure in his balls. The risk to his dick wasn't as important as the risk to his heart. One of his greatest fears was that once he got back to the prison hospital and they drugged him up, he'd forget everything. He'd forget Sarah.

Closing his eyes, he made a pact with God. He'd do whatever was necessary, including sacrifice his freedom and/or life, to keep her and his men safe. He'd lie, cheat, steal, kill, and die, but he wanted one thing in return: he wanted to remember this moment.

He wanted to remember Sarah forever.

Sarah trembled with aftershocks and was grateful for Nate's arms around her. But while he'd more than satisfied her, she could still feel his need beneath her hip. "Nate?"

"Hmm?"

"Don't move." She untied the blanket and tossed it aside. Moving quickly, she straddled him, his sweatpants the only thing separating them.

He opened his eyes, and she put one finger on his lips. "Shh." Using her other hand, she gently lowered the waistband of his pants until his erection sprang free. After kissing his jaw, his cheek, and eventually his mouth, she rose and lowered, taking all of him inside her.

His length filled her completely, and she tossed her hair over her shoulders. The curls almost reached her hips. A fire built within her lower stomach, and she ached for his hands around her waist to drive her up and down. Ached for his rough breath on her neck as he pistoned into her. But she had something else in mind.

"Sarah." Her name edged with his North Carolina drawl sounded like a prayer, maybe even a confession.

She tilted forward, keeping her motions slow and short, rocking more than riding. His breaths turned into short, hot puffs, and when he touched her breasts, she took his hands and placed them on the floor, palms down. Then her fingers traced the random scars on his chest partially hidden by the light hair.

His swallow made his body jump, but she touched his hot skin, feeling his heart bang around. "No." She nipped his nose. It was her turn to give orders. "Don't move."

Braced on his hands, his forearm muscles bulged with the effort to keep his body still while she increased the tempo of her tight rocking movements. The pressure built low in her womb, and she contracted around him. He hissed, "Sarah."

She gripped his shoulders and lengthened her strokes, desperate for relief. When his hands found her waist to take over the rhythm, she gave in to his strength. His own need for relief apparent from his lifting and slamming her down again, from his deep, guttural growls, from the way he threw back his head and arched his hips. The moment he convulsed and emptied himself, an intense explosion of pleasure left her shaky, breathless, and exhausted.

She fell onto him, barely remembering him kissing her head, picking her up, or tucking her into bed, him around her. The only thing she did remember was wishing they could stay like this forever.

At four thirty a.m. Sarah double-checked the clock on the microwave. She sat on the apartment floor surrounded by photographs, the ledger, and her journal. Colored pens and note cards were thrown about like jimmies on a cupcake.

She drank her chamomile tea and let the hot water burn her throat. She'd woken half an hour ago with a racing heart and a mind that wouldn't shut off. She was so overwhelmed with everything that'd happened, she needed time and space alone while Nate slept.

She closed her eyes. No man in her life had ever made her feel as beautiful and sexy and loved as Nate had. She hadn't known that sex could be so…incredible. Amazing. Sacred. She bit her lower lip. Considering what she'd experienced tonight, she'd been crazy to think she'd known anything about sex.

Yet—and, yes, there was a *yet*—he'd hardly let her touch him. He probably thought she hadn't noticed because what they'd experienced had been *shattering*. But she had. He'd done most of the touching, tasting, and taking, while she'd received the most intense pleasure she'd ever experienced.

How could she have fallen in love with a man who was going to leave her in a day and a half? Her heart broke for both of them, but mostly for Nate. The amount of pain he kept inside was so much larger than the body he inhabited, it amazed her that he could carry it all. Which was why she'd woken up determined to solve the cipher. She was going to use it as leverage against the Prince and Remiel.

It was a dangerous game, and she had to let Hugh Waring know. Not wanting to call this early, she texted him. I've decided to solve that cipher. Do you have any other information that could help? Text or call when you get this.

Her phone buzzed with a call from Hugh. She answered, "Why aren't you asleep?"

"I could ask you the same question." Hugh's voice sounded tight and stressed, similar to her father's when he was on a case.

She also heard ambient noise in the background, including loud male voices. "You're working at this hour?"

"Yes. Are you sure about this, Sarah? It could get dangerous."

"I know. I also know a man from Charleston was murdered in a cemetery where I was taking photos yesterday morning."

"Thank God you're alright." Hugh paused. "That murder is my missing persons case. Sheriff Boudreaux has been handling the investigation. I was supposed to be there later today, but I can't get away. We're having trouble with the Russian mob. You don't know Russian, do you?"

"Only Latin, French, Welsh, and Old Gaelic." She paused for his laugh. "Why are the Russians in Charleston?"

"No idea. I called the hospital to check on your dad. He's been moved out of the ICU?"

"Yes. They won't let me see him, but my lawyer is working on it."

"Who did you retain?"

"Calum Prioleau."

Hugh whistled. "When you go in, you go big."

"I'm hoping to see my dad today."

"Good. Wait. There's something else." Papers shuffled in the background. "My MC sent over more paperwork regarding Nate Walker's prison hospital commitment. A Colonel Jack Keeley accused Walker of the ambush, and Kells Torridan signed the commitment order. According to the prison hospital's paperwork, Walker is still there."

She hit her journal with her red pen. "Can you send me the commitment papers?"

"I'll email them." Hugh paused for more finger tapping. "How do you know Walker?"

"I need to go, Hugh. Thanks for emailing me those documents. I'll text as soon as I have info on the cipher. Bye." She hung up and held the phone to her chest.

A text came in from Hugh. *Be careful and keep in touch.*

She drew up her legs and rested her head on her knees. Did Nate know about Kells's and Jack's betrayals?

"You left the bed." Nate's voice drifted over, and she looked up. He wore his sweatpants, and his hair hung loose. He was bare-chested, and she couldn't help but watch his muscles ripple with each breath in and out.

"I know." She picked up her tea and waved at the mess. "I couldn't sleep."

He squatted and read a few note cards. "What are you doing?"

"Solving the cipher." His eyes darkened, and she scrambled to stand up. "I have an idea. I tried to tell you earlier, but we got, uh"—she licked her lips because his interest had slipped to her breasts—"distracted."

He picked up the ledger and flipped through pages. "You can't solve that cipher."

"I have to." She grabbed his wrist. "We have to. It's the only way to save you."

"It's my job to protect you, not the other way around."

She squeezed his wrist until he put the book down and looked at her. His eyes were weary and bleak. "You're not going back to that prison hospital."

"I'm not letting anyone else get hurt."

She released him. Now they stood a foot apart, her research spread on the floor between them. "You're a soldier, Nate. You know we have to risk everything if we're going to save everything. We're either all in or all out. But we can't play it safe and try to mitigate the damage at the same time. Those scars on your body, the ones you don't talk about, are a witness to that truth."

"You haven't lost everything, Sarah. You've never felt that kind of despair."

"Haven't I? I went all in on my research, and people I trusted used it to betray me. I lost my job, my reputation, everything. And what did I do? I came to Savannah to hide. Now my father is paying the price for my cowardice."

"Are you calling me a coward?"

"No. I'm saying I know what it's like to feel powerless, like a failure. I know I didn't suffer the same way you did, but I understand what it's like to be betrayed and abandoned." She held up the map he'd brought to the SPO weeks ago. The map that was the reason they'd met in the first place. "I'm not losing you or my father. I'm not going to be afraid anymore."

"No." Nate's nose flared. "Because of my recklessness, my arrogance in thinking I knew what was best, ten of my men were tortured for two fucking years."

"I know—"

"And now they're in prison, and one of them has a price on his head because of that cipher." He took the map from her, folded it up, and shoved it in her straw bag. "We're not solving this cipher. We're going to my men, and we'll come up with a plan together."

"We can't trust them."

"What are you talking about?"

She exhaled and ran her hands through her messy hair. It was a mass of tangles from the top of her head to the curls at the ends. "I had a friend of mine do a background check on you."

His hands landed on his hips, and he tilted his head. "You did what?"

"Two weeks ago, after you kissed me in the station, I asked Hugh Waring—"

"That detective from Charleston?"

"My father's old partner, yes." Nate advanced, and she raised a hand. "Hugh has a military contact who told him something."

"What? That I'm a murderer? That I planned and executed the Wakhan Corridor Massacre? That I led my men into an ambush? I know the rumors, Sarah. I'm living the nightmare."

"Did you know that Jack Keeley, your friend who has a price on his head, is the one who accused you of poor decision-making that led to the ambush? That Kells is the witness who signed your prison hospital papers committing you?"

"Bullshit."

She picked up her phone and showed him Hugh's email. "It's true." She softened her voice as Nate read it. He sat on the couch, one hand behind his neck, the other holding the phone. She knelt and gripped his knee. "I'm sorry, Nate. Kells and Jack betrayed you. Remember the envelope the hooded man gave you? The message inside?"

"Don't trust Kells Torridan."

She squeezed his leg. "Now what are we going to do about it?"

CHAPTER 29

NATE RAN A HAND OVER HIS HEAD, NAILS SCRAPING HIS scalp. He hated his long hair and wanted nothing more than to cut it. Except he'd been ordered—by Kells—to keep it long. Even in the prison hospital, it hadn't been cut. Had that been Kells's order as well?

Nate reread the emails, focusing on the signatures at the end of each document. Every step of the way Kells had signed away Nate's honor, reputation, and life.

But why? Kells had been Nate's CO since he'd become a Green Beret. Kells was the strongest commander in all of Special Forces. Everyone knew it, and every man wanted to serve under him. Kells was tougher than most but also fairer than all.

As far as Jack's accusation? Yes, Jack had been there the night of the ambush, but there was no way Jack would've betrayed Nate. They were friends. They were brothers.

"Nate?" Sarah squeezed his knee again. "We've been pitted against each other. Your need to protect versus my need to reveal. Yet if we want to save you, we have to solve this cipher."

"You mean save you, right?" He rose and stepped over her research. "If you solve this cipher, you save your career."

"This isn't about me. This is about your fear that you can't save everyone you love."

He held up her phone. "Everyone I love is only out for themselves or in danger, and I'm not strong enough to save them."

"That's not true." She took the phone and tossed it onto the couch. "I've spent my life studying the sixteenth and seventeenth centuries with their massive societal upheavals and wars. And there are two things I've learned. First, the people we admire in history are never defined by their deeds but by their enemies. The stronger the enemy, the stronger the person must be to succeed."

"Sarah—"

"Second, men of war begin their careers with a moral certitude, a belief that what they're fighting for is true and just. Yet almost all end their careers steeped in cynicism that destroys their souls. Look at the pirate captains and privateers who'd once been proud officers in the British Navy. Look at the Fianna."

His sigh carried the sorrow of the damned. "What does this have to do with me?"

"You became a soldier and, for some reason, the target of an enemy whose stealth, intelligence, and cunning were beyond anything you could've anticipated. Whose machinations landed you in a POW camp, all horrors and tortures included."

He didn't want to talk about this anymore. "It broke me, Sarah. When it was all over, I could barely walk. I had little memory of the years in the camp, and I didn't speak the entire time I was in that prison hospital."

"You're wrong, Nate. You didn't come out broken. You came out more determined than ever to protect and save those you love." She cupped his face with both of her hands. He wanted to moan when her cooler fingers caressed his hot, scratchy skin. Instead, he closed his eyes. "You came out a man of honor. A man worth saving. But to prove it, we need time."

He opened his eyes and took her wrists to lower her hands. "We need my men."

She waved a dismissive hand. "We can't trust them or Kells or Jack."

"Not true." She knew nothing about his men. She wouldn't know what teamwork looked like even if it was featured on the History Channel.

"What's true is that you and your men are being crushed

between two powerful forces. Kells is playing both sides, and we're on our own. We've less than a day and a half to figure out a centuries-old cipher and use it as leverage to save you. Unless you have another idea?"

He sat on the window seat, one leg up, and watched the rain puddle around the courtyard. "Remiel gave me an out, if I help you solve the cipher."

"When you met in the alley?" She sat in front of him. Her rising breasts betrayed her shallow breathing. "Why didn't you tell me?"

"Because it doesn't matter."

She touched his knee and scooted until she sat between his legs. Her hand rested on his chest. "Everything we do matters."

He picked up her hand and kissed the palm. She made a fist, as if saving the kiss for later. "Remiel said that if I help you, he'll protect Jack in prison."

She tilted her head. "Can Remiel do that?"

"I wasn't sure—" Nate shook his head. "But now that I know for sure that Remiel was responsible for taking down two A-teams, I think it's possible."

"How do you know for sure what he did?"

"Tonight, with Remiel, I saw Fletcher Ames, lead torturer in Remiel's POW camp."

She scrambled off to pace the room, arms flying. "Why didn't you tell me this before?"

"Remiel's promises are bullshit." Nate stood and took her shoulders to keep her still. "Remiel would never help me. He's a psychopathic liar who kept me and my men in that POW camp for years. If Kells and the rest of the unit hadn't rescued us, we'd still be there." Nate moved his hands across her collarbone to caress her smooth neck. "The whole thing is a ploy to get me to help you."

She gripped his wrists and whispered, "Or maybe it's a one-upmanship ploy against the Prince. Remember, if we're the pawns, then the real battle is between the Prince and

Remiel and Kells. That means there's a good chance Remiel will keep his word and protect Jack for no other reason than to strike at the Prince. But only if we solve the cipher."

Nate chewed the inside of his cheek. *What if she was right?* She might not know how to work on a team, but she had a talent for assessing situations. He nodded to the colorful notes, journals, and pens on the floor. "Do you have a plan?"

"The beginnings of a plan." She wrapped her arms around her waist, and he wanted nothing more than to take her to bed. To bury all of his pain and stress and worry inside her. To make this all go away.

He sighed. "I'm not going to like it, am I?"

"You're going to be furious." She picked up her papers and stacked them on the couch. "I started my plan earlier this evening. When we were at the hotel, after we saw Rebecca's diary, you went to the bathroom, and I asked Miss Nell to do something for me. And she did."

Oh. Hell. No. "Tell me you didn't."

She picked up the ledger and put it in her straw bag. "I gave Miss Nell my report and asked her to mail it to the granting agency before midnight. It's on its way."

He paced the room. Since the area was small and he was large, he turned every eight steps. He flexed his hands, and his chest heaved in and out. Oh, he was angry. She'd lied to him, done what she wanted, Nate and the rest of his men be damned. Not to mention putting her own life in danger. He watched her pick up note cards and pens. His stubborn, willful historian had disobeyed his orders. "When were you going to tell me this?"

She cleared her throat. "At the club. But then you met Remiel…" She sat on the couch and grasped her knees. "I never had the chance. But it's okay."

"How is any of this okay?" He stopped in front of her, hands on hips. He stared at her hands but wouldn't meet her gaze. He didn't want her to see how betrayed he felt. "Why would you do that knowing how dangerous it was? What do you not understand about Fianna warriors? They're straight-up killers, Sarah. They told you not to."

"No, they told me to stop my research." She stood to face him. "They didn't tell me specifically not to apply for the grant to study the diary. But it's part of my plan. If we can go to Remiel, tell him I need time to win that grant money before solving the cipher—"

"No." Nate started pacing again. "We're not going to Remiel. We're not asking for more time. Even if we knew how to find him, he'd never agree to it."

"How do you know?"

He hit the wall with his fist, and she flinched. His hand left an indentation in the drywall, and now his knuckles ached. "Because I spent years being tortured in his fucking POW camp. Remiel does *not* negotiate."

"Then we'll go with my second plan."

Nate shook out his hand and looked up. "Heaven have mercy."

"We don't need mercy." She spoke with such matter-of-factness that he almost believed her. "We need luck. We're going to go to the auction and steal my diary."

He threw himself in the armchair. "The one that's surrounded by guards and alarms?" He snorted. "With U.S. senators in attendance? That's a great plan."

"Sarcasm noted." She picked up her colored pens and added them to her bag. "The diary is my best clue to solving the cipher."

"I thought it was unreadable. Hence applying for the grant?"

"It was unreadable because I didn't want to touch it without restoring it. I didn't have the money or equipment or proper conditions to study it." She threw a small journal into her bag. "Now I'm going to tear those diary pages apart and hope we can find clues to help us."

This idea was insane, and they were on a course destined for epic failure. By attempting to solve the cipher, they were putting themselves in the middle of a war between the Prince, Remiel, and possibly Kells. No way was this going to end well.

"Sarah—" A noise at the front door stopped him mid-thought. It was still dark outside and at least an hour before sunup.

Sarah whispered, "What's that?"

Someone jiggled the handle. "Wait here." He went into the bedroom to get the gun, and when he came out he found Sarah near the front door holding an envelope.

"Someone shoved this beneath the door."

He went to the door's security window and didn't see anything. He moved to the window seat overlooking the courtyard. Sarah came up behind him. Her scent made it difficult to focus, but he kept his attention on the area below. A figure passed the fountain and headed for the alley. He was only in view for a moment, but it was enough for Nate to recognize him.

"It's the hoodie guy," she said into his shoulder.

He turned to her, keeping his face hard and his voice low. "Next time I tell you to stay put, you stay."

She held the envelope to her chest. He recognized the hurt in her eyes, but he didn't have the luxury of caring.

"If we're going to do this—"

"Go to the auction?" Her eyes widened. "Steal the diary? Solve the cipher?"

"Yes. If we do this, we do it my way. My rules. That means if I tell you to get down or run, you do it. No questions. Agreed?"

She waited a moment before pushing her hair over her shoulders, before licking her lips, before her scowl turned into a smile that made him wonder who was in charge. "One condition."

He frowned and took the envelope from her. He wasn't used to negotiating orders. And he sure as hell didn't like it. "What?"

She kissed him on the cheek. "You drink another cup of tea."

Sarah felt like twirling around the room. Instead she put more water on to boil. Despite Nate's anger, she'd won. Nate was going to drink another cup of tea and help her solve the cipher. She hadn't worked out all the details, but they were sure to follow. "What's in the envelope?"

Nate took out a stack of eight-by-ten photos.

She looked over his shoulder. *Her* photos. "They're my pictures from yesterday morning on the Isle of Grace."

"The ones I had developed at that pharmacy?"

"Yes." She sat in the armchair near the couch and sorted them on her lap. "Why did that hooded man drop them off?"

"I don't know." Nate turned the envelope over. "Look."

Like the envelope the previous day, words were written on the flap.

JCH Room 424. 0530 Hours. 802419.

She took the envelope. There were no other identifying marks.

Nate was looking something up on her phone. "JCH means Joseph Candler Hospital."

"That's where my father is."

Nate checked the clock. It was ten to five. "How quickly can you be ready?" He found a set of keys on a hook next to the front door.

"Twenty minutes."

"Make it ten." He kissed her hard and grabbed her hand to lead her to the bedroom. "We're going to see your father."

Etienne stood by the *Brigid*'s railing and stared into the dark water below. This quiet time between the moon's sleep and the sun's awakening was his favorite part of the day. Few people were out, and no one was around to judge.

A few hours ago he'd found Antoine, but the punk had been no help. Etienne had even offered serious bills, but Antoine had barely twitched. With no other choice, Etienne returned to the *Brigid*. He was hours past check-in, and it was time to face his cousin.

The Warden came up next to Etienne. "Remiel has made changes."

Etienne closed his eyes. In Remiel's world, changes were never good. "What changes?"

The Warden's oversize black hood covered the eyes and kept the rest of the face in shadows. "Remiel is waiting."

Etienne took a deep breath and went below. Remiel sat at his desk studying a map and eating strawberries. Fletcher Ames lay on the floor, mouth duct-taped and hands cuffed to a ring mounted to the wall. His eyes were closed, and his body twitched. It was hard to tell if he was asleep, in pain, or both.

Two men sat in the chairs flanking the desk. The taller, wider man wore all black and had a gun strapped to his chest. His arms and fingers were inked with random designs, and teardrops were tattooed below both eyes. Another merc. Awesome.

It wasn't until the second man in a tracksuit shifted that Etienne knew he was fucked. Antoine clasped his hands behind his neck as if he belonged in Remiel's inner circle. As if he was one of the *fucking family*.

Remiel raised his head. His blue, dead eyes offered no clue as to his mood. "You're late."

"I know." Etienne wasn't about to apologize in front of Antoine.

"What happened with Leroy?"

"He didn't show." It was the truth, after all.

The unknown man laughed, and Etienne clasped the handle of the knife he kept strapped to his belt. Didn't this guy know the help kept quiet?

"I told you," Antoine spoke in a sniveling, suck-up voice. "Etienne lost it."

"Is it true, Cousin?" Remiel said. "Did you lose your encrypted cell phone? The one thing the Prince, not to mention Kells Torridan, could use to find me?"

Since they both knew the truth, Etienne answered, "Yes, sir."

"You've no idea where you lost it? Or who could've taken it?"

"No, sir. I've looked everywhere." Etienne fought the panic in his voice. "I need time—"

"No." Remiel came over to clasp Etienne's shoulder. "There's a tracker on the phone. I know where it is."

Thank you, God. "I'm sorry, Coz. It won't happen again." Etienne blinked a few times as relief rushed through him. "Where is it?"

Remiel pushed on Etienne's shoulder until his knees hit the wood floor. "Walker has it."

Etienne stopped breathing until it felt like his lungs were going to explode.

The mercenary bent down in front of Etienne. The monster truck of a man stank like cabbage. His eyes showed no other emotion than barely controlled violence.

"This is Igor." Remiel smiled as if pleased with a pet. "He's one of Leroy's men."

A Russian? Etienne closed his eyes.

Remiel whispered in Etienne's ear, "Igor will be my head of security until our business with the Russians is done."

Igor had taken Etienne's job? He swallowed before opening his eyes and croaking out, "I can find my phone. I can handle—"

"You can't handle shit," Antoine said.

"Fuck you." Who the hell was Antoine to be passing judgment on anyone?

"No," Remiel said in a measured, careful voice as he went back to his desk and put on his reading glasses.

"Antoine is correct. It's been a stressful few weeks, and we've lost a lot of men, paid as well as family members. You, Etienne, need time away. Time to remember why the stakes are so high." Remiel nodded to Igor, who grabbed Etienne's arm and forced him up. "Before I allow you to kill Walker, you need time in the box."

"No!" Etienne fought to break free, but Igor's grip threatened to snap Etienne's arm. "Cousin. Please. I promise—"

"It's for the best." Remiel nodded at Fletcher still on the floor. "I can't allow any more mistakes. Not now that I've come this far." Remiel nodded to Igor. "Take Etienne away."

"Cousin!" Etienne screamed until his voice was hoarse. "Please! No!" He fought Igor by kicking and dragging his heels, but the Russian was far stronger and forced Etienne up the stairs.

Once above, Igor threw Etienne onto the deck, and he hit his nose. Pain drove into his head, and blood tracked down his face. Igor laughed and kicked Etienne in the ribs. Agony ripped through him, and he curled into a ball. If Igor wanted him, Igor would have to carry him.

Igor kicked him again, and Etienne moved toward the edge of the yacht. Every breath was like driving knives into his face and ribs, and he rolled until he could almost see the water below.

Rain started, and he raised his head. It was still dark, and he'd have even more cover if the clouds hung around. If he did this, he'd be on the run from his cousin forever.

Was the box that bad that he'd risk spending the rest of his life in hiding? Hell, yes.

Igor stomped over, and Etienne pretended to be knocked out. He was *not* going into the box. He found the knife at his waist and stopped breathing because things hurt less that way. Igor lowered himself on one knee. When he rolled Etienne over, Etienne attempted to drive the knife into Igor's neck. Except Etienne missed and hit Igor's arm instead.

Igor grunted and backhanded Etienne. His head hit the

metal handrail, and everything blurred. As he used the railing to pull himself up, Igor advanced, hands fisted.

Etienne swung his legs over the rail and dropped. The
cold water stripped the breath from his lungs, and his
muscles numbed. But he forced himself to swim. He'd
made the choice to leave, and he'd be hunted forever.
Shore lights shone ahead. He had one choice left. To
kill Walker and save his own ass, he needed leverage. He
needed that historian.

CHAPTER 30

SARAH SAT IN THE SENTIENT BEAN COFFEE SHOP ACROSS THE street from the hospital and cradled her coffee mug. She was curled up in a green velvet chair while Nate waited for the rest of their order. He wore black combat pants, combat boots, and his jacket to cover his weapon. All she'd had was a pair of jeans, Keds, and a pink sweater set. Not quite *sneaking into hospital* or *stealing million-dollar manuscript* clothes. Maybe she should've been more specific with Samantha. On the other hand, Sarah had had no way of knowing how her life would change from yesterday to today. At least the shop's aroma of mocha, with undertone of mildew, eased the bitter taste of worry.

Nate had driven them here and hidden the Juliet's Lily truck a block away, near a construction zone. She'd forgotten he shouldn't be driving until they'd arrived. She'd said something, but he'd dismissed her worries.

Nate returned with a plate of two croissants, a piece of strawberry pie, and some napkins. "It's early. They don't have much available." He placed everything on the table in front of her.

The buttery croissants smelled heavenly, and the piece of strawberry pie looked delicious. Since leaving the apartment, he'd been polite yet distant. She wasn't sure whether to blame post-sex awkwardness, his driving when he knew he shouldn't have been, or his focus on their next task. Considering what she knew about men like her father, she figured the latter. She hoped for the latter. She preferred the latter. "Thanks."

The female barista with long blond hair came over with two takeaway coffee cups and two forks and placed them on the table.

"Here you are." She spoke directly to Nate, her attention on his upper arms. "Anything else I can do for you?"

"No," Sarah said more sharply than she'd meant to. Well, not really.

Nate put a hand on Sarah's shoulder and squeezed. "Thank you for the coffee, ma'am."

Seriously, did Nate have to be polite to everyone?

When the woman returned to the counter, Sarah took another sip of her coffee and wiped her lips with a napkin. "Why do you need two takeaway cups?"

Nate sat on the edge of the chair across from her, elbows on forearms, hands clasped.

She stiffened. She knew male nonverbal lecture clues well.

"I want to chat up the security guard. I need intel on the hospital's layout." He reached out to palm her cheek. "I'll be back soon. In the meantime, eat everything."

"There are two croissants. And a piece of pie."

He kissed her nose. "I'm sure you can finish them by the time I return. You must be hungry." He picked up the coffee and left the shop.

Sighing deeply, she drank her coffee, and a few minutes later had eaten the two croissants and was staring at the pie. Scanning the shop, she noticed the newsstand with the paper's headline: RUSSIA BLAMES U.S. FOR STOLEN ARMS.

Sarah turned toward the window and saw Nate near the emergency entrance, talking to someone.

Since she still had time, she ate the pie. She was hungrier than she'd realized. She also had reason to be.

After wiping her hands with many napkins, she sank into the velvet and closed her eyes. She wasn't sure what she loved most about Nate. His arms. Yes, those were nice arms to have. His powerful thighs that could spread hers. The things his lips could do. And his fingers...*Good golly Moses*...his fingers.

"Sarah?" Nate's voice startled her, and she opened her eyes to find him kneeling in front of her. "Let's go see your father."

∾

"I talked to one of the guards," Nate said as they waited for an elevator in the hospital's lobby. "The newer part of the building has security cameras. But they haven't finished updating the older part where your dad's room is."

Because of the large number of patients and small number of staff, no one paid attention to them. When they got onto the elevator, Nate pulled out a card from his coat pocket, held it to a magnetic keypad, and pressed 4.

"What is that?"

"A key card. We need it to get to the fourth floor to access the older part of the building."

The doors opened, and they got out. "Did you steal that key card?"

"Yep." He walked toward the end of the hall. They passed a few rooms with closed doors and, thankfully, no nurse stations or employees. He used the card again to get to the stairway.

"Are you even a little bit sorry?"

"Not when it comes to the safety of those I love." He kept climbing.

Since she couldn't argue with that, she followed him up the stairs to the eighth floor.

"The guard said this door isn't alarmed yet. In case he's wrong, be prepared to run."

Nate opened the door slightly, and she peeked under his arm. This area smelled older, like new paint over mildew. He shut the door quietly.

They were at the end of the hallway, near a waiting room and a nurse's station. Six rooms were clustered around the station, and a hallway led to the next station and another six rooms, and finally a third similar configuration was at the end. The length was lit with overhead lights.

"My dad's room is at the far end of that hallway?"

"It's also locked." He checked his watch. "The nurses change shifts in one minute. There are no visitors allowed on this floor, and the elevators are locked. No one comes here without an escort."

"If we're seen, we can't claim we're lost?"

"No. Once the change starts, the guard said the staff converge on the nurse's lounge for coffee. We'll have a minute, maybe two, to get to the other end."

"And my dad's locked room?"

"I think that's what the six-digit code is for."

"You *think*?"

"It's a best guess." He rubbed his chin with his fist. "Maybe you can ask Augustus."

There was a tinge of laughter in his voice, and she hit his arm. Except he probably didn't feel it. No man should have that many muscles in his arms.

He kissed her quickly and opened the door an inch. When he slipped out, she followed. They knelt behind a low wall that separated the waiting area from the rooms. Sure enough, when the clock on the wall struck five thirty, three nurses left their stations and headed for a door in the hallway between the first and second cluster of rooms. The nurses from the second and third clusters were headed in their direction.

Nate kept a hand on her shoulder while they stayed crouched. When he nodded, they ran around the station and down the hall until he raised a hand. The lounge door had a glass window, and they had to crouch below the line of sight to pass it.

Once on the other side, he took her hand and ran. His legs were longer than hers, and she struggled to keep up. By the time they hit the third station, he was almost dragging her.

The last door had a metal plate with the number 424. Below it was a keypad with a red indicator light. Nate typed in *802419*, and the light turned from red to green. They rushed in and Nate closed the door behind them.

Nate locked the door while Sarah went to her father's bedside. Machines flanked Mr. Munro's bed, blinking colors and bleeping sounds.

"Dad?" Sarah reached over the bedrail and took her father's hand. "It's me. Sarah."

Joe opened his eyes. Unlike Sarah's brown eyes, Joe's were a deep, dark blue. "Sarah?"

"It's me, Dad." She kissed his palm. "I'm going to get you out of here."

"You shouldn't be here." Joe threw a hard scowl in Nate's direction. "Who's this?"

"This is Nate," she said. "He's my friend."

Joe stared at Sarah before his head shook, his eyes rolled, and his fingers clawed.

Nate moved her aside. "Your dad's having a seizure."

"We need to call someone."

"We can't without being caught." Joe started convulsing, and Nate took Joe by the shoulders and rolled him to his side. His eyes blinked rapidly, and his breath was choppy. "Get his cannula." While Nate turned off the silent alarm button on a machine, she found the cannula behind the bed and hooked it around Joe's ears and beneath his nostrils.

Joe's seizure stopped as quickly as it'd come on. He lay on his side, but his eyes were clear, and his breathing had evened out. Hopefully Nate had turned off the alarm in time.

"Dad?" Sarah lowered one of the side rails so she could sit on the edge of the bed and hold Joe's hand. "Are you alright?"

Joe sat up again and fixed that cranky blue gaze on Nate. "Who are you?"

"Nate Walker," Sarah said patiently. "He's a friend."

"Augustus isn't here, is he?" Joe scrunched his face. "He's a pussy. And I'm sure as hell not walking you down the aisle to meet him." Joe coughed before adding another, "*Pussy*."

Nate laughed while Sarah frowned. "I'm not engaged to Augustus anymore. And stop saying that word."

Joe frowned at Nate. "Are you a pussy, son?"

"No, sir." Because, really, what else would one say? "I'm here to protect Sarah."

Joe nodded. "Then talk her out of this foolish Augustus nonsense." Joe looked around the room. "Hugh should be here. He'd know what to do."

Nate knew it was petty, but he was annoyed by the Hugh Waring lovefest.

"*Dad.*" Sarah touched his face. "Have you heard of Remiel Marigny?"

"*No.*" Joe reached for a paper cup of water, but his hands shook and the water spilled. Sarah held the cup, and once he finished drinking, she placed it on the table.

Nate squeezed her shoulder. Joe was fisting and unfisting his hands.

"I wish I had some tea to give him," she said. "It always eases the headaches that come after his seizures. When he drinks it regularly, it lessens the seizures."

Joe's fists hit the bed on either side of his hips. "That tea tastes like shit!"

"Dad!" Sarah looked at Nate. "My father doesn't normally curse. At least never in front of me."

Nate took one of her hands. "It's okay. Cursing and other outbursts can be caused by seizures. Besides, your tea does taste like—"

She put a hand over his mouth. "No more cursing."

"Yes, ma'am." He wanted to kiss her hand but didn't want to embarrass her in front of her father.

Joe yanked off his cannula. "Get me the hell out of here."

"I'm going to solve the cipher, Dad." Sarah rehooked her father's cannula. "If I can solve it, I can get you out."

Joe squinted at Nate again. "Who are you?"

"Nate Walker, Dad. He's my friend."

"Can't he speak?" Joe sneered at Nate. "You a cop? Or military? Except for the pussy hair, you got the look about you."

"Ex-army, sir."

"You going to marry my daughter? If so, you gotta get rid of the pussy hair."

Nate coughed on his own spit.

"Oh my gosh. *Dad*." Sarah pressed her face into her palms. "This is embarrassing."

"Duly noted, sir. I promise, before the wedding, to cut the pussy hair."

Sarah dropped her hands and stared at him.

"Augustus," Joe said irritably, "he had pussy hair *and* a pussy name."

Nate laughed again.

"Please stop saying that word." Sarah glared at both of them. "It's not polite."

"She's bossy," Joe said to Nate. "Smart, though. And stubborn. Likes her own way."

No kidding. "Good to know."

"Dad, please." She poured him another cup of water. "Do you remember anything else from the night behind O'Malley's Pub? Anything unusual you saw before you passed out?"

This time Joe took the cup on his own. "Hugh got the call about a disturbance in the alley behind O'Malley's Pub. Since the owner was a buddy of mine, I rode along." Joe closed his eyes. "We went around back and found six duffel bags and two guys beating each other. One had a gun, and I pulled my weapon. The thug wouldn't put it down. Hugh and I called for help and..." Joe's voice trailed off.

"What else do you remember, Dad?"

"I fired my weapon and felt a sting in my neck. First Hugh fell to the ground, then I did. It was like I was trapped in my own body until everything went black. When I woke up, days had passed. Four officers were dead. The two dealers were dead. The duffels had been filled with heroin. The prosecutor accused us of running drugs and killing other cops."

Nate dragged over the only chair and sat next to Joe

on the other side of the bed. He had a sick feeling in his stomach. "Joe, do you think someone stuck a needle in your neck?"

Joe swung his head from Sarah to him. "Who are you?"

"That's Nate," Sarah said softly. "He's my friend."

Joe nodded. "A needle in the neck is possible."

Nate pressed his elbows into his thighs. "Do you remember seeing a man right before getting stuck? Maybe two men with an odd walk? They would've hit their chests and—"

"Yes. Our backup hadn't arrived yet, and I was paralyzed but not completely unconscious. Two men came out of the shadows. No one believed me. Our defense attorney told me and Hugh not to say anything." Joe grabbed Nate's arm. "I'm not supposed to say anything. Someone will get hurt."

Fuck. "What. Did. You. See?"

Joe threw himself onto the pillow, one arm with a trailing IV over his eyes. "Right before everything went black, I saw them bow."

CHAPTER 31

SARAH STOOD TO PACE THE ROOM. "DAD, ARE YOU SURE YOU saw two men bow?"

"Of course." Joe kept his eyes covered with his arm. "I was told not to tell anyone."

"Who told you that?" Nate asked.

"Those same two men came to see me in the hospital. They said if I told anyone what I'd seen, Sarah would be killed. Then before they left, they bowed again."

Nate clasped his hands behind his neck. "Did they bow to the waist?"

Joe nodded.

"Good," Nate said. "That's good."

"How is that good?" Sarah whispered. "My father saw Fianna warriors bow. We both know what that means. We have to get my father out of here. Now."

He took her shoulders and pressed his forehead against hers. "It's possible Remiel was behind the drug deal and your father got in the way. I also think Remiel's men injected your father with…something before the Prince's men showed up to stop the drug deal."

"I knew something terrible had happened to my dad because after that night, he was never the same. I'd just never realized he'd been deliberately poisoned."

Nate's jaw was moving as if he was grinding his molars. "My headaches and seizures started in the POW camp when the guards shot me up with something. The doctors thought it was an opioid but could never identify it. At the prison hospital in Maine, they had to stupefy me with drugs just to keep the seizures under control."

"If Remiel was responsible for both the POW camp and the O'Malley Pub massacre—"

"It means your dad and I were injected with the same compound."

"Except my father's situation is getting worse." She shook Nate's arm. "Look at me."

When he did, she saw the truth in his eyes. His situation was getting worse too. Her breath shortened, and she felt light-headed. "They told my father there's no cure."

"They told me the same thing."

She closed her eyes. This couldn't be happening.

Nate took her hand. "Sarah—"

Noises outside the door startled her, and she opened her eyes. Two voices came through the door.

"Nurse?" a man asked. "Have you checked on Mr. Munro yet today?"

"Not yet." The female nurse's voice had a soft Southern drawl. "Mr. Munro gets his next dose of meds in fifteen minutes."

Sarah glanced at the clock on the wall. It was almost six.

"Who are you again?" Joe's voice boomed, and Nate rushed over to whisper in his ear.

Sarah watched the door handle, waiting for the nurse to type in the code and unlock it.

"There's nothing to worry about," the nurse said. "Mr. Munro has been quiet all night."

"And you're giving him all of the meds?"

"Of course."

"Fuckers!" Joe threw his cup at the door, barely missing Sarah's head.

The paper cup fell to the floor, and Sarah grabbed tissues to wipe up the water.

"What was that?" the man asked.

"Occasional outburst," the nurse said. "Side effect of the drugs you prescribed."

"He shouldn't be having outbursts if you'd given him enough sleeping pills."

"You didn't prescribe sleeping pills."

"I need to talk to your supervisor." Footsteps echoed until they both walked away.

Sarah dropped the wet tissues in the trash. "What are we going to do?"

"Joe?" Her dad turned toward Nate's low voice. "You don't mind getting wet, do you?"

"What the hell do I care?" Joe grabbed Nate's arm. "No pussy hair at the wedding."

"Got it." Nate smiled. "No pussy hair."

Sarah shook her head. She was both disgusted by her father's newly acquired language skills and brokenhearted because it meant his neurological condition was declining. Nate leaned in to say something else to her father. But she couldn't hear and didn't care because the lock had clicked. Someone was outside trying to come in. "Nate?"

"Remember," her father said to Nate. "Augustus was a pussy. No pussies allowed."

"I promise." Nate took out his gun and nodded to her. "Time to go."

A moment later a female nurse entered with a pill cup. She stopped, her focus on the gun. "You two shouldn't be here." She looked back over her shoulder as if not sure she was in the right place. "How'd you get in?"

"Long story." Nate pulled the fire alarm.

Three things happened at once. The alarm was so loud the nurse fell to her knees, hands over her ears. The sprinklers turned on, spraying everyone and everything. And Nate dragged Sarah out of the room.

She glanced back to see her father sitting up, soaking wet, and smiling.

Nurses ran around, yelling for help. She and Nate slipped as they ran toward the exit. No one noticed them since everyone was running into different rooms. The patients were now screaming, some were crying, and the mobile ones had come into the hallway.

They made it to the stairwell. Just as the door shut, she heard someone yell, "Stop them!"

She raced down the stairs behind Nate, not stopping until they reached the basement. She slipped on the concrete floor, and Nate gripped her elbow to keep her upright. "Where are we?"

"The morgue." He pointed to the EXIT sign down the corridor. "Run."

Their footsteps echoed in the empty space until Nate pushed the emergency door handle and another alarm sounded. They ended up in a receiving lane behind the hospital, shimmying between food trucks, parked ambulances, and hearses until reaching a main road.

Luckily, it was still dark and raining again. They crossed two more streets and found the truck. She prayed her father would be okay. She hated leaving him in that chaos. Although, from his smile, it seemed like he had been enjoying himself.

Nate opened the passenger door for her, and it wasn't until he turned on the ignition that she realized he was driving again.

"Nate—"

His cell phone rang, and he answered it on speaker. He then tucked it into the center console so he could maneuver the truck out of the parking space. "Walker."

"Nate?" Detective Garza's voice sounded *tranky*—tired and cranky, like her father's used to get. "Tell me you're not at the hospital."

"Not at the hospital." Nate slammed on the brakes, and she gripped the dash. Fire trucks had blocked the way, and he had to do a six-pointer to turn around.

"Were you at the hospital this morning?"

"Yes."

"Dammit, Nate. We talked about public disturbances—"

"We went to see Sarah's dad and ran into trouble."

Garza sighed like Nate was the most bothersome kid in class. "How is Mr. Munro?"

"Not great." Nate waited for the light to change before turning left. "Can you find the evidence files used to build the case against Chief Munro and Detective Waring?"

"For the O'Malley Pub case?" Garza scoffed. "That was a national scandal. I'm sure those records were sealed." Garza paused. "Oh. Right. You weren't here then."

Sarah studied Nate's clenched jaw. He'd been in the POW camp.

"You're from Jersey. Surely you have some clout."

"Okay, brother. You do know that Trenton and Boston aren't in the same state. Right?"

Nate scowled and worked his way around a garden square. There was a surprising amount of traffic. Then she remembered today was the opening day of the Summer Arts Festival in the Historic District and the police were redirecting traffic to public parking areas.

"Dude," Nate said as they passed a horse-drawn carriage. "Any chance you can meet us at the apartment at seven?"

"Us?"

"Me, Pete, and Zack. I'm calling Samantha and Calum too."

"Why?"

"Let's just call it a check-in."

"*Fuuuuuuuuuuuuuck.*"

Nate hung up and, at a stoplight, dialed another number. Instead of using the speaker, he held the phone to his ear. "Calum, can you come to the apartment at seven?" Nate paused. "Seven a.m." Another pause. "There will be donuts."

When Nate was done, she touched his arm. "What are you doing?"

"Rallying the troops. We need help."

"We don't need help." She turned to face the window. "We don't need anyone."

"Did you see the situation back there? We barely got out."

"We did get out, Nate. We're both smart and capable. We can do this together."

"My men, our friends, won't betray us."

"How can you say that? Jack accused you, and Kells signed your commitment papers. And we just confirmed that the Prince and Remiel have been at war for years. We're better off on our own."

"I can't protect you without help." He parked across from a bakery not far from the apartment. "And I'm not too proud or afraid to admit it."

"It's not pride or fear. It's experience. We can't trust anyone." She pointed to his soaking-wet clothes and then to the donut shop. "You can't go in there like that."

"It's pouring. No one will notice." He took her hand and gently drew her in for a kiss. He smelled warm and masculine and wonderful. Why couldn't they have stayed in bed, tucked away from the world and the weather? "It'll be okay. I promise. We'll solve the cipher. Save your father and my men."

Now that he was all in, she had doubts. But instead of speaking them, she kissed him. His words, full of promise, made her want to believe him. Believe in the trust he had for his men. She just wished he'd included himself in that list. That he believed himself worth saving.

CHAPTER 32

ZACK STOOD IN THE GYM'S OFFICE POURING HIS SECOND CUP of coffee. He'd gotten Nate's text and needed the caffeine.

Turns out that Nate's run-in with Remiel, which Zack still wasn't sure how to process, wasn't the highlight of the night. From the moment the two Russian men demanded entrance to the VIP lounge, the club's vibe changed from boozy to violent. Zack had tried to discover if either of the Russians was Leroy, but a fight over a blond stopped that plan. Then one of the Russians hit a dude dressed like a vampire. The fight led to three cop cars, an ambulance, and Pete closing the club at two a.m.

Pete had wanted to stay with Samantha, but Vane had sent out a text with instructions from Kells—*of course it had been a private text from Kells to Vane*—that all the men were to sleep at the gym. Nate had already left with Sarah, and no one wanted to bother him. Vane had been asleep when they'd returned. As far as he knew, Nate had spent the night as well.

Luke shuffled in carrying two empty packing boxes and went for the coffeepot. "Hey."

"Any word from Kells?"

"Nope." Luke tossed the boxes in the corner and poured coffee into a black Iron Rack's mug.

Pete dragged his ass into the room and threw himself into a chair, one arm over his eyes, the other hand stretched out. Zack put a cup of hot black coffee in Pete's hand. Pete grunted his thanks.

Vane appeared with a box of donuts and wearing the wide-awake look on his face that screamed *I got a solid eight hours* that made Zack want to slam his mug on the table. Or into Vane's perfectly straight, white teeth. Either would work.

"All set, Luke?" Vane put the box down on the table and opened the lid. "I have a full teaching schedule today."

Luke grabbed a jelly donut and finished his coffee.

"What's going on?" Zack asked, not sure if he wanted the answer.

Vane answered first. "Nate wants us to clear out that back room. Where is he? I haven't seen him since yesterday."

"Nate's up and gone already," Luke said without blinking. "He's got a ton to do before…you know."

"Right." Vane chewed the inside of his cheek as if not sure what emotion to show: sadness, regret, general concern.

"Where are you going to put everything?" Zack asked. The back room was filled with at least sixty years of old equipment, furniture, and storage boxes.

"I rented a Dumpster from the trash company," Vane said. "It'll be here in thirty."

"With what money?" Pete said with his arm still covering his eyes. He hadn't made a move to drink his coffee.

"The trash company said they'd throw the charge on the quarterly bill. I figured we'd worry about it in two and a half months."

Pete grunted and took his first sip of the hot java. "Fuck. This stuff tastes like piss."

"I bought it at that discount grocer near the train station," Luke said, taking another donut and eating it in three bites. "Much cheaper than the stores in town."

"Why does Nate want you to clean house?" Maybe it was some kind of male nesting since Nate knew he'd be leaving them soon. Scratch that. *Tomorrow.* Zack closed his eyes and let the hot coffee burn his throat. *Fuck.*

"Calum's IT guy is coming by later today." Luke measured dried coffee grounds into another filter. "Nate wants us to set up the comm center in the back room, complete with doors that lock. Maybe even some kind of key code. Courtesy of Calum Prioleau, of course." Luke took the pot and left the room.

Vane added, "Nate also wants us to clear the office of anything pertaining to our real situation and move it all into the new comm center. Office is for gym business only."

Made sense. "You might want to get an exterminator in as well."

"Why?"

"Mice." Pete lifted his arm to take a chocolate donut. Only Zack could see his buddy's smile.

Zack bit into a donut to hide his laugh. The mice were rats bigger than cats.

"Oh." Vane took out his phone, started dialing, and left with a brusque, "Thanks."

Luke returned with a pot filled with fresh water. He dumped it into the coffee maker, inserted fresh beans, and hit the start button. "Where's Vane going?"

"Calling the exterminator." Zack took Pete's free hand and dragged him up.

Luke grimaced. "Forgot about that." The water perked, the scent of coffee hit the air, and Luke closed the office door. "I got a text from Kells. We have two problems. The first is that, apparently, Sarah Munro asked a detective friend of hers in Charleston to run a background check on Nate. Somehow Kells found out, and he's pissed."

Pete drank more coffee. "Can't say I blame her."

That niggling feeling in Zack's gut that had started yesterday grew. It'd been obvious that Nate was falling for Sarah, but could he—or any of them—trust her? Didn't appear likely. "The second problem?"

"Kells is in Minnesota. At Leedsville prison."

"Kells went to see Jack and the other men in prison?" Zack shook his head like he needed to clear the water from his ears. "Leedsville doesn't allow visitors."

"Kells didn't see Jack or the other men."

Pete grabbed a second donut. "Then why the fuck did Kells go up there? And how'd he pay for the flight?"

"Dunno. His secret contact? The one keeping us out of

prison?" Luke found the clipboard on the desk and flipped pages. "Kells is returning with someone he got released from Leedsville. And this man is going to live with us here. Alex Mitchell."

"Fuck," Pete said.

Zack tossed the rest of his coffee into the garbage can and finished his glazed donut. Nothing Kells did surprised Zack anymore.

"I don't know the hows or whys," Luke said. "Just what is. And the *is* includes Alex living with us. That reminds me, I need to redo the bunk arrangements."

Zack poured himself a new cup of coffee. He had to give his boss credit for being a brilliant strategist. "Years ago, Alex was charged with Remiel's murder. Now that Remiel isn't dead, Alex is free."

"How many people know Remiel isn't dead?" Luke said. "That's black ops classified bullshit. And why is Kells bringing Alex here?"

"Holy. Shit." Pete's eyes went wide. "The Prince."

Luke's questioning face smoothed out. "*Of course.*"

Jeez, one would think from Luke's breathy voice that a limo filled with bikini-clad supermodels had pulled up. "What does the Prince have to do with this?"

Luke shook his head. "The Prince is not going to be happy about this."

"Why the fuck not?" Zack was getting annoyed now.

"Because," Pete said in his own breathless voice, "Alex Mitchell is the Prince's younger brother. His *real* brother."

Good Lord. "No way is Alex a Fianna warrior. Alex couldn't follow an order if you promised him millions and all the women a man could want. Besides"—Zack tasted his coffee and, just for the hell of it, added a shitload of sugar—"Alex has two older brothers."

Pete jammed his elbows into his thighs, the heels of his hands pressed into his eyes. "The Prince is Aidan Mitchell, Alex's oldest brother. But no one's supposed to know that except for me, Nate, and Luke. We figured it out, by accident, two weeks ago. If the Prince discovers you know, Zack, we're screwed."

"Kells knows," Luke said.

"No." Zack poured this cup out as well. The sugar had done shit to cut the bitterness. "Kells *knew*. He's known all along."

Luke tilted his head. "Kells also knew Remiel was alive when we thought he was dead."

"Which means that Kells, from the very beginning, knew that this fucked-up situation wasn't about us. It was about a war between Remiel and the Prince which we got sucked into."

"Maybe." Pete stood. "Maybe not. What time is it?"

Zack checked his phone. He had two texts from Nate. "Shit. It's ten after seven."

"Let's head there now," Pete said. "Luke, just…keep Vane busy—"

Zack laughed out loud. He'd just thought of something. Everyone in the Spec Forces community knew that Vane and Alex despised each other. Something about a fistfight in a Moroccan hotel. "I think it's time to give Vane a break from Cain's pigsty."

Luke erased something on his clipboard. Then he smiled. "Vane should room with Alex."

Pete laughed until Vane appeared with the newspaper. "What's going on?"

"Nothing," Luke said. "Pete just told a dirty joke."

Vane, who'd never tell a dirty joke, frowned. "Remember last night when you told us about Etienne and that meeting with the Russian *vor* named Leroy? I thought you should see this." Vane handed the newspaper to Zack. "Now we know what Remiel wants."

Zack read the headline and had just one thing to say. "*Fuuuuuuuuuck.*"

CHAPTER 33

Nate opened the door for Zack and Pete. "You're late."

Pete breezed in. "Yep."

While Zack went for the coffee, Pete beelined for Samantha. She sat at the table with Garza, Calum, and Sarah, who'd been relating the history of the cipher.

Sarah had been unusually quiet since their return. While waiting for the others, she'd had two cups of coffee and sorted through the photos they'd received under the door. She'd twisted her hair into a bun that sat low on her neck. A forgotten pencil stuck out of her hair, but Nate didn't mention it. He thought it was adorable and wanted to remember her this way. In her pink cami and sweater, jeans, bare feet, and glossy lips, she appeared confident and approachable. And so damn sexy, he almost threw everyone out so he could take her back to bed.

Instead, he grabbed another jelly donut. Between now and tomorrow he was eating whatever the hell he wanted.

Pete kissed Samantha on the head. Today she wore a black lace dress and black combat boots and had twisted her hair into a side braid. "What are you doing here?"

"Nate invited me." She tilted her head to kiss Pete on the lips. "Nate said once a target of Remiel, always a target."

Pete glared at Nate. "You told her that?"

"Yes." Nate shut the door. The truth was true whether one wanted it to be or not.

"Uh-huh." Pete got a mug of coffee and sat at the kitchen table.

"I'm glad Nate invited me." Samantha touched Pete's wrist. "I'd rather know what's going on than worry about what might be happening."

"That's why you're teaching her Krav Maga, right?" Nate had every intention of signing Sarah up for that class before he left.

"I guess." Pete nodded at Garza. "What're you doing here?"

"I'm here to discuss the radical idea of no public disturbances." Garza topped off his own cup and sat next to Pete. "It's a concept Nate has trouble comprehending."

Zack drank his coffee and rested his ass against the counter. "What's going on?"

"We went to see my father." Sarah tucked her feet beneath the chair and cupped her mug between her palms. "When we were almost caught, Nate pulled the fire alarm."

Calum lifted an eyebrow. "Can it be traced to you?"

Nate hoped not. "*No.*" With Calum, confidence was everything.

"Before I forget, this is from Luke." Zack handed Nate a Post-it note and went back to mainlining caffeine. "The weapons inventory you asked for."

Please be a joke. "On a Post-it?"

Zack pointed to the list. "There are two stuck together."

Nate turned it over to read the most depressing list ever. Then he handed Zack a notepad and pen he'd found in one of the kitchen drawers. "Make a list of weapons and ammo we need."

"Don't you have credit cards?" Sarah asked.

"The government took everything we had," Zack said as he wrote with one hand and balanced his mug with the other. "Froze our bank accounts and our credit."

Sarah turned to Calum. "Is that legal? Can the government just take everything?"

"Apparently," Calum said. "My firm has looked into the situation, but everything surrounding Kells Torridan's men is classified."

"And my military contact can't get any info either," Garza said.

Sarah threw up her hands. "Can't you hire lawyers?"

"If we do," Zack said, "we go to prison. That was the deal. We take dishonorable discharges and leave everything behind, including service weapons, personal accounts, and vehicles."

"My motorcycle," Pete said, "was stored at an offsite garage. Zack's bike is still in New Orleans. Our two cars are from Cain's wife and Vane's nana."

"You have a blue minivan and a black Escalade," Garza said. "Which one belonged to the grandmother?"

"The Escalade," Zack said.

"Nate," Pete said, "you don't have to do this before you leave. We'll be okay."

"It's important that we have a plan. Right now all we're doing is reacting to threats. I told Luke I want to see the most recent gym numbers. I want to make sure we have a budget and that any extra money goes to the things we really need like food, weapons, and ammo." Nate pointed at Zack. "You're in charge of the armory. You do all of the purchasing as well as keeping track of range time for everyone. We can use Pops's range on the Isle of Grace."

"We don't have time." Pete intertwined his fingers behind his head, his tattoos flexing beneath his black shirtsleeves. "Between clearing the back room and setting up a CP, running classes, managing the gym, clearing tunnels, and working the club, we're getting four hours of shuteye."

"I know." Nate looked at Samantha. "Would you consider quitting the club and working at the gym part time?"

"Sure. As long as the hours are flexible so I can keep my job at Juliet's Lily and do candlelight ghost tours."

Nate exhaled with relief that came from one plan working out. "You'll manage the front desk and monitor the website and social media stuff. You can even order the men around, keep them on task and on budget—"

"How are we going to pay her?" Pete said.

"I'll pay her salary," Calum said, "until the gym makes enough to be self-supporting. It'll more than make up for her lost income from the club."

Samantha looked at Pete. "Would you mind?"

Pete kissed her hand. "Do whatever you want."

"Then yes. I'd love to work at the gym." Samantha blew Calum a kiss. "Thanks."

Great. Nate went for the coffeepot. Although he'd already had three cups, he poured a fourth. And this one he loaded up with cream and sugar. "Next on the list is a phone call I got from Jack. Kells showed up at Leedsville last night."

"And Kells is returning with Alex Mitchell?" Pete chuckled. "We already know."

Nate rubbed his chin. "So much for being the looped-in XO."

Garza scoffed. "How'd Kells get the money to fly to Minnesota and home in a day?"

The hot coffee burned Nate's mouth, but it tasted better than Sarah's tea. "Same way Kells kept Zack and the other men out of prison. Kells has a contact we don't know about."

Garza stared directly at Calum. "Gotta be someone with power and money."

Calum threw up his hands. "Not me. And it's not Carina either. I already asked."

Pete sighed. "This means we'll have another mouth to feed. Besides the fact that Alex has an aggressive streak and an intense dislike for Vane."

Nate had forgotten about the issues between Alex and Vane. "I'll text Luke to make sure he doesn't put Vane and Alex in the same bunk."

Pete and Zack gave each other a look that Nate ignored. He didn't have time for drama.

"Who is Alex Mitchell?" Garza asked Pete.

"Nate and Zack's Ranger buddy. Alex is also the Prince's brother who was convicted of killing Remiel."

Calum took out his phone and texted. "That means Kells knew the Prince's identity and never mentioned it."

"And that Kells has been lying to you," Sarah said softly. "Again."

Nate glanced at her bowed head. "I'm sure Kells had his reasons."

"I have to admit," Pete said, "having Alex is a hell of a bargaining chip if we need leverage over the Prince."

Nate exhaled and got to the main point of the meeting. "Sarah and I have decided that the only way to save Jack and her father is to solve her cipher."

All gazes landed on Sarah, who straightened her shoulders and nodded. Nate had to give her credit. When she believed in something, she didn't retreat.

"Do you mean that Prideaux pirate cipher you just told me about?" Samantha asked. "The one that protects those hide sites?"

"Yes," Sarah said. "If I solve the cipher for Remiel, he'll release my dad from the hospital."

Pete stood and pressed his fists on the table. "It also means the Prince will kill Jack."

Sarah stood as well. "Remiel promised Nate that if we solve the cipher, he'll protect Jack in prison."

The room went silent, and every pair of eyeballs landed on Nate.

Of course, Pete went first. "When the fuck did this convo take place?"

"Last night," Nate said. "Behind the club. Remiel confronted me, confirmed that he was responsible for the ambush and POW camp, then told me he'd protect Jack if we solved the cipher."

"*Whoa.*" Zack placed his mug on the counter and faced Nate directly. "Remiel admits to all of this, and you trust him with Jack's life? Are you insane?"

"I've run through every scenario," Nate said slowly to make his point. "This is our only option. We have to solve that cipher in order to save Jack and Sarah's father."

"No." Zack clasped his fingers behind his neck. "Just no."

"Unfortunately, Nate might be right." Pete picked up the newspaper on the table, still wrapped in a plastic sleeve, and threw it at Nate. "Read it."

Nate slipped the paper out of the sleeve and read the front page aloud. "Kremlin accuses U.S. of stealing 12 SA-24 MANPAD missiles."

"What are MANPADs?" Samantha asked.

"*MANPAD* stands for 'man portable air defense.'" Nate dropped the paper onto the table. "They're shoulder-fired, heat-seeking anti-aircraft missiles."

Pete pointed at Zack. "Your turn to share."

Zack crossed his arms and told them about Etienne's connection with the Russians and ended with "Remiel may be buying MANPADs from the Russian mob. But he needs a safe place to hide them."

"The hide sites." Sarah laid out the paper so she and Samantha could read it. "That's why Remiel wants the cipher solved. He needs a place to store his weapons."

Garza stood and slipped on his jacket, covering his holster. "Finding these hide sites by solving this cipher may be the only way to find these weapons."

"For the record," Zack said directly to Nate, "this is insanity."

"Then you're going to hate the next part of our plan," Nate said. "The reason I asked you here."

Pete dropped his large body onto the couch. "Fuck me."

Samantha went over to sit next to him. "Just listen to what Nate has to say."

Calum slipped his phone in his jacket pocket. "As a concerned citizen who doesn't want missiles floating around his city, I'd like to hear this plan."

"It's simple," Nate said. "We're stealing a diary. We need your help. And you can't tell Kells."

Zack held his breath while Nate laid out the plan. When Nate finished, Zack exhaled until he felt light-headed. "You want to go into an auction, with a U.S. senator—"

"There'll be two senators there today," Calum said.

Okaaaaaay. "At noon. And steal a diary worth fifty thousand dollars."

"We barely avoided prison." Pete still sat on the couch, with Samantha curled up next to him. "If we're caught—"

"You won't be caught," Sarah said. "I'm the one doing the stealing."

Zack contained his rising temper in his fisted hands. This plan was not only crazy, it could land them in jail. Even worse, if Kells found out, they'd be in a mountain of trouble they'd never recover from. What was Nate thinking going with Sarah's plan? No, what was he thinking *with*?

Zack couldn't help but notice how Nate's focus hovered on Sarah. How he followed her every movement, as if the rest of them weren't in the room. "Helping with the getaway counts as a crime too."

"You're not helping us get away," Nate said, "just watching the getaway route."

"I don't like it," Garza said. "If you're caught, I can't help you."

"I'm not asking you to," Nate said. "I'm only asking you to look the other way after I hit Calum. I gotta knock him out to make it look real."

Calum nodded. "I like the plan."

"I don't," Pete said. "It screams *failure*."

Garza studied the ceiling. "Fuck."

"Are we voting?" Samantha asked. "Because if we are, I vote yes."

"How can you agree?" Pete yanked her braid. "After everything that's happened to you?"

She slapped Pete's hand away. "That's why I'm voting for it. If this plan helps to forestall any more violence between Remiel and the Prince, I'll help however I can."

"Good," Calum said. "Then you can take Sarah to Dessie's and help her pick a dress." He turned to Sarah. "If you're going to do this, do it in style."

Sarah clasped her hands and said, "Thank you, Calum."

"Help me understand," Garza said to the room. "How is a diary going to help us find a hide site?"

Sarah took over the convo with "The Prideaux pirate cipher uses two-part substitution encryption. It was hugely popular from the fifteenth through the eighteenth centuries. The first part is the code, like the sequence printed on these heroin bags." She handed Zack a photo of a crime scene with dead guys and white blocks of heroin printed with I9A4B8M5C6. "The second part is the key that decodes the sequence. I know from reading that diary that the pirates used a specific book as their substitution key. I just don't know which one. I'm hoping the diary will tell us."

"And if it doesn't?" Pete asked.

"There may be other clues that can lead us to a hide site. If we find one, maybe we can solve the cipher backward."

"This plan is sketchy as hell." Zack handed the photo to Pete.

Nate held out his hands, palms up. "Do you have a better idea?"

"Fuck yeah." Pete let the photo drop on the floor. "Do nothing."

Sarah moved closer to Nate, and he took her hand. "Not an option anymore."

"I disagree." Zack's voice sounded raw, and he took a deep breath before continuing, "This plan hinges on the word of a woman we don't know and I don't trust. And I'm not sure, Nate, that you're in any position to realize what the hell is going on. Not with all the...stress you've been under." There. He'd said it.

From Nate's wide nostrils and thin lips, the truth wasn't going over well. "What are you talking about?"

"Zack is just looking out for you, brother." Pete moved next to Zack, their shoulders almost touching. "Sarah stole a file—"

"Photographs of me and Nate," Sarah said in a thin, high voice.

Zack focused on the pretty woman in a pink sweater, with a great figure and brown eyes that a man could fall into. A woman who may or may not have trapped one of Zack's best friends into a scheme that could ruin them all. "Sarah also ran a background check on Nate with the help of a Charleston detective."

Nate moved first until Sarah put a hand on his arm. "It's okay, Nate. I'll handle this."

She moved until she stood so close she had to look up at him. Zack could even smell her gardenia perfume. Good thing he preferred jasmine.

"Two weeks ago, after I met Nate, some horrible things happened. My assistant at the Savannah Preservation Office was murdered and books were stolen from the collection. As the daughter of a police chief, as well as an intelligent, level-headed citizen, I asked Detective Waring—my dad's former partner in the Boston PD—to do a background check on Nate. There's nothing wrong or strange or betrayally in that."

Betrayally? "I'll be honest, Sarah. I don't trust you. I don't like how Nate has come to rely on you. And I don't think this plan serves anyone other than your own ambitions."

Her eyes widened with a fierceness Zack reluctantly admired. "You know nothing about me, and your lack of trust in Nate's judgment says more about your inability to judge the situation than his."

Nate came over and gripped Zack's shoulder. Nate's

green eyes were clearer than they'd been in weeks. "I appreciate your concern, brother, but we don't have time to argue. Are you in or out?"

Calum gently pushed Zack and Nate apart. "I say we vote."

Zack shook his head. "No."

Samantha took Sarah's hand and said, "Two yesses here."

"Yes," Calum and Garza said together.

"I vote yes," Nate looked at Pete. "Bro?"

Pete kicked a blue-striped pillow that'd fallen off the couch. "I'm in. With reservations."

"*Dude*," Zack said to Pete. "Are you serious?"

Pete picked up the pillow and threw it onto the couch. "You weren't here two weeks ago. This is beyond law enforcement. Their bureaucracy can't deal with Remiel's brand of nightmare."

Zack moved to the window overlooking the courtyard. He also had reservations, but...by tomorrow, with Nate gone, none of this would matter. "Okay. I'm in. But I'm not happy."

"Before we start planning," Calum said, "I have to ask. Why aren't we going to the feds about these weapons?"

"We can't," Pete said. "If the feds figure it out on their own, good for them. But if the Fianna are involved and we bring attention—you know the consequences. Besides, we're not even sure Etienne's meeting was about those missiles."

Calum nodded. "Now what?"

Nate checked his watch. "We have two hours to plan. The auction is at noon, and that will give us another twenty-four hours to make this happen. We have to be done by noon tomorrow."

Samantha tossed her braid and asked, "Why?"

"Because"—Nate looked at Samantha, then at Sarah—"that's when I have to leave."

CHAPTER 34

SARAH WAS SITTING IN THE BACK OF CALUM'S BENTLEY WHEN her phone buzzed with a text from her boss.

> We need to talk about your employment situation. Call me ASAP.

It was the second text he'd sent her within the hour, and she didn't have the emotional energy to deal with him now. She turned over her cell and stared out the window as Calum's butler Ivers drove them to the Mansion on Forsyth Park Hotel.

With Nate and his men, they'd discussed what was going to happen at the auction. Then she'd gone to her house, where she'd packed clothes, hiking boots, her dad's weapon, and her research materials. She'd also added more tea and salve. After their escape, they were heading out to the Isle of Grace to hide in one of Pops's hunting cabins.

Garza had intel on the hotel's security setup. Zack had staked out the escape route. They had Juliet's Lily's truck for their getaway. Calum had ensured an invitation for Nate would be waiting at the door. Nate had shopped for food and ammo.

They'd worked through countless details she'd never considered. She'd honestly thought she'd walk in, take the diary, jump out the window, and worry about the rest later. Apparently, Green Berets didn't work that way. Zack had kind of come around. She got why he didn't trust her, but she didn't understand why he didn't trust Nate. This was as much Nate's plan as hers.

"You look beautiful." Calum sat next to her while he texted someone about something. "Dior suits you."

She smoothed the skirt of the white dress Samantha had helped her choose at Dessie's shop. It had a tight waist, full skirt ending at the knee, and fitted bodice with cap sleeves. The skirt was made with layers of *extremely sheer* white silk organza. A taffeta-and-tulle petticoat gave the skirt a fullness that belied its whisper-weight fabric.

White silk lined the bodice, but the sleeves remained sheer. The neckline was edged with silk-embroidered strawberries, and small Swarovski crystals graced the center of each one. It was the most feminine dress Sarah had ever seen, and she'd fallen in love with it instantly. It wasn't until she'd been outfitted with a new strapless bra, leather ballet flats, and lace panties that she even dared to look at the price.

"Calum? Please don't faint when you see the bill." Seriously, her purchases had cost more than most wedding gowns.

"I promise I won't faint." He grinned while he typed. "Whatever the cost, it's worth it. You look stunning. I love the Swarovski crystals."

She laughed and touched her hair, which Samantha had twisted into a complicated knot and decorated with gardenia blossoms. "Remember that when you're considering never speaking to me again."

He slipped his phone in his jacket pocket. For the auction, he'd changed into linen pants, a pale-blue dress shirt that matched his eyes, and a blue silk tie decorated with purple and green turtles. "It can't be close to what Carina spends."

"Are you sure?"

He placed his hand over hers, smiled, and squeezed. "Everything will work out. I promise. You have to stop fretting."

"No fretting." She gave him a half smile. "I promise."

"Good." He took something out of his leather briefcase on the floor. "I wanted to give you these before the fun starts." He handed her a paperback copy of Shakespeare's

Othello. "This belonged to your mother. Remember when I told you that your mother and mine had been friends?"

"Yes." She opened the book to find a stack of old photographs. They were all of a group of three girls, each around fifteen or sixteen. "What are these?"

Calum pointed to the name scrawled inside the cover. *Meg Theroux.* "My momma, who's in Paris, told me about the book and photos. She'd stored them in our cottage on the Isle of Hope for safekeeping."

He held up a photo of three girls at the beach. They stood by the ocean, their arms linked, smiles wide. "The blond that looks like Carina is my momma. The black-haired girl is Isabel Rutledge."

"Is Isabel related to the Rutledge family who stole your diary and gave it to the Savannah Preservation Office?"

"Yes. There are members of the Rutledge family in Charleston, Savannah, and New Orleans." Calum ran his thumb over the third person in the photo. "This girl with long brown hair is—"

"My mother." Sarah covered her mouth with her hand.

"Your momma was from one of oldest families in Savannah."

"Is that why the Habersham sisters chose me to work on the Prioleau/Habersham collection despite my *issues* at the Smithsonian?"

"Along with your impressive résumé." Calum lifted one of the photos up to the light. "I also support rebels. After reading your article in *The British Journal*, I knew you were my girl. I loved the fact that you hypothesized that not only were the Prideaux hide sites real, but Thomas didn't betray Rebecca in spite of the historical records saying otherwise."

She dropped the book and photos onto her lap. A few fell on the floor. "*You* chose me to manage the collection?"

Calum picked them up. "And to keep the Habersham sisters in line."

Not sure what to say, she went back to the photo of three girls sitting in the reading room at the SPO. "Do you know anything about my mother?"

"She was a smart girl with lots of friends." He sifted through the photos he'd picked up. "According to my momma, they were all obsessed with Anne Capel's recipes and Rebecca Prideaux's love life."

"I know my mother never let the story of Rebecca and Thomas go."

Calum handed her another photo of two girls in sundresses drinking iced tea in a courtyard filled with flowers. They wore sunglasses and bright smiles. "This is your momma and Isabel Rutledge. While all three girls were close, your momma and Isabel were like sisters. They were desperate to prove that Thomas didn't betray Rebecca. Although they never succeeded."

"The girls wanted to redeem the love story, but they grew up before making their great discovery." Grew up and got pregnant, to be precise.

"Sarah? Do you want to redeem Thomas and Rebecca's love story for their sake? Or your momma's?"

"Both, I guess." She ran her thumb over her mother's image on the photo. "My mother was betrayed by my biological father, I was betrayed by my fiancé, and my father was betrayed by his station when they refused to believe in his innocence. I think, all along, I needed to prove to myself that loyalty—and true love—is real."

"A noble purpose." Calum showed her a photo of the girls wearing aprons in a kitchen surrounded by mortars and pestles and stacks of dry herbs. "Besides love stories, the girls were committed to finding all of Anne Capel's herbal recipes."

Sarah smiled at the girls with wide grins holding spoons and whisks. "I have a box of Anne's recipes my mother and grandmother left me. Some work quite well."

Calum handed her another photo of the three girls in

black T-shirts with Latin phrases printed in white. She covered her mouth with one hand so she wouldn't laugh. Because if she laughed, she'd cry. "Do you know what these T-shirts say?"

He pointed to Isabel Rutledge. "*Luke sum ipse patrem te.* Luke, I am your father."

Sarah pointed to Calum's mother. "*Sona si Latine loqueris.* Honk if you speak Latin." But she paused when she got to her mother's. "*Hic est finis iter est scriptor.* Here is my journey's end." The same phrase written on the envelope the hooded man had delivered.

Calum took the photo and turned it over. "Isn't that the quote from the tomb where the body was found yesterday?"

"Yes. It's Shakespeare." She read the back. "Look at the date. This was taken a few months before—"

"Your mother became pregnant." Calum cleared his throat. "My momma mentioned that your mother confided in Isabel. If you want information about your father, you could ask her. I believe she lives in New Orleans."

"Thanks." Not wanting to think about that now, she sorted through the other photos. One was taken in the Cemetery of Lost Children in front of Anne Capel's crypt. It was barely daylight, and they were holding beer cans, which meant they'd been playing "Dare the Witch," a game in which teenagers slept in front of Anne's crypt all night and drank a beer in the morning.

Sarah's mother had been full of life, so not-caring-about-the-rules, while Sarah had always been...focused and disciplined.

"Sarah"—Calum flipped through her mother's copy of *Othello*—"do you know anything about your birth father?"

"Not much." She stacked the photos and placed them into the white beaded handbag that Calum had bought her as well. "My birth father was eighteen with brown eyes. He worked as a lifeguard that summer on Tybee Island and used to call my mother his *fair warrior.*"

"From *Othello*." Calum took out a photo from the book. "I've not seen this one before."

Sarah took it and squinted. Her mother, who was obviously pregnant, stood with her hand on a tomb covered with white-spotted lichen. Perched on top, a weeping angel clutched a young girl in its wings. The angel's moss-cloaked face gazed up at Heaven with eyes so round and sorrowful, Sarah's heart swelled. That's when she realized her mother's face was tear-streaked. She'd been crying.

Sarah wiped her face with her fingers until Calum handed her a handkerchief. She smiled. Nate and Calum had to be the only two men left in the world who carried handkerchiefs.

"Look at those dates carved into the headstone," Calum said. "1683 to 1699."

She inhaled sharply. "Those are the supposed life and death dates of Rebecca Prideaux." She glanced at Calum, who now wore reading glasses and was studying the photo. "Do you think this is Rebecca's tomb?"

"It's possible. That monument is in the Cemetery of Lost Children, but it's tucked away on the outer edge."

"Why?"

Calum removed his glasses and raised an eyebrow. "Rebecca may have been innocent, but she was still burned as a witch."

Of course. "Rebecca is buried in unconsecrated land." She touched the angel's face. "Look at those words beneath the dates. *My Soul's Joy, My Fair Warrior.*"

Calum took the photo and returned it to the book between the same pages from where he'd removed it. "Looks like Thomas, as well as your biological father, were also *Othello* fans."

She couldn't guess anything about her birth father but had an idea about Thomas. "Thomas probably knew that history would cast him as the treacherous lover who'd betrayed Rebecca."

"That's depressing." Calum found a pen and, on the

inside cover of the book, drew a crude map. "This is the location of Rebecca's tomb." Then he put the book into her beaded purse and said, "Time to focus on our mission. Steal the diary, get away, solve the cipher."

She straightened her shoulders. "And save Nate and my father." Because saving the men she loved was the most important mission of all. Her phone buzzed again with a text from Cassio. She showed it to Calum.

> Beware, Lady Sarah. I have told your father to be not blind, from hence this time, trust not your daughter's mind.

Calum squeezed her hand as another text came through. This one was from her boss. *You're fired.*

CHAPTER 35

AT ELEVEN A.M., NATE STOOD IN THE SECURITY LINE TO enter the Mansion on Forsyth Park Hotel lobby. He felt weird wearing dress slacks, a dress shirt, and a tie. He couldn't remember the last time he'd worn shoes that weren't combat boots. He'd tucked his handkerchief into his back pocket but had hidden his gun in the truck with their other supplies.

Pete had left to teach his class, while Garza returned to the station. Since there wasn't much Garza could do to help them without jeopardizing his career, the best place for him was at work. Although he'd texted that the roadblocks would be temporarily lifted at noon for thirty minutes to let local traffic get by. They had until 1230 hours to get away.

Nate and Zack had scouted the external security cameras, trying to figure out the best way to escape from the office window and dodge the cameras' lines of sight. It would've been much easier to hack into the security systems and shut them down.

Nate's phone buzzed with a text from Zack.

Set up a position. Ready when you are.

Once Nate entered the lobby, he grabbed a seltzer from the bar and a catalog from a table and made his way to the pool deck. Nate had no clue about the camera situation. If anyone studied the tapes afterward, he wanted everything to appear as normal as possible.

Not having access to state-of-the-art equipment sucked.

He worked his way around a stage with a podium flanked by flowers. Display cabinets stood along the patio's perimeter. And it was hotter and more humid than summer had a right to be. If this heat kept up, they'd be in for a hell of a storm later. Another problem for another hour.

While he waited for Sarah, he studied the cases and read the catalog entries. Except for the diary, all of the artifacts were weapons from the seventeenth and eighteenth centuries. The catalog had a photo and a detailed physical and historical description of every sword, gun, knife, garrote, and other lethal-looking weapon available for auction.

He matched up artifacts with catalog descriptions until he noticed the last page. Sarah's black-and-white professional headshot showed her with her hair down and wearing glasses. The bio, describing Sarah as the authenticating historian of the Prioleau/Habersham collection, repeated what he'd read in Kells's file. The woman he loved was a brilliant historian whose career had been sidetracked by betrayal.

The area was filling up with women in cocktail dresses and high heels. The men all looked hot and uncomfortable. As he studied a group of seventeenth-century pirate cutlasses, he got another text. This time from Calum.

We're on our way.

Nate made his way to the lobby. More people had entered and were waving their auction signs as fans to move the air. Even with the AC, the hotel couldn't keep up with the humidity.

"Nate?" A female spoke, and he turned to see Calum's twin sister Senator Carina Prioleau standing with a tall, distinguished man in a fitted dark-gray suit. He had gray eyes and blond hair and wore a sense of entitlement with ease.

"Hello, Carina." Nate took Carina's outstretched hand. Grudgingly, he had to admit that she was beautiful in a skinny, off-putting way. She wore a long yellow sheath dress, and her blond hair had been twisted into a bun. The rope of diamonds around her neck competed with the diamond drop earrings larger than nine-millimeter bullets.

"What are you doing here?" Although Carina tried to keep the sneer out of her voice, her condescension leaked through. "Shouldn't you be managing Calum's new gym?"

"Carina, you shouldn't tease," the man said in a Boston accent, similar to Joe Munro's.

"I don't take it personally." Nate met the man's gray eyes that carried a deep coldness. "Carina speaks like that to everyone except Calum." Nate didn't feel bad about embarrassing Carina because it was true, and everyone knew it. Including Carina.

Carina snorted delicately while the man smiled and offered his hand. "David McGuire."

"David," Carina said with a little less condescension, "is the U.S. senator from the great state of Massachusetts."

Nate shook. "Nathaniel Walker."

"Are you here for the auction?" David asked, although from the way he scanned the room, he wasn't interested in the answer.

So Nate didn't give him one.

"Well"—Carina glared at Nate—"David is the high bidder for Rebecca Prideaux's diary."

"How interesting," Nate said. "Are you a history buff, Senator?"

"Of course. I'm from Boston." David watched Carina with a gleam in his eyes that sickened Nate.

Carina moved her shoulder slightly, as if trying to get away, and Nate stepped in.

"Carina, may I speak with you for a moment? If Senator McGuire doesn't mind?"

"Not at all." David kissed Carina's hand, and she yanked it away.

Without thinking through the consequences, Nate

gripped David's arm and whispered, "When a woman backs away from you, it means she doesn't want you. Keep your hands *off*."

"Nate?" Carina hissed.

He let go of the senator, took her arm, and led her away. Once by the pool, she said, "What was that?"

"Senator McGuire is an ass."

"David McGuire is chair of the Senate Appropriations Committee. He's agreed to help finance my reelection campaign."

"You're going to let him grope you?"

She waved a hand. "Of course not!"

"I know from experience that once you give up your own power, you have to fight like hell to get it back. No election or committee assignment is worth giving your power away." Nate exhaled like he'd been running sprints. "The Carina I know would *never* put up with that. She would *never* give up her power to another. Especially a toad like David McGuire."

She stared at him. No insults. No condescension. Just a wide-eyed gaze that held some as-yet-to-be-named emotion. When things got awkward, he led her around the room. He stopped in front of a case filled with muzzle-loading pistols. Sometimes he just needed to stop and be thankful for modern guns. "Carina, what do you know about Rebecca Prideaux and Thomas Toban?"

Carina licked her lower lip. "Are you asking for your girlfriend Sarah Munro?"

"How do you—"

"I know all about the people who work for me."

"Sarah works for the Savannah Preservation Office."

"She was hired to manage the Prioleau/Habersham collection. She also works for me."

"Is that why you called her boss yesterday? To get her to stop looking for her hide sites?"

"They're not *her* hide sites. They belonged to my

family." Carina took a glass of champagne from a passing waiter. "I never called her boss. He called me almost a year ago, and I told him to stop her search for the hide sites. When he called me yesterday, I suggested he fire her."

"Does Sarah know that?"

Carina shrugged. "I know you think I'm a bitch, but I don't want anything else to happen on Capel land. My husband died out there, and I'll do anything to protect my brother."

"You think being around me is dangerous for Calum?"

"For everyone." She moved in closer. "I'm a U.S. senator with some access to black ops intel. I know about Kells Torridan and his men—*your men*—here in Savannah. I also know your former CO Kells is in the middle of a war with dangerous men, and I don't want Calum involved."

"I don't either, Carina. I'll do my best to protect him."

"Then stop Sarah from looking for those hide sites."

Nate swallowed, but his mouth was dry. When another waiter walked by, he asked for a ginger ale. "I'm just curious about Rebecca and Thomas."

Miss Nell came over. "Are we talking about love?"

"We are." Nate took his soda from the waiter and studied the two women. Despite their age difference, both were beautiful and wealthy. Miss Nell wore a green fitted suit and scarf with green and purple turtles. Although she was eightyish, the light in her eyes and stylish clothes made her seem two decades younger. The diamonds around her throat helped. "Sarah doesn't believe that Thomas betrayed Rebecca."

Carina sipped her champagne. "Sarah is right. Thomas didn't betray Rebecca. They were betrayed by Anne Capel."

Miss Nell wiped her lips before tasting her drink. "You can't know that for sure, dear. The only proof refutes what you believe."

Carina waved a hand. "The men of the isle killed Anne's lover, burned her home, and hanged her for being a witch. When the rope broke and Anne survived, she was forced to make her own living on the Isle of Grace. She carried a grudge against all of the families on the isle, including the Tobans and Prideauxes. Anne hated all men. It makes sense she'd want revenge."

"But to use a young girl like that?" Miss Nell tsked. "That's barbaric."

Nate snagged a shrimp toast and popped it in his mouth. "How did Anne use Rebecca?"

Carina finished her own shrimp toast and wiped her fingers on a napkin. "When Rebecca, the teenage daughter of Anne's greatest enemy, came to Anne for an herbal remedy, she saw an opportunity. Anne befriended Rebecca, teaching her about Puritanism and medicines, and earned Rebecca's trust.

"When Rebecca admitted her love for Thomas Toban, Anne knew Rebecca and Thomas's love affair would humiliate the Prideaux family. Anne told Rebecca she'd help her and Thomas elope. In return, Anne wanted the locations of the hide sites where the Prideaux pirates hid their loot."

Nate tried not to laugh. "Loot?"

"Stolen goods," Miss Nell corrected. "The Prideaux pirates stored their goods in the hide sites until their fence could move the goods to the white market."

Carina scoffed. "It didn't hurt that the Habersham family was *the* fence for the piracy and privateering that went on in Charleston, Savannah, and New Orleans until the Civil War."

"Miss Nell!" Nate gently admonished.

Miss Nell raised an elegant eyebrow. "My family also consisted of rogues and thieves."

And that explained Miss Nell's wealth. "Anne wanted the locations of these hide sites?"

"Actually," Carina said, "Anne also asked for the cipher and the encryption key. When Rebecca said yes, Anne set up Rebecca and Thomas's escape. Anne's plan was to humiliate the Prideaux family *and* get the hide sites.

"The night of the elopement, Rebecca, with the cipher and key, met Anne at the meeting spot with two mysterious men and their boat. These men were to take the lovers up the coast where they'd get on a ship, *The Blue Lady*, bound for Cyprus. But Rebecca refused to give the cipher and key over to Anne without an assurance that Thomas's family wouldn't be ruined, and Anne turned on Rebecca.

"An enraged Anne had the lovers arrested. When Rebecca's family discovered she'd betrayed them, they burned her as a witch. But the mysterious men rescued Thomas, and they all disappeared on the frigate *Sea Dog*. Years later, Thomas became a ruthless pirate who took on the Prideaux pirates directly, using the hide sites and cipher to fight them. There's also a legend that says Thomas hunted down the two mysterious men that allowed Rebecca to be killed."

"What do you mean, allowed?"

Carina finished her champagne, and a waiter appeared with a new glass. "Supposedly, Anne promised the mysterious men access to the hide sites. These men, angry at the loss of the hide sites, let Rebecca die and made Thomas watch. When Thomas found these men years later, he murdered them in a ruthless show of brutality. Some say Thomas even bowed before he killed them because they bowed before Rebecca died."

Nate stared at the dying ice cubes in his glass. The mysterious men were Fianna warriors? Of course they were. "If Thomas didn't betray Rebecca, why do others believe he did?"

"Because the only written account about their love story tells a different tale. According to a letter written by Captain Fripp of *The Blue Lady*, Thomas learned Rebecca was willing to sacrifice his family for their love. Furious at the betrayal, Thomas gave her back to her family, and they killed her."

"I hope that story's not true." Miss Nell shivered. "Can you imagine how terrified Rebecca would've been? A sixteen-year-old girl betrayed by her lover and burned at the stake?"

Nate found himself wanting to avenge the injustice done to this young woman. "Why don't you believe the story where Thomas betrays Rebecca if it's the only one with a written account?"

Carina looked past his shoulder, and he turned to see Senator McGuire prowling the area. "Anne Capel had the stronger motivation. The Prideaux family adored Rebecca. By turning the family against their daughter, Anne got her revenge for the death of her own lover."

"And," Miss Nell lowered her voice to conspiratorial levels, "Captain Fripp was distantly related to the Prideaux pirates, through the Charleston branch of the family. His letters were written after Rebecca's death, and he could've been paid to write them."

And Nate had his ah-ha moment. "Those letters rewrote history. The Prideauxes would rather be seen as villains than fools played by Anne Capel."

Carina tapped him on the shoulder. "Now you're thinking like a politician."

That didn't make him feel better. He finished his drink, the ice sending a pain through his molars. "You mentioned that years after Rebecca's death, Thomas used the cipher and hide sites to destroy the Prideaux family. But if Rebecca was killed, how did Thomas get the information?"

"No one knows for sure, dear," Miss Nell said.

"Since the lovers were running away together," Carina said, "Rebecca probably told him."

"Hello, Miss Nell," Calum appeared to kiss her hand, leaving her flushed, before turning to his twin sister. "Conquer any nations today?"

Carina smiled. "Not yet."

"Where's Sarah?" Nate asked Calum.

"With the auction manager." Calum took a glass of club soda from a passing waiter. "The auction company would like Sarah to speak for a moment about the collection."

Carina ate a chicken skewer, then dabbed her mouth with a napkin. "I'm not sure why Sarah is upset about that diary. It's ours to do with as we please."

"Actually, Carina," Calum said in that smooth, even tone he only used with his sister, "it belongs to the Savannah Preservation Office. It was a gift from the Rutledge family."

"Which wasn't theirs to give in the first place. Besides, do you know how much it's worth?"

"Sarah said the starting bid was fifty thousand dollars. An extreme amount for a diary no one can read."

"That was the auction company's appraisal. I had another one done last night, and it's now about eight hundred thousand."

Calum coughed on his club soda. "*Why?*"

Carina shrugged. "The appraiser contacted me on behalf of Grayson Insurance. They insure collections for the largest museums. And the auction manager here agreed to go with the new opening bid."

"As in Grayson Trust?" Calum made Carina hold his glass while he took out his phone to start texting. "That financial firm in Boston?"

"I guess." Carina frowned while Calum typed. "Does it matter? The diary will go for whatever someone is willing to bid on it."

Calum glanced at his sister. "Did you ask this appraiser why his numbers were higher?"

"No. I had my campaign manager handle it all."

Calum blew out a breath and texted while Carina tapped her nails on her glass.

"Carina." Nate spoke with his softest drawl. "Does this appraiser have a name?"

"I don't know his last name, but I remember his first because it was unusual."

Calum put away his phone, took his club soda and her champagne out of her hands, and gave them both to a waiter. "Care to share?"

She sent her twin a smile. "Augustus."

CHAPTER 36

A LOUD BUZZING SOUND PIERCED NATE'S EARS, AND HE flinched.

Maurice, the auction manager, stood at the podium, tapping the microphone. "Welcome to the Prioleau/Habersham auction of the largest private collection of sixteenth- and seventeenth-century pirate weapons in the United States."

The man droned on about historical facts and saving the turtles, but Nate had stopped paying attention. Sarah had come up on stage. She wore a dress that made her look so exquisitely feminine he turned away to breathe. Her hands were clasped in front, and her hair had been tucked into a knot at the back of her head and decorated with live gardenias.

Her white dress made her seem…utterly beautiful and unattainable.

When she moved to the podium to speak, her voice sent chills down his arms, and he stared at the marble floor. She spoke about the history of the weapons, the desperate and violent world these men lived in, and the political betrayals and upheavals that led them to form a brutal society that shaped the New World.

Flanked by Calum and Carina, whose ancestors had been knee-deep in that society, Nate realized everything Sarah was willing to give up on his behalf. She still had a job, even if it wasn't the job she wanted. She still had her freedom, even if it was at the expense of her father's. She still had a life outside this war between Remiel Marigny and the Prince. But once she stole that diary, her life would change forever. And she was willing to do that not just to help her father but to save him.

He was both humbled by what she was willing to sacrifice and disgusted with himself for allowing it. What kind of man let the woman he loved save him?

Calum took Nate's arm and said to Carina, "Excuse us for a moment."

As she left to talk to another couple, Nate said, "I'm not sure we should do this."

"It's too late to change your mind." Calum nodded toward Sarah on the stage. "Her boss found out she applied for a grant and fired her."

Nate wished he had something stronger to drink than ginger ale. "She has nothing left." And when he returned to Maine tomorrow, she'd be alone.

Sarah left the stage and followed Maurice into the hallway that led to the manager's office.

"It's time," Calum said. "Let's help your woman."

Sarah made her way down the hallway to the hotel manager's office. Security guards stood in front of the door until Maurice waved a key card. Her hands were sweaty, and she felt nauseated. Within the past hour she'd lost her job and was about to become a felon. She barely remembered what she'd said up on stage since she was still in shock over her boss's curt text. Thank goodness Maurice hadn't heard the news yet.

She tossed her beaded handbag on the desk and used two fingers to wipe her damp cheeks. The diary sat on the felt book cradle as if waiting for her to save it.

"The pre-bid price has gone up considerably since getting another appraisal," Maurice said, taking off his jacket to expose his soaked shirt. "The diary is now going for eight hundred thousand."

"*Dollars?*" She coughed on the word. "Why?"

"I found something you missed." Maurice paused when the door opened again.

Calum and Nate entered, and she breathed deeply for the first time in hours. Despite everything going on, she couldn't help but notice how handsome Nate looked in his dress trousers and shirt. His long hair was pulled back, and he even wore a tie. When his green gaze landed on her, small tremors started in her lower stomach. Just having him nearby made her feel better. Made her feel as if everything would be okay.

Except for the fact that he was leaving tomorrow.

She shook her head. "What did I miss that would put this diary at eight hundred thousand?"

Nate whistled low and moved closer to the diary.

"That's a lot of money for a moldy book," Calum said.

"Who are you?" Maurice asked.

"Calum Prioleau. The senator's brother."

"Oh." Maurice put on his jacket and puffed his chest. "I didn't realize."

Calum's polite smile didn't come close to reaching his eyes. "Most people don't."

"*Maurice.*" She pointed to the diary. "What did you find?"

Maurice opened his briefcase on the desk. "I…we…may have been hasty in our decision to publicly mock your thesis."

She checked her watch as Nate's hands moved to her shoulders. Ten minutes until noon.

With a huff, Maurice took out a velvet bag and black zippered case. After opening the bag, he handed her the magnifying glass that clipped onto her glasses. Then, from the case, he gave her a pair of cotton gloves, a dusting brush, and a bone folder. "Tell me what you think. Just remember the pressure alarm."

Nate pointed to the lens she attached to her right eye-glass lens. "What is that?"

She put on the gloves and glasses. "A monocular. It magnifies up to three times." She held a stick that looked like a tongue depressor. "The bone folder allows me to turn pages without touching them."

Nate smiled. "Sexy."

Calum laughed as he took out his phone and texted.

She studied Rebecca's diary. It was open to two pages she'd never seen before. Pages that had been stuck together and were now sliced apart. "Who did this?"

"I did," Maurice said. "The secondary appraiser requested I do so."

Nate snorted. "You mean Augustus?"

"Excuse me?" She raised her head too fast, and because of the monocular, her vision was wonky.

"Who is Augustus?" Calum asked.

"Sarah's loser ex-fiancé," Nate scoffed. "A short, betraying sack of shit."

"Really?" Calum stared at her, one eyebrow cocked. "You have a loser ex-fiancé?"

"*Short* loser ex-fiancé," Nate said again. "Did I mention he's a betraying sack of shit?"

"We broke up." She returned to her inspection. "Maurice, why would Augustus appraise *my* diary?"

"Since Augustus is now with Grayson Insurance, the company underwriting this auction, I asked for his opinion."

"Does Senator Prioleau know you've been appraising her almost-million-dollar manuscript in a hotel manager's office?"

"I sure as hell didn't know." Calum crossed his arms and assumed an indignant air. "I'm not sure how I feel about it."

"One must do what one has to," Maurice said in a sheepish voice.

"I bet." She ran the brush over one of the cut pages. Her vision fixed on the Latin phrase written on the bottom. *"Hic est finis iter est scriptor."*

"Here is my journey's end." Calum stood close enough for their shoulders to touch. "The T-shirt?"

"No," Maurice said. "Shakespeare. *Othello*, I believe."

Calum rolled his eyes, while Nate's nod told her he recognized it as well.

Mildew filled her sinuses, and she tasted the mustiness. Using the brush, she swiped it over the opposite page.

Along the edges, Rebecca had sketched five-petaled roses and five-pointed stars. At the top was a notation: *520TH310332*. Below that were alphanumeric sequences she recognized as part of the cipher. Despite her hands perspiring through the gloves, she took photos with her phone. If Maurice could break the rules, so could she. "Maurice, I'm not seeing anything that would make this worth more money."

"A piece of paper had been folded up and shoved between those two pages. Mold and damp had glued it in place."

"And you *unfolded* it?" Her boss would have locked her in an underground storage vault if she'd attempted something like that outside the lab.

"Needs must." Maurice pointed to a document lying on a piece of muslin on the desk.

She went over to look at the document and covered her mouth so she wouldn't scream.

"What is it?" Nate said, coming up behind her.

She took off the gloves and monocular and dropped them on the desk. "It's a marriage license." She pointed to the signatures on the bottom. "Thomas and Rebecca were married."

Etienne wandered around looking at the weapons and trying not to fidget in the suit he'd borrowed from his brother. After making it to the shoreline, he'd returned to his family's cabin on the Isle of Grace. Thankfully, none of his brothers had been around to ask questions.

Exhausted, he'd taken a shower and drunk a pot of coffee while figuring out his next step. He had a radical idea that could get him killed. But it meant he had to get close to Sarah, which wouldn't be easy with Walker around.

Etienne had known Sarah would be here since the

Warden had been tracking Sarah's every move for the past
few months. And he'd been able to get into the auction
because one of his second cousins was a security guard.

After Sarah's speech, he watched her go through a side
door to the admin area of the hotel. Walker and Calum
Prioleau followed her, and Etienne followed them. Luckily,
his cousin and a high school buddy were both on duty and
appreciated the smoke break. His cousin had even offered a
security walkie-talkie to keep track of everything.

Now Etienne had his ear on the door, listening.

Sarah took out her phone and photographed the license.
She still couldn't believe that Thomas had *married* Rebecca.
Not betrayed her. Although the information didn't matter
for her career—because that was burnt toast—it was valida-
tion on behalf of her mother who'd always believed that
Thomas had loved Rebecca.

Would the information change the world? Or even
make the nightly news? No. It meant her mother's trust in
true love had been well placed.

Meanwhile, Maurice clasped his hands and rocked on
his heels. "I think you'll agree that this marriage license
significantly increases the value of this diary."

"You're right." She checked her watch and nodded at
Nate. "And I'm sorry."

Maurice frowned. "For what?"

"For this." Nate hit Maurice on the chin, and he dropped
like a cinder block until Nate caught him and lowered him
to the ground.

Meanwhile, Calum had opened the windows and was
texting. "Zack knows you're on your way."

"Sarah," Nate said. "Out. Now."

Sarah took the marriage license, folded it, but before
she could shove it in her purse, Nate took it. "What are
you doing?"

"You're leaving now and I'm taking the diary and this license." Nate dragged her toward the window. "I don't want you involved in stealing anything. I'm not arguing about this."

"But—"

Nate kissed her hard and then went back to Maurice's body on the floor.

Calum pointed out the window. "Do you see that flash of light from an alley on the other side of the garden and across Abercorn Street?"

"Yes."

"That's Zack. He'll take you to the truck. You should be able to get out of town from there, but you only have half an hour."

She glanced at Nate, who was rummaging through Maurice's pockets.

Calum shook her shoulders. "Nate will meet you."

No. She wasn't going alone. "This isn't the plan we agreed to."

"It's the plan that's in motion."

She peered over the window's ledge and she saw box-woods three feet below.

Calum pushed her shoulder. "Go."

Once her dress skimmed the window ledge and her feet hit the ground, she ran across the garden and through a parking lot. The heat shocked her. It'd gotten at least ten degrees warmer since she'd arrived. She wanted to look back. Instead, she slowed to cross the street like a normal person and walked until she fell into Zack's arms.

"In the truck." Zack pointed to the work truck parked at the end of the alley. "*Now.*"

While Zack returned to his position, she climbed into the cab and started it. As she waited with the AC blasting, she clasped her fingers behind her neck and closed her eyes. She was supposed to be the one to steal the diary. She was supposed to take the blame. She didn't want to give anyone more reasons to send Nate away.

A loud alarm rang out. While she didn't see anything resembling panic, a loud noise started that sounded like a car alarm on steroids. Then she heard a gunshot.

CHAPTER 37

ETIENNE, WITH HIS EAR PRESSED ON THE DOOR, HEARD CALUM say, "She's crossed Abercorn Street."

Static came from the radio, then a voice. "We need an escort to take Senators Prioleau and McGuire to the hotel manager's office."

"On it," another man answered.

"Go to Pops," Calum said. "He'll give you directions to the cabin on Black River."

Etienne smiled. He knew that area well because it was on Capel land where he and his brothers poached wild boar. It was a desolate, desperate area. A perfect place to kidnap a beautiful woman.

"This way, Senator." Carina's voice carried down the hallway. She turned the corner with a man in a suit and a security guard.

Etienne kept his head down, and as he passed her, an alarm sounded.

The security guard ran to the office, opened it, and yelled, "Stop!"

Gunshots rang out, and Carina hurried into the room. "Calum!"

Etienne sprinted down a service hallway and hit the EXIT door. He crossed the parking lot and went for the alley that led to Abercorn Street.

The walkie-talkie in his hand screeched. "Calum Prioleau is down. Diary is gone."

Sarah had *definitely* heard a gunshot. Her heart rate jacked up, and she made sure the doors were unlocked. Zack paced near the entrance to the alley, fisting and unfisting his hands.

Where was Nate?

She faced front again, gripping the wheel and checking the road. She'd have to push her way into traffic and was worried about delays due to the arts festival. And she'd not thought about the effects of adrenaline. She was shaking and hadn't even started driving yet.

She leaned forward to watch the streetlight, praying it would turn green when she needed it to. Her foot tapped the cab's floor. Nate should've been there by now.

ComeOnComeOnComeOn.

A moment later, the side door opened, and Nate fell in. The diary and license dropped onto the floor, and Nate slumped to the side. Blood ran down his arm, pooling on his sleeve's cuff.

Zack shut Nate's door and came around to her side.

She rolled down the window. "What's wrong?"

"Nate's been shot in the shoulder. It's a graze, but it'll need to be taken care of."

"He's been *shot*?"

"I'm fine," Nate groaned.

She turned toward him until Zack grabbed her arm. "Follow Garza's directions. Drive to Pops's trailer. Don't stop for any reason. Got it?"

She looked at Nate again. "I…uh—"

"Sarah!" Zack's harsh order made her face him. "You wanted us to trust you. Now you need to finish this mission. If you don't, we'll have much bigger problems." Sirens sounded, and blue and red lights flashed behind them. "Go. Now. Nate will be fine until you get to Pops's house. And for all of our sakes, solve that damn cipher."

Zack ran in the other direction, and she put the truck in gear. She pulled into traffic and waited at the red light. Police cars cruised by on the cross streets, sirens and lights blaring. She gripped the wheel as if that would make the light change faster.

Then, across the street in front of a mailbox, she saw Cassio standing in jeans and a T-shirt. He stared at her with such anger, she felt its heat. With one fluid movement, Cassio wrapped an arm around his waist and bowed until his head almost hit the ground.

A honk behind her reminded her to go, and she hit the accelerator. She didn't know much about Fianna warriors, but Nate had confirmed a head bow was a greeting, a waist bow was a warning, and a full bow was a sign of imminent execution.

Just as she passed the corner, she saw another man beneath a pink crepe myrtle tree holding a walkie-talkie. She shivered and hit the door locks. Etienne.

Sarah drove the speed limit until reaching the bridge connecting Skidaway Island to the Isle of Grace. Her hands ached from gripping the steering wheel. Every breath coming out of her tight chest hurt. Her plan had sounded logical when she'd suggested it, but now that she was in it, now that Nate and his men had chosen her over Kells, she realized the amount of danger she'd put them all in.

She stopped at a red light and checked Nate. His eyes were closed.

"I'm okay."

"You don't look okay." The light turned, and she headed over the bridge. Rain started, and she turned on the wipers. They squeaked and left a stream of dirt across the window.

"We knew this wasn't going to be easy."

"It never occurred to me that you'd be shot." He laughed, and she frowned at him. "It's not funny."

"Maybe not. But I always assume I'm going to get shot."

"How did this happen? Who fired a gun at you?"

"One of the security guards, I think. I was kind of busy stealing the diary and jumping out a window."

"What a horrible way to live." Yes, she was being judgy, but her plan hadn't included him getting *hit* by a *bullet*.

"It's a graze."

She wasn't so sure. "Why were you going through Maurice's pants before I left?"

"I stole his cell phone and gave it to Zack." Nate licked his lips, and she glanced behind. He'd loaded the cab with supplies and groceries, with a case of water on the floor. She couldn't reach it while driving. "There might be something on it we can use if Luke can hack into it."

She exited the bridge and drove through the center of the Isle of Grace, the tiniest town ever. Thunder hit, the rain picked up, and the hand-dug storm drains on either side of the road filled. The storm had come in suddenly, not just with flash flooding but with dark skies that made it look like dusk instead of midday. "I didn't know thievery was a necessary skill in the army."

Nate coughed. "Covert operatives do things that most soldiers aren't allowed to do."

"No wonder you all look like criminals."

He barked out a laugh and then winced. "We grow our hair for undercover work, to help us blend in." He threw her the lamest leer ever. That alone told her how much pain he was in. "Most women think we're sexy."

She ignored him and focused on the road and the increasing rain. Not only was he hurt, he was flirting with her. Maybe that's how he handled stress.

"Sarah? Do you fish?"

"Excuse me?" She hated how pale his face appeared. The shakes started in her legs and worked their way up her spine. She slowed when she noticed the lights shone through the windows of the isle's white church, St. Mary of Sorrows. And someone stood on the front step, hands in jean pockets, wearing a black hoodie.

Maybe it was the adrenaline. Maybe it was because she was tired of being followed and threatened. Or maybe she was ready to take back some control after being fired. But she made a sharp right and drove as far as she could go. Massive oak trees with sweeping branches covered with

Spanish moss squeezed the church from all sides. Only the white steeple cut through the dense foliage.

The hooded man stood there, unmoving.

She slammed on the brakes and heard the branches drag along the roof. Nate's eyes were closed, and as desperate as she was to help him, she might not get this chance again. She got out and stepped into the rain.

The humid air was tinged with the isle's unique smell of honeysuckle, seagrass, and marsh mud. Her shoes sank in the spongy ground, and her wet dress clung to her body. Water dripped down her face and her neck, pooling between her breasts. She was tired of being watched, hunted, afraid.

She paused at the bottom of the stairs. The hooded man stood beneath the overhang in front of a black, arched double door. She wasn't scared, although her mind told her to be. She didn't want to run, although her legs felt restless. She didn't want to lose Nate, yet she was running out of time. "What do you want?"

The man said nothing. His hands were still in his pockets. His face still covered. He wasn't threatening her, just... watching her.

"Why are you following us?"

The man raised an arm and pointed. She turned to see a patrol car parking next to her truck. A man got out, ran to Nate's side, and peered in. When she faced the hooded man again, she wasn't surprised to discover he'd disappeared.

She hurried to the truck. "Who are you?"

He adjusted his hat. "Sheriff Boudreaux."

Oh. Right. "Did you see him?"

Sheriff Boudreaux frowned. "See who?"

She motioned to the church. "The man on the steps. He's been following us."

"No." Sheriff Boudreaux opened Nate's door and reached in to lift him up. He'd slumped over into the driver's side.

"Then who turned on the lights in the church?"

"They're on a timer." Sheriff Boudreaux grunted under Nate's weight. "Detective Garza called me and told me about your plan. Then Zack called and told me Nate had been shot on the getaway."

"You're okay with all of this?" She waved toward the church again.

"It's not a matter of being okay. Nate is one of us. As is Garza." Sheriff Boudreaux still struggled with Nate. "Help me."

She got into the driver's seat and pushed Nate up from her side. He was heavier than he looked.

Nate's head rolled. "Kells mentioned fishing."

"He's delirious." Sheriff Boudreaux buckled Nate into his seat. "Follow me. I'll take you to Pops Montfort. He's waiting." Sheriff Boudreaux shut the door and returned to his patrol car.

She switched on the ignition and followed. Her body shook, probably because she was soaked. Once they left the protection of the trees, she adjusted the wipers. The deluge made it impossible to see, and she was grateful for Sheriff Boudreaux's red and blue flashing lights to guide her.

Nate groaned. "Kells said there'd be fishing."

"He also said you could trust him." She slowed because the tire ridges in the dirt road had turned into mud. She adjusted the AC to defog the windows. That's when she saw the sign on a tree: PRIVATE PROPERTY. P. MONTFORT.

She made a right turn onto a dirt road, then two lefts and a right that led to a trailer tucked between pine trees with a red barn behind it.

"Don't worry, Nate," she said, bringing the car to a stop. "We're safe. For now."

An older man appeared on the deck around the trailer. He wore a red T-shirt and overalls and carried an umbrella in one hand and a shotgun in the other. His appearance matched the scowl stretched across his wrinkled face.

This couldn't be the right place, could it?

Sheriff Boudreaux parked, came to Nate's side, and opened the door, both of them getting soaked. "We gotta get him inside."

"Nate?" She touched his shoulder. His body was hot, but he was out cold.

CHAPTER 38

NATE SWUNG HIS LEGS OVER THE EDGE OF THE TWIN BED IN Pops's trailer. He wore only dress slacks, and his hair was undone. As he ran his hands over his head, his left shoulder ached. He dropped his arm and held it against his chest.

There was a bandage on his shoulder, and his arms had been coated in Sarah's burn salve. Then he remembered: *Sarah. The diary. Getting shot.*

Getting up was a wobbly experience. Once he gained his equilibrium, he felt better. His shoulder hurt like it'd been dislocated, yet his burns felt…better. And he hadn't woken with a headache. Since he'd no idea where his clothes were, he followed the sound of Sarah's voice.

"I've got Pops's truck packed," Sheriff Jimmy Boudreaux said. "You'll drive here, not far from Boudreaux's Restaurant. Down this dirt path, there's a landing with a johnboat."

Nate entered the family room to find Sarah and Jimmy sitting next to each other on the couch, a map laid out on the coffee table. Pops stood behind, watching. "Hey."

Sarah ran over and threw her arms around his neck. "Are you okay?" She'd changed into jeans, a blue T-shirt, and a matching hooded sweatshirt.

"Yeah." He hugged her tight, ignoring the ache in his shoulder. "I'm good."

Pops *harrumphed* and went into the kitchen.

Jimmy stood. He was in full uniform, and his hat lay on the chair nearby. Another reminder of how much Nate's friends were risking. "I've been giving Sarah directions to the cabin on Capel land."

Nate nodded, and Pops returned with a glass of water and four ibuprofens that Nate swallowed in one gulp. "Tell me."

He lowered himself on the couch next to Sarah, while

Jimmy sat on her other side. Pops went into the kitchen and banged around. The scents of garlic and onion filled the trailer, and Nate's stomach grumbled.

Sarah squeezed his hand. "Pops is making jambalaya."

Nate squeezed back. Pops's jambalaya was even better than his fried fish.

Jimmy pointed to a hand-drawn map of the isle. "Park near Boudreaux's restaurant, and you'll find a johnboat tied up to a small boat landing behind the cooking shack. Head south on Black River. When you spot the *No Trespassing* sign, turn right and navigate the estuary until you see a dock on your right. The cabin is on the rise above the dock." Jimmy used a finger to trace a section of Snake Creek. "To get to the cemetery, go back to Black River and turn right. When the river splits, bear left and continue on Snake Creek. The cemetery starts along the creek here. There's no boat landing, so you'll have to find someplace to tie up."

Pops appeared, wiping his hands on a hand towel. "The current in that area is brutal." He nodded to a handmade tidal chart next to the map. "Keep track of the times. The water goes out as quickly as it comes in."

Nate nodded. "Got it."

"Son?" Pops asked. "You up for managing a boat with your arm?"

Nate stretched out his arm and flexed it. The entire upper area of his shoulder was covered with white gauze. "Did I need stitches?"

"No," Jimmy said. "Sarah and I cleaned and bandaged it."

"I'll be fine."

"Pops even had antibiotics." Sarah threw a smile at the older man. "Thank you for that."

"No need." Pops tossed the towel onto his shoulder and headed into the kitchen.

Jimmy smiled at Sarah. "Don't mind Pops. He's always like that."

Sarah chuckled. "He reminds me of my father. He's the king of cranky."

Nate rubbed her neck. He had so many things he wanted to talk to her about, but time was ticking. "How long before we get to the cabin?"

"Between driving and river time, about an hour. Depending on the tides, it's a forty-minute boat ride between the cabin and cemetery." Jimmy checked his watch, then looked out the window. The sun was peeking out from behind dark clouds. "It's almost two p.m. The storm has passed, but the tide is high. There's no time to waste if you want to see that cemetery today."

"Sunset's at eight forty-three," Pops said from the kitchen.

Nate stood and pulled Sarah up. "I need weapons and clothes."

Sarah pointed to a bag from the floor near the couch. "Your combat boots are in the truck."

"Nope." Pops came in holding a spoon. "Gotta wear snake boots." He pointed through a window to the deck outside the back door. "You can wear Rafe's and my Tess's." Pops returned to the kitchen.

"Tess?" Sarah asked Jimmy.

"His wife." Jimmy went to the deck and brought in the two pairs of boots. The brown pair was bigger than the other, which had ladybug faces on the toes. "Nate, I put a shotgun and a bolt-action rifle with a thermal scope in the truck. There's extra ammo for all the weapons, along with two knives and a machete."

"Pops gave me the keys to cemetery mausoleums." Sarah picked up an iron ring from the coffee table with jangly, old-looking keys on it. "Not every large tomb has a key, but most do."

A knock sounded on the door as it opened. Grady Mercer came in wearing hunting camo gear. "We've got a problem."

"What's that?" Jimmy asked.

Grady's interest slid to Sarah. "Ma'am." He took off his hat before saying, "You must be the historian everyone is talking about."

"Sarah," Nate said, "this is Grady Mercer. He lives on the isle. He's a friend."

She offered her hand, and Grady shook it. "Nice to meet you, Mr. Mercer."

"You're much prettier in person."

"Excuse me?"

Pops came into the family room, this time with a faded flower apron over his overalls, just as Grady found the remote and turned on the television. He switched channels to the local news running a NEWS ALERT.

Two photographs appeared side by side, one of Nate taken from an outside security camera he and Zack must have missed and the other of Sarah in her white dress. Both shots were of them crossing Abercorn Street.

A voice said, "Earlier today, a valuable diary owned by the Prioleau family was stolen from the Mansion on Forsyth Park Hotel. We have security camera footage of the suspects. If anyone has any information, contact the Savannah Police Department."

Grady shut off the television.

Nate held Sarah close, her head on his chest and beneath his chin. Her heart beat faster than his, and she let him hold her weight. "We knew that was a possibility. We'd no way of knowing which of those cameras were active."

"Enough chitchat." Pops clapped his hands. "Let them eat so they can leave."

Nate kissed Sarah gently and said, "Go in. I'll be right there."

Once she disappeared, Grady said, "Son, when you get to the cabin, there's Morse code on the ham radio. My call sign and directions are in the drawer. You need me, you start clickin'."

"Thanks." Nate knew from experience how adept Grady was at Morse code.

Grady nodded and left.

"I'm glad you know Morse code," Jimmy said, grabbing his hat. "I suck at it."

Nate wasn't great with it either.

Jimmy paused, one hand on the door. "How long will you two be gone?"

"Not long."

Jimmy chewed the inside of his cheek. "If I don't hear from you by tomorrow afternoon, I'm coming after you. That reminds me." He took a SAT phone off his utility belt. "Take this. Not sure it'll work way out there, but there's no cell service. No other way to contact me."

Nate couldn't respond. Jimmy was going beyond the bounds of friendship. "Thanks."

"I don't know all that's going on, but I saw what happened two weeks ago at Capel Manor. If you hadn't been there, Juliet would've died. And there are a lot of people on this isle who'll never forget that." After clapping Nate on the back, Jimmy left.

"Nate?" Pops came out of the kitchen wiping his hands on a towel. "Come in and eat with your woman."

CHAPTER 39

ETIENNE TURNED OFF THE SHOWER, DRIED HIMSELF WITH A towel before wrapping it around his waist, and opened the door of his motel room to see the Warden holding a key. Etienne was surprised but not unhappy.

He stood aside so the Warden could enter. "I wasn't expecting you."

The Warden stopped at the mess. Remiel's Russian thugs had already come and gone. All the drawers had been emptied, the blankets dragged off the bed, the few pieces of crappy furniture thrown on their sides. "I thought you were dead."

"I did too." Etienne shut the door. The irony of the messy room was that he'd inherited a neat and tidy gene. "You here to kill me too?"

"No." The Warden picked up a chair. "Remiel is searching for you."

"Obviously." Etienne found a pair of jeans, dropped the towel, and yanked them on. He put on a gray T-shirt, grateful for one clean thing to wear. "Since Remiel's besties have already searched my room, I figured I had a few minutes."

The Warden closed the window shutters. "What are you going to do now?"

"Not going into the box." Etienne threw clothes into a duffel. The box was his cousin's sick, sadistic venture into deprivation torture.

The Warden tossed him a black T-shirt to pack. "How're you going to avoid that?"

Etienne shoved in his other dry pair of jeans. "I have a plan."

The Warden scoffed. "It'll never work. Remiel always wins."

Etienne found his phone on the bed and opened his contacts list. He'd bought a new burner half an hour earlier and had uploaded the info from his laptop. The same laptop Remiel's men hadn't found because Etienne had hidden it in his cache, along with extra weapons and cash, not far from the motel. Working for Remiel required one to always be prepared. "Before my nephew Eddie died, he sent me a list of all of the contacts he'd collected. Kid was smart. Somehow he found this."

The Warden came over to read the list, brow furrowed. "Is that the number for the Prince?"

"Yes." Etienne tossed the phone onto a pillow. "And I called the Prince and proposed a deal."

"You did *what*?" The Warden dropped onto the edge of the mattress. "No one calls the Prince and proposes anything. Not unless they want to be dead."

"I've nothing to lose." Etienne gathered the rest of his clothes from the floor. He dumped them on the bed and started folding. "I offered the Prince Sarah Munro and the diary *before* she solves that cipher. The Prince agreed, but he also wants Fletcher Ames."

The Warden rose to pace the room. "If the Prince wants Sarah, why don't his warriors just take her?"

"Not sure. Maybe because Walker would die protecting her." Etienne went into the bathroom to grab his toothbrush and deodorant. "And the Prince still wants to recruit Walker."

"Do you have a plan where you stay alive?"

"I do." Etienne put the cap on the toothpaste and stuffed it into his backpack. He scanned the room. There wasn't much else to take, other than his weapons hidden in his motorcycle jacket lying on the floor near the anemic AC. "It's a good plan."

The Warden grabbed his arm. "Why are you telling me this when you know I'll go to Remiel?"

"Because you're helping the pretty historian." Etienne

peered into the Warden's face, close enough to see skeptical eyes beneath the hood. "When you dropped off that envelope with the map, you added an extra clue to the envelope. You gave Sarah her photos. You sent her that old ledger. You've been watching over her because you're helping her solve the cipher."

"I work for Remiel." The Warden dropped Etienne's arm. "Remiel needs that cipher solved, and I don't know how to do it. I'm helping her by sending all the clues I know about. He *knows* I'm helping her. And he knows why."

"Except Remiel doesn't care about Sarah. If she doesn't solve the cipher, she's dead. And I know that, despite your illogical loyalty to Remiel, Sarah's death is the one thing you won't allow."

The Warden returned to the window and this time opened the shutters to stare at the train tracks along the riverbank. One hand gripped the casing; the other was shoved in the hoodie pocket.

Etienne zipped his duffel. "I want you to help me kidnap Sarah, retrieve the diary, take Fletcher Ames, and hand them all to the Prince."

"Remiel will kill us both."

"I'm already dead to him." Etienne sighed. "I know your other goal, besides protecting Sarah, is to take down the Prince. It's the only reason you're working for Remiel, right? The enemy of my enemy is my friend?"

"Remiel isn't my friend. He's my distant cousin."

"You're family."

"And families don't betray each other."

Etienne scoffed. "Which is why Remiel wants to put me in the box? Remiel isn't just dangerous. He's a brilliant, narcissistic sadist."

"I'm not excusing Remiel's behavior."

Of course not. The Warden, for as long as Etienne could remember, had always been Remiel's guardian. Telling Etienne and his brothers that they'd no idea what Remiel had suffered, as if the suffering of others meant nothing. "Remiel wants to put me in the box because I lost my cell phone? After everything I've done for him? Bullshit."

"I'll talk to him." The Warden turned with crossed arms. "See if he'll change his mind."

"Remiel won't." Etienne ran his hands over his damp hair. "Our only chance is to work with the Prince. If we give him Sarah and the diary, before she solves the cipher, he'll let her live and he'll protect all of us from Remiel."

"Except I don't need protection from Remiel. In fact, if I tell Remiel where you are and what you're planning, he'll trust me even more."

Etienne found his phone again and scrolled his contacts. "If you do that, you'll be the one who loses." He'd highlighted one particular name, number, and email on the list.

"How'd you get this?" The Warden's voice dropped to a low drawl.

"From Cassio." The warrior had whispered it in Etienne's ear before he'd run from Sarah's house. "My brothers have instructions. If something happens to me, an email goes to this man telling him all about Sarah. Telling him all about his daughter."

"You're an ass." The Warden reached for the phone, but Etienne shoved it in his pocket. "You don't know shit about Sarah's *real* father."

Etienne threw the Warden onto the bed and yanked off the black hood. The Warden, with her lush red lips, flashing brown eyes, long dark, braided hair was, truly, a beautiful woman. He laid his body on top of hers. "I know you'll do anything, including betraying Remiel and seeking asylum from the Prince, to save Sarah."

The Warden shook her head, her eyes wide. "If we betray Remiel, he'll hunt us down for the rest of our lives."

"I'm already hunted." He placed his palms on the mattress on either side of her head. Despite their fifteen-year age gap and different backgrounds, their sufferings had given them something to bond over. "I need your help. No one else can know."

The Warden closed her eyes. "What do we do?"

Etienne stood and tossed his duffel next to the door. Then he closed his backpack. "I'll kidnap Sarah. You grab Fletcher Ames and meet me on the Isle of Grace."

The Warden scooted off the bed and tossed her braid over her shoulder. Her eyes flashed with indignation, annoyance, anger, and every other possible emotion. "There's no way I can take Fletcher without getting caught."

"We'll distract Remiel." Etienne slipped on his coat, then found his weapon to check the clip. Fully loaded, with a spare magazine in the backpack. "I have two bums waiting to take photos of a new man in Iron Rack's Gym."

She tilted her head. "Why?"

He shoved the clip into the gun and pulled the slide until a bullet entered the chamber. "Torridan went to Leedsville last night. And, according to my source in the prison, Torridan brought *him* to Savannah."

"Alex Mitchell?" She began to pace again. "The man who tried to *kill* Remiel?"

"Yes."

The Warden stopped by the window, her focus on the outside world she'd never be a part of again. "If we do this"—she spoke so softly he had to move behind her to hear—"you'll keep Sarah safe."

"I promise...Isabel Rutledge...to protect Sarah Munro." He put his hands on her shoulders and whispered, "If you help me, I'll save your best friend's daughter."

In the back room of Iron Rack's, Zack said goodbye to the exterminator and moved a stack of rusted metal folding chairs. The gym's storage room was still filled with stuff, but it was less stuff than Luke and Vane had started with.

They'd cleared out enough so the exterminator had been able to set rattraps, even catching a few along the way.

Now the center of the room was clear. The doors leading to the outside and to the main part of the gym needed new locks, but a locksmith was on his way. Luke had also moved in the metal filing cabinet to use as their armory. That was getting a new lock as well.

Operation Command Post was progressing. Hopefully that would make Nate happy.

At the moment, Pete and Vane were teaching classes. Luke was busy searching through the cell phone Nate had stolen, Samantha was teaching herself how to run the front desk, and Cain and Ty were clearing tunnels.

Since Calum's IT guys could arrive anytime, Zack offered to keep working on the back room. He was salvaging as much furniture as he could so they'd have someplace to put the computers. He'd found folding tables, metal chairs, and an old dresser.

After watching Nate and Sarah drive away with the diary, Zack had spoken with Garza and then returned to the gym and filled in Pete. Zack just hoped Nate would be okay. While he'd been grazed by a bullet, he'd also had a partial seizure. It'd taken all of Zack's strength to get Nate into the truck.

And the last thing Zack wanted to think about? What Nate had told him, during their stumble to the truck, about Kells and Jack. Because if it was true that Jack had made the accusation and Kells had signed Nate's commitment order, Zack didn't know if the unit would survive.

Garza stormed in. "I told Pete to cut his class short and meet us here."

"Okay." Zack set up a folding table he'd found and locked the legs. It should hold three of Luke's laptops. "What's wrong now?"

"Have you seen the news?"

"Nope." Zack had stayed away. It helped that the gym didn't have a TV. "Why?"

"Calum and a man named Maurice are in the hospital because Nate hit them both."

"Nate had to knock out Maurice and make the attack on Calum look real."

Garza blew out a gust of breath and ran his hands over his head. "There's a BOLO for Nate and Sarah. They were ID'd by a security camera as well as Maurice."

Fuck. "It really sucks not having any high-tech gear." Hell, not that long ago he and his men had been in a high-tech command post, *in the fucking desert*, with the best data supplied by every intelligence agency the U.S. government had. Now? They had nothing.

Garza helped him drag another folding table from beneath a stack of rotting gym mats. Rodent droppings fell off the table. It would need to be scrubbed with bleach.

Correction: Their *nothing* was covered with rat shit. *Hooah*.

Together they unfolded the table and locked the legs. "Forensics is looking for the bullet the security guard fired at Nate."

"Will they find it?"

Garza took it from his pocket. "It hit a bench outside the escape window. I dug it out when I responded to the scene."

Zack started moving the wet and moldy gym mats and tried not to sneeze. "Anyone see you?"

"No." Garza helped with the stinky mats, and together they were able to maneuver them out the door and into the Dumpster. Then Garza tossed in the bullet.

"Were there any cameras in the office?" Zack asked.

"Luckily, no. I'm working with Elliot on the case, but I let him take the lead."

They went inside, where Pete was waiting with bottles of cold water. "Any word from Nate?"

"Yes. I talked to Sheriff Boudreaux." Garza drank most of his bottle in one long gulp. "Nate and Sarah are on their way to the cabin. They know people are looking for them."

Zack wiped water off his chin. He hadn't realized how parched he was. "Nate's arm?"

"He'll recover." Garza finished his bottle and threw it into a black plastic contractor bag used for smaller trash. "I also spoke to Detective Hugh Waring in Charleston."

Zack finished his bottle and tossed it. Any news, even bad news, would be a welcome distraction. "Any intel about Stuart Pinckney?"

Pete stared hard at Zack. "Stuart Pinckney? Allison's husband?"

"Yes," Zack said.

Pete opened and closed his mouth three times before he said, "Oh."

"Stuart Pinckney is the other Charleston banker who went missing," Garza said.

"And you didn't tell us?" Pete clasped his hands behind his neck. "Hell, Zack. We can only help each other if we tell each other what the *fuck* is going on."

Garza's glare was in total agreement with Pete.

"Alright," Zack said. "Next time the husband of the woman I love is kidnapped, I'll call a staff meeting."

"Screw you."

Zack held out his hands. "Look, man. I'm sorry."

Garza cleared his throat and put his hands on his hips. Full-on, Kells-inspired lecture mode. "Does Nate have a medal of Saint Michael the Archangel?"

"He did," Pete said. "It was taken from him in the POW camp."

The stress in Zack's stomach turned sour, tightening his gut, making him nauseated. "Why?"

"Because sometime between midnight and six a.m., someone murdered Stuart Pinckney. His body was found in a churchyard in Charleston. The letter *B* had been carved into his left hand, and the only clue found on the body is a medal of Saint Michael the Archangel with the name Nathaniel Walker engraved on the back."

Fuck. Me.

"This is bullshit," Pete said. "Nate lost that medal years ago and is being set up."

"That medal belonged to Nate's father," Zack added. "They share the name."

Pete paced, arms flailing in different directions. "There's no way Nate could've driven up to Charleston, killed Stuart, and returned."

Garza scoffed. "It's only an hour and twenty minutes away. He had plenty of time."

"Except Nate can't drive," Zack reminded them.

"Yet Nate *does* drive." Garza raised a palm before Pete could protest. "Nate is innocent. There's no motive, no witnesses. Just that medal. But that medal could implicate Nate in two murders. He drove to the isle yesterday, and this diary theft doesn't help his case. Which brings me to our next problem. Kells."

Pete shook his head. "You gotta be shittin' me."

"Wish I was, brother. Kells landed in Charleston and, while renting a car to drive to Savannah, was taken in to be questioned by Detective Waring."

Zack and Pete shared an *oh God no* glance.

"According to Waring," Garza said, "they talked about yesterday's dead man on the Isle of Grace, Pinckney's murder, Nate's medal, and Nate and Sarah's BOLO." Garza snapped his fingers. "And, just for kicks and giggles, a Shakespearean quotation had been cut into the ground near Pinckney's body."

"The Fianna," Pete said, looking up at the ceiling. "They do shit like that."

Zack wanted to curl up and cry.

Luke appeared in the doorway. "Hey. Just heard from Kells. He and Alex should be here in an hour. I also got into that cell phone Nate stole."

Garza crossed his arms. "Nate stole a cell phone?"

"From Maurice," Luke said. "There's not much on it

except for a few calls between Maurice and a man who I believe is Sarah's boss at the Smithsonian."

When Luke left, Pete said, "Great. More useless intel."

"I'm needed at the station." Garza clapped Zack on the shoulder. "I'm sorry about your girlfriend's husband." Garza scrunched his nose. "That sounded weird, didn't it?"

Zack nodded because he didn't have the courage to mention that Allison had never actually been his girlfriend.

Stuart was dead. Nate was a suspect. Kells knew they were running an unauthorized operation and was on his way home to skin them. And the one thing Zack knew to be true? He was an ass. Because the only thing he could think about was the fact that Allison was free.

CHAPTER 40

"I CAN'T BELIEVE YOU WERE SHOT," SARAH SAID AS NATE maneuvered the boat along the river.

He wasn't concerned about the wound. He'd suffered worse pain.

The sun had come out, and she'd put on her straw hat and had Grady's map in her lap. Nate steered as they motored by miles of undisturbed coastline edged with banyan trees, marsh grass, and dense swamps. Despite the desolation and humidity, it was beautiful. Maybe it was the isolation that appealed to him. Or the white birds skimming along the water shimmering in the heat.

They'd had no problem finding and loading up the boat. Although they'd had to make hard choices about what to bring. They'd both agreed on clothes, food, and water. But Sara had wanted to take *boxes* of research until he convinced her the boat would sink. She'd finally agreed to take what would fit in her straw bag. Which, unsurprisingly, was a lot.

She pointed to a cut in the river. "Turn right there."

This estuary was narrower and shallower, and he had to guide the boat carefully. He didn't want the outboard motor to get caught in seagrass. As they went deeper into the isle, the trees along the banks formed canopies above them, cutting off the sunlight.

Sarah had been quiet since leaving Pops's house.

"Sarah? Are you okay?"

"I'm not sure I have enough information to solve the cipher." She sighed. "Everyone has given up so much to help us. I can't believe what they're risking. Especially Sheriff Boudreaux and Detective Garza. They could lose their jobs."

"I know." That was a truth Nate lived with every day.

She touched his knee. "How are you feeling?"

He knew she wanted to know about the seizure he'd had after being shot as well as how his arm was doing, but he didn't want to worry her. "I don't have a headache, so I'm good."

"I'm glad you drank another cup of tea before we left Pops's."

His stomach wasn't. "I know you were fired."

She nodded and stared at the map again. "My boss warned me not to apply for that grant, but I did it anyway."

"Any idea how he found out?"

"No." She pointed to a dock on their right. "It was a foreign granting agency, but I keep forgetting that the world of historians seeking grant money isn't just competitive, it's small."

He guided the boat to the dock and handed Sarah the rope. She got out and tied them up. Keeping the boat balanced, he handed her supplies, which she stacked on the bank. The cabin sat sixty yards away, on a crest of land, surrounded by the encroaching forest.

"Does this cabin belong to Pops?"

"Kind of. Grady and Pops are Capel land caretakers, and they use it whenever they're out here."

"I'm hoping *primitive* refers to *no cell service* and not *no indoor plumbing*."

He was worried about the same thing. Once their supplies were unloaded, he picked up the case of water and led the way to the cabin.

She grabbed the duffels and a bag of groceries and followed. "Once we're unloaded—"

"We'll go to the cemetery." He saw her biting her lower lip. "Don't worry. You can do this."

She went up the four steps to the porch of the rough-hewn cabin. Opening the door, she said, "*We* can do this."

He lowered the case of water onto the porch, took her bags out of her hands, and dropped them. Then he removed her hat and drew her in for a kiss. It was a long, lingering kiss. The kind that promised breakfast in bed, Sunday picnics, and snuggling by the fire on winter nights. The kind that promised forever. Because forever was what he wanted. Forever was what he'd dreamed of even when he hadn't been dreaming. Forever was what he knew he'd never have.

He lifted his head and looked into her brown eyes. Every time he was close to her, the humming in his body that foreshadowed a seizure eased. She wasn't his cure, she was his hope.

"Nate?" She wrapped her arms around him. "I can't lose you."

"I know." He kissed her head and gently undid her arms. "If we're going to see that cemetery—"

"Alright." She wiped her face with her fingers. "Let's get settled, and I'll grab my things."

Before she moved, he swept her up and carried her over the threshold.

She wound her arms around his neck. "What are you doing?"

What I will never have another chance to do. "What does it look like?"

She pressed her forehead against his and whispered, "It looks like Heaven."

An hour later, Nate tied the boat to a mangrove tree near the Cemetery of Lost Children.

Luckily, the cabin hadn't been too primitive. It had a bedroom with a queen-size bed, a bathroom with a shower and a tub, and an open kitchen and family room with a fireplace. They'd found clean sheets, a homemade quilt, and towels in the closet.

While Sarah made the bed, he searched the cabin for weapons. Water and power were provided by a generator on the side porch. There was gasoline as well as a canoe in the shed. He'd found wire and rattraps with which to make trip wires. And he'd checked out the ham radio. Thank goodness there was a Morse code book in the drawer. Although he hoped he wouldn't need it.

Nate helped Sarah out of the boat. "Do you have a camera?"

"I'll use my phone. It's in the backpack with the water, ammo, and knives." They both had pistols, and he also carried the shotgun and machete. "Can you locate us on our map?"

Now they were using the map of the cemetery the hooded man had dropped off at the gym yesterday.

"Yes." He studied the map, looked around, and started walking. "I always liked math and things like orienteering because I'm dyslexic and hated to read."

She followed. "I didn't know."

"It's not a big deal. That's why you're solving the cipher and I'm protecting you. I'm your muscle."

"Oh, Nate." Her voice sounded so low, and he watched a blush rise from her neck to her cheeks. "You're much more than that."

More than anything else in the world, he wanted that to be true. "Come on. Let's find a hide site."

Sarah followed Nate up a ravine, not liking how heavy her breathing had gotten. She really needed to exercise more. "Are we close?"

Nate read the map and then scanned the area. "Soon."

"I'm not sure what the scale is on that map, but it's a pirate map. It could be anything."

"What do you mean?"

"Pirates measured distance—on land—in feet, yards, paces, and leagues. It was part of their ploy to make their treasure maps difficult to decipher."

Nate paused to study the map again. "Good to know."

When her stomach rumbled, she regretted not eating more of Pops's jambalaya. But she'd been too wound up to eat more than a few bites. "I wish we had strawberry pie."

He laughed. "Is that your new comfort treat?"

"It's my new everything treat."

"I thought that's what I was." Laughter leaked out of his voice.

"How can you not be freaked out right now?"

"Because"—he reached down to help her up the steepest part of the ravine—"I've been in much worse situations."

"I'm not sure I want to know about those."

Once she stood next to him, he kissed her hand. "I can't tell you anyway."

Of course not. Still, it hurt her heart to think that he had painful memories he couldn't share with her.

"You're going to be okay, Sarah. I'll make sure of it."

She stopped because she was sad and angry at how unfair all of this was to him and his men—but mostly him. "What if we ran away together? I don't have a job, but I have money saved. We could change our names. Live our lives together, forever."

He caressed her face with one hand, while the other held the shotgun on his shoulder. "We can't do that, sweetheart."

"Why?" She blinked quickly so she wouldn't cry. "This is all...*wrong*. You weren't responsible for that massacre. You were kept in a POW camp. Your men are in prison. You were tortured and poisoned until you lost most of your memories." Her voice broke. "Haven't you given enough?"

He pulled her in until her head rested on his chest, his chin on her head. "I can't leave because if I do, my men will pay the price."

She sniffled. "I don't understand."

"If I don't return to Maine, the men in Savannah join the others at Leedsville."

She backed up until he dropped his arms. She wanted to

see his green eyes, make sure he was telling her the truth. "Says who?"

"Says Kells. I knew the rules—that I had to return or my men would be punished—before I left the prison hospital."

"Kells," she scoffed. "The same man who signed your commitment papers."

"I can't leave my men. I won't let them face the consequences of my cowardice."

"You're not a coward. Why can't you see that about yourself?"

He kissed her softly. "I don't want to argue. I want you to trust me. Can you do that?"

He was right. She didn't understand, but she wanted to. "Yes, Nate. I trust you."

Twenty minutes later, they stood in front of a tomb with yellow police tape blowing in the wind.

"Look." She pointed to the *Hic est finis iter est scriptor* carved along the top of the stone crypt. The name *JONES* had been cut below the phrase. The building was four feet deep by six feet wide. A wrought iron fence surrounded the plot.

Nate walked the perimeter, and she followed. They stopped in the back where the dirt looked clumpy and congealed. Someone had stuck yellow marker flags in the ground. "This is where the banker was found."

She shivered and focused on the five-pointed stars and five-petaled roses carved into the stone. They were so worn and covered with lichen, they were almost invisible. "Can you hand me that ledger from the backpack?"

A moment later, he handed it to her. "This book looks old."

"It is." She flipped through the pages, looking for a Jones entry. "The even stranger thing is that someone sent it to my house and didn't leave a note."

"Huh."

"This mausoleum was built by Thomas Toban in 1750, yet the people inside died between 1630 and 1703." She handed her phone to Nate. "Will you take photos for me? Especially the stars and roses?"

"Sure."

While he took photos, she read. "Thomas commissioned at least six tombs in this cemetery, most of them for families who'd died decades earlier. I wonder if Thomas built these tombs to hide—maybe even protect—the older Prideaux hide sites."

"Makes sense." Nate finished taking photos. "Ready?"

"Yes." She followed Nate to the front door. It took a few tries to find the right key, but the doors swung open easily. "One might think the hinges had been recently oiled."

Nate used the backpack to prop open one door, re-slung the shotgun onto his shoulder, and handed her a flashlight. "Shine the flashlight into the room, but my pistol and I go first." He didn't wait for her response. He drew his weapon and entered the crypt.

She was, by now, used to his ordering-people-around style. He motioned her in, and she gagged on the stench of decay.

"Sarah, breathe through your mouth."

It took a moment for her eyes to adjust and see…no caskets. "Where are the bodies?"

Nate walked the perimeter. Slime covered the walls, probably causing the disgusting odor. "No idea."

Her foot caught on something metal on the floor. An iron ring attached to a trapdoor. When they opened it, the light shone into pitch-blackness, barely outlining stairs.

"I'll go down first," he said. "I'm not sure about the stairs."

She handed him the flashlight. "Be careful."

A minute later, he said, "It's wet, but the stairs are safe."

She counted twenty steps, then felt Nate's hands on her waist. He lifted her and she landed on a plank floor covered in water up to her ankles. Nate swung the light around a room that was four times the size of the crypt above them.

Tabby made from sand and crushed oyster shells covered stone walls. "My research was right. The walls are lined with *opus signinum*."

He pointed the light to where the floor sloped down toward a dark corner. Water flowed under the planks, and there was a door nearby with another padlock. "We're at the water level, if not lower, of the estuary this place backs up to."

She walked the room. "These rivers and streams change with the tides and the seasons, and according to my research, the hide sites were only dry two to four weeks a year. The pirates who built them didn't have access to them at the same time, which is why they built so many."

"That's smart. Missions run out of the same safe house for weeks aren't a good idea. You want to keep moving." He shone the flashlight on the door again. "More roses and stars."

"In classical navigation, they mean time and distance." She paused. "The ledger entry for this tomb had the numbers *0519* written in the margins." She touched his arm until he moved the light between them. "The numbers could indicate time. The months and weeks the sites were dry before they were flooded again." She counted on her fingers. "This hide site is dry in May, starting the nineteenth week of the year."

He pointed the light along the bottom edge of the room. "See those clay tubes? That's how the water flows in and out. This cellar is flooded for most of the year, except for a few weeks from mid-May to mid-June." He swung the beam around again. "Except this is the fourth week in June and the hide site is just now filling up."

"Maybe the tidal patterns are changing. And tonight is a new moon. The tides should be even higher."

"Or Thomas got the dates wrong."

Dates? She moved his light to shine on the door's stars and roses. "You're brilliant!"

He smiled. "How's that?"

"Time. Specifically, thirteen days." She took his hand and led him to the stairs. "We're missing thirteen days from 1752."

They got out of the hide site and shut the door. Nate locked up, put away the light, and shrugged on the backpack before saying, "What are you talking about?"

"These tombs were built before 1752."

"So?"

She started the trek to their next stop. "In 1752, the British government dumped the Julian calendar for the Gregorian calendar." She waved a hand around the cemetery. "The colonies lost ten days, like, *poof*." She snapped her fingers for effect. "Because of the way leap years work, which is math that's way too complicated for me, those ten days in 1752 are equivalent to thirteen days now."

Sarah sank onto a flat tomb, feeling more light-hearted than she had in days. "We haven't solved the cipher yet, but we found a hide site. We proved they actually exist and to hell with *The British Journal*. I know it's stupid, but I want to call my boss and tell him I was right all along."

Nate knelt, placed his gun on the ground, and held her hands. "It's not stupid. You've been searching for these sites your entire adult life. You should be proud."

She cupped his face in her hands and kissed him. She loved the feel of his lips, his woodsy smell like pine and freshly cut grass, the happiness she felt in his arms. "We did it, Nate." This time she spoke so softly, it wouldn't even count as a whisper. "We found a hide site. Now we're going to save you."

CHAPTER 41

NATE STOOD IN FRONT OF SAINT MICHAEL THE ARCHANGEL while Sarah took photos. The archangel, with his white marble washed in a green mildew haze, stood on a plinth block. He gripped a shield in one hand and a sword in the other. He was also naked, with his manly parts making up for the fact that he no longer had a head.

Nate focused on the *TT* carved into the front of the plinth. His emotions were hard to pinpoint. He was happy for Sarah because she'd found the thing she'd been searching for her whole life. And while that thing may or may not be able to save him, she'd still defied all of her naysayers and betrayers.

The problem was while she'd found what had given her life meaning, so had he. Yet he was expected to give her up to live a life locked away as if his heart hadn't been ripped from his chest. The only thing he knew for sure was that this next twenty hours were the most important he'd ever live. They were the last hours he'd ever have with the woman he loved.

"Come on!" Sarah came back for him. "You're dawdling."

"I'm carrying the backpack and the weapons."

Her laugh was like cold water running over hot stones. It both soothed and sent a surge of steam through him.

She tugged his arm. "I want to show you something."

He let her lead the way.

"Look at the statue's plinth block." She knelt, pushed away wildflowers, and pointed to the stone. "Five-petaled roses and five-pointed stars."

"Thomas had both tombs built. Maybe the builder gave him a break on the design."

She stood and wiped her hands on her jeans. "I never thought of that. I'd just assumed the designs connected them."

He hadn't meant to be harsh. Walking around the statue, he searched for something that would help. He came to the front again. The angel had been carved in a masculine way, and he smiled. He'd seen many classical statues, but this one was *well endowed*. He placed his hand on the shield to peer closer. Maybe the *fullness* was a representation of Thomas's insecurities.

"What are you doing?"

Startled, he looked up at the sword, then the shield. "Checking out the weapons."

"Really."

"Yep." He ran his hand down the shield. "I was curious—" He felt something beneath his palm and smoothed his hand over the mildew. "I think there are words written on the shield."

Sarah moved in next to him and used her fingers to feel the soft indentations in the stone. "You're right. We can do a rubbing." She reached for the zipper of the backpack and found a journal and a pencil.

"Do you carry everything you own everywhere you go?"

"Usually." She stuck the pencil in her ponytail and ripped out a page from the journal. "But you made me leave things behind, both in the truck and at the cabin."

"You didn't need to bring a textbook to the cemetery."

"You don't know that." She stood on the plinth and pressed the paper to the shield.

"You're also not the one carrying everything."

She rubbed the pencil over the paper, and both dark and light edges appeared. "For *muscle*, you complain a lot."

He couldn't help but laugh and held her waist to keep her steady.

When she was done, he helped her down. Then she showed him the paper. "*Hic est finis iter est scriptor.*" She tucked the paper into the journal. "Now do you think there's a connection? Or is it still a design discount?"

"You're the historian." He kissed her on the nose. "You tell me."

She smiled wide. "I do."

"Then I believe you." He took her hand. "Where to next?"

She pulled away to retrieve a book from the backpack. "Calum made us a crude map we can use to find Rebecca Prideaux's tomb. This was my mother's copy of *Othello*. My mother was a fan."

Nate opened the worn paperback copy of *Othello* and studied the truly awful topographic drawing only a lawyer could make. "Alright." He shrugged on the backpack and arranged his weapons. "Follow me." She fell in next to him, and he said, "Maybe that phrase is the key to the cipher."

"I hope not!" She wrote in her journal as they walked. "My Latin isn't *that* good."

"I was teasing." He took her elbow as she erased something at the same time she stepped over a broken headstone.

"Oh." She smiled and tapped her lips with the pencil. "Besides, the phrase isn't long enough. The pieces of the cipher I've seen use twenty-two different letters."

He stopped and kissed her. Despite the backpack, rifle, and gun in his jacket pocket, he grabbed her shoulders and pulled her close. He didn't just want her in his bed. He wanted her laughter and her joy and her love.

When he finally let her go, she wobbled. "What time is it?"

He checked his watch. "Tide goes out in less than an hour."

She offered her hand, and he took it. "Then let's find Rebecca and go home."

What am I going to do without Nate?

She watched him as he slashed his way through the brush on their way to Rebecca's tomb. Even though he wore a jacket and carried a backpack and a shotgun, she could see his graceful strength with each swing of the machete. He was so much more than muscle. In a short period of time, he'd become *everything*.

A few minutes later, they stopped in front of the tomb with the weeping angel and the carving of *My Soul's Joy. My Fair Warrior*. Seeing it now, knowing she was her mother's joy and might lose her own warrior, her eyes filled. She blinked away the burning.

"Wow," he said, trying to read the name. "This is sad. Are you sure it's Rebecca's?"

She rubbed her face with the cuffs of her jacket. The angel's face seemed not just sorrowful but angry at the injustice done to this child. "The ledger marked Thomas as buying a tomb for 'my soul's joy' with the initials *RP* next to it." She walked around the tomb, tearing a page out of her journal. "Nate, can you hand me a pencil?"

"You have one in your hair."

Embarrassed, she yanked it out. "Thanks." She and Nate knelt, with him holding the paper while she rubbed. "This limestone is fragile, and I don't want to chip it."

"We still have time."

Except we don't. She used the long side of the charcoal pencil and floated it over the paper. It was painstaking, but when she lifted the paper she'd transcribed *52OTH310332*.

She found her phone in her jacket and went through her photos. "Look." She showed him the photo she'd taken of the diary. "It's the same sequence Rebecca wrote in her diary. I just wish I knew what it all meant."

Nate checked his watch. Then he stowed the rubbing and journal in the backpack. "We need to get home."

She opened *Othello* to the page bookmarked by the photo of her mother. It was hard to believe that her mother had once stood in front of this tomb, pregnant and weeping for her lover. While her mother had never talked about

Sarah's birth father, her mother had also made Sarah feel like she was the most wanted child ever born.

Sarah ran her fingers over her mother's sad face and followed Nate. "I hope this is enough to solve the cipher."

He watched her, his face a study of hard angles and firm jawline. It made him look even more masculine, even more dangerous. "A friend once told me you can't live in the wreckage of the future and the past." He cupped her cheeks. "All I want, right now, is to be with you until I leave. If we solve it, wonderful. If not, I need to know you're going to be safe. Alright?"

She swallowed and nodded.

"Good." He kissed her—on the forehead this time—and started walking again.

Sarah stepped carefully on the spongy ground. They were skirting the edge of the cemetery, closer to water, and there were pockets of marsh mud. She tried to keep up, but she'd noticed a notation on the page her mother's photo had bookmarked. Her mother had starred line 318, which began with "Here is my journey's end." Then she noticed the act and scene numbers. "Nate?"

He raised a hand. Slowly, he dropped his backpack and machete and aimed the shotgun into the grove of resurrection ferns. "Boars."

His attention was focused on something she couldn't see, his head tilted as if listening to something she couldn't hear. "Take the path by the Jones tomb and get to the boat. No noise."

"But—"

"If I say run, you run and climb the nearest tree you can find." He looked at her, his eyes intense and determined. "Got it?"

She shoved the pencil into her hair, clutched her book, and moved, only to crack a branch.

"Sarah?" Nate primed the shotgun, the loud double-clicking sound making her wince. "Go. *Now*."

She turned and walked fast and quietly. Once she passed two columns draped in wild honeysuckle, she heard him say, "Run!"

She took off, looking for a climbable tree while at the same time trying not to trip. Loud snorting sounds told her the feral hog was coming.

Suddenly, a shot ripped through the cemetery. A flock of birds panicked and flew away. A second shot sent a sound wave that silenced the chatter of the woods. She hid behind a tree and waited.

Finally, Nate emerged with the backpack over one shoulder, machete attached to his hip, the shotgun ready to fire.

She ran to him. With one arm, he held her close. His breath was fast but steady, unlike hers. She was a hyperventilating mess.

"It's okay. Let's get to the boat." He pulled the pencil from her hair and said in a voice laced with laughter, "I wonder what Augustus would've done."

Her laugh sounded like a snort. "You're unbelievable. And covered in marsh mud."

His grin brightened his eyes. "Unbelievably sexy?"

"Whatever you say." *Although he really, really is.* She just didn't want to make his head any bigger than it already was. "What happened?"

"I killed a boar." He lifted a branch for her. "I wanted to drag it to a mud pit. But since it was too heavy, I covered it in branches."

"Does it matter?"

"Pops and Grady have been fighting off encroaching boars. Since dead ones will attract predators, including other feral hogs and coyotes, maybe even wolves, I wanted to do something." They reached the ravine leading down to the boat, and he helped her in. "I'll send Grady a message on the ham radio and let him know."

Once they were on the river, heading to the cabin, he

handed her a bottle of water. "What were you telling me before the boar showed up?"

She drank her water, not caring that half of it trailed down her chin. "I know how to solve the cipher."

CHAPTER 42

ZACK ENTERED KELLS'S OFFICE AND CLOSED THE DOOR.

"You're late." Kells stood near the window, arms crossed, eyes blazing.

"I was helping Samantha deal with a difficult member."

Pete, who sat in a chair near the desk, added, "Hiring Samantha was Nate's idea because we need the extra help. Calum agreed to pay her salary."

Zack felt a burning in the back of his head and turned to see Alex Mitchell near the filing cabinet. He sat in a chair, ankles crossed, tossing an apple into the air and catching it again.

Alex wore a scowl that would scare the devil. His black hair had been shorn, and bruises covered his face. His dark-blue—almost purple—eyes carried more anger and anguish than should be legally allowed.

Zack nodded, and then saw Garza, shouldering the map of Afghanistan on the wall.

"Tell me again," Kells said slowly because, obviously, he thought they were all in preschool. "Where is Nate?"

Zack raised his hand. Again, because preschool. "A lot's happened since you've been gone, sir."

"It's been one day." Kells nodded at the cop. "Detective Garza filled me in on what he knows."

Garza offered a classic had-no-choice-brother shrug.

Zack rubbed his sweaty palms on his thighs "Yesterday..." He started with Nate going to the Isle of Grace, being attacked, and having a seizure, all the way up to Nate getting shot after stealing a valuable diary and doing the hightail to the Isle of Grace to solve the cipher. Because maybe if Nate and Sarah solved the cipher they could use it as leverage against Remiel Marigny and the Fianna to save both Jack and Sarah's father. Zack also told Kells about

Remiel taking Sarah's father, the Prince's threat to kill Jack, and Remiel's counter-promise to protect Jack.

Then Zack added the missing Russian missiles problem. Which wasn't their problem, but Kells would want to know.

Once Zack finished, he sat in the chair next to Pete.

Kells, to his credit, hadn't said a word during the recitation. He'd just watched Zack with those goldish-brown eyes that could spot bullshit a battlefield away.

Finally, Kells let out a long-suffering sigh. "Do the other men know what's going on?"

Zack shared a glance with Pete before saying, "Some. Since the Fianna were involved, we didn't want to—"

"What?" Kells shook his head. "Put them in more danger?"

"No, sir."

Kells turned away to stare out the window. "Did any of you, at any time during this escalating mess, think to call me?"

"No, sir," Pete said. "Nate wanted to handle this on his own."

"Nate is sick, suffering from memory loss, seizures, and Lord know what else." Kells squeezed the bridge of his nose. "I just spent an hour with Detective Hugh Waring in Charleston. He wanted to know Nate's whereabouts last night until this morning."

"Nate was at the club and then with Sarah all night," Zack said.

Kells faced them again, hands on his hips. "The same Sarah who sent Waring a list of our men in prison that she found in my office? The same Sarah who took one of my files? The same Sarah who encouraged Nate to steal that diary?"

Zack wasn't sure what to say to that except "Sir, Nate isn't a murderer. His medal was stolen in the POW camp."

"We know that." Kells waved an arm around the room. "But Detective Waring doesn't care. All he's worried about is a murdered banker in his town and a second man killed on the isle where Nate *drove* to yesterday morning."

"Remiel killed that man on the isle." Pete said sullenly.

"The problem is," Kells said, "no one in civilian law enforcement knows who Remiel is, that he was supposedly dead, but that he is in fact alive. It's all classified, remember?"

"With all due respect," Garza said, stepping into the convo, "Sarah was with Nate on the isle yesterday morning."

"Can she account for all his time?" Kells asked. "Was she with him at every moment until he returned to town?"

"I'm just saying—"

Kells raised a hand. "I appreciate your help, Detective. I'm only just realizing how valuable an asset you are. What I don't know is why you're doing this. It's hard to trust a man when you don't know his motivations."

Garza's face turned to stone. "If you'll excuse me, I need to return to the station." With a nod toward Zack and Pete, Garza left, making sure to shut the door behind him.

"That's one ally down," Alex said from his chair as he started to peel his apple with a bowie knife. "Well done."

"Alex?" Pete threw an empty soda can that missed Alex's head and fell onto the floor. "Shut the fuck up."

"That's enough." Kells began to pace, and Zack exhaled. Kells's pacing meant he was moving beyond his anger into fix-it mode. "Did anyone try to stop Nate from putting us all in danger, especially himself?"

"Of course we did." Pete's face twisted into a scowl Zack had never seen before. "Sir, why did you have Sarah and Nate followed? We know about the file that Sarah took with the photos and background info."

Kells ran a hand over his short, ginger-red hair. "I had reason to believe Remiel was targeting Sarah. I discovered the connection a few weeks ago, which is why Nate is in some of those photographs."

"Yet you didn't tell us?" Pete pointed at Kells. "Weeks ago, you knew Remiel might've been behind all of this, and you didn't mention it."

Kells stopped pacing and returned to the window. "I didn't *know*. I *suspected*. I was protecting you."

"Is that why you signed Nate's commitment papers?" Zack hated the sneer in his voice that bordered on insolence but couldn't help himself. "And Jack leveled an accusation against Nate? To protect him?"

"Whoa," Alex said with a smile Zack wanted to rip off the ex-convict's face. "Now that I didn't know."

Kells crossed his arms. "I did what I felt was best at the time. And I am doing the same now."

Pete stood. "You've no idea what's best for Nate. You haven't seen him in action in years. You haven't—" Pete shook his head as if reorganizing his words. "You haven't heard his stories of the POW camp. Of what they did to him or Jack or any of the other men. You don't even know why Nate lost his medal at the camp. Or that he saw a Fianna warrior the night of the ambush. You don't have a right to be pissed *at* him because you weren't around when guards were pissing *on* him."

Kells closed his eyes for a long moment. When he opened them again, they weren't as fierce. He'd used his infamous self-control to dial back his temper. "None of you told me what was going on yesterday or today. I have a right to be angry."

"Agreed," Pete said. "But Nate needs to fix this before he returns to that prison hospital."

"How? By breaking into another hospital? By stealing a priceless diary?"

"No, sir," Zack said. "By helping Sarah solve the cipher."

Kells muttered a number of curses under his breath. "We can't negotiate with Remiel or the Prince. And Nate, more than any of you, should understand that no leverage can fix this."

"You're wrong." Pete said. "In a screwed-every-which-way sitch like this, our only option is leverage. That cipher is all we've got."

Kells went to his desk and sat, his attention on the files and paperwork scattered on top. "I need to talk to Nate."

Pete sighed. "Sir, there's no cell service out there."

"Figure it out." Kells raised his head and speared Zack with a don't-question-any-more-of-my-fucking-orders gaze. "And tell Nate I want him in. *ASAP*."

⁓

Etienne had a second safe house. He'd learned that lesson from the Fianna. Always have backups for your backups, including three safe houses, one of which your cousin doesn't know about. This one was in an abandoned building not far from Iron Rack's Gym, with access to Calum Prioleau's tunnels.

Etienne handed Isabel his phone, with the photo of Alex Mitchell that the two bums who lived in the alley near Iron Rack's had taken. "What do you think?"

She sat on the table laid out with weapons and cleaning supplies and studied the photo. Tonight, her long hair was in a high ponytail. "It's Alex. I recognize those amethyst eyes and that pissed-off frown."

If Etienne wasn't in such a desperate situation with such a desperate timeline, he'd take her on the floor, surrounded by concrete and brick walls and metal beams. In all the grittiness that represented everything his life had become. He craved the smell of her skin, her tongue—

"I'm still not sure about this." Her voice brought him out of his daydreams. "Remiel hardly lets Fletcher Ames out of his sight."

"It's too late to change our minds." Etienne paced the industrial area. "We move forward with the plan."

Isabel stayed quiet, her head lowered while she read their futures in the pine floorboards.

"Isabel?" When she raised her head, he said, "This is how we save Sarah."

Isabel blinked. "You're sure if we bring Sarah, the diary, and Fletcher to the Prince that he'll protect her?"

"He'll protect all of us." Etienne traced a series of scars along her forehead. "The Prince doesn't make deals lightly. If we renege—"

"We die." She intertwined her fingers behind her neck. She was signaling either defeat or resignation. It didn't matter which because either would get her to do what he needed done.

"As soon as you return to the *Brigid*, I'll send the photo of Alex to Remiel." Etienne put on his motorcycle jacket and found his phone and his weapon, shoving both in the pockets. "You'll have a short window to take Fletcher."

"No." She took his hands, her gaze pleading. "This won't work."

"It will. Once Remiel sees Alex, he'll go insane and take it out on someone. He won't choose you because he adores you. He won't choose Fletcher Ames because that piece of meat's already been broken. Escape while Remiel is occupied. His *episodes* last twenty minutes. Make sure you're gone by then."

She swallowed hard. "It'll be too dark to take the river."

"I know Capel land almost as well as I know your body. When all this is over," he said, "we'll go away. Live our lives the way we want to. Together."

She pressed a hand to her mouth and said in a muffled voice, "Do you know what Remiel did after he discovered Fletcher Ames's betrayal?"

"I was there when Remiel tortured him."

"Remiel killed Ames's niece. She was three months old."

Shivers left scorch marks on Etienne's back, as if he'd been burned with dry ice. "All the more reason to do this. If we give the Prince what he wants, we'll never see Remiel Marigny again."

CHAPTER 43

SARAH PUT ON WATER TO BOIL FOR MAC AND CHEESE, THE tomato soup was heating in the microwave, and she'd started a pot of coffee. She also needed to make Nate another cup of herbal tea.

She'd already bathed, and Nate was still in the tub. They'd considered doing it together but they'd both agreed they didn't need to get distracted. She'd also changed into her PJ pants, camisole, softest zip-up sweatshirt, and fluffy socks she wore as slippers. She'd towel-dried and braided her hair because she wasn't sure what else to do with it.

"I smell food." The deep, masculine voice came from nearby, and she turned to see Nate with only a towel around his waist.

Her mouth went dry. For some reason, he looked larger than last night. Maybe because, for the first time, it was light. Or maybe it was his newly re-bandaged shoulder. His muscles were so defined that water from his long, wet hair followed the rivulets of his cut body. Down his neck, working their way across his chest, disappearing beneath the towel slung low on his hips, then reappearing as they traveled along his calves.

There was nothing soft about him. Her heart began a staccato beat that made breathing difficult. If she pressed herself against him, his body would give no quarter.

"Sarah."

His voice and the beeping microwave snapped her out of her stupor. "Food is almost ready."

"I need you to do something first."

She bit her lip and faced him again. He was closer now, and she could see the scars on his chest, beneath the dusting of hair. Burns. Cuts. Long stripes that looked like they could've been whip marks. *What had this man suffered?* "Yes?" There were so many frogs in her throat she was amazed she got one word out.

He held up a pair of haircutting scissors, a comb, and a battery-powered hair trimmer she'd not noticed. She'd been too distracted.

"You want me to cut your hair." *Nice going, obvious girl.* What was wrong with her?

Nate placed everything on the table and used a finger to tilt her head until their gazes met. "They may or may not do this in the prison hospital, but I want you to."

"Don't you need permission?"

"I'm not in the army anymore. From now until tomorrow, I'm making my own decisions." He handed her the tools. "You know how to cut hair, don't you?"

She smirked. "I'm a cop's daughter. I know how to cut a man's hair."

"Good." He went out to the porch.

She followed to find him sitting in a rocking chair, towel still around his waist, waiting for her. The sun was setting behind them, but the sky had a pinkish hue, with all signs of the storm gone. It was hot and humid but not as buggy as it'd been in the cemetery. "I thought it would be easier to sweep up out here."

She laid the tools on an overturned fishing bucket nearby. "How short?"

"Keep buzzing until I say stop."

She combed his hair from crown to end, trying to ignore the scars on his back. She'd felt them last night, but seeing them now—much worse than the front—made her hands shake in sadness and rage. She'd like nothing better than to seek retribution on his behalf. But knowing Nate, he'd never let her do that. "I can't use the trimmer until it dries."

"Cut as much of it as you can."

"I don't know how I feel about this." She started

combing again. It wasn't fair. His hair was thicker than hers. "I've only ever seen you with long hair."

"I can assure you"—his voice rumbled as if holding in his laughter—"I'll be even sexier."

No doubt. "Well, you can't have a long pompadour."

His fingers gripped the chair's handrails, and he planted his feet so he wouldn't rock. "I don't know what that is, but it doesn't sound badass."

Nothing was as badass as Nate Walker. Or as gentle. And loving. "A pompadour is a medium-length cut with long bangs combed up from the forehead in a high roll." She worked the comb through one more time. "It was named after Madame de Pompadour, King Louis XV's mistress."

"No real man would have such a lame haircut."

"I knew a man once who did." She smiled and began cutting. "Augustus."

༄

An hour and a half later, Nate came in from setting trip wires around the cabin and couldn't help himself. He stared in the mirror and ran his hands over his head. He honestly couldn't remember the last time he'd had short hair, and it felt...freeing.

He went to the CD player in the corner, next to the ham radio he'd already used to message Grady, and found a Nat King Cole album inside. He turned it on, listening to the strains of "Sweet Lorraine." Sarah sat cross-legged on the floor surrounded by research.

After his haircut, he'd changed into jeans and a T-shirt for dinner. While macaroni and tomato soup weren't his favorites, he'd been hungry, and the food hot. Then they'd gone back outside with her coffee and the tea that tasted like sludge so she could finish his haircut with the trimmer.

"How do you feel about your hair?" She sipped her coffee, but he could see the smile hidden behind the mug.

He ran his hands over his head again. "Glad I don't need a brush anymore."

She smiled. "Come help me."

He sat on the couch, close enough to take one of the three pencils sticking out of her hair. "I thought you were doing this on the table."

"I need to be in the center where I can see everything." She handed him her mother's beat-up copy of *Othello* and a piece of paper. "Open up the play to Act 5, Scene 2, lines 310 to 332."

"Why?"

She scanned her circle of research, which included all of the photos they'd collected, Rebecca's diary, their cemetery map, and the ledger. There were also notebooks, pens, pencils, and multicolored Post-it notes. It looked like a huge mess, but he wasn't about to doubt the woman with the PhD.

She handed him the rubbing from Rebecca's tomb. "See that sequence? 52OTH310332?"

"Yes."

She held Rebecca's diary and turned it to the page that had the same number written on top. "Rebecca wrote the same sequence in her diary."

"What does it have to do with *Othello*?"

Sarah opened her journal and wrote *52OTH310332*. "This is an old citation format for the play." Then she rewrote it as *OTH 5.2.310–332*. "This is the citation format we use now. I think this passage, where Othello is lamenting the fact that he killed Desdemona, is the substitution key."

He took a pencil out of her hair and turned to Act 5, Scene 2. "Now what?"

"Starting on line 310, alphabetically label the beginning of each line until you reach line 332. Start with *A* and end with *W*."

He gave each line a letter. "Done."

She peered at the diary, unaware of how lovely she looked with her messy bun, PJs, glasses, and hair pencils. "We know the Jones tomb covers a hide site, soooooooo… can you find a J anywhere in the passage?"

He scanned until he hit the line he'd marked as the letter *I*. "The line 'I' reads, 'Here is my journey's end.'" He raised an eyebrow. "That can't be a coincidence."

"It's not. It's also the line my mother starred." She paused to write in her journal. "If you start counting with 'H,' the first letter in the phrase 'Here is my journey's end,' the 'J' in 'journey' is the ninth letter in. That means the letter J is represented by the notation I9: I for the line it comes from, 9 from the position of the letter in the phrase."

"Makes sense." Kind of. "There are a million O's."

She picked up the diary again and, using the eraser end of a pencil, gently skimmed the pages filled with alphanumeric sequences.

"Is that killing you?" he said, trying not to tease her too much. "Working on a three-hundred-year old journal without muslin gloves or bone folders?"

"You've no idea," she said as she scanned. "Here's a cipher sequence that starts with I. It's I9A4B8M5C6."

She handed him her journal, and he started comparing the sequence to the play. She shifted so she could watch while he wrote. He tapped her on the nose. "Do you mind?"

"You're slow."

He raised an eyebrow. "I'm dyslexic."

"I forgot." She kissed him on the head. "What is A4?"

He chuckled. Her insistence told him she wasn't as sympathetic as he'd expected, but as long as she kept kissing him, he didn't care. He went to the first line and counted four letters until landing on…"O."

She smiled wide. "B8?"

That one was easy. "N."

Her shoulders shook, and he wasn't sure if she was laughing or crying. "Nate!"

"Right. M5 is E." He paused. "C6 is…S." He'd just spelled out JONES. "Sarah?" Was that awe in his voice? It sounded like it. Because, apparently, they'd just solved the cipher.

She wore the widest smile he'd ever seen on a woman's face. "We did it, Nate. We solved it."

"Let's do another one. Just to make sure."

She picked up Rebecca's diary and started reading off alphanumeric sequences. Thirty minutes later, while the crooner sang through his greatest hits, they'd identified twenty-four names. She'd also transcribed the sequences and corresponding tomb names on the bottom of their map.

She shut the diary and slipped it, along with their map and the copy of *Othello*, into a gallon-size Ziploc bag she'd found in a kitchen drawer. Then she stood and stared at him. "I still can't believe it." Her voice was breathless with joy or wonder or awe. He wasn't sure which, but it didn't matter. They now had something to bargain with.

When Nat King Cole started singing "Unforgettable," Nate stood and pulled her into his arms. Moving them away from her research, he swung her around and started to dance. "You're amazing. How did you figure it out?"

"All the pieces were there. That quotation we've seen everywhere—*Here is my journey's end*—is from *Othello*. As are the phrases *My Soul's Joy* and *My Fair Warrior*." She pointed to the rubbing of Rebecca's tomb with the sequence *52OTH310332*. "But it was when I saw my mother's notation in the book on line 318 of Act 5, Scene 2, that I realized the rubbing was an old citation. I just needed to figure out the pattern."

Nate swung her around again and then brought her in, closer this time.

"Anyway," she continued in a whispery voice, "one of the few things I know about my father—my real father—is that he used to call my mom his *fair warrior* and she used to call me her *soul's joy*."

"The same phrases on Rebecca's tomb."

Sarah smiled. "We had all of these disparate pieces, and we just needed my mother's notation to bring them all together."

"Do you think your mother figured out how the cipher worked?"

She leaned into him, and he tucked her head beneath his chin. "I don't know. It's possible. She never mentioned the cipher. She was always more interested in the love story."

"*Hmm.*"

She lifted her head slightly. "What?"

"It's just that the someone who came up with this cipher—before Rebecca and Thomas stole it—must've had a broken heart. That passage is beyond sad. It's almost suicidal. The cipher's author must've been in a bad place too."

"I've never thought of that. Anecdotal evidence places the cipher's beginnings around 1642." She paused. "It's attributed to a Prideaux pirate who probably lived a brutal life."

Nate closed his eyes. He didn't want to think about death or sadness or broken hearts. The crooner's voice lulled Nate to a place he was afraid he'd never be able to leave. "What I'm not sure about is how to find the other hide sites. We have names but no locations."

She wrapped her arms around his neck and kissed his chin. "I was only asked to solve the cipher. Now we just have to use it to save Jack, my dad, and you."

Nate stared into Sarah's eyes. "Why do you want to save me?"

"That's a ridiculous question."

"I need to know."

She rubbed the back of his neck, staring at the scar on his cheek. "Because I love you." She closed her eyes. "And I don't want to lose you."

He dropped kisses on her forehead, trickling them along her cheek to her neck. "I don't want to lose you either."

"Why?" The hitch in her voice made him smile.

"Because I love you too."

"Nate?" He could feel her shortened breath, see her wide, panicky eyes, hear her shaky voice. "What are we going to do?"

"We have the cipher key." His hands moved up her side until coming dangerously close to her breasts. "We have to come up with a plan to use it."

"Now?" She kissed his chin.

"No." His lips trailed down to her neck while he undid the sweatshirt zipper. "Not now."

And that's when static came through the SAT phone. "HQ…to base."

∽

Sarah wanted to throw the SAT phone out the window. Instead, Nate grabbed it from the kitchen table and responded. "Base to HQ. Go ahead."

She frowned. This was their time. And the sand was slipping through the glass quickly.

"Nate," Jimmy's voice came through the static. "Zack—"

"Repeat," Nate said, clicking the button.

She turned off the CD player. She knew she was being selfish, but Nate would be gone soon, and she'd be alone. Swallowing hard, she stripped off her sweatshirt and knelt in front of Nate, dragging her fingers along his denim legs.

Nate's eyelids lowered, and the bulge in the front of his jeans grew. Her hands rested close to the very large, very masculine part of him that moved. Her stomach tightened from the memory of his weight on top of her, his body deep inside hers.

Nate clicked the button again. "Repeat?"

"Kells wants—" And the phone went silent.

Nate threw it onto the couch. "*Sarah*."

"What do they want?" The heat coming from inside the denim was almost enough to scorch her, and she kept her gaze at zipper level. All it would take was a simple tug of the zipper. And her mouth was right there.

"I don't know."

She looked up and licked her lips. "Should we call

back?" She cupped him, enjoying the weight of his erection through his jeans.

His larger hand immediately trapped hers, forcing her to hold him harder. He growled. "*No.*"

Slowly, despite his hand covering hers, she undid the zipper. *Would he let her?*

"*Sarah.*" The word held so much weight it sounded like his emotions were more than he could carry. Which was why it was time for her to take some of the burden.

Aaaaaaaaaaaaand he didn't wear underwear. She gripped his erection, her thumb running over the top while her fist began to pump. She heard him swallow, and she smiled as her tongue ran over his hard ridge. Back and forth, up and down, in a rhythm set by her hand and tongue. His scent surrounded her, making her feel safe and loved.

"*Fuuuuuuuuuuuuuck,*" he moaned. "Sarah, I can't—"

She took him into her mouth, and his entire body contracted. His legs were now wide apart, his hands gripped her hair, and his hips thrust forward. She slipped a hand into his jeans to hold his balls. He was so warm and tight and hard. His hands encouraged her, his breath sounding like a low-flying jet.

"*Sarah.*" The way he drawled her name, like a deep yearning, sent shock waves through her. Her lower body clenched until the pain made her catch her breath. "I *need* you."

She stood, took his hand, and led him to the bedroom. They might only have a few hours left, but he wasn't going to leave her without understanding what he meant to her. He wasn't going to rot in that prison hospital without believing how much she loved him.

CHAPTER 44

NATE FOLLOWED SARAH INTO THE BEDROOM, WATCHING her hips sway while she unbraided her hair. When she reached the bed, she drew down the quilt and stripped off her camisole and then the PJ bottoms, leaving her in the tiniest white-lace panties he'd ever seen.

He ran his hands over his head, still surprised at the feeling of his short hair and uncertain what to do next. He knew what he wanted to do but also knew what he should do.

He should return to Kells and give him Sarah's research, her cipher, everything Kells would need to keep Sarah safe. While Nate should be preparing for his return to the prison hospital.

"Nate." Her breathy voice made his dick jump involuntarily. *That* part of him didn't give a fuck about *should*. *That* part of him only understood raw, selfish need.

He reached for one breast with a hard, pink tip. When his finger teased, she threw back her head with a sexy moan. He did it again and again, smiling at her reactions. When he added his other hand to her other breast, her eyes closed and she almost fell on the bed.

That's when it hit him that this would be the last time he'd be with her. A fierce heat swept through him, a hot anger at the injustice. He'd finally met the woman of his dreams at the same moment he was losing his freedom. Desire drove away away thought and regret and everything that kept him from being inside her, taking her, making her his.

With a grace the Fianna would be proud of, he swept her into his arms and laid her on the bed. He removed the white panties, then his own clothes. She watched with half-open eyes but didn't press him. She waited because she knew that's what he needed. And how many of the women he'd been with had done that? Had seen to his needs before theirs? *None.*

He stood at the end of the bed, holding himself, while she raised her arms to him. He hesitated only because once he started he'd be that much closer to leaving her.

"Nate." She was now on her knees, on the bed, holding his face in her hands. "Does your shoulder hurt?"

"*No.*"

"Then *please.*"

Before he knew it, she was on her back, and he was driving into her. The tight, intense pleasure overrode all of his other fears. He pistoned with a ferocity he'd never experienced. Her nails scraped his ass until he rolled over, forcing her to straddle him.

She smiled and set the pace. Since it wasn't fast enough, he held her hips and increased the speed. She arched her back, and he sat up to tease her breasts with his tongue and teeth. He used his legs to force her thighs farther apart so he could drive even deeper. It took all of his strength to keep them both upright until his last stroke when she cried out and his world—his heart—shattered.

He fell back, holding her on top of him. He kissed her head and rubbed her bare shoulders, loving the fact that her breath was choppy.

"I've never been so happy and sad at the same time."

"I know." His fingers trailed over her silky skin, and she shivered. "You're cold."

She snuggled into his chest. "I'm not."

He reached around until he found the edge of the quilt and covered them. Then he saw his jeans lying on the floor, a smidgen of white cotton hanging out of the pocket. "I want to give you something."

She kissed his chest. "You already have."

He laughed as he reached for his jeans. Once he'd

grabbed what he needed, he returned to his position with her lying on top of him. "I want you to have this."

She raised her head to look at him. Her breasts smooshed on his chest, her long hair flowing over her shoulders. "Your handkerchief?" She shook her head. "It belonged to your mother. I can't take it. You'll need it in the prison hospital."

"I can't take it with me." He handed it to her. "Keep it safe."

She gripped the white handkerchief trimmed in embroidered strawberries, and he remembered the dress she'd worn earlier.

He pushed her hair away from her face. "You looked beautiful today. I'll always remember you like that and like this and like the girl on the floor with pencils stuck in her hair." He kissed her nose, then her lips. "If things were different, I'd be asking you to marry me."

Because as crazy as it seemed, he already *felt* married.

"If things were different," she said softly, still holding the handkerchief, "we'd already be married."

Oh, God. "Keep it, and yourself, safe." He pressed her head down again because he wanted to feel all of her on all of him.

"I promise."

Her soft words made his body harden again.

He loved her, but he was also a selfish bastard. In a single move, he turned her onto her stomach. He splattered kisses down her spine while his fingers fondled. When she was ready, he lifted her hips and drove into her again. And again. And again. He took every ounce of pleasure from her body with one goal: to return it tenfold so she'd never forget him.

She cried out in pleasure, still gripping the white handkerchief, as he emptied himself inside her. On his final thrusts, two thoughts were uppermost in his mind.

He'd do anything to keep her safe. Even if he had to betray her.

❦

An hour later, Sarah sat in the tub, nestled between Nate's hard thighs. She was sore all over. But in a good way. In an adored sort of way. She rested her head on his chest. "Should we call Jimmy?"

"Probably. But I don't want to." Nate's lips fell on her shoulder, leaving shudders in their wake. "Thank you."

From the tension in his voice, something was wrong. "For what?"

"For being with me despite my seizures and all the horror that comes with my past." His eyes were lowered and difficult to read. "I can't keep my hands off you. I sure as hell can't let you go. Yet I have no future." His hands traveled down her arms, across her stomach, then up again until they raised her breasts above the waterline.

She wanted to moan at his touch, but she wondered if his touching her was more about staying focused in the moment. "We solved the cipher."

One of his hands moved down to touch the soft center between her legs. She shifted so he could reach more easily, and heat flared from her lower stomach to her breasts. Every muscle contracted, and the pressure built again. How could she have anything else to give him? She tilted her head to stare at his hard jaw and grinding teeth.

"I've no idea what to do next," he whispered while his fingers caught a rhythm and built on it. "But I don't know how to let you go."

With the pressure rising, she reached down with one hand to cover his larger one and helped him press against her core. He was hard, and she lifted herself up until his erection was just under her bottom. She felt him hiss while her breath became short and shallow.

When one of his fingers slipped inside her, the waves began. Hot, heavy vibrations that swept through her body, forcing her legs to close even tighter and their combined hands to press even harder. His finger entered deeper, and the highest wave peaked, leaving her breathless and shivering. She cried out as the last convulsion ripped through her. As quickly as she could in the tub, she turned around and straddled him.

She needed him deep inside her where she could keep him safe.

He gripped her hips while she lowered herself over him. The tight, powerful feel of him filling her up, stretching her to the limit, made her gasp. "You barely fit."

He tightened his hold on her hips and forced her all the way down. "I fit perfectly."

She rose up slightly, only to have him slam her down. After another up and down, she found a slow, riding rhythm that made him growl. And that made her smile. "What if I decide to keep you here? And never let you go?"

"Fine by me," he said between his teeth just before he latched on to a nipple.

Her body had turned into a single nerve ending, sparking and jumping, while he lavished nips and sucks on one rosy tip, then the other, before reaching up and bringing her lips down to his. "Come with me, Sarah"

She rode him hard for another long moment. Fire began in her toes and traveled up, tightening her leg muscles, until her body contracted. She heard his breath shorten, saw his eyes squeeze shut just before his body exploded in one long, final thrust.

While shudders traveled the length of her body, the last of her strength gave out. She fell onto his chest, not caring that they'd splashed water everywhere. She rested her head beneath his chin. His heartbeat ran the half-minute mile while his arms tightened around her shoulders. It took another long moment before the shaking stopped and the shivering began.

That's when she noticed the bath water had gone cold.

∽

At eleven p.m., Sarah padded around the cabin, restless and unable to sleep. It was a dark, moonless night that made her wary and uncertain. She'd left Nate asleep in the bed and put her PJs and sweatshirt on. She'd even slipped the handkerchief in her pocket. Now that he'd given it to her, she'd never be without it.

Something was wrong with Nate. She could feel it. Their lovemaking had been amazing, even better than the night before. Still, he'd been hesitant. And when she'd asked him about it after their bath, he'd shut down. She'd even encouraged him to call Jimmy back, but there'd been no answer on the SAT phone.

She paced the room, looking at her research on the floor. She focused on the photos of Thomas's tomb she'd taken.

Why was she uncertain? They had the cipher. They had leverage. Maybe it was because they didn't have a plan for what to do next. They'd both been so wrapped up in the present, she hadn't wanted to think about the future.

Needing something else to focus on, she rummaged through a kitchen drawer until finding a switchblade. Then she sat on the couch and took Rebecca's diary out of the Ziploc bag. Although she knew she shouldn't, she cut pages that had been stuck together by water damage and mold. The damage was extensive, and she gave up after separating only two. Gently, she turned them with the eraser end of a pencil and saw something new:

$$32\,\frac{^{22}}{_7}\,/\,4502\,10\,\frac{^{22}}{_7}\,/\,4473\,6\,\frac{^{22}}{_7}\,/\,4528\,17\,\frac{^{22}}{_7}\,/\,4362$$

How odd.

She heard a snapping noise outside and turned off the light. It sounded like the mudroom door had been left open. As she moved into the kitchen, a masked man snagged her.

His hand clamped over her mouth, and his other arm tightened around her waist.

She kicked and bit his hand, but the man wouldn't release her. She tried to knock over a kitchen stool to make some noise and wake up Nate. Except the man moved too quickly, dragging her through the mudroom and out the back door. The night was pitch-black, and the generator's roar meant Nate would never hear them.

The man threw her against the side of the cabin. She shook her head despite the hand over her mouth and the one keeping her wrists above her head.

"Where's the diary?"

Etienne Marigny? She fought him until he slapped her. She fell to the side, and brilliant pain flooded her head. He forced her up, his arm on her throat. A second man wearing a hooded sweatshirt appeared out of the darkness and covered her mouth with tape. Then Etienne spun her around to wrap her wrists together behind her back.

Etienne threw her over his shoulder as if she weighed nothing. "Find it," he said to the hooded man. "*Hurry.*"

The hooded man slipped inside.

She kicked at Etienne as he rounded the cabin, but it was hard with her being upside down and her arms behind her. She could tell from the way the land sloped that he was headed for the dock. Her ribs felt like they were going to crack, and every breath was agony. The further away he took her from the cabin, the more she screamed into the tape.

Once at the dock, he threw her down. She hit the wood planks hard, her head taking the brunt. Her vision blurred, and it hurt to breathe. Bile built up in her throat, and she began to hyperventilate.

If she vomited with tape over her mouth, she'd choke to death.

Etienne dragged her into a boat where theirs used to be. A dim lantern on the dock provided the only light. "Get in."

Tears rolled down her face. She tried not to cry, but exhaustion and fear were too much. Etienne pushed her, except her hands were tied, and she fell forward. Her shins hit the seat, and her legs buckled. She had to lie down in order to shimmy onto the seat.

Someone grunted, and she turned to see another man sitting in the boat.

Even in the dark, she could tell this third man was missing an ear. He wouldn't look at her. He was wrapped in a blanket and kept his head down.

Etienne untied the rope holding the boat to the dock. "Be friendly to Sarah. She's Nate's lover."

The man lifted his head, and she flinched. It wasn't just the deep scars circling his eyes that made her move away. It was the absolute fear in his face. Like he'd been tortured by a host of demons.

The hooded man ran down the ravine holding a Ziploc bag, grabbed the lantern, and boarded.

He'd taken the diary?

Etienne jumped in while the hooded man started the ignition. The boat rocked, and Sarah prayed Nate would hear the motor. Etienne took control of the wheel, turned on the headlights, and headed down the creek toward the river.

As they motored away, the hooded man sat near Sarah, still holding the lantern. The light cut through the darkness, and the last thing she saw on the dock was her white handkerchief.

CHAPTER 45

NATE FELL OFF THE BED AND HIT THE FLOOR. HE DRAGGED his naked, sweat-soaked body to the edge of the mattress and forced himself to stand. Unlike other nightmares, this one left fragments of memories behind. But glimpses of torture didn't do anyone any good.

He shook out his arms. Sarah was covered by blankets and pillows, and he didn't want to wake her. *Why was it so hot in here?* He gathered his clothes and hit the bathroom to rinse off. The cold water helped erase the lingering visions. At least this nightmare hadn't left a headache behind. Maybe miracles were possible.

He dried off and slipped on his jeans and T-shirt. When he went into the kitchen to make coffee, he noticed Sarah's tea bags and put on water to boil. Not wanting to wake her, he used the battery lantern on the counter. While the water heated, he stared out the window. Without the moon, he couldn't see the dock. He didn't check the time because he didn't want to know how many hours he had left with Sarah.

He really should call Jimmy again...but didn't want to.

As he poured water over a tea bag and sucked in his stomach to fight the stench, he heard a noise in the mudroom. He carried in the lantern. The back door was open and banging the wall. He returned to the family room and turned on the lamps. Then he froze.

A letter with his name on the front lay on the floor near the door. He tore it open.

Nate,

I've solved the cipher, but now I have to leave to save my father. If I don't, Remiel will kill him. I'm sorry about Jack.

Sarah

What the hell? Blood pounded in his veins, and he rushed into the bedroom. He yanked off the quilt to find that Sarah was a pile of pillows and blankets.

He shoved his pistol in his waistband and grabbed a flashlight and rifle. Once outside, he headed toward the dock. He didn't care that he was barefoot. Hell, he could've been naked and it wouldn't have mattered. His trip wires had been cut, and his boat had disappeared.

A crippling pain gripped his heart, and he dropped. His knees sank in the sandy soil, his mind in turmoil. He couldn't believe she'd left him. Not after what they'd shared. He ran a hand over his head, trying to make sense of it all.

Could Sarah have betrayed him while he'd been having a fucking nightmare?

He shone the light on the river, dispersing the darkness. The beam reflected the water, scattering shadows along the moving surface. It didn't make sense. Why would she leave in the middle of a moonless night?

He stood and swung the light around the dock until it caught something white. *His handkerchief.* He picked it up as his body hummed and the headaches he'd not had since yesterday wound their way through his head again. Sarah hadn't *left*. She'd been *taken*.

He sprinted to the cabin and sent a message to Grady. Then he tried to call Jimmy on the SAT phone. After four tries, he gave up and found his boots. While tying, he received Grady's message in Morse code. *Meet at Pops. Will contact Jimmy, Garza, and Pete. Use canoe.*

Nate gathered his weapons and drank the disgusting tea in one scalding gulp. As he packed up Sarah's research, he realized the diary was gone. Then he grabbed the letter and shoved it in his pocket with the handkerchief. As he left the cabin, he checked the clock. It was 0030 hours, and the pit churning in his gut told him he was running out of time.

Sarah marched through the cemetery with Etienne behind her. Although her socks were ruined, she was grateful for them and the penlight Etienne hung around her neck with paracord. If she got the chance to run away, she'd have light. The only thing better? A gun.

She inhaled and exhaled to keep the panic under control. Now that the initial adrenaline had worn off, she needed a plan. She tripped, and Etienne pushed her. "Keep moving."

They were in the cemetery, but it was dark, and she was lost. Nothing looked familiar, and the area was even creepier at night. Etienne walked behind her with a gun, and she'd no idea what had happened to the hooded man. Once they'd landed, the hooded man had taken the tape off Sarah's mouth and disappeared with the lantern.

The scarred man walked next to her. Although he also had a penlight around his neck, his feet were bare, and his hands clutched the blanket. He'd yet to speak. She shivered and wished she'd zipped up her sweatshirt when she'd put it on. With her hands behind her back, her sweatshirt hung open. Her white cami didn't hide anything, and she'd gotten wet. "Where are we going?"

"Be quiet. Keep walking."

She focused on avoiding sunken headstones. "When Nate finds me, you'll cry."

Etienne pressed the gun to her head. "Shut. Up."

She swallowed and kept walking until Etienne stopped in front of a mausoleum. She couldn't see well, but the land behind sloped down, probably to an estuary. Etienne unlocked the tomb's door. "Get in and sit."

She and the scarred man sat near a stone casket. Etienne handed his gun to the scarred man. "If she runs, shoot her." Then Etienne disappeared, the door shutting them in.

"Quick." She shifted so her back was to the man. "Undo my hands." When nothing happened, she realized he pointed the gun at her. Seriously? What was wrong with this guy? "I can get us out of here." Exaggerations were necessary in emergencies.

The man stared at her. Even in the dark she could see death in his eyes. He had a new-growth beard, and his hair had been recently shorn because there were razor marks on his head.

"*Please*." Desperation made her voice shaky and hoarse.

"Do you love Walker?" The words were tinged with a southern Turkish dialect.

Okaaaaaaay. She looked around to make sure there wasn't someone else speaking. "Excuse me?"

He looked at the gun, as if not sure what to do with it. "Do you love Walker?"

"Why don't we talk about it when we're *free*."

"I tortured him."

Whoa. "Are you Fletcher Ames?"

"Yes. I also poisoned Walker." Fletcher raised his head, and his brown eyes held no empathy or compassion or love. If evil had a scent, it would be the acrid stench of Fletcher Ames.

She swung her legs around and kicked him the chest. Except her hands were still behind her, and she tipped over. She shimmied upright to spit in his face. "You *bastard*. You tortured and poisoned the man I love? You better not untie me, or I'll—"

"I can save him." Fletcher kept the gun pointed at her, but his hands shook.

She scooted away, hitting a tomb. "You're a monster."

"I know where to find the antidote." He played with the

gun as if it were a fidget toy. "Remiel told me not to, but I kept it." His low laugh was so hollow, so sinister, her stomach roiled, and she tasted bile. Fletcher placed a finger on his lips in a silent *shush*. "Remiel doesn't know. But *he* does."

"He?" At this point, she didn't care. Between struggling with her taped hands and trying not to vomit, she could barely bring in enough air. Her vision wavered from light-headedness and dehydration. Her burst of righteous anger had exhausted her. "Are you going to tell me about this *he*? Or the antidote?"

He lowered his gaze to her breasts. "For a price."

"Oh, hell no." She kicked at him but tipped over again. It took precious energy to scramble upright.

Fletcher grimaced. "Not *that* kind of price. The kind that kills."

"You want me to kill someone?"

The wonky neck lights deepened the scars around his eyes. "Yes."

She closed her eyes. "Who?"

"Me."

She laughed until she realized he was serious. Opening her eyes, she said, "Sure." Because why the hell not. She started fighting the bindings on her wrist again and felt a shard of metal on the floor. *Could it cut the tape?* Carefully, she rubbed the tape with the metal, praying it was sharp enough and that Fletcher wouldn't see.

Except his head was so bowed down, he wouldn't have noticed if she were naked. "You have to promise."

"Fine." She kept up the subtle sawing motion. "I promise. Who is *he*, and where's the antidote?"

"Your father knows—"

The door blew open, and Etienne stormed in. "Get up." He took the gun from Fletcher and forced him to his feet.

She rose, keeping her shoulder on the tomb as leverage. Her wrists were still bound, and she hated the fact that she wanted to cry again. Etienne went behind the tomb in the center and opened a trapdoor. There was a hide site in here. And she didn't even care.

Etienne dragged her by the arm to the opening. "I'm not untying your hands. You'll have to jump. Or I'll push you."

She sat on the edge and swung her legs into the hole. "It's eight feet down."

"Good thing there's water." He kicked her, and she fell.

She hit the cold water, and the breath rushed from her lungs. She clung to the metal in her hands and struggled to stand. The water had helped cushion the fall, but it was up to her thighs. "*Please*. You can't leave me."

"Actually, I can."

A moment later, the door shut, and the only light came from around her neck. She manipulated the metal shard and started cutting. Her shoulders burned from the movement. When she felt the tape give, she cut faster until her hands cramped and she dropped the shard.

That's when the realization hit. Nate had no idea where she was or how to find her. Because she'd asked him to trust her instead of his men, he was working alone. Because she feared being betrayed yet needed his protection, she'd inadvertently made Nate betray his own instincts. Because she'd been so desperate to save him, she may have lost him forever. And at the rate the water was rising, she was going to die in a hide site.

But the worst part? She'd never be able to save Nate.

CHAPTER 46

NATE SLUNG THE RIFLE ONTO ONE SHOULDER, CARRIED THE shotgun, and walked into Pops's trailer with Grady. Grady had been waiting for Nate with a thermos of coffee and croissants at the truck he'd left near the boat landing the day before. He'd no idea where Grady had come up with the pastries, but Nate was grateful.

He stopped when he saw the room. The couch had been pushed aside, and someone had set up a folding table covered in maps. Jimmy and Garza stood shoulder to shoulder, heads down over the maps. Zack was nearby, talking to Pete.

Ty, Vane, and Cain were with Pops next to another table filled with weapons. Kells looked like he was having a heated argument with Calum until Luke came out of the kitchen with two coffee mugs and gave them each one. Alex Mitchell hung out in a corner.

Garza noticed Nate first, then Calum and Kells turned toward him. Like falling dominoes, Nate's men stopped their conversations to stare at him.

"Son," Grady said with a hand on Nate's shoulder, "tell them what's been going on."

Suddenly, being in the POW camp with Fletcher Ames seemed far more appealing. When had Nate become such a damn coward? Or maybe it wasn't cowardice. Maybe Sarah was right. Maybe it was his fear of not being able to protect those he loved.

He cleared his throat. "Sarah is gone. I think Etienne Marigny has taken her."

"Where?" Pete asked.

Nate propped the shotgun near the door and gave the rifle to Grady. "I don't know."

A low murmuring filled the room until Garza said, "Nate,

your Saint Michael medal was found on a banker's body yesterday in Charleston. You're a suspect in that murder."

Of course I am. "I didn't kill anyone. Fletcher Ames, the lead torturer in the POW camp, stole my medal years ago." Nate took the offered water bottle from Luke. "I've been with Sarah since Friday."

"Except Sarah isn't here." Garza scratched the back of his neck. "And you don't know where she is?"

Nate stared at the white ceiling. "No."

"Also," Calum said while texting, "Maurice filed assault charges against you."

Of course he did. "Least of my worries."

"Still," Calum said, finishing his text, "I've put another lawyer from my firm on your case. If I take it, there may be a conflict of interest. Because you hit me too."

Kells put his coffee on the table. "I had an interesting meeting with a Detective Hugh Waring in Charleston. Did you know Sarah had you investigated?"

"Sir." Nate coughed because his throat was closing up. "Sarah didn't betray us."

"Then what the *fuck* happened." Kells's words, spoken in the harshest tone Nate had ever heard, ricocheted around the room. The sentence wasn't a question. It was an order.

After finishing his water, he told them almost everything that'd happened since he'd stolen the diary. He left out the private events between him and Sarah but ended with "Sarah used the diary and a copy of *Othello* to solve the cipher."

Ty stepped forward, hands fisted. "Which means Jack is a dead man."

Nate held up a hand. "Not if we save Sarah and trade the cipher to the Prince in exchange for lifting the bounty on Jack's head."

"Except," Kells said, "you don't know if the Prince will agree to that, and Sarah is gone. You're sure she didn't leave on her own?"

"Yes. She left a handkerchief." Nate yanked it out of his back pocket. "She never would've left it behind."

Garza's cell phone rang, and he excused himself to go to the kitchen.

"What's this?" Vane picked up the paper that had fallen out of his pocket.

Fuck. Nate reached for it, but Vane had read it.

"It says that Sarah left you to save her father."

Nate yanked it out of Vane's hands. "It's not true."

Kells held out his palm. After a long moment, Nate gave it to him. "I know Sarah. She'd never betray us."

"She solved the cipher when she knew Jack's life was on the line," Kells said.

"She solved the cipher for leverage." Nate's voice reeked of frustration, and he took a few deep breaths to control his heart rate.

"Why are you defending this woman?" Vane frowned. "Are you fucking her?"

Nate threw Vane into the wall, one arm pressed on his windpipe. "*Apologize.*"

It took both Pete and Zack to drag Nate off Vane.

Vane moved away, rubbing his neck. "What the *hell* is wrong with you?"

"Don't *ever* talk about her that way again." Nate knocked off the other men. "She didn't leave me. She was *taken.*"

"Did she cut your hair?" Kells asked.

Figures that was the thing Kells would be concerned about. "I asked her to."

"*Jeeeeeeeeeeeeeez*, Nate," Pete said. "What the hell were you thinking?"

"What was he thinking with?" Vane added.

Nate moved again until Zack got in his face, both hands on Nate's chest. "I believe you, brother."

Vane scoffed while the other men murmured. Cain and Ty wouldn't look at Nate. Jimmy, Pops, Calum, and Grady were off to the side, not saying anything, as if they knew this wasn't their fight. Luke just watched everyone. As did Alex.

"No." Kells came out with a flat statement. "We're not saving Sarah."

Nate turned his attention to his boss. "Because she went to Hugh Waring for help? She did it because you were having her followed. Having *us* followed."

"I was protecting you."

"You can bend the rules to protect us, but I can't to protect Sarah?" Nate waved a hand in disgust. "Jack can accuse me of something I didn't do? What kind of hypocritical bullshit is that?"

A deep, resonating silence bomb dropped on the room. The only thing Nate could hear was his own pounding heart. The only thing he could see were Kells's furious eyes and flared nostrils.

Yeah. Nate had told Kells off in front of the other men. But Nate hadn't been the only one keeping secrets to protect those he loved. *Hell.* Kells was the king of secrets, and Nate was sick of there being different rules for him and his men. And, right now, Nate didn't have the time to deal with this emotional shit. He needed to find Sarah.

"We have a problem," Garza said, returning from the kitchen. "Or maybe it's a good thing. I'm not sure." He put his phone away and scanned the room. "*Whoa.* What happened?"

"Nothing." Kells faced Garza. "What's wrong?"

"Just got a call from Detective Elliot."

"Jeez," Pete said. "Don't you two ever sleep?"

"I could say the same thing about you and your men." Garza focused on Kells again. "Homicide's been called down to the Savannah River front. Those two Russians from the club the other night? Dead. With puncture holes through the neck."

"Fuck," Pete muttered.

"That's not all," Garza continued. "Two more Russians were just found dead in Charleston. Same cause of death."

The men spoke at once until Kells crossed his arms. "What does that mean?"

"It means," Nate said as calmly as possible, "the Fianna killed them with a retractable blade called a misericord. It slips in through the neck and takes out the brainstem. Or under the arm to pierce the heart."

"It's a close quarters weapon," Pete said. "It's quiet and not as messy as a gunshot or knife."

"You think the Fianna stole those MANPADs?" Zack asked.

Garza glanced at Jimmy. They both shrugged.

"When will you dipshits learn?" Alex's deep voice came from the corner where he stood with his arms crossed, sardonic stare up and running. "This isn't about weapons. Nate's girlfriend is right. This is about leverage. The missiles were never the end for Remiel. It was the power they represented."

Vane sneered at Alex. "You don't think Remiel would use them?"

"Uh, *no.*" Alex might as well have said *duh.* "Remiel has no interest in mass murder. It's not personal enough. He'd rather torture the one person he holds a grudge against than take down an airliner full of strangers." Alex stared at Kells who looked away. "The missiles are also a form of currency. Need ten .50 cal machine guns? Trade a missile. Need a chicken sandwich from a fast-food joint? Trade a missile." Alex stared at the front door behind Nate's shoulder. "Isn't that right, Cassio?"

Nate and the rest of his men turned to see a man emerge from the shadows and fill the doorway. He wore jeans and a motorcycle jacket.

"Indeed, Master Mitchell." Cassio hit his chest with a fist and bowed his head. "Gentlemen. I bring greetings from my Prince on this desperate night."

The tic above Nate's eye kicked in. Pete, Garza, Calum, Jimmy, Pops, and Grady had seen a Fianna warrior two weeks ago. But the others hadn't. From their wide eyes and open mouths, they appeared shocked. Except for Kells and Alex, who did not react.

So much for Nate's pledge not to discuss the Fianna with his men. At least this revelation had been the Prince's doing, not Nate's.

Since no one said anything, Nate took charge. "I believe Etienne has Sarah."

Cassio nodded. "He's trading her to the Prince tonight."

"*Why?*"

"She solved the cipher, did she not? Your own words admitted this."

Cassio had snuck up on them and listened in? So much for their improved operational security. "Why is Etienne trading her? I thought Remiel wanted the cipher."

"He does." Cassio's attention landed on Kells. "Sometimes loyalties change. Since Etienne seeks asylum with the Prince, he needs to offer something in return."

Kells moved until he stood next to Nate. "Etienne is trading Sarah for asylum?"

"Indeed," Cassio said. "Except the Prince prefers another." Cassio nodded to Nate. "I'm to escort you. We should leave now."

"Wait," Kells said in a sharp voice that cut through the bullshit. "Why does the Prince want Nate?"

Chills went down Nate's spine. "Now that Sarah has solved the cipher, the Prince is offering an exchange."

Kells got into Cassio's face, putting himself between Nate and the warrior. "What does that mean?"

"'Tis the only way to put the world to rights."

Kells looked at Nate. "Explain."

"Sarah solved the cipher. Jack's life is forfeit unless I trade mine for his."

Kells paled. "The Prince wants to execute you?"

"*No.*" Cassio's denial resonated. "'Tis a trade of service for life."

It took a minute for Kells to speak. "The Prince is *recruiting* Nate? You want me to give up one of my men?"

Cassio hit his chest with his fist. "Aye."

The room erupted. Male voices all spoke at once with panicked questions until Kells raised a hand. The room went quiet, and he said, "No."

"'Tis not a request." Cassio looked at Nate. "Ready, my lord."

Kells grabbed Nate's arm. "You don't have to do this."

Not only did he need to do this, he had the sickening realization that this had been the Prince's plan all along. "I'm protecting those I love."

Kells tightened his hold. "We just need time to figure this out."

"If I don't do this, we all die." Nate stared directly at his friends, at his brothers, then Kells. He needed them to understand the new threat to their unit, to their lives. "Now that the Prince has allowed you to see Cassio... speaking means death. For all of us."

"Indeed," Cassio added.

"Wait." Vane shook his head. "If you don't return to the prison hospital, do we go to prison?"

Kells ran his hands over his head and closed his eyes. It was the closest Nate had ever come to seeing Kells lose control. "I don't know."

"'*Tis time*." Cassio's order made everyone turn to him. "Saint Michael awaits."

"What about Nate's second?" Alex hadn't moved from his corner, but his voice dispelled some of the tension. "A potential Fianna recruit is allowed to bring a second to a parlay with a warrior."

Cassio pointed at Calum. "All weapons stay behind. We leave now."

"Calum stays here." Nate handed Kells his and Sarah's pistols and the two knives he carried in his boots. Then he followed Cassio outside.

Kells followed. "Nate—"

"Colonel." Cassio pointed into the darkness. It was hard to see, but after a moment, when his eyes adjusted, Nate saw outlines of men around the yard. Cassio whistled, and the men hit their chests and bowed their heads in unison. There were at least four, probably more.

Kells took Nate's arm in a strong grip that made him wince. "You don't need to do this."

"I need to fix what I messed up five years ago."

"How is *this* going to do *that*?"

Nate disengaged his arm and looked away. He couldn't bear to see the pain in Kells's eyes or in the gazes of the other men in the room. "By protecting those I love."

Zack was freaked out. And considering what it took to freak out Green Berets, they were in serious shit. He'd never believed the Fianna existed. Then when he'd learned they did exist, he hadn't absorbed the truth until now. Not only were the Fianna *really* real, they'd made themselves known and were taking Nate away.

Fuck. That. Zack watched Nate from the window. Zack wasn't sure how to help, but one thing he knew was that this wasn't going to end with Nate becoming a part of the Prince's *fucking Fianna army*.

Zack blinked. Were those men outside the trailer, hidden within the shadows?

Cassio whistled, and the men hit their chests with their fists and bowed their heads in unison. Then Cassio and Nate walked away.

Calum met Zack at the window. "I should've gone with him."

"No." Zack gripped Calum's shoulder. "Nate needs to face these monsters on his own." Unfortunately, it'd taken weeks for Zack to comprehend that Nate's demons weren't just in his head. They walked the earth and had been haunting him since his release from prison. "Nate needs to take back control. He needs to find himself again."

Kells came inside, his face paler than Zack had ever seen it. Even more than the night when they'd gotten the news about Nate's and Jack's teams being ambushed. All of the men in the room remained silent. The only sound was from the clock ticking on the wall.

"Sir?" Zack asked. "What are we going to do?"

Kells looked at Grady. "What did Cassio mean by *Saint Michael awaits?*"

Grady smoothed a hand over a map on the table. "Saint Michael is the tomb in the center of the cemetery."

Pops added, "It's the fixed point on Capel land. In the dark, it's a good hour's hike."

Kells focused on his men. "We're going to that cemetery to save Nate."

"And the warriors outside?" Vane asked.

"Diversion," Zack said, coming over to the map table. "We'll set a diversion, and three of us—me, Pete, and Ty— will escape and head to the cemetery."

"You'll get lost," Grady said. "There's no moon and no GPS."

Right. "Then we navigate the old-fashioned way."

"That's not enough men," Kells said. "You've no idea what you're walking into."

"The Fianna are watching us." Zack loaded up a nine-mil on the table in the corner. Pete and Ty joined him. Luckily, Pops and Grady had extra weapons and ammo they were willing to lend. "We'll leave most of the men here so the Fianna won't know we're gone."

"We won't have any comms," Pete said. "The SAT phones are shit. And forget cells."

Zack wanted to throw something. Instead he slammed the clip into the gun and loaded a bullet in the chamber. "Not long ago, soldiers managed without tech and comms. I'm sure we can figure this out." He shoved the gun in his jacket pocket. "If we don't, we lose Nate forever." Zack caught Kells's nod, and that was all the go-ahead necessary. "Who's in?"

Every man raised his hand.

"Good." Zack studied the map again. "Time to make some noise."

CHAPTER 47

"I NEED TO FIND SARAH." NATE FOLLOWED CASSIO through the woods toward the cemetery. As he trudged, he fisted and unfisted his hands. He'd never felt this powerless before.

Cassio didn't answer. Despite wearing a backpack and carrying a penlight, he moved with a gait that looked like water sliding over glass.

Nate grabbed the warrior's shoulder, making him stop. "Tell me the plan."

Cassio threw off Nate's grip. "Should we attack with swords out, tilting at one another's breast in bloody opposition?" He waved a hand toward the dark, swampy vegetation around them. "Would you prefer that which would bring certain death?"

"Of course not. But you don't know that *bloody opposition* is what's waiting for us if we attack Remiel's men and save Sarah."

"Don't I? I should question the Prince's actions and knowledge?" Cassio started walking again. "If I ever dream of such a matter, abhor me."

Nate followed, breaking branches and kicking rocks along the way. He acted the brat in order to leave a trail. Just in case. "No soldier is required to follow bullshit orders without question."

"'Tis true, brother. Not all masters can be truly followed. But the Prince"—Cassio glanced back and struck his chest with a fist—"the Prince's heart attends to his men and their missions. His thoughts are true, his answers just."

Not in the mood for a Prince lovefest, Nate swallowed a bitter taste and realized he wasn't going to get any intel out of Cassio that the Prince hadn't previously authorized.

"I'm telling you true, Cassio. I'm not going with you until I know Sarah is safe."

Cassio shook his head. "'Tis an act of honor to give your life up for a brother's. Especially one who betrayed you."

Whatever. Right now Nate didn't feel honorable. He felt like a failure. The Prince had manipulated Nate's greatest weakness—his need to protect those he loved—and cornered him. "I'm not bluffing."

Cassio jumped a small creek. "I do not play the villain."

Nate didn't cross the water. "Where is she?"

When Cassio continued walking without answering, Nate jumped the creek and followed because, really, what the hell else was he going to do? If he didn't, Jack would be killed. He had to come up with a plan ASAP.

Finally, Cassio said, "Once you become one of us, both of your hearts will mend."

Oh yeah. Nate knew all about the brutal, almost pagan Fianna training that included running around naked in the winter and walking through the gauntlet that consisted of forty warriors on either side of an aisle, each holding two weapons. And the giving up of everyone and everything a man loved.

Then there was the learning how to walk with that eerie gracefulness he despised and the speaking in Shakespearean English thing. His dyslexia was going to love that. "Can't wait."

Cassio sighed and finally stopped to face Nate. "If you do not abide, Heaven will hurl out your soul for the fiends to feast upon."

Oh. Come. On. "Meaning?"

Cassio resumed his hike. "This is no time to be at one another's heels. We have proceedings to meet, and time is fleeting."

There was a plan and they needed to stop arguing because they were running out of time? Nate scoffed. "This would be so much easier if you spoke normal English."

Cassio's frown, oh so similar to Kells's, screamed annoyance. "Will you attend?"

Nate stared up at the dark, moonless sky and sighed. "Yeah. I'm coming." *Hooah*.

Etienne waited behind a glory cross with Fletcher. When Etienne heard Isabel's whistle, he dragged Fletcher toward the statue of Saint Michael, where Isabel stood four feet from Cassio.

Fletcher had a penlight around his neck, and Isabel carried the battery-powered lantern. Despite the dim light, the warrior's hard eyes glittered.

"How now." Cassio hit his chest with his fist and bowed his head. "Have you what the Prince requested?"

"Yes." Etienne threw the diary in a Ziploc bag on the ground. It landed near Cassio's feet. Then Etienne shoved Fletcher in the same direction.

Cassio took Fletcher's arm and made him sit on a flat tomb. "And the historian?"

Etienne shoved his hands in his pockets. "I'll tell you where Sarah is when we're off this godforsaken isle."

Male laughter came from Etienne's left side. Igor and one of his thugs appeared with flashlights, stinking of cabbage.

Etienne almost retched. "What the fuck?"

Igor stopped a few feet away, his flashlight wavering. "Remiel made a side deal with the Prince. Twelve MANPADs in exchange for the torturer. I believe the Prince has taken the missiles?"

"'Twas confirmed." Cassio dragged Fletcher by the arm and threw him at Igor.

"No!" Fletcher landed on his knees near Igor's feet. "Please. God. No!" Fletcher's blanket fell off, exposing burns and cuts on his bare chest. He didn't stop screaming until Igor slapped him.

Etienne took out his gun. He didn't give two shits what

the Prince did with Fletcher or those missiles. "Cassio, you get the historian as soon as we're gone from here, safe and sound."

Igor laughed. "You're a fool."

Etienne turned to the Russian, ready to fire, when Isabel touched his arm.

"I'm sorry, Etienne." She kissed his cheek and walked to Igor. She'd taken her light, which left him in deep shadows.

"Isabel?" Heat built in Etienne's veins as she stood with Igor. "You lying *bitch*."

"You know why, Etienne," Isabel said in her low, melodic voice. "I'd never make a deal with the Fianna, not after what they did to Sarah's mother. Meg was my best friend, and they destroyed her. I'm not going to let them hurt Sarah."

What did Isabel not understand? Remiel was an even bigger freak show than the Prince. "I told you I'd keep Sarah safe."

Isabel pointed to Cassio. "You can't if you're making deals with *him*."

If Isabel thought that Remiel was a safer bet than the Fianna, the bitch deserved the box. Since she was no longer his concern, Etienne said to Cassio, "Let's go so I can tell you where to find Sarah."

"You're not leaving with Cassio," Isabel said. "I told him where Sarah is hidden. He doesn't need you."

"'Tis true." Cassio drew his weapon from his jacket. "You will not be coming with me."

Etienne hissed low. Without the Fianna's protection, he was dead. Thank God he had a backup plan for his backup plan. "Sarah isn't where you think she is." He chuckled, more to himself since he was the one who'd written the punchline. "I put her in a *new* hide site. One Remiel and I recently cleared that none of you know about. And since there's no cell service out here, by the time you contact Remiel, Sarah will have drowned."

"Drowned?" Isabel pushed the hood off her face, exposing her red lips and brown eyes. "What do you mean?"

"The hide site she's in?" Etienne laughed again. "It's filling as we stand here scratching our asses."

Her inhale could be heard in Atlanta. "Where is Sarah?"

"Not telling you." *Bitch.* "Just wait until I tell Sarah's birth father what's been going on. Think Remiel will save you when a Fianna warrior finds out he has a daughter? And that you knew about it and didn't say anything? Good luck with that, you *fucking whore.*"

"You bastard!" Isabel moved forward until Igor held her arm. Igor's man grabbed Fletcher and disappeared. Then Igor picked up Isabel and tossed her over his shoulder. She dropped her lantern to kick him, but he laughed and went into the darkness. Her cries echoed around the uncaring tombs.

"Good riddance." Etienne laughed in fake relief to alleviate the tension. The lantern rolled toward Etienne's feet, leaving him and Cassio illuminated by fractured light. "Back to our agreement. I give you Sarah, you guarantee my freedom."

"No." Cassio hit his chest with his fist, nodded, and walked away.

Etienne ran over and grabbed Cassio's shoulder. "Sarah will die."

Cassio threw Etienne off and kept walking.

Etienne's elbows and ass hit the ground. If he couldn't trade Sarah for his life, his life was worthless. Remiel would have him hunted down within days. Etienne scrambled to his feet, his weapon raised. If his life was about to end, so was Cassio's.

"Cassio!" A male voice came from the shadows.

Walker?

Cassio turned as Etienne fired.

Cassio got off a round before landing on the ground. Etienne's leg burned, and he dropped his gun. With his

hand over the wound, he stumbled away. He'd betrayed
Remiel, Isabel, and the Prince. If Etienne couldn't make a
new plan, he'd be dead by dawn.

Nate grabbed the backpack and ran toward Cassio. The
warrior lay on the ground, and Nate tripped on a headstone
before landing on his knees nearby. A lantern offered some
light, and he opened the bag. "Are you hit?"

"Nay. Just a scratch."

From behind a mausoleum, Nate had watched *the plan.*
Which had been nothing more than a showdown between
Etienne, Cassio, and the hooded man-who-was-a-woman.

And the issue of Sarah's birth father being a Fianna warrior? That had to be a later time-and-place thing. He'd no
mind space left even to think about that. Everything in him
was focused on saving Sarah. And, to a minor extent, Cassio.

In the backpack, Nate found a small combat medic
pouch.

"'Tis minor," Cassio said in a strained, gaspy voice.

Nate grabbed the lantern and brought it closer. "Let me
see."

Cassio opened his coat and lifted his shirt. His side
had been grazed. The wound wasn't fatal, but it required
tending.

"You need help, and I need to save Sarah." Nate took
Cassio's wrist to check his pulse. It was strong yet erratic.

Cassio struggled to sit. It didn't take long for Nate to
wash and bind the wound. But by the time he'd finished,
Cassio's face had paled. "My brothers have convened near
the river—"

"I'm going after Sarah."

"She is lost."

Nate retrieved Etienne's gun, the lantern, and the Ziploc
bag with the diary. "I'm going after Etienne. He knows
where Sarah is hidden."

Cassio's voice stuttered, "Leave her. 'Tis for the best, brother."

The horror finally made sense. "You *want* Sarah to die?"

"She solved the cipher."

"No." Nate checked the clip. Thank God it was full. "I agreed to go with you, and I will. But I'm not joining you until I save her."

"If you save her, Jack dies. Such a choice to save a lover's breath."

"Tell the Prince if he kills Jack, he loses me." Nate shoved the diary into his jacket, then held the lantern high and the gun against his hip. "Did you bring me here to show me that the hooded man was a woman named Isabel? That there's an *Igor* who'd take away the man who tortured me for years? That you were never going to let Sarah live?"

"Yes."

Nate wanted to scream *fuck you* and *fuck the Prince*. Mostly he wanted to yell *why?* Instead, he bit his tongue and reined in his temper. He didn't have the time to deal with Cassio's psy-ops bullshit. On cue, a huge clap of thunder rocked the sky. More rain meant rising estuaries.

"Once I find Sarah, I'll return for you. But if I don't find her, you can tell the Prince I'm coming after him next." Nate headed for the Jones crypt. It was the only hide site he knew of, and as he ran, he begged God to keep her alive.

I'm going to die in one of my hide sites.

Sarah shuffled her feet to find the metal shard under the water. She couldn't save herself if she couldn't get free. And the water had made the tape gooey. How had she ended up in this disaster?

If she was being honest with herself, which she always tried to be, this nightmare was her fault. If she'd not been so afraid of being betrayed, if she hadn't insisted on doing this only with Nate, she'd be in Nate's arms right now. Not in an underground room with water up to her waist.

She felt something with her toes, held her breath, and went under. The problem was trying to grab it with her hands behind her back. On the third try, she got it and came up for air. Her lungs hurt, and she was thirsty, but the brackish water wasn't safe to drink. The worst part was the heavy-eyed exhaustion she fought as she sawed through the tape until she was... *free*.

After rubbing her wrists, she waved the light around the ten-foot-square room. She hadn't seen a door leading to the river. She dove down to look for another entrance. When she emerged, the flashlight went out, leaving her in pitch darkness. Water must've leaked into the casing.

Her breaths shortened, and she spun in circles. *Keep it together, Sarah.*

Many minutes later, she found the door. It was only three feet high, but the lock was underwater. Forcing her metal shard into the opening took time. It wasn't until the water reached her breasts that the lock unclasped. Relief poured through her, and she yanked the iron handle. The door opened a few inches and got stuck. Water flowed in, and she fought to close it. Except the door, which wasn't open enough for her to get out, wouldn't move in either direction.

She'd just hastened her own drowning.

Zack motioned for Pete and Ty to stop. Thanks to Pops's fireworks stash, they'd set off a fire show that had allowed them to get away.

Zack had memorized Grady's map, but the woods were dark, and they were under light and sound discipline. They'd no idea what they were walking into and couldn't risk being ambushed.

Thermal scopes on their borrowed-from-Pops rifles helped them maneuver. They'd also added infrared glow tape to their jackets to ID each other in a gunfight. They walked single file with quiet footfalls.

For a while they followed a trail of broken branches and disturbed rocks, but when the tracks ended, they headed for the cemetery entrance.

Forty minutes later, they hit the gates, and Zack heard snuffling. "What's that?"

Pete motioned to the right, and they squatted behind a tomb. "Boars."

"No one mentioned *boars*." Ty used his outdoor whisper instead of his indoor one.

"Pops did," Pete said. "*Five* times."

"We need to head to Saint Michael's tomb," Zack said. "ASAP."

Ty spat. "What if Nate's gone already?"

"Then we head for the river," Zack said. "They may have brought a boat."

"This plan sucks," Ty said. "We need ear radios. We're not dressed properly, we're using borrowed rifles, and we have no way to keep track of our position."

"When the plan sucks," Zack said, "we suck it up." Ty opened his mouth, and Zack shut that bitch storm down. "I know we're not prepared."

When Jimmy had called Pete earlier, they'd all jumped in their two vehicles and gone to Pops's. They'd had no idea they were walking into a paramilitary situation. But they should have. Not only was Zack carrying another man's rifle, they were all wearing an assortment of hunting jackets Pops had found in a closet and the cedar smell irritated Zack's nose. Nate was right. They'd allowed their self-pity to wear down their self-discipline. Now they were paying for their terrible OPSEC and lack of preparation.

"I know," Zack continued, "that we don't have the tech we're used to and we're attacking an enemy we know nothing about."

"With boars," Pete added.

"We also have no idea how many of them there are," Ty said. "Or what they want."

"They want Nate," Pete said. "And we can't let that happen."

"*Hooah*, brother." Zack stood. "Follow me."

Twenty minutes later, they were lost, and the boars were following them. They passed a crumbling mausoleum covered with plastic sheeting.

Ty kicked a headstone. "This su—"

A gunshot hit the tree near Zack's shoulder. "Down!" He crawled behind a chest tomb. More gunfire sounded, and he saw flashes coming from the other side of a crypt.

Pete moved next to him, and Ty was nearby behind a tree. Shots rang around them, spewing limestone and bark.

"What the hell is this?" Pete whispered.

Good question. "No idea."

"Fianna?" Ty asked.

"Nah," Pete said. "These guys can't shoot for shit."

"They must have thermal scopes," Ty said.

The firing paused.

"They're probably reloading," Zack said. "Any idea how many?"

"Two shooters. Maybe three." Ty squinted. "I wish we had grenades."

"Dude." Pete shook his head. "Civilian operation. No grenades."

Ty scowled. "Says who?"

"The law." Pete pointed to the crumbling mausoleum five feet away. "If one of us can get up there with the rifle—"

"We have thermals, and they have thermals." Ty crawled over just before the bullets started flying again. "It might as well be broad daylight."

Zack heard more grunting noises. "We need a distraction."

A bullet hit the top of the tomb they hid behind, and Pete slid down farther. "Any ideas?"

"Cover me," Zack said. "When I signal, we advance."

"Advance?" *Bullshit* was written all over Ty's question.

"It means charge." The bullets were coming more slowly this time, as if the enemy's weapons were jammed or they were still reloading.

Pete and Ty started firing, and Zack ran. A bullet whizzed by his head, but he made it to the crumbling mausoleum and used his rifle to snag the plastic. That'd been the easy part.

Zack shoved broken limestone pieces into his jacket and headed toward the grunting sounds, dragging the plastic. His eyes had adjusted to the dark, but he was still tripping over low headstones and holes in the ground. This was a crazy plan, and he'd no idea if it'd work.

Two boars dug in the ground near a tilted cross. He threw a stone, and they lifted their heads. He threw another, closer to his location. They followed the sound. He walked quickly, making more noise than usual, and the boars followed. Forty yards away, Ty and Pete were still trading bullets with the bad guys . Zack scrambled up a tree with the plastic. Once the boars came close, he shook out the sheeting. As they passed beneath him, he dropped the plastic on the first animal.

The boar kicked the ground, and its grunts turned to growls. Zack fired a shot toward the enemy. The animals took off toward the bad guys, making horrible squealing sounds.

A man with a thick accent said, "Run!"

Zack sprinted toward Pete and Ty and motioned *follow me* with one arm. When the bad guys started firing in a different direction, toward the boars, Zack and his men took the advantage and charged.

CHAPTER 48

GUNSHOTS?

Nate ran toward the sounds, the lantern throwing beams in some directions and leaving shadows in others. He'd not found Sarah in the Jones tomb. Now he was looking for Etienne or Remiel's men. Nate prayed the gunshots were coming from the Russians. Something he could honestly say he'd never prayed for before.

Ten minutes later, he found Ty, Pete, and Zack in a clearing. Ty held a red-lens flashlight on two dead men. *Remiel's Russians.*

Nate sank to his knees because they wouldn't hold him anymore.

Zack planted a hand on Nate's shoulder. "You're okay?"

Nate threw him off. "*Why?*"

"Why did we kill these men?" Pete came over. "Because they were firing on *us.*"

Ty wiped his forehead with his arm. "They were no match for the boars, though."

The words caught in Nate's throat. He could barely speak. Barely breathe. Barely see.

"Hey." Zack knelt in front of Nate. "What's wrong?"

"They were my last chance." The last word fell apart like a hammer crushing ice.

"Nate?" Pete's voice sounded more concerned. "What's going on?"

"Sarah is in a hide site beneath one of these crypts. It's filling with water, and I've no way of finding her except for the Russians, who I'd hoped would lead me to her before she drowned." He fell forward, his palms hitting the dirt, crushed shells cutting his hands.

He was so tired and scared and desperate. "I don't…can't… find her."

Pete dragged Nate to his feet and picked up the lantern. "We'll figure this out."

Nate pulled Etienne's gun out of his back waistband, then put it in again. And took it out. "I have to find Sarah."

Zack stopped Nate's hand. "It's okay, Nate. We'll find her."

"How?" Ty asked. "There are hundreds of tombs—"

"Shut up, Ty," Zack said.

Nate started walking. He was getting to know every inch of this cemetery. It killed him that he could be passing above Sarah at this moment and never even realize it. A dread unlike any he'd ever known filled him with such physical pain he could barely walk. His men followed.

"Where are we going?" Ty asked.

"No idea," Pete said, still carrying the lantern.

Twenty minutes later, Nate stopped in front of Saint Michael the Archangel. Cassio was gone, and Nate had no idea what to do next.

Zack came up next to Nate to stare at the naked angel. "Explain again about the hide sites."

Nate told them about Sarah's hide sites and the cipher and how she solved it. He finished with "She deciphered the parts of the cipher she had, which gave us names but not locations."

"Where'd she get the original cipher from?" Pete asked.

Nate took the Ziploc bag from his jacket. "A diary written by a sixteen-year-old Puritan girl who was burned for witchcraft and buried in this cemetery."

Zack undid the bag and took out the diary, the copy of *Othello*, and a folded page. "What's this?"

Nate laid the page on top of a flat tomb. "It's an old pirate map of Capel land and this cemetery." Along the bottom, Sarah had written the alphanumeric sequences they'd deciphered and the corresponding names of the tombs that covered her hide sites.

Pete and Ty came over with the lantern.

"These alphanumeric sequences," Ty said. "They were translated into these names using *Othello* as a substitution cipher key? Made by pirates and maybe used in the Revolutionary War?"

"Yes." Nate ran his hands over his short hair. *What am I going to do?*

"Cool." Ty picked up the three-hundred-year-old diary and started flipping through it like it was the Sunday sports section. "What are these?" He pointed to numbers Nate had never seen:

$$32^{22}_{7} / 450210^{22}_{7} / 44736^{22}_{7} / 452817^{22}_{7} / 4362$$

"No idea." There were more numbers, but they were smudged.

Pete used a stick to poke the map. "Walk me through these hide sites one more time."

As Nate talked, Ty read the diary.

A minute later, Ty said, "Hey. This Puritan girl is in love with pi."

"What are you talking about?" Pete took the diary. "It says, 'RP loves TT.' How do you get pie out of that? *Idiot.*"

"Two capital T's next to each other resembles pi, you know, like in Greek."

"*TT* stands for *Thomas Toban*," Nate said. "Rebecca, the girl who wrote that diary, ran away to marry him. In fact, Saint Michael is Thomas's tomb…" Nate grabbed the lantern and ran over to the archangel. There were no birth or death dates on the plinth block. Only *TT*, which did resemble the symbol for pi.

Ty used the red-lensed light to illuminate the plinth block. "Look at these stars and roses."

"Sarah said in classical navigation that roses and stars represent time and distance."

Time and distance…and pi?

Nate returned to the diary to study the numbers. After a minute, he realized every sequence followed the same pattern. *Of course.*

His dyslexia might've messed with his words but never with numbers. And everything he'd ever wanted to know about patterns, he'd learned from Sarah.

Some of the tightness in his chest lessened, and he found one of Sarah's pencils in his coat pocket. Then he turned over the map. Taking the first sequence, he rewrote it as $32\frac{22}{7}/4\,|\,502$.

"See? Every sequence has twenty-two over seven in the middle, which is about 3.14, the early notation for pi. In each sequence, twenty-two over seven is followed by a four." He tapped the pencil on the tomb. "The four is in the first half of the sequence, not the second."

Pete shouldered him. "So?"

"I read this as thirty-two pi divided by four, which is eight pi."

"This sounds like math." Ty appeared with his red light. "Tell me this isn't calculus."

"Nope. Trigonometry." Nate drew a circle. "Two pi is a full circle. Eight pi just means you go around the circle four times...but you still end up at a zero bearing." He scoffed lightly. "I bet the pirates were trying to make it more confusing."

Pete's hands landed on his hips "It's working, because I don't know what the fuck you're talking about."

"Stick with me." Nate started transcribing the other numbers. "These sequences are polar coordinates that will tell us where the hide sites are from some starting point."

"Polar...what? Oh, jeez." Ty closed his eyes. "I hate math."

Zack and Pete studied the numbers while that dull feeling in Nate's head cleared. Logic started kicking fear's ass. Logic would find the woman he loved.

Zack shook his head. "What do you mean?"

Nate met Zack's confused gaze. "Remember basic land nav training? We moved from point A to point B on a map by determining the compass direction from A to B in degrees, zero to three sixty, measured from magnetic north as zero degrees. Then we measured distance in meters."

And the crowd went silent.

So Nate continued. "These numbers are giving us a direction—a bearing—and a distance to take from some point of origin."

Ty sighed heavily. "How?"

Pete and Zack just stared at Nate, and he could almost hear their eyes glazing over.

Nate pointed to the numbers he'd transcribed:

$$32 \tfrac{22}{7} / 4502 = 8\pi \mid 502$$

$$10 \tfrac{22}{7} / 4473 = 5\pi/2 \mid 473$$

$$6 \tfrac{22}{7} / 4528 = 3\pi/2 \mid 528$$

$$17 \tfrac{22}{7} / 4362 = \pi/4 \mid 362$$

"Angles can be measured in degrees *or* in radians, which are usually written in terms of pi. That's what clued me in." He pointed to the circle he'd drawn. "A quarter of a circle is ninety degrees, or pi divided by two radians. Half a circle is one hundred eighty degrees, or pi radians. A full circle is three hundred sixty degrees, or two pi. Get it?"

Zack leaned in closer. "The first part of the sequence is a bearing in radians—"

"What are radians again?" Ty asked.

Zack pushed Ty away. "The second number is a distance…what is that supposed to be in…feet?"

"I'm not sure," Nate said. "Sarah said pirates described distances using measures like *leagues* and *paces*."

"Why?" Ty threw up a hand. "Why would anyone

complicate their lives like this? Why would anyone make math even more confusing?"

"Because"—Zack picked up diary—"pirates didn't want people finding their shit. They buried their treasure and made confusing maps only they could use."

Nate considered whether to explain how—unlike compass directions, which were measured clockwise, always from magnetic north as zero degrees—radians were measured counterclockwise, from any point on a circle chosen as the "zero line."

Instead he said, "To use these coordinates, we need to figure out where the starting point is and decide which direction from that point should be considered zero degrees, or zero radians."

"You mean a zero line that isn't magnetic north?" Pete asked.

And Pete got a gold star. "Yes. Then we take our bearings off that zero line, walk the right distance…hopefully find the sites, which we'll know by the names Sarah deciphered."

Zack snorted. "Another way the pirates made it hard as hell to find their loot."

"Oh, *hell* no." Ty stomped around, his red light flashing everywhere. "I'm throwing the too-much-trig flag. I don't do sines and cosines."

"We're lucky Nate was a math major." Pete pointed to the diary. "How do we find the point of origin for these coordinates, figure out a zero line, and determine the distance?"

Nate felt rising panic again. "I'm not sure."

No one mentioned that Sarah had transcribed over twenty hide site names, yet they only had four possible coordinates.

"Wait." Zack moved toward Thomas's tomb. "Didn't Pops call Saint Michael the *fixed point* of Capel land?"

Nate looked up. "When?"

"Earlier tonight when we decided to save you."

"Grady also said Saint Michael marked the center of the cemetery." Pete walked around the tomb with the lantern and shone it on the TT engraving. "Slice of Greek pi, anyone?"

Nate hurried over with the map to stand in front of the TT. Then he turned toward the direction of the Jones tomb hide site.

"Could Thomas Toban's tomb be our starting point?" Zack asked. "And…maybe this side of the tomb is our zero line?"

Nate reread the distance numbers, mentally translating them into possible lengths. With the cemetery no more than half a mile on a side, the lengths could only be in feet or yards or—as Sarah had mentioned earlier—paces. Which, if he remembered correctly, were about 2½ feet. His breath hitched, and then, for the first time since waking from his nightmare, he smiled. "Yes."

"That means"—Ty slapped the angel's ass—"Thomas, my man, *you* are our compass rose."

Hooah, brother. *Hoo-fucking-ah.*

Nate put one foot along the base of the tomb and walked in the direction of the Jones hide site, counting paces aloud.

Too many minutes later, he returned.

"What are we dealing with?" Pete asked.

"Paces. I walked the distance off at 520 paces, close enough to 528." His legs were probably longer than the pirates'. "I also marked the Jones site on this map."

"Can we kill some boars now?" Ty asked. "Or search for Sarah?"

"In a few, brother," Zack answered. "Right, Nate?"

"As soon as I check the alignment of the Jones tomb to the sides of Thomas's tomb." He lay the map on the flat tomb and drew a line between his penciled dot marking the

Jones site and Saint Michael's tomb, which, thank goodness, was already on the map. "Three pi divided by two is three-quarters of a circle. If I go clockwise from this line by three-quarters…"

He marked a line perpendicular to his first line, put an arrowhead on it, and wrote a large *0* next to the arrow. After staring in the direction he'd just paced, he turned the map, and…bingo! "My zero line here lines up with this side of the tomb with the TT on it."

He took a precious moment to close his eyes and take a few inhales and exhales. The deep breaths evened out his heart rate, and a spiral of hope pushed aside his exhaustion.

He opened his eyes and, on the map, recorded the bearings and distances for the other three tombs. They weren't perfect or precise, but it was all they had.

Ty read over Nate shoulder. "You're sure Sarah is in this cemetery?"

"Yes." Nate divided a gym flyer he'd found in his jacket pocket and, on the back, drew two crude maps of the cemetery. Then he listed the tomb names and marked the four approximate hide site locations.

After explaining to the men how to use the coordinates with Saint Michael as the starting point, he said, "The hide sites are beneath large, mausoleum-type structures and sit along creeks or estuaries. Maybe even a river. We're splitting up into pairs, each taking two hide sites."

Zack grabbed one of the rough maps, and Pete took the other.

"There's another thing. These hide sites are only dry during certain weeks of the year, and then they fill up again." Thunder rumbled again. "Etienne said that Sarah's is filling now."

Although the water wasn't that cold, Sara was shivering. Because of her mistake with the door, the water had risen to her neck. Pretty soon she'd have to tread water, and she wasn't sure she had the strength.

She heard thunder through the open door. The rain made echoey sounds on the water, and she screamed again.

"Sarah?"

She spun around in the water, in the dark, having no idea which way she was facing.

"Sarah!" A woman's voice was definitely calling her.

"I'm here! I'm here!" she screamed, but it came out as a throaty cough. She'd no voice left.

"Sarah! Swim to the door in the wall."

"It's stuck." Except all that came out was a hoarse bark.

"Swim to the door."

It wouldn't budge.

"Sarah!" The voice was now coming from outside.

Sara gripped the edge of the door until she couldn't feel her fingers and yanked again. *It's not working.* Although the door was only open a few inches, mud rushed in with the water. She rested her head against the wall and felt a pain in her hand. She still clutched the shard.

She dove down, using the edge of the door as a guide. She couldn't see, but she'd gotten used to that. Her hands told her the bottom metal edge of the door was bent and had dug into the wood flooring. Using the blade, she cut the wood around the bent metal. She had to come up twice for air, but on the third time she got the metal edge to bend up. The door shifted a few more inches. Water came in faster, so she pushed harder.

"Sarah!" The voice sounded desperate.

That desperation spurred her to force the door open even a few more inches…she was able to slip her arm and leg through. The river flowed in faster, rising above her head, and she coughed. Suddenly, something grabbed her wrist. A strong hand with a tight grip. She coughed and swallowed what felt like a bucket's worth of brackish water.

The door pushed in, like the person on the other side

had kicked it. The hand on her wrist drew her out, but she struggled to breathe. The more water she gulped, the more she felt faint. The more light-headed she became, the more she panicked. The more panic took over, the more she fought the person who held her arm. Finally, when she had no more strength and could no longer breathe, she slipped into darkness.

CHAPTER 49

SARAH WASN'T THERE.

Nate and Zack left the first hide site, which probably hadn't been used in years. The crypt covering it was unlocked. Inside, they'd found so many caskets, they had to move three outside to get to the trapdoor in the floor. Once they opened it, they found the hide site filled in with stone and debris.

It was raining steadily now, and they were both soaked. Nate had no idea what hour it was or how much time had passed since he'd woken to find Sarah missing. It felt like an eternity.

Zack used his forearm to wipe his face. His long, wet hair molded to his head. "Nate?"

Nate took a deep breath and ran. "This way."

Fifteen minutes later, the next tomb on their list was locked. Zack blew the lock with his rifle, and the sound cut through the night. Nate and Zack went in, guns ready.

"Nate." Zack motioned to the corner, where a metal ladder lay on its side.

Nate's hands shook. She had to be here. He could feel it.

Another fired shot broke the lock on the trapdoor. The gunshot inside the stone room left a ringing reverb. He opened the door, but it was so dark he almost didn't realize it was filled with water. "Sarah!"

No answer.

Zack brought the ladder over, and they dropped it in. Nate handed Zack his pistol and flashlight and went down. The rain had made him wet, but the water soaked his bones. His hands shook, and he could barely hang on. "Sarah!"

No answer.

Oh, God. No!

"Nate!" Ty ran in. "Down by the river. Behind us."

Zack shifted, taking the light with him. "What?"

"We left the second hide site," Ty said between coughs. "I saw a light."

Nate came up, soaking wet, and took his weapon. "Sarah?"

"Maybe. Someone was carrying a body out of a creek."

Nate ran out of the tomb and around. Maybe it was because his eyes had adjusted to the dark or the reflection of the rain on the white tombs or a combination of anger and fear making him desperate to see, but twenty yards away, he saw four people near the bank. The tall one was Cassio, who knelt over another, who was lying down and not moving. The hooded man-who-was-a-woman stood near Cassio with a flashlight, and a fourth person, Fletcher Ames, sat on a tomb, holding a penlight.

Nate stumbled down the ravine and pushed Cassio aside. Nate fell on his knees next to Sarah, who lay prone on the ground. "Sarah?"

He pressed his ear to her chest and exhaled in relief. She was soaking wet, her breaths were erratic and shallow, but she was alive.

Gently, even though he wanted to do it fiercely, he cradled her in his arms and held her close. Her eyes fluttered, but she didn't open them.

"She needs rest," the hooded man-who-was-a-woman said. "You need to take her away from here. Away from Savannah." The woman, like the rest of them, was soaking wet. "My name is Isabel. I was a friend of Sarah's mother."

"Advice from the woman who stalked us and kidnapped Sarah?"

Who may have kept her from her birth father?

"I was helping Sarah. Her mother was my greatest friend, and I swore to her that I'd protect Sarah."

"Know what that sounds like?" Nate's laugh sounded like a bark. "*Horseshit.*"

Cassio placed a hand on Nate's shoulder. "Passing judgment on things you know nothing about is a pursuit for lawyers and politicians, not men of honor."

"I was there when Sarah was born," Isabel said. "There when her birth father left her mother. There when——"

"I don't care." Nate cradled Sarah, wishing he had a blanket. He was as cold and wet as she was, and he'd nothing to offer her. "I'm taking her——"

"That's not about to happen," a man said.

Etienne?

The light shifted, and Nate turned to find Etienne holding Isabel, her back to his chest, a knife on her throat. She'd dropped the flashlight, and it had rolled away.

The tic above Nate's eye started up again. "Let her go." He'd no reason to protect Isabel other than his need to take care of Etienne for good.

Zack appeared. "Let me take Sarah. She may be hypothermic."

Nate handed her over, and Zack hurried up the ravine.

Nate took off his jacket and threw it on the ground. His gun landed on top, and he kept his gaze on Etienne. "Cassio? I need a knife."

Cassio handed Nate a hunting knife because the warrior understood. This was personal. It should be dealt with in a personal way. Knife to knife. Fist to fist. Man to man. "Let her go."

Cassio took the flashlight and moved toward Fletcher Ames. *That* was another emotional landmine for another night.

Cassio kept the light on Etienne, leaving Nate in the shadows.

Etienne backed into the dense foliage, dragging Isabel. The light followed him as he limped. Had he been shot?

"Do you want to die slowly or quickly?" Nate asked.

"I'm not dying tonight." Etienne halted, and Isabel gripped his arm. "I just want what's mine. Asylum in exchange for the historian."

"Working for Remiel not what you thought it'd be?" Nate nodded in Fletcher's direction. "Remiel has a habit of turning on those closest to him."

"Fuck Remiel," Etienne said. "All I want is out of here!"

"You don't deserve to be out of here," Isabel said in a hoarse voice. "I know you shot at Sarah yesterday in the cemetery. You shot that banker from Charleston. You killed those cops behind O'Malley's Pub. You even cut their hands with the letter *B*."

"The situation in Boston wasn't my fault," Etienne sneered. "Things were going as planned until the fucking Fianna showed up. I had to kill those men."

"And poison Joe?" Nate asked.

"No different than what Fletcher did to you."

None of this mattered now. Nate had been approaching the entire time and had forced Etienne up against the creek bank, his shoulders barely fitting between two trees. Now all Nate needed was a diversion.

Nate steadied the knife in his hand and made a show of glancing over his shoulder. Except instead of moving forward with his plan, he paused.

At the top of the ravine, near the mausoleum, Sarah lay on the ground, both Pete and Zack covering her with jackets and rubbing her arms. Behind them were *all* of his men, many of whom were holding flashlights. Ty sat on a tomb next to Cain, who had his arms crossed. Pops and Grady carried their bolt-action rifles, while Jimmy and Garza had lanterns. Vane was on the far right, near Luke and Calum. Alex was so far on the left Nate almost didn't notice him.

Kells stood in front, hands in the pockets of his field jacket, staring at Cassio.

Nate faced Etienne again. *Now or never.*

Nate threw the knife, and it hit the tree next to Etienne's head. The surprise made Etienne jerk, allowing Nate to yank Isabel out of Etienne's arms. Then he went for Etienne's knees.

Isabel ran while Nate and Etienne both hit the ground. Nate ended up on top and punched Etienne in the jaw. Pain flooded his hands and knuckles. He pounded again.

Etienne threw a left hook and rolled away, protecting his left leg. Nate's jaw throbbed, and he kicked Etienne in his wounded thigh. He howled and rolled down the bank even more.

Nate followed. It was darker here, but he heard a distinct whistle of a knife swinging. He jumped aside just as Etienne's blade skimmed his chest, slicing his shirt. Then Etienne disappeared.

"Sarah is like Isabel. Like all women." Etienne's voice came out of the darkness. "She'll betray you."

Nate heard sounds off to his left, like heavy breathing. "Sarah will never betray me. She believes in me." Even when he didn't believe in himself. Her strength and bravery had taught him that.

Etienne came up fast, but Nate lowered his body and used his good shoulder to slam Etienne into a tree. Nate felt the reverb in his body. The terrain was slippery and dark. Normally not an issue, but since he'd been shot in the shoulder and hit in the jaw, everything hurt.

Needing to get out of the muddy ravine, he worked his way up the bank. Etienne followed with his knife out. Once on flatter ground, Etienne charged. Nate tripped on a root and fell onto his back. The air blasted out of his lungs, and Etienne straddled him. Nate saw the blade fly and grabbed Etienne's neck with both hands.

Nate rolled until he was on top with his hands around Etienne's neck. Etienne kicked and clawed at Nate's fingers to peel his hands away, but Nate had self-righteous anger on his side and put all of his fury and frustration and fear into crushing Etienne's neck. Etienne was a tough bastard though. He gripped Nate's head and used his thumbs to dig out Nate's eyeballs. Nate closed his eyes and pressed harder—until he heard a gunshot next to his head.

He fell off, covering his ears with his hands. The blast left him disoriented, deaf, and shaking. When he opened his eyes, Isabel was walking away, holding a gun against her thigh.

Cassio helped Nate up.

"Cassio." Nate stumbled, and Cassio used his shoulder to prop him up. "What the fuck just happened?"

"Lady Isabel killed the fiend." Together, Cassio and Nate limped to the tomb where Fletcher Ames had been sitting.

Except the fucker had disappeared, taking the penlight with him. Nate dropped to his knees. "Where the hell is Fletcher?"

Cassio clutched his side with one hand, his wide shoulders heaving. "I know not."

Nate scanned the darkness. "Isabel is gone too. She and Fletcher must have taken off together."

Cassio lowered himself to the tomb Fletcher had sat on. "They'll return to Remiel, and we'll meet them another day."

"Why?" There were so many questions wrapped up in that one word. "Why did you save Sarah? Why didn't you let her die like you'd threatened?"

"The Prince wants a willing recruit, not one who'll harbor resentment."

Cassio spoke true. If the Prince had allowed Sarah to die, there was no way Nate would ever willingly join the Fianna. "You're letting us both live?"

"Her stopped heart paid the price." Cassio shifted and winced. "The Prince only requires one death per lifetime."

Her heart stopped? "How did you—"

"With hand to heart."

CPR. Nate stood and picked up his coat and gun. Then he offered a hand to Cassio. "And Jack?"

Once Cassio stood, he said, "Your lord will be free from the death sentence."

"And me? Do I go with you?"

"No." Cassio started walking. "Since you're not prepared to forsake the world, the Prince has decided you'll return to your prison until you're ready to join us."

He wasn't mature enough to be in the Fianna? Nate followed, not sure how to feel about *that* news and also unsure how to ask the final question. So he just said, "Sarah's birth father?"

"A tale for another day." Cassio put a hand on Nate's shoulder and squeezed. "Come. Your brothers—and your love—await."

＊

Sarah felt herself lifted in strong arms and rested her head on a hard chest. She didn't have the strength to wrap her arm around his neck, yet she smelled pine and summer breezes. She heard a fast but steady heartbeat and a whisper in her ear.

"Stay with me, sweetheart."

Nate. She wanted to open her eyes, but she was cold and shivery. He walked while male voices floated around her.

Pete's came first. "Seriously, dudes. Every woman we know is signing up for my self-defense class. This. Is. Ridiculous."

"This is also why," Vane said, "*we* need to retrain in all forms of hand-to-hand combat."

"And primitive survival and orienteering skills," Zack added. "With a side of trig."

"Great," Cain said. "Why don't we all become Eagle Scouts?"

"Personally," Garza said in his New Jersey accent, "I think you should all learn Latin and read Shakespeare. I can help with that."

"How?" Ty said.

"I have a Masters of Letters degree. And if you don't

know what that is, you can ask Sarah when she wakes. She has one too."

Sarah smiled, and Nate tightened his hold.

"Tomorrow," Sheriff Boudreaux said, "after Garza and I deal with these bodies, investigations, and police reports, I'm shutting this cemetery down."

"Good luck with that, son," Grady said.

Pops *harrumphed*.

"Sir?" Luke asked. "Does this mean Nate still has to return to the prison hospital tomorrow?"

The men went silent, and after a long moment, she heard another new voice. This one lower, straining with confidence and power. "Yes."

CHAPTER 50

ZACK ENTERED THE FOYER OF CALUM'S MANSION. HE'D knocked, but since no one had answered, he'd let himself in. He was the last one to arrive because he'd drawn the short straw and was the last to shower. *Aaaaaaaaaaand,* because he'd been the last, he'd only had cold water and had missed his ride.

Pete, probably because he was too tired, offered Zack the use of his motorcycle.

He followed the voices to an upstairs sitting room. Calum stood by a window, watching a line of pink tinge the horizon, arms crossed. Pete sat on a couch, in Iron Rack's sweats, one arm over his eyes. Vane sat next to him with his head back.

Cain was sprawled in a club chair with his phone, probably texting Charlotte. Ty was on the floor, leaning against an ottoman, arms crossed. Luke sat at a desk in the corner, writing on a legal pad.

Ty's sprained ankle and Pete's gash from a piece of rebar had been the team's only physical damage. Except for Sarah and Nate, of course.

Pete tossed Zack a bottle of water "Where's Alex?"

"At the gym. Asleep."

Kells arrived with Detective Garza. Kells sat in another chair, legs spread, his hands clasped. He hadn't shaved, and his stubble looked redder than ever.

"How's Nate?" Pete asked.

Nate and Sarah were being checked out by Doc Bennett and his staff who, apparently, were on 24/7 call for Calum.

Garza answered first. "Nate has bruised ribs, a gunshot graze on his shoulder, and numerous cuts and abrasions." He glanced at Kells before continuing. "Nate missed an appointment yesterday. Doc Bennett ran some more blood work. That stuff they pumped into Nate in the POW camp was far more powerful than the street stuff he'd been taking. Yet, when the doc took blood an hour ago, the compound in his system had lessened."

"What the hell does that mean?" Pete finally took the arm off his eyes. They were swollen and bloodshot.

"It means," Garza added, "that Nate may not regain all of his long-term memories, but with rest and time and an herbal tea he's been drinking, his seizures and headaches should lessen."

"Those seizures could be affecting his executive functioning," Kells said. "It might explain his choices lately."

"Bullshit," Pete said.

Every head turned toward Pete. *Had Pete just called out Kells? Again?*

"Nate might have headaches and seizures," Pete said, "but he's not crazy. He *saw* that hooded man on the isle the other day. He and Sarah *were* chased through the historic district. Sarah *had been* kidnapped. You *were* having them followed. What I don't get is why you can't believe him!"

Guilt. Zack watched Kells's posture straighten while his hands fisted. Did Kells feel guilty over the doomed operation? Because, seriously, it wasn't any of their faults. Or... Zack's heart felt like it was turning itself inside out. Did Kells feel guilty because he *blamed* Nate for the failure? And hated himself for the blame at the same time?

Zack clasped his hands behind his neck. If that was the case, then they were all screwed. Kells was their leader, the man they needed to trust—more than anyone—at this moment.

Before Kells could answer, Nate arrived in jeans and bare feet. Zack was still getting used to Nate's *short* hair. Yet it suited him. All of the men stood, with varying versions of "How's Sarah?"

Ivers came in with a tray of coffee. "Breakfast will be served buffet style in the dining room in ten minutes."

After everyone took a coffee and thanked Ivers, Nate sat in an armchair.

"Doc Bennett is with Sarah. She suffered mild hypothermia, but her body temp is almost normal. Cassio said her heart stopped, but her EKG is normal. She's also been vomiting. It's possible the water she swallowed is making her sick. But with rest and care, she should be okay."

Zack said a silent prayer of thanks.

"Nate?" Pete asked in his typical straightforward style. "What the fuck?"

Nate's elbows dug trenches in his thighs as he stared at the blue-and-green Turkish rug on the floor. "Sarah solved the cipher, and we were going to use it as leverage to bargain with the Prince for Jack's life. Unbeknownst to us, Etienne had a falling-out with Remiel. He and the hooded man—who is a woman named Isabel—decided to trade Sarah, the diary we stole, and Fletcher Ames to the Prince in exchange for asylum. Except the Prince then traded Fletcher Ames to Remiel in exchange for those missiles."

"So," Zack said, "Alex was right about the missiles being a commodity to trade instead of a weapon to be used?"

"Yes."

"The Prince also took out four Russians tonight," Garza said. "Two in Charleston, two in Savannah."

"That's what the Fianna do." Pete had returned to his position with his arm over his eyes. "Besides recruiting Nate."

Nate sighed. "Etienne planned to give Sarah's location to Cassio. But when Cassio decided getting Etienne out of town wasn't worth the effort, we lost Sarah's location. Luckily, with Zack, Ty, and Pete's help, we were able to find her."

"Except Cassio found Sarah first," Kells said. "How?"

"On his way to the boat where other warriors were waiting, he saw Isabel—the woman who was trying to save Sarah. I'm not sure why, but Cassio—reluctantly—decided to help."

"What about Sarah and Jack?" Kells said. "She solved the cipher."

"The Fianna lifted the bounty on Jack's life when I joined them. But, apparently, since I'm not *mature enough* to be recruited yet, I'm returning to the prison hospital until I'm ready."

Vane waved a hand. "What about Sarah?"

"She died." Nate's voice became softer than slippers on carpet. "When Cassio rescued her from the hide site, he had to do CPR to get her heart started. Technically, since she died once for solving the cipher, she fulfilled the terms of the contract and will be allowed to live her second chance."

"Jeez, Nate," Cain said, throwing his phone onto the pillow next to him. "How did you find her? That cemetery wasn't just dark as shit, it was freakin' *huuuuuuuge*."

Nate let Zack tell the story about polar coordinates and Thomas the Compass Rose.

When Zack finished, Ty added, "We did math. *Hard* math."

"Did Etienne kill those bankers from Charleston?" Luke asked.

"I know Etienne killed the banker found on the Isle of Grace. And that he was involved in the O'Malley Pub murders."

"*Fuck me*," Cain said. "The O'Malley Pub murders made national news."

Nate nodded. "That was Etienne's operation until it was interrupted by Sarah's father Joe Munro and Detective Waring. They, in turn, were interrupted by the Fianna. As far as the murdered banker in Charleston who was found with my medal? All I know is that it was a Remiel kill. I'm just not sure which of Remiel's minions did the deed."

Calum finally turned to face them all. "What's happening out on the isle now?"

"To make everything look legit, Jimmy called in the

SPD," Garza said. "Jimmy also told me that when Etienne doesn't show tomorrow, his brothers will search for him."

"What about Etienne's body?" Zack asked.

"We moved Etienne next to the two Russians Pete, Zack, and Ty killed." Garza crossed his arms and looked away. "Did you know there are boars on the isle?"

"Are you saying"—Zack swallowed hard—"that the boars, uh—"

"We have feral hogs in the Pine Barrens of New Jersey. They do the same thing. They clean up. Even if they don't finish, it'll be clear to the investigators that the Russians— and Etienne—were eaten by wild animals. There's nothing left to investigate."

"Their weapons? And other evidence of a gunfight?" Kells asked.

Zack tried not to laugh. That question was classic Kells.

"Jimmy and I cleared the scenes as best we could in the dark. It's pouring out there now, and that should muck things up. The cemetery is large, and since we moved Etienne's body, no one will know where he was shot. Even if Etienne's brothers find his body, and other evidence, it will look like the Russians killed him. Luckily, thanks to Nate, we have Etienne's weapon. That will prove he murdered that banker on the isle."

"Are you the lead on the case?" Calum asked Garza.

"Yes. I'm confident that, in a few days, the investigation out there will wrap up. I also got a call from Maurice, the auction manager. He dropped the assault charges against Nate. You wouldn't know anything about that, would you, Calum?"

Calum smiled at Nate. "Possibly."

"Detective," Kells said, "will Detective Waring still want to talk to Nate about the Charleston murder victim?"

"He was killed the same way as the one out on the isle. Even though we can't ID an actual killer, I'm sure we can tie Etienne to that death as well. Like Nate said, even if

Etienne didn't do it, it was still a Remiel kill. And while it's true that Detective Waring knows too much about Nate, that'll make it easier for him to believe that Nate lost his medal in a POW camp." Garza gripped Nate's shoulder. "I'll call Detective Waring tomorrow and take care of it."

Zack scoffed silently. *That victim* had been Allison's husband, and Zack's emotions were still in free fall.

"Waring won't let this go," Kells said.

"I'll talk to Waring," Garza replied in a firm voice that said *no contradictions allowed*. "My worry is Remiel's next move. Does anyone have any idea about that?"

"All I know," Pete said from beneath his arm, "is that Sarah went all in on solving that cipher, even when everyone told her not to, and gave us a win. By knowing how to find those hide sites, she's taken them out of play for both the Prince and Remiel."

The men murmured their agreement and their admiration until Zack said, "The murdered man in Charleston is Stuart Pinckney."

It took Kells a minute, but when his eyes widened, it was clear he'd made the connection. And then the rest of the male choir chimed in with questions and concerns.

But Nate was the one who put a hand on Zack's shoulder. "*Allison's* husband?"

"Yes."

"Is that a problem?" Garza asked the room.

"I don't know," Kells said to Zack. "Is it?"

"No. But I'd like permission to check on her."

Kells nodded. "No physical contact. Got it?"

"Yes, sir." It was more than he could've hoped for.

"You can take my bike," Pete said. "Just don't get a ticket."

The doctor poked his head in. "Nate? Sarah's awake."

Nate left, and the rest of the men stretched and moved, all of them—except for Kells and Calum—talking about breakfast.

"We should eat and return to the gym," Vane said in that all-knowing way of his. "We've got a lot to do today."

As the men left, Luke handed Zack the legal pad he'd been writing on. "Remember you asked me to talk to Charlotte and Abigail about the night of the ambush? They called me because neither wanted to send anything by email. I wrote down what they said. I hope it helps."

"Thanks."

"Oh, and Vane contacted *you-know-who*." Luke looked behind him. Kells was still talking to Calum. "She said she'd be in touch."

Vane talked to Kells's wife Katherine? "In touch with you?"

"*No*. With you." Luke left the room, shaking his head. *Wonderful.*

"Zack?" Kells came over. "I need an executive officer."

XO? The air rushed out of Zack's lungs, and he gripped the chair next to him. "Why?"

"Because in six hours, two MPs are picking Nate up and taking him to Maine. He's returning to the prison hospital."

CHAPTER 51

SARAH SAT IN THE GIANT BED, SURROUNDED BY BEEPING medical equipment. Tall windows overlooked the garden below and the river beyond. Nineteenth-century furniture and rugs decorated the room. She was in a hospital gown, and her hair was a mess. She vaguely remembered taking a bath and having her hair washed. But she must've gone to bed with it wet.

The clock said six a.m. Although she was exhausted, a mind niggle told her there was something she needed to do.

Nate entered. Before she could move, his arms were around her, his kisses on her face, her lips, her hair. He sat on the bed so he could lean against the headboard, stretch out his legs, and cradle her in his arms. She lay partially on top of him, her head on his chest, beneath his chin. She loved his warm, solid heartbeat. "Where were you?"

He pointed to the loveseat near the window with a pillow and blanket. "I was sleeping there but needed to talk to my men."

"About not going to prison?" He kissed her hair, and she raised her head. "I'm not giving up. We have the cipher. Someone somewhere must be willing to trade for it."

"Sarah." He kissed her lips. "There's nothing anyone can do."

Her eyes burned, and she tasted salt. She wrapped her arms around him, desperate to breathe in his scent until it became her own. "Run away with me. Calum has money. He'll help."

"If I run, the rest of my men go to prison."

She pressed herself closer until all of her was touching all of him. "I don't care."

"Just let me hold you until I leave."

She stifled her cry, and they tightened their hold on each other. She was never, ever going to let him go.

"Sarah?" he whispered into her hair. "I love you."

"Oh, Nate." The sob escaped, along with a rogue tear. "I love you too."

Nate closed his eyes and held Sarah until she fell asleep and his arms went numb. Until the sun rose higher in the sky and he smelled coffee wafting up from the dining room. Until short shadows turned to longer ones and he heard a knock on the door.

"Come in," he said quietly.

The door opened, and Zack came in and stopped a few feet away. "It's time."

Nate disengaged himself from the woman who was now his entire world. Her hair was spread out across the pillow, her face covered with bruises and scratches that the doctor said should heal quickly. He laid a white throw blanket on top of her. After kissing her head and breathing in her gardenia scent for the last time, he took the handkerchief out of his pocket. He placed it in her hand, and she involuntarily clutched it to her breast.

Zack gripped Nate's shoulder. "I'm sorry."

Nate nodded and wiped his face with his forearm. *Sorry* was such a useless, meaningless little word that left blood everywhere it went. "So am I, Zack. So am I."

When he got downstairs, Calum and Garza were waiting for him. Zack stood by the front door.

Nate spoke to Calum first. "Tell Jimmy, Pops, and Grady that I appreciate everything they've done for us. And that I'll miss them."

Calum shook his hand but wouldn't let go. "Carina

wanted to be here to say goodbye, but she's in Washington doing senatorial things."

"I doubt she's interested in my issues."

"My twin might be a bitch, but she has a heart. She just keeps it hidden in an iron safe surrounded by barbed wire. Besides"—Calum tilted his head and half smiled—"she has this crazy idea that I hired you, and the rest of your men, to watch over me. As the oldest by eleven minutes, she's overprotective and doesn't like it when she thinks I'm in trouble. She's quite upset about you leaving me unprotected."

Nate laughed. He'd not known that Carina was older than Calum, but it didn't surprise him. "Tell Carina...not to give away her power."

"I will." Calum gripped Nate's shoulders, and his eyes shone. "I'm going to try my best, legally, to get you free."

"This is out of your jurisdiction, Calum. Oh, and please say goodbye to Miss Nell for me." Nate closed his eyes and struggled to get the words out. "And watch over Sarah. She loves strawberry pie."

"I promise." Calum hugged him before handing him off to Garza.

"Take care of yourself." Garza stuck out a hand. "I'll miss you."

"Me too," Nate said as Ivers appeared to drive him and Zack to the gym. "Me too."

This is much harder than I'd thought it'd be.

Nate stood in the gym's classroom. A duffel sat on the floor. It's not like he had much, and he certainly wouldn't need much. All of his men were there, and once he'd said goodbye, the MPs would take him away. They'd agreed not to cuff him until he got to the car. Then they'd start the car ride up to Maine.

He went down the line shaking hands and clapping backs as if he were just being deployed for an indefinite amount of time instead of going away for seventeen years. Which might as well be forever.

"Remember," he said to Luke, who could barely look at him. "Weekly movie night for the men. And the bowling league on Sundays. A few things to keep us—you all—together."

"Got it," Luke said. "And we're going with the laundry service you chose."

Nate wanted to laugh at their conversation but was afraid he'd lose it. He'd spent years with these men in some of the worst combat zones in the world. And now they were talking about movies and bleach.

When he got to Pete, they just hugged. Hard. They'd been through so much together, there were no words.

Zack stayed still with his hands in his jeans. "This sucks."

"I know." Nate exhaled. "You'll be a great XO. Just remember, you're in charge. Don't let the men push you around."

"I'll be sure to tell Kells."

Nate said goodbye to Cain, Ty, and Vane, and even Alex shook his hand. Suddenly, the door swung open, and Samantha raced into the room and threw herself into his arms. She wore a black-and-purple sundress and had dyed her hair with purple streaks. He hugged her tight. She was crying and unafraid who saw. "Please don't leave us," she said into his neck.

"I wish I didn't have to."

She released him and then kissed him on both cheeks. "You saved my life, Nate Walker. As well as Juliet's and Sarah's. I'm going to make sure no one forgets that."

Pete came over and took her hand, knowing that if he didn't, Nate might never make it out on his own. Nate grabbed his duffel and left the classroom to see Kells.

Kells was in his office, staring out the window at the closed-up T-shirt place across the street. "I'm sorry."

Nate wasn't sure he'd heard correctly. "None of this is your fault."

"Isn't it?" Kells half-turned toward Nate.

"No. All of this is, and always has been, my fault. I need to take the punishment." Although, despite the gravity of his sins, losing Sarah and being banished seemed overly harsh and unjust. But that was just his opinion.

"I'm doing everything in my power to save you and Jack and the rest of the men. You also need to know that Jack didn't want to accuse you. I made him do it."

"Why?"

"Because I didn't have the courage to do it myself." Kells finally looked directly at Nate. "I didn't want to, but I blamed you. And in dumping most of the blame on you, I was able to make a deal and get the other men's sentences reduced from life in Leavenworth to twenty years in Leedsville."

Nate sucked in a roomful of air. Kells had betrayed him. To protect the rest of the men. Because that's what Kells did.

"Although"—Kells's sigh carried exhaustion and worry—"considering the state you were in when I rescued you, I thought the prison hospital was a better choice than the U. S. military's prison at Leedsville."

Nate looked away. He understood, but not really. Instead of digging into the pain, especially since Kells was apologizing, he studied the wall. The map of Afghanistan had been taken down and put in the back room. They were bringing order and discipline to their ranks. That alone told him they'd be okay. That alone gave him peace.

But there was one last thing. "Sir, I mentioned this before, but now that the Fianna have made themselves known—"

"I know. Secrecy or death. And I understand why you couldn't say anything the other day. I just wish—" Kells sighed and handed Nate a tin from the desk. "Pops said this tea was helping your headaches. I thought you could take it with you."

"Thanks." Grateful for the subject change, Nate took the *Chocolate de Paris* tin and packed it. He also had the tea bags Sarah had made for him. "I'll never forget you. Nor Jack or any of our men."

Kells rearranged the files on his desk, then shoved pencils into the tomato soup can he used as a holder. "They're here. I'll walk you out."

Nate left the office, carrying his duffel, and when he saw the MPs standing there in full uniform with their sidearms, his legs wobbled. But he held his head high and left Iron Rack's and Savannah and Sarah. Forever.

Sarah curled up on the couch Nate had slept on and watched the sun lower. He'd disappeared, and she didn't know whom she was angrier at: him for leaving without saying goodbye or herself for falling asleep.

She heard a knock. "Come in."

A man wearing khaki combat pants, a white T-shirt, and combat boots entered. He was exceptionally tall and wide, but it was his short, ginger-colored hair and day's worth of stubble, along with his intense brown eyes, that made him so intimidating. He dropped a backpack on the floor and carried over a dressing chair. He sat and stared at his clasped hands.

"You're Kells." No point in being vague or polite.

"Yes."

"Is Nate gone?"

"He left earlier."

Now it was her turn to study her hands. She wanted to scream, but that wasn't going to help her case. "How could you send Nate to jail?"

"I didn't send him. He was sent."

Kells was playing word games? That just irritated her

even more. "I know you have high-powered contacts. That's how you got him free to start with. Please. Talk to this person."

"The decision can't be changed." Kells stood to pace, his long legs eating up the floor in both directions. "I spoke with Doc Bennett. The herbal tea you made for Nate helped."

She adjusted the blanket over her lap. "It helped my father too. Even though he can't drink it because he's still in the psych ward."

"The doctor would like to see the recipe. It's possible that reviewing the contents of the tea might help him ID the compound that's making Nate sick."

"I'm seeing the doctor later. I'll give it to him."

Still, Kells paced. She was familiar enough with men to know when they had something else to say but couldn't find the words. Finally, he took a Ziploc bag out of his backpack and handed it to her. It contained Rebecca's diary, her mother's copy of *Othello*, and the map that'd brought her and Nate together. She opened the bag and removed the map to find a circle with perpendicular lines on the other side. "What's this?"

"Your hide sites." After explaining how radians worked, he said, "Nate discovered four coordinates in the diary, but we know there are more." Kells pointed to the moldy book. "You're the only one who can help us. We need you to read what else is in there. Calum said he'd give you whatever restoration money is necessary."

"You think the diary might lead you to Remiel's overall plan?"

"Possibly." Kells stopped pacing at the end of the couch to look out the window. With his arms crossed, his profile appeared hard and unrelenting. She had the feeling he didn't often ask for help. "Then there's the cipher. You know you can't tell anyone that you solved it."

"It could save my career."

"That cipher has been hidden for more than three hundred years and is protected by the Fianna."

He'd no right to ask her to do this. "Did it ever occur to you that if I made the cipher public and all the hide sites were found, then Remiel couldn't use them?"

"Then Remiel would move on to another plan. This cipher and these hide sites are *known* entities. My men and I can use them against Remiel."

"How?"

"I don't know yet. But if they're made public, I've lost any advantage I have." He ran his hands over his head in a nervous gesture that reminded her of Nate. "You've no reason to trust me, but I'm asking for your help."

"Why did you have me followed?"

"I knew about your grant proposal and believed Remiel would contact you."

"How? And why?"

"The granting agency, RM Foundation, was funded by RM Financial, a group I've been watching for a while because it's owned by the Prince."

She struggled to stand until Kells put a hand on her shoulder. "The Prince knew I was applying for the grant?"

"Yes." Kells moved away. "The Prince has been keeping tabs on your research. He also convinced your colleagues to publish your thesis in that British history journal. Luke was able to trace phone calls between a man named Maurice and your boss. From there, Luke was able to determine that five people you trusted were paid by the Prince to destroy your career."

"I thought it was Carina."

"She knew about your grant proposal and wanted to stop it for her own reasons. But she had nothing to do with the Prince or his plans. I doubt she's ever even heard of him."

Sarah honestly didn't know what to say. She'd known about Maurice and Augustus and the others, but her boss? How could he do that to her?

"Sarah? Will you help us?"

She could only imagine what this request cost Kells. She also knew he was right. He needed her. If helping him kept her close to Nate, she was in. "I don't want you following me. Or lying to me. Or not telling me when you hear news about Nate."

"One condition." Kells threw his backpack over his shoulder. "When you're better, you take Pete's Krav Maga class for women. It'll make Samantha happy to have you there."

"Agreed." And because Sarah was annoyed that he seemed to want the last word, she added, "I need you to get a message to someone."

"I can't contact Nate."

"Not Nate." She got off the couch, wrapped the blanket around her shoulders, and padded in bare feet to the desk. She'd already written the note. She just never thought she'd have a chance to send it. "It's for the Prince."

Kells laughed, and that made her even more annoyed. "I don't know how—"

"Nonsense." She handed it to him. "If you know where he banks and that he staged the destruction of my career, you know how to contact him. If you do this, I'm in."

When he left, she clutched the diary, *Othello*, and the map to her chest. She'd finally achieved her goals: redeem Thomas and Rebecca's love story, solve the cipher, and find the hide sites. But where she should've felt happiness, all she knew was bleakness. Because without Nate, everything she'd achieved meant nothing.

CHAPTER 52

A FEW DAYS LATER, SARAH SAT IN CALUM'S STUDY AND SIPPED a cup of tea. She was still reeling with the news that her father was being released tomorrow. Apparently, Calum's law firm had been able to prove that the social worker and the doctor who'd signed off on her father's commitment had accepted payments from a sketchy law firm in New Orleans that had ties to Remiel.

She didn't know anything about the law firm, but Calum did, and he'd used the info to blackmail the doctor and social worker into releasing her father. Honestly, she didn't care about Calum's machinations. She was just happy her father was coming home.

Calum had also told her about her mother's childhood friend Isabel Rutledge—the hooded woman—who'd been helping Sarah yet working for Remiel. Sarah wished she could've questioned Isabel; after all, she'd given Sarah the map and photos and possibly the ledger that she'd used to solve the cipher. But since Isabel worked for Remiel, it was probably best to let that one go too.

Her phone rang, and her heart hammered. She answered, "Hello?" praying it would be Nate but knowing it couldn't be. Kells had told her she'd never hear from Nate again.

"Sarah," Hugh Waring said, "I just finished talking to Detective Garza. This story about Etienne Marigny. It's... almost unbelievable."

"I know." She stared out the window at the garden with a spray fountain.

"There's a witness who heard Etienne's confession to the pub murders and our Charleston bankers. I'm still unsure about some details—"

"I don't know, Hugh." And she didn't. She'd left all

the details of these spinning stories up to Detective Garza and Calum. She'd no idea what they'd told Hugh and what they'd left out. Garza and Calum said they'd stuck to the truth, but it was often the gray area around the truth that hid the real story. Rebecca and Thomas had taught her that.

"Sarah, did you solve the cipher?"

"The cipher wasn't as important as I'd thought." And look at her now. Sticking to the gray areas. "Guess what? My father is being released tomorrow, and I've accepted a new job."

"Really? Doing what?"

She smiled when she remembered Calum pitching the idea to her in such a nervous way, as if afraid she'd say no. "Since the auction was canceled, Calum and Carina Prioleau, as well as Miss Nell Habersham, have decided not to sell their collection of pirate weapons. They've also decided to create a new Prioleau/Habersham Art Foundation. They want the foundation to search the city and surrounding areas for historical artifacts to buy and preserve for their collection. Eventually, there'll even be a museum. The foundation will collect, authenticate, and preserve."

"And they asked you to work at this foundation?"

She moved into the sunlight streaming through the window. She needed to feel the sun's heat on her face. "Calum asked me to be the director. My first project is a diary owned by a sixteen-year-old Puritan girl."

"I'm so glad for both of you, and I'm even happier to have friends like you and Joe living less than two hours away. Charleston isn't Boston. The South isn't as easy-going as they want everyone to believe."

She laughed for the first time since Nate had left. "Maybe not. But they make up for their earnestness with friendship and…" She smiled at the empty dish on Calum's desk. He'd been bringing her a plate every day.

"And?" Hugh prompted.

"They have this fabulous thing called strawberry pie."

༶

Two weeks later, Sarah and her father stood behind the tiny St. Mary of Sorrows Church on the Isle of Grace. Her father had settled into his daily routine. Now that he was home and drinking her tea four times a day, his memory was improving and his seizures lessening.

"This was a good idea." Her father took her hand and squeezed. "How did you coordinate this, again?"

"Sheriff Boudreaux suggested it when he realized Mom was from Savannah and her maiden name was Theroux." Apparently, the Boudreaux and Theroux families had been friends. "Calum managed the actual move."

Her father kissed her cheek and said, "I'll wait for you in Mamie's Café across the street. Sheriff Boudreaux said Mamie's has the best barbecue in Georgia. And strawberry pie."

She tried not to cry but ended up wiping her eyes with Nate's handkerchief.

Once her dad disappeared, she knelt in front of her mother's grave. When Sheriff Boudreaux had offered the burial space in the cemetery behind St. Mary of Sorrows Church on the Isle of Grace, Sarah had said yes immediately. Now she and her father could visit her mother anytime.

"I received your message." The male voice underscored with a South Boston accent came from behind.

Sarah stood and faced the Prince. Calum had told her that the Prince, when speaking to civilians, didn't hold to the Fianna's formal speech patterns. And she was grateful. She was too tired for word games.

The Prince wasn't as tall as Kells or as handsome as Nate, but he was distinguished in a European kind of way. His short brown hair was styled, and he wore dark dress trousers, a red silk shirt, and a conservative red paisley tie. His hands were in his front pockets, and dark sunglasses covered his eyes.

He took off his glasses and stared at her mother's tomb. Sarah had had *Hic est finis iter est scriptor* carved above the name *Meg Theroux Munro*. *My Fair Warrior* was carved below.

"I want you to free Nate."

The Prince's laugh was both confident and condescending, and she fisted her hands. "Even if I could do such a thing, which I can't, I wouldn't."

"*Why?*"

"Because not everything is under my control."

She couldn't help but notice that his brown eyes were similar to his brother Alex's. Samantha had told Sarah what little she knew about *that* drama. "Did you know the prison hospital where Nate is being kept has agreed to let him drink herbal tea twice a day? It helps with his headaches and seizures. I was allowed to send some to Nate, and I think you're the reason."

The Prince crossed his arms over his chest. "Why would I do that?"

"Because you want to recruit Nate. You're punishing him now, but you're just waiting until things change, and then you'll turn him into a monster."

"Like Cassio?" The Prince raised a sculpted eyebrow. "My warrior who saved your life? Twice?"

A good point, which irritated her even more. "Cassio may be the exception. But what if I told you there was a cure for the poison Fletcher Ames pumped into Nate?"

"How do you know this?"

"Fletcher Ames told me. He told me he'd give me the cure if I agreed to kill him. Now that he's with Remiel, I'm wondering if he wouldn't make you the same offer."

"And what do I get in return?"

"First, you save Nate, the man you want to recruit. Second, I'll give you the cipher and the hide site locations and any other pertinent information I learn from Rebecca's diary."

"Does Kells know about this offer?"

"Yes. He agreed. Information in exchange for the cure."

"I'm…intrigued." Thunder ripped in the sky above, and the Prince raised his head. "Who else knows how to solve the cipher?"

"Kells and his men. It's a simple substitution cipher, and I trust them completely."

"That's never a good idea, Miss Munro."

She was tired of his warnings and wanted to go home. "There's one more thing. Fletcher Ames, when he was talking about the cure, mentioned my father. I wasn't sure if he was saying that my father has the cure or needed the cure. I'm guessing the latter. While I'm not sure that my dad was poisoned the same way Nate was, I'd like my father to have access to the cure as well."

"Actually, Miss Munro, Fletcher Ames meant both." Before she could ask for clarification, the Prince offered his hand, and she shook it. "Information for a cure?"

She nodded.

"Then Cassio will be in touch."

As the Prince turned to walk away toward a black Mercedes waiting near the church, she said, "Fair warning, Mr. Mitchell."

He looked at her and put on his glasses.

She doubted anyone called him that, but she hoped it annoyed him. "You can save Nate, but you'll never recruit him. I won't let you."

"As you wish." After he bowed his head, he stepped into his car and drove away.

Nate finished his tea, sat on the porch of the prison hospital, and watched the seagulls fly over the uninhabited Maine island. God, how he envied them. He'd been here for three weeks, yet the nurses hadn't drugged him. He wasn't sure why and didn't want to ask. He was just appreciating the time before the mind numbing began.

At least his headaches had lessened. And he hadn't had a seizure since the night before he almost lost Sarah. He closed his eyes and tried not to remember. Remembering only led to sleepless nights and restless days. As far as he knew, he was going to be here for seventeen years. Or forever. They were the same thing.

He raised his face to the sun and the breeze. If he opened his eyes, he'd be able to see the lighthouse overlooking Frenchman's Bay.

"Walker." One of the orderlies came out. "You have a visitor."

Visitor? He opened his eyes. This was a no-visitors-allowed-ever prison. "Who?"

"Me." Carina Prioleau came onto the porch and sat on the edge of an Adirondack chair. She took off her oversize black sunglasses that matched her black pants, white blouse, and low black shoes. Her long blond hair was caught in a clip and hung over a shoulder. It was the most casual he'd ever seen her.

He reached out to touch her arm, just to make sure she was real. When he felt the silk of her blouse, he dropped his hand into his lap. "What are you doing here?"

"Looking for you." Except she wasn't looking at him. She was staring out over the rugged hills covered in purple and yellow wildflowers. Birds of prey dipped in the wind. "Do you remember the auction?"

"My short-term memory is still intact."

She nodded. "Do you remember what you said to me? What you asked Calum to remind me? About not giving away my power?"

"Yes. Although I shouldn't have yelled at the senator." Nate didn't need any more time added to forever.

"Senator McGuire deserved it." When she met his gaze, he was surprised to see none of her haughtiness. "I wanted to thank you for reminding me of who I am. I know people think I'm a bitch who didn't love my husband, but I did.

That I couldn't wait to take over his senate seat, although that's not at all true. It's been almost eleven months since his death and I still miss him terribly."

He reached over to hold her hand, surprised to find it freezing cold. "I know that pain well, Carina. And I wish you didn't have to live through it too."

She nodded before standing. "Anyway, we can go as soon as you're ready."

He stood and shoved his hands in his pockets. "What are you talking about?"

She smiled. "I reclaimed my power like you told me to. I knew something about Senator McGuire that the president found interesting."

"What did you do?"

"I gave the president *something* with which to coerce the senator into voting a certain way on a defense bill. In exchange, I got you a reprieve." She put on her sunglasses. "I wanted to get you a pardon, but that required more leverage than I had."

"When I said take back power, I wasn't talking about blackmailing a U.S. senator."

"Now you sound like Calum." She took a piece of paper out of her bag and handed it to him. It had an official seal on it. "It's a temporary postponement of punishment until I can get you a pardon. I don't know how long it will last, but the last man who received a presidential reprieve has had his punishment postponed for sixty years."

He stared at the paper until the words blurred and the edges tore from his sweaty hands. "What does this mean?"

She hiked her bag on her shoulder. "We're going home. And once we're there, you're going to promise to watch over my brother." She went inside. "Hurry. My private launch is waiting."

∽

Sarah stood in front of Saint Michael in the Cemetery of

Lost Children at dusk, appreciating the breeze that preceded the rainstorm thundering in the distance. She knew
she shouldn't be here. Sheriff Boudreaux had absolutely
forbidden it. As well as Kells and his men. And Pops and
Grady and Garza. Calum would probably have a hissy as
well, but she didn't care. She needed to be where she'd last
been happy with Nate. And since she couldn't get back to
the cabin on her own, she went to the place where they'd
solved the cipher.

Part of her wished she could return to the time before she
knew Nate. Before she'd loved him. Before she'd lost him.
Because wishing that none of this had ever happened was
so much less painful than wishing for what would never be.

"Sarah? Are you trespassing?"

She turned to find Nate backlit by ghostly shadows, in
jeans, a white T-shirt, and his black combat boots. "I am."
Her soft voice settled around her like the falling mist. "And
you still found me."

"I will always find you." He opened his arms. "Because
I love you."

In a heartbeat, she was in his embrace, planting kisses all
over his face. "Don't leave me again."

"I promise." With his hands holding her head, his lips
stole her breath and took command of her heart. "I love
you," he whispered between more kisses. "I'll never let
you go."

Suddenly, he swung her into his arms and sat on a flat
tomb. Then he arranged her on his lap. "I'm sorry. I almost
failed you like I failed my men."

She loved the sensation of his heartbeat beating beneath his
T-shirt. "You didn't fail. You found my hide sites, and you
saved me. If I hadn't been worried about being betrayed—"

"Shh." He closed his eyes and rested his chin on her
head. "There's never been a woman who's touched me the
way you have."

"You're the bravest, most loving man I know. I was

worried you'd fade from my mind, like our time together was a dream." When her arms encircled his neck, he opened his eyes. They were stark and hungry and masculine. His lips traveled her neck and down to her shoulder until she captured his face, loving his scent, his stubble, and his obvious arousal. "Are you home for good?"

"According to Carina Prioleau, yes."

She kissed his nose. "Do I want to know?"

"Probably not. Although I think we're good for at least sixty years." He stood both of them up. "Before we commence with more kissing, I want you to see what we found when we realized this tomb was the compass rose."

After he brushed away wildflowers, she saw a rough inscription carved around the base. The stone had sunk into the ground, but the rain had washed away the mucky buildup around the sides. He took a small penlight out of his pocket and handed it to her.

As she walked around the perimeter, she read the verse aloud: "*For she had eyes and chose me.*"

A tear escaped. "Rebecca and Thomas never had their happy ending. They didn't live the life of happiness and love for which they were destined."

Nate's hands were now on her shoulders, his lips in her hair. "They did live, sweetheart. To love with all your heart is to live fully, no matter how short the time."

"They married, but they couldn't escape their tragic fate."

Nate gently turned her around. "Their fate isn't our fate. We've been given the chance they never were, and I intend to take it." After another hard kiss, he knelt down and took a diamond solitaire out of the pocket of his jeans. He slipped the ring on the fourth finger of her left hand. "I can't promise I'll be a perfect husband. But I can promise, for the time we have together, a life filled with love. A life fully lived. Without fear or regrets. Sarah, will you marry me?"

Happiness filled her with light until she felt weightless. "Yes, Nate. I'll marry you."

EPILOGUE

SARAH TOOK THE CHAMPAGNE GLASS FROM NATE AND brushed her veil away from her face. It'd been a beautiful ceremony in St. Mary of Sorrows. Now they were in the garden of Calum's *cottage* on the Isle of Hope. The court-yard and parterre garden with symmetrical fountains had been decorated with white roses, gardenias, and green ferns. White fairy lights were strung throughout the trees. The colonial-era mansion behind them had been lit with candles and gardenias.

Her father had given her away, and Nate had waited for her at the altar.

"Are you thinking about our honeymoon?" Nate ran his hand up and down her spine. Nate, like the rest of the men, wore a black tuxedo. Calum had insisted. "Because I am."

She hid her nervous smile behind her champagne glass. They hadn't been together since he'd come home a few days ago. They'd been too busy moving him into her house, helping her father settle, and getting the wedding together. "Will you be okay living with me and my dad in my mother's house?"

"You mean will I mind leaving the gym to live with the woman I love and the father-in-law who thinks I'm not a pussy?"

She hit him on the arm. Of course, he barely noticed.

He laughed and kissed her neck. "I'll manage."

Female laughter came from the dance floor, and she smiled. The other women here included Miss Nell, Samantha, Carina, and Cain's wife Charlotte, who'd just arrived from North Carolina.

Now Pete and Samantha, who'd been Sarah's maid of honor, as well as Cain and Charlotte were dancing to a local

Cajun band. Vane, Ty, and Luke were eating at a nearby table. Miss Nell had cornered Alex, while Pops and Grady stood with Garza, Jimmy, and her father at the bar. Calum and Carina appeared to be arguing, and Zack had walked away to look at his phone. Sarah had no idea where Kells had gone.

Samantha walked over with an envelope. "This is from Calum, but he's too shy to give it to you."

Sarah pulled out a piece of paper and said, "We can't—"

"Yes, you can," Samantha said.

Nate took the document. "Calum is sending us to Charleston. He's reserved the honeymoon suite at the Mills House. With Ivers providing transportation."

Samantha waved a hand and walked toward Pete. "Enjoy it."

A moment later, Charlotte appeared in a pink silk slip dress that skimmed her petite figure. She'd intertwined pink rosebuds into her white-blond curls. "The wedding was beautiful."

"Thank you." Sarah brushed away a stray hair that had come lose from her French braid. A comb adorned with fresh gardenias fastened her veil in place. "I'm grateful to Samantha and Calum. They did most of the wedding planning work, and the flowers came from Juliet's Lily."

"I *love* that place. Cain and I are looking at an apartment near that store." Charlotte took Sarah's hands. "I just wanted to say that your dress is beautiful."

Nate kissed her head. "Yes, it is."

"Thank you." Sarah smoothed down the skirt of the white silk organza dress she'd worn to the auction. "I thought it'd been ruined, but Miss Nell sent it to a dressmaker in Charleston who was able to repair it. She even fixed the embroidered strawberries."

Sarah had also tucked Nate's handkerchief between her breasts because she wanted it close to her heart.

"Are those crystals in the strawberries?"

Sarah whispered, "Swarovski."

Charlotte's eyes widened, and then she smiled. "Did you know that Othello gave Desdemona a handkerchief embroidered with strawberries? Apparently, they're a powerful symbol of love and fidelity."

"I'd no idea." Sarah looked up at Nate, who smiled down at her. "But I'm not surprised."

Zack came over, with Cain close behind. Cain took his wife's hands, and handed Nate an envelope. "Kells returned to the gym, but he wanted me to give you this."

Nate took out a letter. "Kells gave me two weeks' leave. And left Cain in charge as temporary XO."

"*What?*" Cain grabbed the letter and frowned. "When you're not around, that's Zack's job."

Zack clapped Cain on the shoulder. "I'm going to Charleston for a few days."

"Just remember, brother," Nate said to Cain, "you're in charge."

Charlotte kissed her husband on the cheek. "Isn't that what I always say?"

Laughter sparkled, and once Cain and Charlotte went back to the dance floor, Zack shook Nate's hand. "Before you leave, I want to thank you for reminding me to believe in second chances."

The men went in for a hug and once they separated, Zack kissed Sarah on the cheek. "I'm sorry I didn't—"

"No more sorries," she said. "We all had reasons not to trust each other, but once we took that risk, we proved that we can beat Remiel. We proved that regardless of our mistakes, we're stronger when we work together."

Zack swallowed and said to Nate, "You're a lucky man, brother."

"I know." Nate held Sarah by the waist and pulled her closer. "Lucky and grateful."

When Zack walked away, she stood on her toes and kissed her husband. Surrounded by him, their friends, and

garden filled with laughter and music, she'd finally started
own family.

~

tes later, Nate found himself alone on the dance floor
his new bride. Music floated around them, and she
d her head against his chest. They danced slowly, her
keeping them in their own private world, his hands on
lower back holding her close.

She'd looked so beautiful walking down the aisle to
et him that all of his words had dried up. He'd barely
en able to say his vows, and Calum—who'd been his best
man and had helped Nate finance the ring—had elbowed
him to speak. He was hot, hard, and desperate to be alone
with his wife. She'd wanted to wait until after the wedding
to be together, and now that they'd said their vows, being
with her was all he could think about.

"Can we leave?" Nate whispered in her ear.

"We leave when Ivers says."

"I can drive," he said while kissing her neck. "I haven't
had a seizure since coming home."

She drew away slightly, a blush staining her face. "We
can't leave until we cut the cake. Or serve the strawberry pie."

Nate stopped the dance, took her face in his hands, and
kissed her. Hard, demanding, unrelenting. Like that night
in the police station. Like that night in the apartment. Like
that night in the bathtub. "*Sarah*."

Laughing, she somehow got out of his embrace and
dragged him away from the dance floor, toward the cake table,
surrounded by all of his friends. Surrounded by his brothers.

As he cut the cake, his hand over hers, he whispered, "I
will always love you, Sarah."

She looked at him, the white veil partially hiding her
face, and he saw tears in her eyes. "Promise me neither one
of us will ever be lost again."

"I promise, my love." He placed a small bit of cake in

her mouth, then kissed the frosting off her lips. "Your wi
is my only command."

His brothers cheered, champagne glasses clinked, and
knew deep in his heart that they would never be lost ag
Because when you're loved, you're found.

ACKNOWLEDGMENTS

I can't believe I'm writing another acknowledgment for a second book. It's been an amazing experience so far and I'm so grateful to all those who've made this book, and series, possible.

First, I'm sending hugs to my agents Deidre Knight and Kristy Hunter. The best hand-holders and calming-downers in the business. This book wouldn't exist if you hadn't taken a chance on me and this series. I, and my characters, appreciate your support and guidance.

Second, if any part of this book made you laugh or cry or feel anything, it's because of the skill and expertise of my extraordinary editor, Deb Werksman. Because of your patience and overwhelming commitment to this book, which started out in a million different pieces, we ended up with a beautiful love story that surpassed anything I could've written on my own. Thank you!

I also want to thank the rest of the Sourcebooks staff, including Susie Benton, Laura Costello, Rachel Gilmer, Stefani Sloma, Stephany Daniel, Kirsten Wenum, Beth Sochacki, and Emily Chiarelli for the many, many hours of hard work you've all put into this book and series. I couldn't have done any of this without you. And if I've forgotten anyone, I apologize and am blaming it on deadline brain!

In case you haven't heard, the Sourcebooks art department is one of the best in the business, and my covers are proof of that. Thank you so, so much for this cover and all of the covers in this series. They are truly amazing!

To Laura Baker, thank you for believing in this book. We worked on different variations of this story for years, and I so appreciate your advice and encouragement.

To Michael Hauge, thank you for giving me courage.

To my sister-in-law Kieran Kramer, thank you for your never-ending love and support.

To my critique partner and dearest friend, Mary Lenaburg, thank you for the endless hours of plotting help and for not giving up on me even when I start talking—and writing—in circles.

To my girlfriends Jean Anspaugh and Jackie Iodice, thank you for being there when I'm both crying and celebrating, sometimes at the same time. A girl is nothing without her BFFs!

To all of my writing friends, including Kimberly MacCarron, Pintip Dunn, Diana Belchase, Kerri Carpenter, Angelina Lopez, Juliette Sobanet, and Christine Glover, thank you for traveling with me on this journey. I never could've done it on my own.

To my brother-in-law and Charleston lawyer, Bill Hanahan, thank you for sharing your family stories, especially those that took place in the Georgia and South Carolina colonies during the seventeenth century. They've inspired the historical aspects of this book and this series.

To my one-eyed rescue dog who sleeps all day by my side, thank you for not judging me when I pull out the Oreos and Cheez-Its.

To my twins, who remind me daily of what's important (love, hugs, and time spent together) and what's not important (laundry, weeding, and cleaning the refrigerator). Thank you for teaching me that life is meant to be celebrated and not just written down as tasks in my day planner.

To my husband, who's always believed in me, thank you for being my best friend, my biggest fan, my maker of maps, and my teacher of land navigation. I will always love you.

Finally, to my readers. Thank you for loving the world of Kells Torridan and his men as much as I do. These books wouldn't be the success they are today without you. I hope I will never let you, or my characters, down.